SCOTTISH LITERATURE INTERNATIONAL

Rethinking George MacDonald: Contexts and Contemporaries

Edited by
CHRISTOPHER MacLACHLAN,
JOHN PATRICK PAZDZIORA,
and GINGER STELLE

Occasional Papers: Number 17
Association for Scottish Literary Studies

Published by
Scottish Literature International
Scottish Literature
7 University Gardens
University of Glasgow
Glasgow G12 8QH

Scottish Literature International is an imprint of
the Association for Scottish Literary Studies

www.asls.org.uk

ASLS is a registered charity no. SC006535

First published 2013

Text © ASLS and the individual contributors

All rights reserved. No part of this book may be
reproduced, stored in a retrieval system, or
transmitted in any form or means, electronic,
mechanical, photocopying, recording or otherwise,
without the prior permission of the
Association for Scottish Literary Studies.

A CIP catalogue for this title
is available from the British Library

ISBN 978-1-908980-01-4

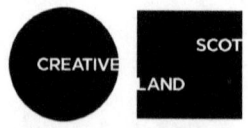

ALBA | CHRUTHACHAIL

ASLS acknowledges the support of Creative Scotland
towards the publication of this book

Contents

Introduction   v

Part One: Belief and Scepticism

One   The Idea of Tradition in George MacDonald   1
Stephen Prickett (University of Kent, Canterbury)

Two   'Divine Alchemy': *The Miracles of Our Lord* in its Context   18
Daniel Gabelman (Eastbourne College)

Three   'With all sorts of doubts I am familiar':
George MacDonald's Literary Response to John Ruskin's
Struggles with Epistemology   36
Jocelyne Slepyan (Duke University)

Four   *Thomas Wingfold, Curate* and the Mid-Nineteenth-Century
Eugenics Debate   52
Ginger Stelle (Morthland College)

Part Two: Social Reform and Gender

Five   George MacDonald's Approach to Victorian Social Reform
in *The Vicar's Daughter*   69
Jeffrey W. Smith (University of Dundee)

Six   Military Bodies and Masculinity in 'The Broken Swords'   84
Jenny Neophytou (Brunel University, London)

Seven   God and Gender in *Robert Falconer*: Deifying
the Feminine   105
Philip Hickok (University of Aberdeen)

Eight   Imagining Reformed Communities: Discussing Social Myths
in George MacDonald's *Princess* Novels and
Christina Rossetti's 'Goblin Market'   121
Christine Chettle (University of Leeds)

Contents (continued)

Nine	Sitting on the Doorstep: MacDonald's Aesthetic Fantasy Worlds and the Divine Child-Figure *Ally Crockford (University of Edinburgh)*	140

Part Three: Ideals and Nightmares

Ten	Stirring the Senses: Identity and Suspense in George MacDonald's *David Elginbrod* *Elizabeth Andrews (University of St Andrews)*	157
Eleven	'La Belle Dame' – *Lilith* and the Romantic Vampire Tradition *David Melville Wingrove (University of Edinburgh)*	175
Twelve	Gothic Degeneration and Romantic Rebirth in *Donal Grant* *Jennifer Koopman (McGill University)*	198
Thirteen	Pictures on a Page: George MacDonald and the Visual Arts *Helen Sutherland (University of Glasgow)*	216

Part Four: Scotland

Fourteen	Speaking Matrilineally (and Especially of Uncle Mackintosh MacKay) *Kirstin Jeffrey Johnson*	235
Fifteen	How the Fairies were not Invited to Court *John Patrick Pazdziora (University of St Andrews)*	254
Sixteen	George MacDonald and the Grave Livers of Scotland *David Robb (University of Dundee)*	273

Introduction

In 1868, only ten years into George MacDonald's prolific career as a writer, a reviewer for the *British Quarterly Review* wrote: 'We do not affirm that George MacDonald has as yet earned a right to be named with these [Robert Burns and Walter Scott]; he is not old as an author, and his genius, much as it has already done, has not, unless we are much mistaken, achieved its masterpiece' (*British Quarterly Review*, 47:93 (January, 1868), pp. 3f). This is but one of many positive assessments of MacDonald's works to come during his lifetime. Among his contemporaries, MacDonald was both respected by the literary establishment and popular with the reading public. This conception of MacDonald was lost in the twentieth century. His ideas fell out of fashion, and the majority of MacDonald's works were relegated to dusty library shelves and visited by only a handful of niche critics. Slowly, this is changing. The past two decades have seen a resurgence of critical interest in MacDonald. While MacDonald's role as literary descendant of the Romantics and an ancestor of modern fantasy writers have been much explored, however, his place in his own time remains virtually untouched.

This omission does MacDonald a grave disservice. By ignoring a fundamental aspect of what made MacDonald the man he was, the critical habit of viewing MacDonald's work only in terms of what came before or what has come since reinforces the long-entrenched assessment that it has a limited value – one only for religious enthusiasts and fantasy lovers. This anthology is an attempt to correct that omission. The essays in this volume look directly at MacDonald the Victorian – at his place in the Victorian literary scene, at his engagement with the works of his literary contemporaries and at his interest in the social, political, and theological movements of his age. The resulting portrait reveals a MacDonald who deserves a more prominent place in the rich literary history of the nineteenth century than he has hitherto been given.

MacDonald's works reflect the complex and nuanced world of nineteenth-century Britain. The nineteenth century is nothing if not complex. To begin to understand MacDonald within the context of his own time, then, necessitates an appreciation for the polyvalence and contradictions of that context. We have attempted to arrange this anthology in a way that is accessible to the casual reader, but that also exhibits the intellectual, literary, and societal complications of the era in which MacDonald wrote.

The anthology begins by addressing ideological cross-currents in part one, 'Belief and Scepticism'. In the opening chapter Stephen Prickett examines MacDonald's role in re-inventing the idea of tradition. Prickett argues that MacDonald was heavily influenced by the wider literary tradition, and that his work profits from careful intertextual reading. He demonstrates this with a reading of *Lilith* (1895), demonstrating how this immensely esoteric and enigmatic work begins to gain clarity when studied as a traditional – rather than merely original – work of Romantic fantasy. The philosophical questions raised by Prickett's conclusion are followed in the second chapter by Daniel Gabelman's study of MacDonald's theology of the miraculous. After explaining the historical development of the controversy surrounding miracles in the eighteenth and nineteenth centuries, Gabelman suggests that MacDonald's view, as demonstrated in his important but neglected book *The Miracles of Our Lord* (1870), brought to a point of culmination the counter-tradition of supernaturalism put forward by Coleridge and F. D. Maurice.

This leads into an epistemological discussion of the novels. In the third chapter, Jocie Slepyan offers possible points of convergence between MacDonald's correspondence with Ruskin and the theories of knowing presented in *Thomas Wingfold, Curate* (1873). Slepyan uses close readings of several key passages to argue that, while MacDonald shared much of Ruskin's concerns about and disillusionment with the organised church, he saw doubt as a stimulant and encourager of faith, rather than its enemy. In the fourth chapter, Ginger Stelle follows with a contrasting reading of *Thomas Wingfold*, looking at how MacDonald used it to discuss science as well as faith. Concentrating on the character of George Bascombe, Stelle presents ways in which MacDonald engaged with ethical and scientific concerns over the then-fashionable theory of eugenics. The picture of MacDonald that emerges is of a canny, sharp-witted cultural critic, unafraid to engage directly and cogently with the pressing issues of his day.

As Stelle's discussion of eugenics suggests, the nineteenth century saw upheavals in social constructs of the individual, and a person's place in society. Not least of these changes were the reconstructions of gender, with the late-Victorian period seeing the rise of both muscular Christianity and the New Woman. So part two, 'Social Reform and Gender', moves from philosophical concerns to how MacDonald engaged with the pragmatic social changes around him. In chapter five, Jeffrey W. Smith argues that *The Vicar's Daughter* (1872), rather than being the rambling, disorganised mess that many critics have accused it of being, is a forthright defence of the role of imagination in social reform. Particularly, Smith connects the character of Marion Clare with Octavia Hill, going beyond Robert Lee Wolff's criticism by using close readings to examine how MacDonald puts forward his own theories of social reform.

This importance MacDonald placed on the imagination is seen again in his treatments of gender. In chapter six, Jenny Neophytou looks at 'The Broken Swords' (1854) to elucidate his struggle with Victorian ideals of masculinity. She places the story within its broader textual and theoretical context, before turning to a close reading that concentrates on the story's contrast between spirituality and physicality. Philip Hickok follows this, in chapter seven, with a presentation of MacDonald's views on femininity, as articulated in *Robert Falconer* (1868). Hickok takes a different approach to the question of gender from Neophytou, emphasising the role of MacDonald's religious convictions, and arguing that in *Robert Falconer* MacDonald was overturning a traditional, patriocentric Christianity to present a feminine, mothering view of God. He concludes by pointing towards the female god-figure of the great-grandmother in the *Princess* novels, and so points forward to chapter eight, where Christine Chettle gives a re-reading of these novels.

In Chettle's analysis, the *Princess* novels develop in parallel with Christina Rossetti's 'Goblin Market' (1862), depicting the struggle both between the sexes, and between classes. She says that by choosing to work in the fairy tale mode, MacDonald and Rossetti both moved outside generic convention, and were thus afforded a greater flexibility in their discussion – and ultimately subversion – of the dynamics of reform within a community. Similarly, in chapter nine Ally Crockford looks at the character of Diamond in *At the Back of the North Wind* (1871) and the children in *Lilith*. MacDonald, Crockford writes, places idealised, even deified, child-figures into desperate social situations as mediators between the spiritual and physical worlds. Childhood serves as an image for MacDonald's ideal society; the divine child figure, then, offers an aesthetic, asexual *evangelium* whereby the social turmoils of the adult world are reconciled in the heavenly and fantastic.

Yet for all his interest in social reform, MacDonald was primarily a literary figure. Nor did he only use literary art to present exemplary characters and societies. So part three, 'Ideals and Nightmares', turns to genre study of his fiction. The section begins in chapter ten with Elizabeth Andrews' new perspective on *David Elginbrod* (1862). Through a series of close readings, Andrews argues that in the novel MacDonald employed the tropes of sensationalist fiction to achieve the didactic aims of religious fiction. By creating a realist sensationalism with logical explanations for Gothic phenomenon, Andrews says, MacDonald uses literature to explore more and more troubling socio-cultural issues than standard realism would have allowed.

Chapter eleven turns from realism entirely, however, as David Melville Wingrove analyses Gothic *topoi* in *Lilith*. Wingrove demonstrates how MacDonald deliberately employed situations and tableaus common to Gothic literature to create his villainess on the frame of Hebrew mythology. Drawing together a number of closely related texts, Wingrove argues that in *Lilith* MacDonald has written one of the most significant vampire novels of the Victorian era, unjustly and inexplicably neglected in the traditional Gothic canon. Jennifer Koopman pursues a related line of inquiry in chapter twelve, assessing the Gothic *topoi* in *Donal Grant* (1883). Koopman, however, is primarily concerned with how the Gothic is used to build literary criticism. She writes that, by employing the Gothic clichés, MacDonald may be satirising and rebuking the English Romantics; her close readings suggest that MacDonald may in fact have been trying to reconstruct a mythologised history of Romanticism more in line with his ideals.

MacDonald, after all, was hardly a passive observer of the Victorian arts scene. So, in chapter thirteen, Helen Sutherland repositions him within the broader artistic contexts of the age. She argues that despite the marked individuality of his better known fantasies, MacDonald shared an aesthetic parity with his contemporaries; she concentrates particularly on his interaction with the Pre-Raphaelites, many of whom were MacDonald's friends. Sutherland focuses on Edward Burne-Jones and

Arthur Hughes, and traces apparent reciprocity of influence through the imagery of several literary and visual works.

While all these cultural and literary influences are important to a full appreciation of MacDonald, he was first and foremost Scottish, and yet this important, simple fact has been widely ignored. So part four, 'Scotland', concludes the anthology by considering MacDonald in his native context. In chapter fourteen, Kirstin Jeffrey Johnson opens the general subject of MacDonald's Scottishness by considering first the role of Scots language in his upbringing and his writing. She then discusses the important influence of his uncle, Mackintosh MacKay, an early champion of Gaelic culture and a colleague of Walter Scott; Jeffrey Johnson further traces MacDonald's homage to MacKay in *What's Mine's Mine* (1886).

Scottish literature comes to the fore in chapter fifteen, in which John Patrick Pazdziora offers a comparison of MacDonald's fairy tales with those of his compatriot, Andrew Lang. Pazdziora traces how both writers followed the example of William Thackeray in re-appropriating the light-hearted French *conte* tradition, MacDonald in *The Light Princess* (1862), and Lang in his Pantouflia stories, particularly *Prince Prigio* (1889). Pazdziora argues that while both men were drawn to the fairy tale mode, they employed it for strikingly different ends.

The anthology concludes with David Robb's study, in chapter sixteen, of MacDonald's view on the importance of being Scottish. Taking his cue from Wordsworth and *David Elginbrod*, Robb gathers a wealth of sources, including writings by authors such as George Eliot and Margaret Oliphant, and news editorials and church meeting reports, to recreate Victorian social attitudes toward Scottishness, both in and out of Scotland. According to Robb, the twin currents of Scottish nationalism and Scottish religious life may have determined not only many of MacDonald's literary efforts, but the course of his private life.

George MacDonald is still too often seen as only the author of a few fairy stories, and even those who are aware of his other fiction are inclined to dismiss it as either uninteresting or made dull by preaching. It was the aim of the conference held in the University of St Andrews in 2011, from which the essays in this book are derived, to expand awareness of MacDonald's place in the life and culture of his times and relate his work to that of his contemporaries. MacDonald had close friendships with many of the leading writers, artists and intellectuals of his time, he had a wide-ranging and adventurous curiosity, and he used his talents as a writer and as a public speaker to comment on the most important issues of his day. It is hoped that this collection of essays will show both scholars of the Victorian period and the general reader interested in George MacDonald that he deserves to be regarded as a distinctive and significant voice in the great debates of his century.

Christopher MacLachlan
John Patrick Pazdziora
Ginger Stelle

Acknowledgements

The image on the cover is reproduced with the permission of the Ashmolean Museum, University of Oxford, UK, and The Bridgeman Art Library. The Editors wish to thank the School of English, University of St Andrews, for help and support in producing this volume; the contributors for making available their chapters; and the Association for Scottish Literary Studies for accepting the collection for publication.

I. BELIEF AND SCEPTICISM

The Idea of Tradition in George MacDonald

STEPHEN PRICKETT

The title of my book, *Modernity and the Reinvention of Tradition* (2009), reflected one of the most extraordinary, and least-observed, linguistic phenomena of the past three hundred years: the virtual disappearance and subsequent re-invention of the word 'tradition'. From Addison and Burke, to Warburton or Wesley, anyone who looks for the word in the eighteenth century will have to look very hard indeed. Paine we might certainly expect to be scornful of the idea, but Burke in his *Reflections on the Revolution in France* (1790), that apparent bastion of traditionalism, uses the word only twice – both times in the same sentence, to describe an obsolete political system. Even Coleridge and his fellow Romantics, who played such a part in the revaluation of the so-called 'middle ages', and were central to the new literary Gothick, were astonishingly chary of the word itself, and use 'tradition', if at all, almost invariably in the sense of an essentially unreliable transmission from the past.

For a variety of causes – the most potent probably being James Marsh's 1833 translation of Herder's *Spirit of Hebrew Poetry* – by the middle of the nineteenth century not merely the idea of tradition, but the word itself, had returned to general circulation in a way that would have been unthinkable a hundred years earlier – allowing it to join that select band of words that have been temporarily dropped from, and then subsequently restored to, the English language.[1] Indeed, by mid-century there were, in effect, at least four overlapping or competing connotations of tradition in circulation. Contrasting with Herder's ideas of creative, aesthetic, and even performative readings of the past, the oldest idea (and still the commonest) was of an essentially unreliable oral transmission of doubtful authenticity or value. This was the view, for instance, of John Henry Newman's brother, Francis Newman. John Henry himself, however, was by the 1840s slowly moving towards the conviction that the best way of understanding the alteration and changes over time of an institution such as the Catholic Church was a developmental conception of tradition, in which new ideas were constantly being assimilated and absorbed as by a living organism. For him, the Catholic Church proved its living nature by the very fact that it was less like the primitive church than those of the Protestant reformers. This interpretation of Catholicism was at the centre of his conversion to Rome in 1845. For his erstwhile friend and fellow-Tractarian, John Keble, however, tradition was essentially a matter of holding fast to what he saw as a precious and unalterable inheritance – never to be altered, changed, or modified.[2]

Such connotations, even where they contradicted one another, were clearly never sealed definitions, and there was – as always – much blurring at the margins. Many who used the word 'tradition' would, no doubt, have been unaware of the degree to which it was contested territory. Others, like the High-Church Christina Rossetti, well aware of the controversy surrounding the word, continue to use it in an almost neutral sense as 'ancient wisdom' but without specific connotations of immutability or doctrinal authority. But the very fact that tradition, and all the complex associations that went with it, were so widely invoked and so fiercely debated, suggests not merely the intellectual flux of the period but the importance attached to the outcome. It is no exaggeration to say that in a society that was undergoing the most rapid intellectual and social changes ever experienced by any comparable country, the understanding of and feeling for continuity with the past represented by the idea of tradition – or, conversely, the rejection of it – was central to almost every major question of the age.

In view of all this, my question here is, of course, where did George MacDonald fit in this debate? What evidence do we have as to his views? The first thing to say is that he uses the word as rarely as any eighteenth-century writer – which is to say, very rarely indeed. By one count the word only occurs about thirty times in his entire writings. This, in itself, may be revealing. If we are to find any clues, in short, they will be indirect ones: signs of practice, not of theory. Equally revealing, perhaps, is that tributes to George MacDonald have tended to perpetuate the norms of Romantic criticism by concentrating on his originality rather than what his devotees might see as derivativeness. As a result, his debt to the past has sometimes been underacknowledged. Thus, in one of the earliest pieces devoted to MacDonald, G. K. Chesterton in *The Victorian Age in Literature* (1913) compares his genius with that of Carlyle:

> [...] he could write fairy-stories that made all experience a fairy-tale. He could give the real sense that everyone had the end of an elphin thread that must lead them into Paradise. It was a sort of optimistic Calvinism. But such really significant fairy-tales were accidents of genius.[3]

If there was connection with a literary tradition, it was best attributed to 'accidents of genius' rather than to what in others might be described as 'subtle craftsmanship' or 'intertextuality'. Other critics were quick to follow Chesterton's thread. For the Inklings, such as Lewis, Tolkien, and Williams, it was his 'mythopoeic' qualities rather than narrative or literary skills that they valued most.[4] Auden, similarly, saw in MacDonald's 'power [...] to project his inner life into images, events, beings, landscapes which are valid for all', evidence of his being 'one of the most remarkable writers of the nineteenth century'.[5]

All this is true, certainly, but it tends to reflect and reinforce our own first readings of MacDonald's fantasy. It is, I suspect, easier for most of us to see the originality – the discontinuities – of his work, than its continuity with a much larger and longer literary tradition. John Docherty, in his analysis of MacDonald's literary dialogue with Lewis Carroll, is one of the few to have stressed the literary context of MacDonald's fantasy. But, of course, the editor of *England's Antiphon* (1870) was influenced even more by the tradition of the past than by any individual contemporary.

Two works in particular stand out in their overt use of literary tradition: I mean the two extended adult fantasies, *Phantastes* (1858) and *Lilith* (1895). Even here, however, in two works consciously studded with references to other earlier writers, critical emphasis has largely fallen on their originality rather than their intertextuality. My main example today will be from the latter, *Lilith* – almost his last work, and in many ways MacDonald's most difficult, misunderstood, and controversial fantasy. Unlike its earlier sister, *Phantastes*, the general critical reaction has been that though it contains poetic or, more often, 'mystical' insights, it is at best a flawed work, and at worst a 'failure'. Rolland Hein admits that it has 'a vivid sense of place' and that 'the aura of the dream, with the startling immediacy of its scenes and the peculiar force of its logic, is maintained with admirable consistency' but nevertheless judges that 'the weight of the idea [...] is not integrated with the symbolism', and that it is generally weak on dramatic quality. Overall it is 'an uneven performance [...] somewhat inferior to *Phantastes*'.[6]

Though, as we all know, Colin Manlove, like Robert Lee Wolff, modified his opinion of MacDonald quite sharply over time, he is only marginally more complimentary to *Lilith*.[7] He recognises much more clearly than Hein the mythopoeic force of the book, but continues to feel that MacDonald, 'a rather nervous seer', has attempted to graft onto a kind of residual mystical Calvinism a belief in free will which it will not take.[8]

Probably the best, as well as the most generous, twentieth-century appreciation of *Lilith* comes from C. S. Lewis. In a letter to his friend Arthur Greeves, of September 1st, 1933, he writes:

> I have just re-read *Lilith* and am much clearer about the meaning. The first thing to get out of the way is all Greville Macdonald's nonsense about 'dimensions' and 'elements' [...] That is just the sort of mechanical 'mysticism' which is worlds away from Geo. MacDonald. The main lesson of the book is against secular philanthropy – against the belief that you can effectively obey the 2nd. command about loving your neighbour without first trying to love God.
>
> The story runs like this. The human soul exploring its own house (the Mind) finds itself on the verge of unexpected worlds which at first dismay it (Chap. I–V). The first utterance of these worlds is an unconditional demand for absolute surrender of the Soul to the will of God, or, if you like, for Death (Chap. VI). To this demand the soul cannot at first face up (VI). But attempting to return to normal consciousness finds by education that its experiences are not abnormal or trivial but are vouched for by all the great poets and philosophers (VIII My Father's MS). It now repents and tries to face the demand, but its original refusal has now rendered real submission temporarily impossible (IX). It has to face instead the impulses of the subconscious (X) and the slightly spurious loyalties to purely human 'causes' – political, theological, etc. (XI). It now becomes conscious of its fellow men: and finds them divided into 'Lovers' [...] and 'Bags' or 'Giants' [...] But because it is an unconverted soul, has not yet died, it cannot really help the Lovers and becomes the slave of the Bags. In other words the young man,

however amiably disposed towards the sweet and simple people of the world, gets a job, or draws a dividend, and becomes in fact the servant of the economic machine (XII–XIII). But he is too good to go on like this, and so becomes a 'Reformer', a 'friend of humanity' – a Shelley, Ruskin, Lenin (XIV). Here follows a digression on Purgatory (XV–XVII).

With the next section we enter on the deepest part of the book, which I still only v. dimly understand. Why do so many purely secular reformers and philanthropists fail and in the end leave men more wretched and wicked than they found them? Apparently the unconverted soul, doing its very best for the Lovers, only succeeds first in waking (at the price of its own blood) and then in becoming the tool of, Lilith. Lilith is still quite beyond me. One can trace in her specially the Will to Power – which here fits in quite well – but there is a great deal more than that. She is also the real ideal somehow spoiled: she is not primarily a sexual symbol, but includes the characteristic female abuse of sex, which is love of Power, as the characteristic male abuse is sensuality (XVIII–XXIX). After a long and stormy attempt to do God's work in Lilith's way or Lilith's work in God's way, the soul comes to itself again, realises that its previous proceedings are 'cracked absolutely' and in fact has a sort of half-conversion. But the new powers of will and imagination which even this half-conversion inspires (symbolised in the horse) are so exhilarating that the soul thinks these will do instead of 'death' and again shoots off on its own. This passage is v. true and important. MacDonald is aware of how religion itself supplies new temptations (XXX–XXXI). This again leads to another attempt to help the Lovers in his own way, with consequent partial disaster in the death of Lona (XXXII–XXXVII). He finds himself the jailer of Lilith: i.e. he is now living in the state of tension with the evil thing inside him only just held down, and at a terrible cost – until he (or Lilith – the Lilith part of him) at last repents (Mara) and consents to die (XXXVIII–end).

[…] I have emphasised the external side too much. Correct everything above by remembering that it is not only the Lovers outside against the Bags, but equally the Lover in himself against the Bag in himself.[9]

I have quoted Lewis at some length here because he enunciates two very important principles of interpretation which few, if any, other modern critics have grasped. The first is that every event in the other world of *Lilith* is purely spiritual – or should we say 'metaphorical'? It is interesting that, though Lewis is well aware of MacDonald's own strictures against allegory 'as everywhere a weariness to the spirit', he reads the narrative of *Lilith* as a systematic allegory rather than simply a loose assemblage of symbols. In support of this reading it is worth noting that events in what one might call the 'internal' narrative are blatantly non-realistic. Not merely is it populated by monsters, shape-changers, and skeletons, but in spite of apparently ferocious violence, few are ever killed – not just Lona, but even, it seems, those trampled by elephants in Bulika.

The second principle follows directly from this: all events in the book are therefore to be read as internal and taking place within the individual psyche. Thus, according to this reading, the children, or Lovers, are not to be seen as 'immature' (as Hein suggests) but rather as 'childlike' (as in the Sermon on the Mount). As his final paragraph suggests, Lewis is not altogether certain about the consistency of his own argument here, especially whether Vane's attempts to help the children are futile gestures towards external philanthropy, or attempts to develop certain qualities within himself – or both. But such a separation is in any case impossible: one cannot consider many so-called 'internal' qualities such as generosity, and helpfulness to others, without also taking into account the corresponding external actions. The psyche does not free-float in a vacuum. What is clear is that, according to Lewis, *Lilith* is to be read primarily as a narrative of self-exploration and self-discovery.

Central to this interpretation is the role played by books, and therefore the library, in the plot. One book in particular – which refers specifically to Lilith – actually spans the two worlds. For MacDonald, self-knowledge is not simply a matter of introspection, of, as it were, internal trial-and-error, but draws also on a huge body of inherited wisdom far greater than any individual can hope to acquire by direct experience. This in turn may give us a further clue as to how we are to understand *Lilith* itself as a book, and the metafictional freight which it carries. One obvious example for later critics might be the presence of what we would now call 'Jungian' archetypes in the shape of the 'wise woman' (Mara) the 'old man' (Mr Raven), and so on – raising the obvious question of how far Lilith herself might correspond to the Jungian 'anima'.

The point is that Jung, like MacDonald, is a product of the European literary tradition: represented by the contents of the library in which Vane finds himself. If Lilith, as Lewis admits to Greeves, remains the most significant gap in his argument and, indeed, is 'quite beyond' him, we should perhaps take up the hint about the significance of books given above and look first for other literary antecedents for Lilith. One immediately comes to mind: Geraldine in Coleridge's 'Christabel'. She, too, has on her side some mysterious and terrible mark:

> Like one that shuddered, she unbound
> The cincture from beneath her breast:
> Her silken robe, and inner vest,
> Dropt to her feet, and full in view,
> Behold! her bosom and half her side—
> A sight to dream of, not to tell!
> O shield her! shield sweet Christabel! (ll. 248–54)

Though she seems more to be a usurper of the mother's role than natural mother (who, we are told, is dead) there is in her attitude to Christabel more than a hint of the Lilith/Lona relationship. Like Lilith also, Geraldine is some kind of vampire who is first rescued by Christabel and then has to be carried over the threshold of the castle by the innocent heroine. Similarly, Lilith's powerful erotic appeal to Vane is repeated in Christabel's mysterious attraction to Geraldine, not to mention Geraldine's for Sir Leoline. Since the poem is unfinished we cannot be entirely certain of the mysterious Geraldine's role in it, but we do know for certain that Coleridge's poem had already been the origin of some of the most powerful myths of the nineteenth century. It was Byron's manuscript copy of 'Christabel' that, we are told, was the inspiration behind the writing of Mary Shelley's *Frankenstein* that fateful evening in Geneva when Shelley's party met with Byron. Less well-known is that Byron's personal physician, a Dr Polidori, also produced a novella as a result of that meeting: *The Vampyre*.[10] There seems little doubt that just as C. S. Lewis was later to appropriate Lilith as Jadis, the Queen and White Witch in his *Chronicles of Narnia*, so MacDonald, a long-time admirer of

Coleridge, has appropriated the figure of Geraldine as a starting point for his own creation of Lilith.

Perhaps the strangest confirmation of Lilith's essentially literary origins, however, is the fact that she herself is apparently the author of the mysterious book in the library alluded to above, one end of which lies in the 'real' world of the novel, the other end of which only exists in the spiritual/internal one. There is a hint here, of course, that it is in the nature of all books to span this gap between external and internal worlds – we recall that MacDonald's first publication, in 1855, was a poem entitled 'Within and Without'. But that hardly prepares us for one of the strangest features of this particular book: that the passage read aloud by Mr Raven is in the form of an autobiographical and confessional poem by Lilith herself. That it is actually *by* her and not the kind of conventional artistic projection we see, for instance, in Milton's first-person portrayal of Satan, is made more probable by the fact that we are told that the book is in manuscript written upon parchment, and is in a language which Vane had never before heard, but which he nevertheless understood perfectly.

In other words, what we are told he is looking at is not a published aesthetic construct at all, but written in some universal language of the soul. What Mr Raven reads, therefore, is not about Lilith, it is in some sense Lilith herself – and what we actually learn about her is very curious indeed:

> But if I found a man that could believe
> In what he saw not, felt not, and yet knew,
> From him I should take substance, and receive
> Firmness and form relate to touch and view;
> Then should I clothe me in the likeness true
> Of that idea where his soul did cleave![11]

According to this, not merely is she in a very real sense Vane's creation – or even, more accurately, his projection – she is a projection not of his worst desires, but, on the contrary, of his highest aspirations. Not for nothing does this passage provide strong verbal echoes of the definition of 'faith' in Hebrews: 'the substance of things hoped for, the evidence of things not seen' (11: 1). Moreover, his initial attraction for Lilith is part of a Romantic hungering for something transcendent and beyond himself:

> For by his side I lay, a bodiless thing;
> I breathed not, saw not, felt not, only thought,
> And made him love me – with a hungering
> After he knew not what – if it was aught
> Or but a nameless something that was wrought
> By him, out of himself; for I did sing
>
> A song that had no sound into his soul;
> I lay a heartless thing against his heart,
> Giving him nothing where he gave his whole
> Being to clothe me human, every part;
> That I at last into his sense might dart,
> Thus first into his living mind I stole.[12]

She is indeed a vampire, but one who sucks not the blood but the soul of her victims. Her appeal is the more subtle and dangerous in that she takes the form of her victim's most cherished and noblest desires. Yet in the end she stands for Death.

This is the second problem which Lewis scarcely deals with. The all-pervading sense of Death in *Lilith* is brushed aside in his bracketed reference to chapters 'XXXVIII–end' – not, as one might think, simply a brief coda, but eight chapters in all which return to what is in effect the central theme of the book: Mr Raven's repeated invitation to come into his house to die. Only those who have already thus 'died', it is implied, will be proof against the temptations of idealism embodied in Lilith. This brings us back to the initial comparison made by so many critics between MacDonald's two great 'adult' romances, *Phantastes*, written at the outset of his literary career, and *Lilith*, written at its close. If the former is, as I have argued elsewhere, essentially a *Bildungsroman*, the latter is something for which the English cannot even borrow a word from German, for it is such a rare phenomenon that there is no such thing in either language. If it existed, or we were to coin such a term, it would be *Todesroman*: a 'death-romance'.[13]

Here we confront what is for me by far the most difficult problem in *Lilith*: the centrality, even the celebration, of Death. As Tolkien once remarked, 'Death is the theme that most inspired MacDonald'.[14]

Yet what we shall from here on call the *Todesroman* is by no means a unique literary phenomenon. Examples would include that very beautiful and other-worldly medieval poem, 'The Pearl', which was incidentally a favourite of both C. S. Lewis and Tolkien. It would include Dante's *Divine Comedy*, parts of Dickens (one thinks of *A Christmas Carol* as well as *Edwin Drood*), the Tolstoy of the *Twenty-Three Tales*, as well as some works by Chesterton, Charles Williams and Tolkien himself. It is a small, but by no means insignificant list of writers, especially if one adds one other, rather more unexpected name, that of Johann Wolfgang von Goethe.

No-one who knows anything of MacDonald's expulsion from the Arundel Congregation for being tainted with German thought could fail to be aware of his interest in German literature, but I confess that it was only having read Goethe's *Wilhelm Meister* in Carlyle's splendid translation, and, more recently, Andrew Bowie's illuminating studies of German Romanticism,[15] that I began to see something of the real extent of the influence of German thought on MacDonald. His debt to *Wilhelm Meister*, especially the second part, *The Wanderings of Wilhelm Meister*, is everywhere present in the fantasies – especially in the two *Princess* books and *The Golden Key*. I have written on this in detail elsewhere, and there is no point in repeating it here.[16] What I did not call attention to there, however, was another aspect of Goethe's elaborate fantasy, the strange Masonic initiation ceremony that Wilhelm undergoes where he is presented with the book of his own life.

Goethe's ambiguous relationship with Christianity and his resolute insistence (still obediently perpetuated by most Germanists) that he was a 'Classicist' and not a 'Romantic' all too easily obscure what is very evidently going on in this scene. At one level, the fictional figure of Wilhelm is being presented with a book which must correspond very closely with the book we, the readers, have in our hands. As Andrew Bowie has demonstrated, the roots of postmodernism and deconstruction lie in what I believe to be distortions of German Romanticism, but, of course, the roots of this particular piece of reflexive intertextuality lie much deeper than that. Not merely was Christianity itself born in an act of literary criticism[17] – the appropriation and revaluation of the Hebrew Bible as the Old Testament as a prelude to the revisionist New Testament – but central to subsequent Christian thought was the biblical 'story' of the world from Genesis to Revelation – that great Book in which we all play our pre-ordained parts. In popular mythology moreover this was accompanied by the image of the recording angel with the book of life in which all our deeds and misdeeds will faithfully be entered. The inference is clear: we are all of us part of some great all-embracing supernatural text. What for Goethe began as the first great *Bildungsroman* ends as one of the first great pieces of Romantic fantasy-writing.

My point is that this is scarcely accidental. Though Goethe would not have considered himself a Christian in any sense necessarily acceptable to the contemporary Church, his work was inescapably steeped in the Judeo-Christian literary tradition. Not merely is this a matter of reading our own lives, and the world in general, hermeneutically, as a text to be deciphered, but it also means that such hermeneutics are richly complex and tensional. Death is not, as it was for the ancient Egyptians, something for which we must be embalmed; nor is it a descent into the classical underworld. As in Dante, it is something to be both feared and rejoiced in: a gateway to an ever-richer eternal life, or to damnation and despair. More specifically, for MacDonald, who was, we remember, a Universalist, it was certainly the transition to an ever-richer eternal life, but precisely because he was a Universalist it was also something demanding complete abnegation of the self. Above all, it is something to be internalised. What is impressive about Lewis's reading of *Lilith* is that he is, as it were, instantly familiar with its terms if not necessarily all its implications. We recall his discussion of the sheer difficulty of internal humility in *The Screwtape Letters*.[18] As a contemporary of Jung, Lewis is able to read *Lilith* not so much as an allegory in the older sense, but as an internal drama of the spirit. But this is my point: what is one of the most startlingly complex and original works of the nineteenth century is also a deeply traditional one. What looks like (and, indeed, is) an entirely new literary form is also something that has evolved by what seems with hindsight like an inevitable technical progression.

Thus the treatment of death in *Lilith* is not quite what we might expect from an old man who knows that he is within a few years – or perhaps even months – of his own death. It is, for instance, strikingly unlike that other great English *Todesroman*, Dickens's *Mystery of Edwin Drood*, which reeks of physical decay and death and was left tantalisingly unfinished by Dickens's actual death in 1870. Death for MacDonald here is not the end of things, but as it were a misplaced beginning. It is the alternative to that subtlest and most insidiously attractive of all corruptions: the human idealism from which Lilith herself feeds. If what we have said so far in support of Lewis's allegorical and internalised interpretation of *Lilith* is correct, then Mr Raven's 'house of death' is primarily a symbolic expression of the spiritual reality of man's absolute dependence on God.

If that sounds more like something out of Schleiermacher than MacDonald we should not be surprised. We recall again that the original charge made against MacDonald when he was compelled to resign his ministry in Arundel was that he was 'tainted with German theology'. There are direct quotations from Schleiermacher in MacDonald's work as early as *Phantastes*. Equally to the point, here is Schleiermacher's proclamation of the essentially personal and first-hand nature of all religion:

> What one commonly calls belief, accepting what another person has done, wanting to ponder and empathise with what someone else has thought and felt, is a hard and unworthy service, and instead of being the highest in religion, as one supposes, it is exactly what must be renounced by those who would penetrate into its sanctuary. To want to have and retain belief in this sense proves that one is incapable of religion; to require this kind of faith from others shows that one does not understand it.[19]

To 'die' in Mr Raven's sense is something you yourself must do. But not merely must Vane learn to move from second-hand to first-hand religious experience; so, I suspect, must the reader of *Lilith*. MacDonald has as it were turned Schleiermacher's dictum on personal knowledge into an aesthetic principle of originality. In true Romantic style, originality in experience begets originality in expression.

In this sense, death in *Lilith* is perhaps best seen as a reversed sacrament. A 'sacrament' is commonly defined as 'the outward and visible expression of an inner spiritual event'. It is a symbolic act. In our world death is not a symbol, but the final event of life. Here, in Lilith's other world, what is in our world the physical reality of death becomes the symbol for the greater reality of human dependence on God. MacDonald has, in effect, followed up Newman's idea of tradition not as a repetition of the past, but as a process of change and development – but experienced now not in terms of theological theory,[20] but of fictional narrative. The only 'traditional' way of understanding death is by way of a totally new perspective on life – and, indeed, of theology itself. As if this were not difficult enough, MacDonald compounds our problems by giving this new meaning of death an almost erotic attraction. Just as the intellectual attraction of what Lilith stands for is transmuted into a strong sexual attraction for Lilith herself, so now the attraction of Mr Raven's 'house of death' carries an almost equivalent erotic charge. It is this, presumably, that gave the first Victorian readers of the novel such problems with it. We know, for instance, that MacDonald's wife was severely 'troubled by the book's strange imagery' and was never really reconciled to it.[21]

But there are other allied elements that have proved equally difficult for later readers to cope with. A similar reversal of inner and outer states makes dreams acquire a greater reality than waking states. The transvaluation of consciousness suggested by the quotation from Novalis with which the book ends, 'Our life is no dream, but it should and will perhaps become one,'[22] goes back as far as that other 'waking dream', *Phantastes*. But here, with the extraordinary ending of *Lilith*, MacDonald's *Todesroman*, the uncompromising nature of this vision is brought home to the reader as perhaps nowhere else in Romantic fiction. The discovery that the first 'waking' is itself only a 'dream' is unsettling enough in itself, but it also gives the second 'waking', where Vane is unceremoniously pushed back into his own library, an even greater ambiguity. If, for instance, the events of the previous chapters were a 'dream' in the above sense, given, as he puts it, 'by Another', are we to conclude that he is at the moment of writing still 'dreaming' (as in the first 'waking')? Or that he is at present waking, and awaiting the return of the dream? This is not an accidental uncertainty, for, as Roderick McGillis has convincingly shown, the uncertainty and ambiguity of the ending is not the result of confusion or sloppy writing but the product of careful and deliberate revisions.[23] We are meant to be left in uncertainty.

But this is what we might have expected from Lewis's exposition of the book to Greeves. If the events of the other world are to be interpreted as a purely internal and spiritual allegory, then by 'dreaming' in the sleep of death in Mr Raven's house, Vane is actually wider 'awake' than in his original state. Moreover, he is not returned to his attic mirror, with its suggestions of self-contemplation, and from where he entered the other world, but to his library – to the world of books, where the collective learning and spiritual experience of others is assembled. That is where this journey into self-exploration must now continue.

His task is not to inhabit one world or the other, but rather constantly to straddle the two and to insist on their ultimate congruity. Once again, that mysterious book in the library can stand for the entire European literary tradition. What is required is a visionary state, like the vision of ordinary sense-perception, which requires not one point of reference, but two. Only when we see with both eyes do we have the stereoscopic vision that enables us to place ourselves in the material world. Similarly, MacDonald implies, we can only place ourselves in the moral and spiritual world by a corresponding kind of 'stereoscopic' perspective. Thus Mr Raven is, and is not, a Raven/a Librarian/a Sexton/and Adam. Mara is both woman and cat. And Lilith? Woman/leopard/leech/vampire; she is surely the hidden pride that masquerades behind the self-sufficiency of fallen human ideals. She is, for MacDonald, the greatest temptation of all, and the last to be relinquished, for she is herself the embodiment of Death. She is, symbolically, the last to enter Mr Raven's house, for only then shall Death die.

What might this then suggest about MacDonald's idea of tradition? We should start, I think, with Lewis's main insight: that tradition is to be internalised. So far from being an external deposit in Keble's sense, handed down from the past, it rather is a way of thinking, a way of using rather than being dominated by history. So far, so good, but there is a corollary: like Lilith herself, tradition is ambiguous – of inestimable value, and potentially very dangerous indeed – and the more valuable, the more dangerous. Not for nothing is Lilith's ambiguous soul to be found in a library – in the book half in one world, half in another. The wisdom of the past can be a liberation, or it can be a drug – giving a quite false assurance, a simulacrum of inherited values that are ultimately valueless; an assurance, if you like, that with their aid one can do no wrong. This is certainly neither Newman's vision of the tradition of the Catholic Church, nor – though MacDonald had read him – is it Herder's. In its resolutely dialectical insistence on antitheses, it is structurally more Hegelian than either; but the moral choices thus posed are more Kierkegaardian. It is, in short, I believe, a vision unique for its period, insisting at once on the value of the wisdom of the past, and its utter valuelessness when confronted by something greater than itself, at once fideistic and deeply sceptical.

But if it is unique for the nineteenth century, there are a few earlier examples. Take, for instance, the disappearance of Virgil in Dante's *Divine Comedy*. At the point of meeting of Dante and Beatrice in the Earthly Paradise, Dante turns to his guide and mentor – only to discover that he has vanished. All the collected earthly wisdom that has brought him through Hell and Purgatory is useless when confronted by the divine vision. That is the correct use of tradition: vital, yet in the end serving to point beyond itself. Lilith is here the opposite of Virgil: instead of pointing beyond, she points back at herself. As I say, there are few, if any, places where this comes in nineteenth-century fiction. But that, surely, is what we would expect from a writer such as George MacDonald.

Notes

1. Stephen Prickett, *Modernity and the Reinvention of Tradition* (Cambridge: Cambridge University Press, 2009), ch 7. In fact the use of the word 'tradition' is the subject of the whole chapter (pp. 129–48).
2. Prickett, p. 189.
3. G. K. Chesterton, *The Victorian Age in Literature* (London: Williams and Norgate, 1913), p. 152.
4. C. S. Lewis, Introduction to *George MacDonald: An Anthology* (London: Geoffrey Bles, 1946).
5. W. H. Auden, Introduction to *The Visionary Novels of George MacDonald*, ed by Anne Fremantle (New York: Noonday Press, 1954).
6. Rolland Hein, *The Harmony Within: The Spiritual Vision of George MacDonald* (Grand Rapids, MI: Eerdmans, 1982), p. 111.
7. Colin Manlove, *Modern Fantasy: Five Studies* (Cambridge: Cambridge University Press, 1975), p. 60.
8. Manlove, p. 62.
9. *They Stand Together: The Letters of C. S. Lewis to Arthur Greeves (1914–1963)*, ed by Walter Hooper (New York: Collins 1979), pp. 459–461.
10. For the relationship between MacDonald and Coleridge see Stephen Prickett, *Romanticism and Religion: The Tradition of Coleridge and Wordsworth in the Victorian Church* (Cambridge: Cambridge University Press, 1976); also *Victorian Fantasy*, 2nd edn (Waco, TX: Baylor University Press, 2005), p. 196.
11. *Lilith*, introduction by Lin Carter (New York: Ballantyne Books, 1969), p. 156.
12. *Lilith*, p. 156.
13. See Prickett, *Victorian Fantasy*, p. 200.

14. J. R. R. Tolkien, 'On Fairy Stories', in *Tree and Leaf* (London: Allen & Unwin, 1964), p. 59.
15. Andrew Bowie, *Aesthetics and Subjectivity: from Kant to Nietzsche* (Manchester: Manchester University Press, 1990); *From Romanticism to Critical Theory: the philosophy of German literary theory* (London and New York: Routledge, 1997).
16. 'Fictions and Metafictions: *Phantastes, Wilhelm Meister* and the idea of the *Bildungsroman*,' in *The Gold Thread: Essays on George MacDonald*, ed by William Raeper (Edinburgh: Edinburgh University Press, 1991), pp. 109-25.
17. See Stephen Prickett, *Origins of Narrative: The Romantic Appropriation of the Bible* (Cambridge: Cambridge University Press, 1996), pp. 56-60.
18. C. S. Lewis, *The Screwtape Letters* (London: Geoffrey Bles, 1942), p. 71.
19. Friedrich Schleiermacher, *On Religion: Speeches to its Cultured Despisers*, trans by Richard Crouter, 1799 (Cambridge: Cambridge University Press, 1988), p. 134.
20. The theme of his *Grammar of Assent*, ed C. F. Harrold, new edn (Longman, 1957).
21. Greville MacDonald, *George MacDonald and His Wife* (London: Allen & Unwin, 1924), p. 548.
22. *Lilith*, p. 274.
23. Roderick McGillis, '*Phantastes* and *Lilith*: Femininity and Freedom', in *The Gold Thread: Essays on George MacDonald*, ed by William Raeper (Edinburgh: Edinburgh University Press, 1990), pp. 49-50.

Bibliography

Auden, W. H. Introduction to *The Visionary Novels of George MacDonald*, ed by Anne Fremantle (New York: Noonday Press, 1954).
Bowie, Andrew, *Aesthetics and Subjectivity: from Kant to Nietzsche* (Manchester: Manchester University Press, 1990).
— *From Romanticism to Critical Theory: the philosophy of German literary theory* (London and New York: Routledge, 1997).
Chesterton, G. K., *The Victorian Age in Literature* (London: Williams and Norgate, 1913).
Hein, Rolland, *The Harmony Within: The Spiritual Vision of George MacDonald* (Grand Rapids, MI: Eerdmans, 1982).
Hooper, Walter, ed, *They Stand Together: The Letters of C. S. Lewis to Arthur Greeves (1914-1963)* (New York: Collins, 1979).
Lewis, C. S., *The Screwtape Letters* (London: Geoffrey Bles, 1942).
— *George MacDonald: An Anthology* (London: Geoffrey Bles, 1946).
MacDonald, George, *Lilith*, introduced by Lin Carter (New York: Ballantyne Books, 1969).
MacDonald, Greville, *George MacDonald and His Wife* (London: Allen and Unwin, 1924).
Manlove, Colin, *Modern Fantasy: Five Studies* (Cambridge: Cambridge University Press, 1975).
McGillis, Roderick, '*Phantastes* and *Lilith*: Femininity and Freedom', in *The Gold Thread: Essays on George MacDonald*, ed by William Raeper (Edinburgh: Edinburgh University Press, 1990), pp. 31-55.
Newman, John Henry, *A Grammar of Assent*, ed C. F. Harrold, new edn (London: Longman, 1957).
Prickett, Stephen, *Romanticism and Religion: The Tradition of Coleridge and Wordsworth in the Victorian Church* (Cambridge: Cambridge University Press, 1976).

— 'Fictions and Metafictions: *Phantastes, Wilhelm Meister* and the idea of the *Bildungsroman*,' in *The Gold Thread: Essays on George MacDonald*, ed by William Raeper (Edinburgh: Edinburgh University Press, 1990), pp. 109–125.

— *Origins of Narrative: The Romantic Appropriation of the Bible* (Cambridge: Cambridge University Press, 1996).

— *Victorian Fantasy*, 2nd edn (Waco, TX: Baylor University Press, 2005).

— *Modernity and the Reinvention of Tradition* (Cambridge: Cambridge University Press, 2009).

Schleiermacher, Friedrich, *On Religion: Speeches to its Cultured Despisers*, trans by Richard Crouter, 1799 (Cambridge: Cambridge University Press, 1988).

Tolkien, J. R. R., 'On Fairy Stories', in *Tree and Leaf* (London: Allen and Unwin, 1964), pp. 9–73.

'Divine Alchemy': *The Miracles of Our Lord* in its Context

DANIEL GABELMAN

In 1873, Matthew Arnold wrote in *Literature and Dogma* 'what we call the Time-Spirit is sapping the proof from miracles. Whether we attack them, or whether we defend them, does not much matter; the human mind, as its experience widens, is turning away from them'.[1] Arnold could have equally said, however, that it was precisely because the Time-Spirit was sapping the proof from miracles that Victorians were so heavily engaged in attacking and defending them. Indeed, since the Enlightenment, miracles had been one of the most contested intellectual subjects as both opponents and supporters of Christianity seemed to agree that its claim to truth and validity rested on these marvellous oddities. Written three years before Arnold's comments, MacDonald's rarely studied *The Miracles of Our Lord* is a fascinating contribution to this cultural discussion for several reasons: first, because MacDonald's work is the culmination of a counter-tradition of miracles initiated by Coleridge and carried on by F. D. Maurice; second, because it avoids rational arguments in favour of imaginative explorations of miracles, not for devotional purposes but – to use Arnold's language – as a means of widening the experience of the human mind in a spiritual direction and turning individuals towards the divine; and finally, because of the way in which MacDonald seems to have applied his understanding of miracles to his own mode of literary creation.[2]

The Counter-Tradition of Coleridge and Maurice
During the Enlightenment, philosophers such as Baruch Spinoza and David Hume threw down a gauntlet against miracles. Hume famously defined a miracle as 'a violation of the laws of nature' and argued that it would be virtually impossible to assemble enough credible witnesses and evidence to overturn the collective weight of universal human experience and affirm that a miracle actually happened.[3] Almost a hundred years earlier Spinoza had claimed that 'miracles cannot make known to us the essence and existence of God, nor consequently his providence' because

according to Spinoza God's attributes 'are far better inferred from the regular and unchanging order of nature'.[4] For God to intervene in nature would be for him to contradict himself.

Christian rationalists such as David Hartley, Bishop Butler, and William Paley responded by vehemently defending the biblical miracles as the necessary 'evidences' of Christianity, evidences which are historical and based upon trustworthy testimony. Paley, for instance, in his influential *The Evidences of Christianity* argued that miracles are 'wrought in the promulgating of a revelation' and that it is because Jesus performed miracles in the presence of so many witnesses that people can be confident that his message is from God.[5] By this account, miracles are primarily about establishing divine authority and about laying the empirical foundations of the Christian faith. These men, in other words, argued that Christianity was an entirely rational and reasonable faith for modern educated people. The Oxford theologian James Mozley – one of many thinkers to carry Paley's line of thinking into the Victorian era – summarised this sentiment when in 1865 he said 'Christianity is the religion of the civilised world, and it is believed upon its miraculous evidence'.[6]

Early in his life when he was a Unitarian, Coleridge subscribed to the arguments of natural theologians like Paley, but after he was reconverted to Trinitarian Christianity Coleridge began to view their ideas as too mechanistic and materialistic.[7] By 1807 when he wrote 'Memorandum on Miracles' Coleridge's view of miracles was almost exactly opposed to both the secular philosophers and the Christian apologists. Whereas Enlightenment philosophers defined miracles as 'suspensions of the laws of nature' Coleridge was incensed by this view: 'suspension – laws – nature! Bless me! A chapter would be required for the explanation of each word of this definition'.[8] In contrast to Christian rationalists like Paley, meanwhile, Coleridge denied that miracles were external evidences to the truth of Christianity upon which a person could build their faith. In *The Statesman's Manual* (1816), for example, Coleridge says:

> In the infancy of the world signs and wonders were requisite in order to startle and break down that superstition [...] which tempts the natural man to seek the true cause and origin of public calamities in outward circumstances, persons and incidents. [...]

> But with each miracle worked there was a truth revealed, which thenceforward was to act as its substitute. [...] It was only to overthrow the usurpation exercised in and through the senses, that the senses were miraculously appealed to; for reason and religion are their own evidence.[9]

Coleridge here uses miracles to criticise both empiricism and natural theology. Miracles overthrow the tyranny of the senses (and thus undermine the supremacy of empirical science), yet precisely because they unsettle the authority of the senses they cannot themselves be the primary evidences of Christianity (as the natural theologians wanted to assert). Miracles are not a prerequisite for faith; rather faith is a prerequisite for miracles. Their value lies not in verifying doctrinal statements but in signalling God's interaction with the world.

A reviewer of this Lay Sermon accused Coleridge of 'heretical boldness' and 'potential infidelity' to Christianity on account of this conception of miracles.[10] Coleridge was so upset by this allegation that he devoted a large portion of the final chapter of *Biographia Literaria* (1817) to refuting it and clearly outlining his view of 'the true evidences of Christianity':

> 1. Its consistency with right reason, I consider as the outer court of the temple [...] 2. The miracles, with and through which the religion was first revealed and attested, I regard as the steps, the vestibule, and the portal of the temple. 3. The sense, the inward feeling, in the soul of each believer of its exceeding desirableness [...] this I hold to be the true foundation of the spiritual edifice. [...]
>
> But 4. It is the experience derived from a practical conformity to the conditions of the gospel – it is the opening eye; the dawning light; the terrors and the promises of spiritual growth; [...] in a word, it is the actual trial of the faith in Christ, with its accompaniments and results, that must form the arched roof, and the faith itself is the completing keystone.[11]

What makes Coleridge's 'true evidences' so remarkable is the relatively insignificant place that he gives to human reason and miracles as historical evidence. Instead of primarily appealing to the metaphysical category of truth ('right reason'), Christianity more heavily relies upon beauty ('exceeding desirableness') and goodness ('actual trial'). Factual knowledge is associated with the 'outer' inessential parts of a temple (its court and vestibule), whereas beauty and goodness are its inner and essential features (foundation, roof and keystone). This is an inversion of the Enlightenment hierarchy of values. Whilst miracles are evidences, they are not the vital supports to the Christian faith that most people take them for – they are merely aids or transitional structures for ushering people into the true temple.

Coleridge wrote more about miracles in his notebooks, but he died before he could publish extensively on this subject and so it remained to F. D. Maurice to pick up on his occasional hints and develop his ideas further.[12] In his long dedicatory letter to *The Kingdom of Christ* (1837) Maurice makes his debt to Coleridge clear and, with specific reference to Coleridge's first Lay Sermon, claims 'I have said very little indeed of which [his] thought was not the germ'.[13] In discussing miracles he notes 'we have been used to speak of miracles as the chief evidences for the truth of Christianity' but that if this means 'a miracle or prodigy, as such, proves the Divine commission of the person who enacts it, we have the strongest reason for rejecting such a notion'.[14] God is a god of law and order, says Maurice, and he would not violate this order for any reason. Maurice here acknowledges the strength of the Enlightenment argument that 'great truths [are] so much better illustrated and proclaimed by the regular and invariable order of nature'.[15] But, he adds, miracles are not violations or interruptions of nature, rather they 'withdraw the veil which conceals Himself the prime worker, and so explains the meaning of His ordinances, the secret of their efficiency, the reason of their abuse'.[16] Like Coleridge, Maurice is primarily concerned with combating a mechanistic and materialistic view of the cosmos. More than anything else, what miracles do is point to God as *the* cause of nature.

Other followers of Maurice and Coleridge also emphasised how miracles primarily point to God as the personal cause behind every effect in the universe. A. J. Scott, a close friend of both Maurice and MacDonald, for instance, argues in his essay 'On Revelation' that 'miracles are no suspension or violation of the laws of the universe. The direct agency of God is as much a law as gravitation. [...] miracles are but one form of the action of the ever-present, everywhere necessary agency [of God]'.[17] Charles Kingsley – perhaps the most successful populariser of Maurice's ideas – devotes a chapter in *Alton Locke* to 'Miracles and Science' in which a wise dean claims that 'to break the customs of Nature is [not] to break her laws' for 'Nature's deepest laws, her only true laws, are her invisible ones'.[18] Science, says the dean, has never and will never explain ultimate or original causes, but miracles point toward the true source of all life and action. Interestingly, the chapter begins with the narrator, Alton Locke, saying that miracles had been his 'greatest stumbling-block' since he 'had read Strauss'.[19]

Kingsley is referring, of course, to David Strauss's *The Life of Jesus* (1835), which along with Ludwig Feuerbach's *The Essence of Christianity* (1841) – both translated by George Eliot – stimulated much religious controversy and discussion in the Victorian era. Whereas Feuerbach claimed that God is a projection of the inner nature of humanity, Strauss argued that the gospels were composed of various myths about Jesus. This mythical school of interpretation agreed neither with the supernaturalists (who believed the gospel events happened as they are recorded) nor with the naturalists (who believed that the miracles could be explained scientifically). Both admitted a historical element, but Strauss believed that the miracles were *mythus* that should be 'considered not as the expression of a fact, but as the product of an idea'.[20] The marvellous stories, in other words, have nothing to do with history or facts but are intended to tell the reader something particular about the nature of Jesus. Strauss did not even consider the possibility that miracles could happen but simply assumed the rectitude of the Enlightenment position.[21]

In a letter from 1863 to Mr Hutton, F. D. Maurice describes how Strauss through his mythical interpretation unwittingly opens up the 'true supernatural origin of all history':

> [Strauss] showed that *no* records of human life can be content with merely naturalistic phenomena. There is always a dream of something transcendent. Follow that doctrine to its extreme in one direction and all history becomes based on falsehood. Follow it to its extreme in the other direction and you come to a true supernatural origin of all history. In the first case the Jewish story becomes one of the myths. In the second it becomes the interpretation of the myths.[22]

The biblical miracles are myths, says Maurice, but they are myths that actually happened.[23] For this reason miracles also become hermeneutical keys to understanding ultimate reality. They show the principles by which God operates and which undergird all creation. 'Miracles', he says, 'are not exceptions but manifestations'.[24]

Hence, miracles are not empirical proofs demonstrating the authority of dogmatic revelation but are themselves revelations of the divine. Maurice and his intellectual followers prefer to speak of miracles as 'manifestations' rather than 'evidences', and as revelations of a higher spiritual law rather than suspensions of natural law, as Maurice expresses in his sermon 'The Miracles':

> They are not arguments to convince the understanding that it ought to suspend its own proper exercises; they are unveilings or manifestations to the whole man, of the nature, character, mind, of the Son of Man; and therefore of the nature, character, mind, of the Father who sent Him.[25]

As with Coleridge, miracles are important not as the rational foundation of the Christian faith but as mediators to an intimate encounter with God – they reveal that the force behind the universe is personal and remains personal. Miracles are visual parables and teaching spectacles. They are not primarily *external* witnesses that give credence and authority to Scripture but *internal* witnesses to the character of God. By Victorian standards, this was a radical redefinition of miracles, one which, along with related ideas, placed Maurice and his followers under the same cloud of 'potential infidelity' to Christianity attributed to Coleridge. They were, however, undeterred, as was George MacDonald.

The Culmination of the Miracle Counter-Tradition in MacDonald

The Miracles of Our Lord was originally serialised in the *Sunday Magazine* from October 1869 to September 1870. This forgotten fact sheds light on the mystery in MacDonald's opening line: 'I have been requested to write some papers on our Lord's miracles'.[26] Who asked MacDonald to write on miracles? There are three possible candidates: 1) Thomas Guthrie, the editor of the *Sunday Magazine* and popular Scottish preacher who shared much of MacDonald's theological outlook; 2) Alexander Strahan, the publisher of the *Sunday Magazine* and a MacDonald family friend; 3) F. D. Maurice, to whom the book is inscribed: 'to F. D. Maurice, honoured of God, I humbly offer this book' (p. 229).[27] That Maurice might have been involved either directly or indirectly in eliciting the work is made more likely by the fact that he too was friends with and published by Strahan and that the three men shared literary and theological circles in London.[28]

Moreover, during the 1860s MacDonald grew increasingly close to Maurice as he made St Peter's, Vere Street (where Maurice preached weekly from 1860–69), his spiritual home whenever he was not travelling or guest preaching. MacDonald named his son after Maurice in 1864 and asked his friend and mentor to be the godfather. Nor was the admiration one-sided. In an undated letter probably from the mid- to late-1860s, Maurice asks MacDonald if he would be interested in collaborating on a work on 'the Unity of the Church' composed of prayers and hymns 'to cheer men's hearts and kindle their hopes of something better to come'.[29] Is it a complete coincidence that in 1868 MacDonald published *England's Antiphon*, his collection of England's religious poetry, with the aim of throwing 'my small pebble at the head of the great Sabbath-breaker *Schism*' and prefaced with the liturgical injunction to 'lift up your hearts'? Whether or not Maurice was the direct or indirect cause of any of MacDonald's works, he was unquestionably the dominant influence on MacDonald's view of miracles. Indeed, as we shall see, *The Miracles of Our Lord* is the flower and fruition of the counter-tradition begun by Coleridge and developed by Maurice.

In the Introduction MacDonald explains his reason for writing about miracles: 'I venture the attempt in the belief, that seeing they are one of the modes in which [Jesus's] unseen life found expression, we are bound through them to arrive at some knowledge of that life' (p. 233). Like Maurice and Scott, MacDonald affirms that miracles are primarily interesting not as evidences but as manifestations of the divine. We should consider them because they will teach us something intimate about Jesus, and this knowing of Jesus, says MacDonald, is 'the immediate end of our creation' (p. 233). MacDonald admits that there are some in his time who would find the New Testament easier to accept 'if the miracles did not stand in the way', but, he says,

> It would be easier for them to accept both if they could once look into the true heart of these miracles. So long as they regard only the surface of them, they will, most likely, see in them only a violation of the laws of nature: when they behold the heart of them, they will recognise there at least a possible fulfilment of her deepest laws. (p. 236)

In a manner similar to Coleridge, MacDonald sets up a distinction between the outer appearance of miracles and their inner meaning, and he claims that miracles are not violations of nature but its deepest fulfilment. The argument is aesthetic and emotive rather than rational. If people could see the beauty and harmony of miracles, then the historical and scientific objections would not have as much force. Yet MacDonald does not think that miracles are especially difficult to believe: 'there are far harder things to believe than miracles. For a man is not required to believe in them save as believing in Jesus' (p. 236). Miracles are not empirical evidences that lead one to believe in Jesus; rather faith in Jesus is prerequisite for believing in miracles. MacDonald concludes, following Maurice, that miracles, as revelations of the inner life of the Son, are also revelations of the Father since the Son came to reveal the Father in miniature. Miracles are the Son doing 'briefly and sharply before their very eyes' what 'the Father does so widely, so grandly that they transcend the vision of men' (p. 234). Miracles condense the workings of nature so that humans with their limitations of time and perception can see the constant connection of all creation to the Father.

This is why MacDonald can partially agree with Enlightenment philosophy about the greatness of the regular workings of nature and say 'miracles are surely less than those goings on of nature with God beheld at their heart', but he rebukes their mechanistic understanding of the cosmos and says that miracles 'are mightier far than any goings on of nature beheld by common eyes, dissociating them from a living Will' (p. 235). Miracles show the world to be governed not by random chance or abstract forces but personal Will. In this way MacDonald simultaneously elevates miracles as intimate revelations (in contrast to Enlightenment thinking) and lowers miracles from being unique demonstrations of extreme power and authority (in opposition to Christian rationalists).

'Power', says MacDonald, 'in itself is a poor thing' for 'no amount of lonely power could create'. He continues: 'it is the love that is at the root of power, the power of power, which alone can create' (p. 247). Without the internal and interpersonal force of love, external power would be 'lonely' and empty.

MacDonald is not, however, just repeating what Maurice and Coleridge had already said. His project is more strange and interesting for he takes the ideas that they had expounded in discursive and apologetic prose and turns them into imaginative explorations of the true heart of miracles. While in several places MacDonald does directly address a sceptical audience, in general he eschews straightforward rational apologetics in favour of a personal encounter with the miracles themselves. For example, after discussing 'the degrading spirit of the commonplace' – a phrase he repeats several times in the book and which he defines as a lowering of the capacity for belief – MacDonald acknowledges that he is speaking to people who at least hope there may be a God. He continues:

> If any one interposes saying that science nowadays will not permit him to believe in such a thing, I answer it is not for him I am now writing, but for such as have gone through a different course of thought and experience from his. [...] But to the reader of my choice I do say that I see no middle course between believing that every alleviation of pain, every dawning hope across the troubled atmosphere of the spirit, every case of growing well again, is the doing of God, or that there is no God at all. [...] The common kind of belief in God is rationally untenable. Half to an insensate nature, half to a living God, is a worship that cannot stand. (p. 257)

MacDonald rebukes Christian and sceptic, saying that both have misunderstood miracles and thereby distorted the character of God. Miracles do not prop up the supernatural; they redefine the natural. They disclose the reality of God's ever-present nearness. But who is the reader of MacDonald's choice if it is not the sceptic and it is not the typical Christian?

With this statement MacDonald seems to be doing something similar to what he later attempts in 'The Fantastic Imagination' (1893) when he says that he does not write for children but for 'the childlike, whether of five, or fifty, or seventy-five' or to what Wordsworth had attempted in *Lyrical Ballads* (1798–1802) when he wrote a new type of poetry in order to create a desire for it.[30] MacDonald, in other words, appears to be trying to construct his own audience not through discursive reasoning but through imaginative encounter, not through direct appeal to rational truth but by revealing beauty and goodness. 'To arouse the hope that there may be a God with a heart like our own', says MacDonald, 'is more for the humanity in us than to produce the absolute conviction that there is a being who made heaven and the earth and the sea and the fountains of waters' (p. 378–79). Hope and desire are more potent than intellectual conviction for motivating and inspiring individuals. MacDonald approaches miracles in a similar way to Coleridge, believing that by arousing an awareness of the beauty and goodness of miracles (Coleridge's 'exceeding desirableness') he can circumvent the fruitless discussions of their truth on both sides, but unlike Coleridge MacDonald does this through beautiful and emotive narrative rather than contentious argumentation. As one of the early reviews of the book says, MacDonald 'everywhere shines out a beautiful spirit of reverence and generous breadth of sympathy' – not something that was often said of Coleridge.[31]

The result is that *The Miracles of Our Lord* is a strange book that does not fit neatly into genre categories. The individual chapters are not sermonic like his *Unspoken Sermons* (1867, 1885, 1889) and *Hope of the Gospel* (1892) but neither are they lectures or essays. MacDonald invites readers to enter into the miracles imaginatively. Even more important for MacDonald than the mythical interpretation of miracles (Maurice's 'miracles as manifestations') is the personal experience and transformation of those individuals who receive the miracles:

> The miracles were for the persons on whom they passed. To the spectators they were something, it is true; but they were of unspeakable value to, and of endless influence upon their subjects. The true mode in which they reached others was through the healed themselves. And the testimony of their lives would go far beyond the testimony of their tongues. Their tongues could but witness to a fact; their lives could witness to a truth. (p. 281)

Miracles are about transformation. The outer transformation (restored sight, cured leprosy, demons cast out), however, while important, is not as significant as the inner transformation that happens when a person encounters Jesus and receives his life-giving love. Miracles are thus almost solely for those who desire them and ask for them. The 'testimony' and 'witness' of miracles to the rest of the world is primarily indirect – through the transformed lives of individuals. Without inner renewal, says MacDonald, there is no miracle: 'a wonder is a poor thing for faith after all; and the miracle could be only a wonder in the eyes of those who had not prayed for it, and could not give thanks for it; who did not feel that in it they were partakers of the love of God' (p. 379). A wonder is a mere show of power and can actually serve to weaken faith, but a miracle is intensely personal and involves the transformation of the whole individual – within and without.

It is for this reason that MacDonald approaches the miracles imaginatively and why he chooses to see a miracle through the eyes of its recipient. Interpreters of miracles can either remain at a critical distance like the spectators whom Jesus rebuked for demanding signs and wonders, or they can humble themselves and enter into the psychological state of the leper, the man born blind, and the sisters of Lazarus. The first group, in MacDonald's view, will probably not even see a lonely wonder; the second might just catch a glimpse of 'the true heart of miracles'.

It should be noted that this is not only a devotional exercise for MacDonald. He also seems to think that it has some legitimate scientific merit:

> There is a wide *may be* around us; and every true speculation widens the probability of changing the *may be* into the *is*. The laws that are known and the laws that shall be known are all lights from the Father of lights. (p. 412)

Instead of fitting neatly into the category given to them by the Enlightenment ('violations of natural law'), miracles escape categorisation and elicit a similarly elusive mode from MacDonald. Miracles don't establish and support a dichotomy between natural and supernatural. They prompt speculation, challenge traditional categories, and reopen possibilities that have been prematurely closed. Miracles redefine our concept of reality.

MacDonald's Divine Alchemy

Another of the things that miracles do according to MacDonald is gesture beyond themselves. Miracles reveal the beauty at the heart of creation, but in so doing they elicit the response of goodness – individuals must follow miracles to their source and enter into a relationship with their author. In an analogous way, allow me to conclude by gesturing beyond *The Miracles of Our Lord* towards the author's more straightforwardly artistic creations.

Speaking of Jesus's first miracle of turning the water into wine, MacDonald says there is a 'glad significance' in this miracle in that

> It is a true symbol of what he has done for the world in glorifying all things. With his divine alchemy he turns not only water into wine, but common things into radiant mysteries, yea, every meal into a eucharist, and the jaws of the sepulchre into an outgoing gate. I do not mean that he makes any change in the things or ways of God, but a mighty change in the hearts and eyes of men, so that God's facts and God's meanings become their faiths and their hopes. (p. 245)

What is surprising about this description of the miracles is how closely it corresponds with MacDonald's artistic practice. MacDonald's fairy tales are not escapist explorations of other worlds or even of a purely interior psychological world as some critics have suggested; instead they attempt to reveal and reorient individuals to the radiant mysteries that are ever-present in common things. In 'The Shadows', for example, when Ralph Rinkelmann returns from his fantastic journey to see the Shadows' church, he finds that 'instead of making common things look commonplace, as a false vision would have done, it had made common things disclose the wonderful that was in them'.[32] Likewise fairy tales for MacDonald do not make the everyday world seem dull and lifeless but rather help reveal the beauty and splendour hidden in the ordinary and the mundane. Thus in *Adela Cathcart*, shortly after hearing 'The Shadows', Adela – who suffers from melancholy and malaise – comments on the effect that playful stories have upon her:

> It seems like magic. I sleep very well indeed now. And somehow life seems a much more possible thing than it looked a week or two ago. And the whole world appears more like the work of God.[33]

Much like miracles, fairy tales open possibilities and make the world seem a more wondrous place. They somehow reinvigorate our perception of reality imbuing the world around us with meaning and significance.

MacDonald's stories 'for the childlike' also appeal to resplendent beauty and lustrous goodness rather than intellectual truth. Indeed, in 'The Fantastic Imagination' MacDonald associates adulthood with avaricious acquisition of truth, and childhood with longing after goodness and beauty:

> We spoil countless precious things by intellectual greed. He who will be a man, and will not be a child, must – he cannot help himself – become a little man, that is, a dwarf. [...] If any strain of my 'broken music' make a child's eyes flash, or his mother's grow for a moment dim, my labour will not have been in vain.[34]

Fairy tales, like miracles, 'arouse' hope and 'wake' desire. They do not add to the storehouse of information, but they elicit emotions and encourage transformation. Fairy tales in MacDonald's view are another way of undermining 'the degrading spirit of the commonplace', the force that saps the life from belief and keeps people from seeing how all creation is a miracle – a personal manifestation of the love of God.

The Miracles of Our Lord also, I think, offers a window of insight into MacDonald's hermeneutics, especially his hermeneutics of fairy tales. In discussing Jesus's first miracle, MacDonald spends several pages imagining what is behind a cryptic exchange between Jesus and Mary. Realising that someone might have a problem with this treatment of the Bible, MacDonald defends his approach:

> If any one objects that I have here imagined too much, I would remark, first, that the records in the Gospel are very brief and condensed; second, that the germs of a true intelligence must lie in this small seed, and our hearts are the soil in which it must unfold itself; third, that we are bound to understand the story, and that

> the foregoing are the suppositions on which I am able to understand it in a manner worthy of what I have learned concerning Him. [...] This interpretation seems to me to account for our Lord's words in a manner he will not be displeased with even if it fail to reach the mark of the fact. (p. 243)

The brevity of gospel narratives is not a woeful deficiency that needs to be filled up by scholarly criticism. On the contrary, the short, abrupt style creates imaginative spaces in which all readers can play. As Erich Auerbach has written, the biblical style is 'fraught with background' in what it leaves out, operates by 'suggestive influence of the unexpressed', and opens a 'multiplicity of meanings', with the result that biblical stories 'require subtle investigation and interpretation, they demand them'.[35] MacDonald clearly feels the force of this demand, but with his second point he also highlights the necessity of readerly good will and participation. The miracle stories are small seeds that only unfold themselves in the fertile soil of a receptive mind, a mind which develops the stories within itself and thereby becomes a participant in the making of meaning.

MacDonald, of course, says something very similar about fairy tales in 'The Fantastic Imagination':

> If there be music in my reader, I would gladly wake it. Let fairytale of mine go for a firefly that now flashes, now is dark, but may flash again. Caught in a hand which does not love its kind, it will turn to an insignificant, ugly thing, that can neither flash nor fly.[36]

In other words, like the lacunae and mysterious brevity of the gospel narratives, fairy tales are intentionally brief and condensed and lacking in psychological drama because this empty space is what invites the readers to join in the meaning-making game. Interpretation for MacDonald thus has less to do with finding a single correct meaning and more to do with whether or not one is interpreting lovingly. MacDonald is without fear that even if his interpretation misses 'the mark of fact' it nevertheless is still a good interpretation because he has arrived at it through love. In this MacDonald – perhaps unwittingly – echoes St Augustine, who in *On Christian Doctrine* says that if 'a man draws meaning from [scripture] that may be used for the building up of love, even though he does not happen upon the precise meaning which the author whom he reads intended to express in that place, his error is not pernicious' (I.36).[37] Love, then, for both St Augustine and MacDonald, is more important than truth in the process of biblical interpretation. But MacDonald even extends this rule beyond the Bible and into fairyland.

The Miracles of Our Lord, then, is not – as most scholars seem to treat it – a peripheral and forgettable book in MacDonald's *oeuvre*. On the contrary, *The Miracles of Our Lord* shows MacDonald at his best: engaging with the concerns of his day and drawing on rich theological and literary traditions in surprising ways to leave his own unique impression on the subject. Perhaps we could say that MacDonald is a sort of 'divine alchemist', taking common teachings and unveiling the beauty and goodness ever-present within them.

Notes

1. Matthew Arnold, *Literature and Dogma* (London: Smith, Elder, 1873), p. 129.
2. The only other extended commentary on *The Miracles of Our Lord* is Roderick McGillis, 'Fantasy as Miracle: George MacDonald's *The Miracles of Our Lord*', in *George MacDonald: Literary Heritage and Heirs* (Wayne, Pennsylvania: Zossima, 2008), pp. 201–16. McGillis reads the book in a Lacanian psychoanalytic light that moves 'between spiritual and psychoanalytic discourses because [he feels] more comfortable with the latter' (p. 207). Whilst pioneering and thought-provoking, McGillis's essay does nothing to contextualise the work, which results in a couple of slight misrepresentations of MacDonald's view of miracles.
3. David Hume, 'Of Miracles', in *Essays and Treatises* vol 3 (Basel: J. J. Tourneisen, 1793), p. 125.
4. Baruch Spinoza, 'Of Miracles', in *A Theologico-Political Treatise* (London: Trubner, 1862) http://www.philosophyarchive.com/index.php?title=ChapterVI_-_A_Theologico-Political_Treatise_-_Spinoza [accessed 10 December 2011].
5. William Paley, *The Evidences of Christianity* (London: T. and J. Allan, 1823), p. 2.
6. James Mozley, *Eight Lectures on Miracles* (London: Rivingtons, 1865), p. 27.
7. For a discussion of Coleridge's early thoughts on miracles see Frederick Burwick, 'Coleridge and De Quincey: Inspiration and Revelation', in *Poetic Madness and the Romantic Imagination* (University Park, PA: Pennsylvania State University Press, 1996), pp. 43–59.
8. Quoted in J. Robert Barth, *Coleridge and Christian Doctrine* (New York: Fordham University Press, 1987), p. 39.
9. Samuel Taylor Coleridge, *Lay Sermons* (London: Edward Moxon, 1852), pp. 10–11.
10. *The Edinburgh Review* vol 27 (Edinburgh: Archibald Constable, 1816), p. 452.
11. Samuel Taylor Coleridge, *The Major Works* (Oxford: Oxford University Press, 2000), pp. 479–80.
12. For a discussion of Coleridge's use of miracles in his notebooks see Stephen Prickett, *Romanticism and Religion: The Tradition of Coleridge and Wordsworth in the Victorian*

Church (Cambridge: Cambridge University Press, 1976), pp. 34–69. Prickett also has some excellent commentary on Coleridge's influence on Maurice (pp. 120–51).
13. Frederick Denison Maurice, *The Kingdom of Christ*, 2 vols (London: J. M. Dent, 1906), I, 9.
14. F. D. Maurice, *The Kingdom of Christ*, II, 156.
15. Spinoza, 'Of Miracles'.
16. Maurice, *The Kingdom of Christ*, II, 159.
17. Alexander John Scott, 'On Revelation', in *Discourses* (London: Macmillan, 1866), pp. 43, 44. Scott's view of miracles is almost identical to Maurice's as he himself seems to admit when he refers the reader to Maurice's discussion of miracles in *The Kingdom of Christ*.
18. Charles Kingsley, *Alton Locke, Tailor and Poet* (New York: Harper, 1850), pp. 349–50.
19. Charles Kingsley, *Alton Locke*, p. 348.
20. David Strauss, *The Life of Jesus*, trans. Marian Evans (New York: Calvin Blanchard, 1856), p. 69.
21. Strauss asserts that 'the absolute cause never disturbs the chain of secondary causes by single arbitrary acts of interposition; but rather manifests itself in the production of the aggregate of finite causalities, and of their reciprocal action' (p. 71).
22. *The Life of Frederick Denison Maurice*, 2 vols, edited by Frederick Maurice (London: Macmillan and Co, 1884), II, 454.
23. Maurice here anticipates the more famous arguments of twentieth-century authors such as G. K. Chesterton, J. R. R. Tolkien and C. S. Lewis. See for example G. K. Chesterton, 'Man and Mythologies', in *The Everlasting Man* (San Francisco: Ignatius, 1993), pp. 101–15; J. R. R. Tolkien, 'On Fairy-Stories', in *A Tolkien Miscellany* (New York: SFBC, 2002), pp. 137–38; and C. S. Lewis, 'Myth Become Fact', in *Essay Collection and Other Short Pieces*, ed by Lesley Walmsley (London: HarperCollins, 2000), pp. 138–42.
24. *The Life of Frederick Denison Maurice*, II, 455.
25. Frederick Denison Maurice, 'The Miracles', in *What is Revelation?* (Cambridge: Macmillan, 1859), p. 57.
26. No bibliography or biography that I know mentions the serialisation, which is odd considering MacDonald also published *Annals of a Quiet Neighbourhood* (1865–66), *A Seaboard Parish* (1867–68), and *The Vicar's Daughter* (1871–72) in the same periodical. The *Sunday Magazine* was an Alexander Strahan publication along with *Good Words* and *Good Words for the Young*, in which three journals MacDonald serialised a majority of his work in the late 1860s and early 1870s. The text is identical to the book, but the *Sunday Magazine* also included several woodcut illustrations of Jesus performing miracles. George MacDonald, *The Miracles of Our Lord* (Whitethorn: Johannesen, 2000), p. 233.
27. This is also the only example of MacDonald 'offering' a book rather than dedicating it.
28. It was Strahan that first delivered the news to the MacDonald family that Maurice had died. Greville MacDonald, *George MacDonald and His Wife* (London: George Allen & Unwin, 1924), p. 415.
29. Greville MacDonald, p. 399. Greville speculates that the reason this project never materialised was Maurice's failing health. In any case, it shows that Maurice respected MacDonald's work and wanted to help out the young writer whose family and financial obligations were burgeoning.
30. Wordsworth wrote: 'every Author, as far as he is great and at the same time *original*, has had the task of *creating* the taste by which he is to be enjoyed'. 'Essay Supplementary to the Preface', in *The Poetical Works* (New Haven: Peck & Newton, 1836), p. xvi.

31. *The Illustrated Review* (December 1870), p. 195. The handful of reviews were entirely positive. See also *The British Quarterly Review*, 53:105 (January 1871), p. 285; *The London Quarterly Review*, 36 (1871), p. 247.
32. George MacDonald, *The Complete Fairy Tales* (New York: Penguin, 1999), p. 64.
33. George MacDonad, *Adela Cathcart* (Whitethorn: Johannesen, 2000), p. 218.
34. George MacDonald, 'The Fantastic Imagination', in *A Dish of Orts* (Whitethorn: Johannesen, 1996), p. 322.
35. Erich Auerbach, *Mimesis*, translated by Willard R. Trask (Princeton: Princeton University Press, 2003), pp. 23, 15.
36. MacDonald, *A Dish of Orts*, p. 321.
37. St Augustine, *On Christian Doctrine*, translated by J. F. Shaw, in *Nicene and Post-Nicene Fathers*, vol 2, edited by Philip Schaff (Peabody, Massachusetts: Hendrickson, 2004), p. 533.

Bibliography

Auerbach, Erich, *Mimesis*, trans Willard R. Trask (Princeton: Princeton University Press, 2003).
St Augustine, *On Christian Doctrine*, trans J. F. Shaw, in *Nicene and Post-Nicene Fathers*, vol 2, edited by Philip Schaff (Peabody: Hendrickson, 2004).
Barth, J. Robert, *Coleridge and Christian Doctrine* (New York: Fordham University Press, 1987).
The British Quarterly Review, 53:105 (January 1871).
Burwick, Frederick, 'Coleridge and De Quincey: Inspiration and Revelation', in *Poetic Madness and the Romantic Imagination* (University Park: Pennsylvania State University Press, 1996), pp. 43–59.
Chesterton, G. K., *The Everlasting Man* (San Francisco: Ignatius, 1993), pp. 101–15.
Coleridge, Samuel Taylor, *Lay Sermons* (London: Edward Moxon, 1852).
— *The Major Works* (Oxford: Oxford University Press, 2000).
The Edinburgh Review vol 27 (Edinburgh: Archibald Constable, 1816).
Hume, David, 'Of Miracles', in *Essays and Treatises*, vol 3 (Basel: J. J. Tourneisen, 1793).
The Illustrated Review (December 1870).
Kingsley, Charles, *Alton Locke, Tailor and Poet* (New York: Harper, 1850).
Lewis, C. S., 'Myth Become Fact', in *Essay Collection and Other Short Pieces*, ed Lesley Walmsley (London: HarperCollins, 2000), pp. 138–42.
The London Quarterly Review, 36 (1871).
MacDonald, George, *Adela Cathcart* (Whitethorn: Johannesen, 2000).
— *The Complete Fairy Tales*, ed U. C. Knoepflmacher (New York: Penguin, 1999).
— *A Dish of Orts* (Whitethorn: Johannesen, 1996).
— *The Miracles of Our Lord* (Whitethorn: Johannesen, 2000).
MacDonald, Greville, *George MacDonald and His Wife* (London: George Allen & Unwin, 1924).
Maurice, Frederick Denison, *The Kingdom of Christ*, 2 vols (London: J. M. Dent, 1906).
— 'The Miracles', in *What is Revelation?* (Cambridge: Macmillan, 1859).
The Life of Frederick Denison Maurice, 2 vols, ed Frederick Maurice (London: Macmillan, 1884).
McGillis, Roderick, 'Fantasy as Miracle: George MacDonald's *The Miracles of Our Lord*', in *George MacDonald: Literary Heritage and Heirs* (Wayne: Zossima, 2008), pp. 201–16.
Mozley, James, *Eight Lectures on Miracles* (London: Rivingtons, 1865).

Paley, William, *The Evidences of Christianity* (London: T. and J. Allan, 1823).
Prickett, Stephen, *Romanticism and Religion: The Tradition of Coleridge and Wordsworth in the Victorian Church* (Cambridge: Cambridge University Press, 1976).
Scott, Alexander John, 'On Revelation', in *Discourses* (London: Macmillan, 1866).
Spinoza, Baruch, 'Of Miracles', in *A Theologico-Political Treatise* (London: Trubner, 1862) http://www.philosophyarchive.com/index.php?title=ChapterVI_-_A_Theologico-Political_Treatise_-_Spinoza [accessed 10 December 2011].
Strauss, David, *The Life of Jesus*, trans Marian Evans (New York: Calvin Blanchard, 1856).
Tolkien, J. R. R., 'On Fairy-Stories', in *A Tolkien Miscellany* (New York: SFBC, 2002).
Wordsworth, William, 'Essay Supplementary to the Preface', in *The Poetical Works* (New Haven: Peck & Newton, 1836).

'With all sorts of doubts I am familiar': George MacDonald's Literary Response to John Ruskin's Struggles with Epistemology

JOCELYNE SLEPYAN

Raised in a Scottish Calvinist home and ministering briefly at a Congregationalist church, George MacDonald had experienced firsthand the turmoil of defining his beliefs and addressing doctrinal tensions inside the church. His own conclusions about faith and interest in Novalis prompted his Congregationalist flock to criticise and question their minister. In response to the letter of a woman in 1866 questioning whether he had any of the old Calvinist faith left, MacDonald confessed that he had many doubts but that each pushed him less to creeds than to the person and message of Jesus. He saw great good coming out of his doubts, finding they resulted in 'a widening of my heart and soul and mind to greater glories of the truth'.[1]

For many of his peers, however, religious doubt was a difficult feeling to be ignored until it could no longer be denied. Inside the church, the undermining of literal interpretations of Scripture caused confusion for both evangelicals and mainstream churchgoers, while the realm of science brought new geological and biological observations, challenging traditional understandings of the age of the earth and man's evolution. By 1862, the challenges posed to churchmen of the Victorian age were summed up by the Bishop of London, Archibald Campbell Tait, as those of 'an inquisitive and restless age' where many 'intelligent Englishmen [were] impatient both of political and still more of ecclesiastical control'.[2] Beyond the political and ecclesiastical, Matthew Arnold, George Eliot, and John Ruskin all addressed their personal doubts in their writing. George MacDonald's concern for the spiritual struggles of many of his contemporaries emerged through his friendship with John Ruskin and this chapter will examine MacDonald's later literary response to Ruskin's doubts, written over a decade after their first correspondence.

At the time of his introduction to MacDonald in 1863, John Ruskin was a household name amid the Victorian middle and upper classes, as he had a prolific career as an art and social critic. Writing the five volumes of *Modern Painters* from 1843 to 1860, Ruskin adopted an evangelical tone, viewing art as praise of God and urging artists to produce true likenesses of nature as the most evident manifestation of a benevolent designer. In the first three books of the series, Ruskin relied heavily on the apologetics of natural design, and paid tribute to his education in William Paley's *Natural Theology* (1802) and the similar arguments of the *Bridgewater Treatises* (1832). Ruskin's Calvinist heritage also supported proofs of God from the creation, and Ruskin argued in *Modern Painters II* that art would raise the higher moral sensibilities of the nation through depicting God's creation.

But by the time Ruskin met George MacDonald, his faith had been shaken and he had experienced what he called his 'unconversion'. Ruskin's loss of faith could be considered exemplary of what many in his generation experienced: from 1802 with the publication of Paley's celebrated *Natural Theology* until the middle of the nineteenth century, many evangelicals relied on nature for proofs of God's existence as a benevolent creator evident to all.[3] George Eliot, in reviewing *Modern Painters III*, appreciated Ruskin's elevation of nature even over Scripture as, in Eliot's words, 'the doctrine that all truth and beauty are to be attained by a humble and faithful study of nature'.[4] But this reliance on nature became uncomfortable for Ruskin and others as nature failed to support literal readings of Scripture, and as advances in geology and biology began to question Scripture-based arguments for the age of the earth and proposed natural selection over a purposeful deity. Higher criticism of the Bible also challenged literalist readings with questions of authorship, sources and the explanations of miracles.

The state of the church in Christendom, however, was the final straw in Ruskin's unconversion, and it was a distressing subject for his contemporaries as well. Though he grew up Calvinist, Ruskin's time at Oxford influenced him in favour of the Church of England, and he retained a strong sense of the church's collective witness to the world. But his high expectations of the church's role as a guide to society drove him to despair over the apathy he noted there. As he wrote to Robert and Elizabeth Barrett Browning in 1858:

> most churches are in a sad way because they all keep preaching the wrong way upwards [...] those people are to be exalted in eternity who in this life have striven to do God's will, not their own. And so very few people appear to me to do this in reality that I don't know what to believe. (pp. 279–80)[5]

Ruskin's spiritual crisis ultimately formed around questions of knowing truth, particularly as the basis of his faith came from proofs from nature, from the authentic claims of Scripture and from the witness of the church. Watching nature's message shift with new science, biblical criticism undermine assumptions of verity, and the church fail in its duty, Ruskin began his friendship with George MacDonald already embittered. Their correspondence surrounded literature and arguments for faith. On the publication of MacDonald's *Unspoken Sermons*, Ruskin called them 'unspeakably beautiful' and lamented, 'if only they were true'.[6] To MacDonald's confidence in the story of Jesus, Ruskin argued that he in contrast belonged among 'poor, wicked people, who sternly think it our duty to believe nothing but what we know to be fact'.[7]

The importance of these perceived 'facts' MacDonald would address in many of his novels. With one novel in particular, I want to look at the way MacDonald manifested and addressed Ruskin's doubts. In *Thomas Wingfold, Curate* (1876), MacDonald asserted a different mode of understanding reality from that on the basis of nature, Scripture or the church's testimony. MacDonald presented Ruskin and his contemporaries with the faith argument of personal investigation of Christ, and the testimony of an internal response rather than external evidences. MacDonald argued for an individualism within Christian experience that allowed for doubts, but didn't insist upon Ruskin's communal proofs. MacDonald used story to illustrate this experiential basis for faith.

Thomas Wingfold, Curate would appeal to Ruskin's doubts on several levels. Wingfold, as a clergyman searching for faith from within the institution of the church, would have had particular significance for Ruskin, who championed the evangelical church in *Modern Painters II* (1843), but reacted to the hypocrisy of the church in letters and memoirs.[8] The arguments of the character Bascombe for the comfortable acceptance of 'prejudices a man has inherited from foolish ancestors' which the church (he argues) propagates, would likely have resonated with Ruskin's own investigation of his childhood doctrines.[9] The arguments for empirical evidence Bascombe brings up would also have mirrored Ruskin's questions. Though MacDonald wrote *Thomas Wingfold* years after his first theological letters with Ruskin, the story encapsulates and challenges Ruskin's struggle with belief and doubt.

In *Thomas Wingfold, Curate*, MacDonald creates a story based on the spiritual crisis and awakening of several characters in the town of Glaston, with the primary focus being the spiritual journey of the local curate himself. When a confirmed atheist challenges the curate, Thomas Wingfold, and questions if he actually believes what his profession requires him to preach, Wingfold is startled to realise that he cannot answer. Realising he has woodenly approached the church as a professional rather than a disciple, the curate is galled into investigating the claims of Jesus for himself. His search is aided by his wise friend Polwarth, the gatekeeper of a local estate, who has studied and affirmed his faith in Christ. To the dialogues between this master and pupil of the faith, MacDonald adds the questions of Mr Drew, the local draper, who addresses the problems of applying faith to economic dealings. Alongside the curate's spiritual journey are those of Helen and her brother Leopold; the kindling of their faith comes through a murder that Leopold has committed and repents of. In giving us a host of characters exploring the credibility of Christian claims, MacDonald addresses rational arguments for faith and questions of knowing truth from various angles. In light of their friendship, correspondence and differing approaches to faith, MacDonald set out characters that modelled and addressed Ruskin's particular doubts. By addressing questions of epistemology, MacDonald confronted his friend's conclusions about the need for a chronological testimony to truth and the limits of external evidence.

An appeal to external evidence, to 'facts', initiates the curate's search. In the novel, the character George Bascombe serves as the evangelising atheist and stimulant to Wingfold's journey. He may also be a gadfly to MacDonald's contemporary readers, as Bascombe presents a materialist's scepticism and the rational arguments they would have encountered in late nineteenth-century England. He contends that empirical data are the only facts, and argues against the intangible foolishness of God and the improbability of miracles. Observing Wingfold's 'sensible' side, Bascombe declares that the curate has too much honesty and rational understanding to adhere to Christian claims. Bascombe also exonerates Wingfold's potentially hypocritical post as a clergyman as merely adhering to tradition and a gentlemanly profession.

MacDonald was deliberate in depicting a sceptic of the age who distrusted faith in anything immaterial and 'seemed most to believe that he had a mission to destroy the beliefs of everybody else' (p. 31). Bascombe argues continually that he values honesty, implying that the other characters that choose to believe in the supernatural have a dishonest or self-deceiving nature. Bascombe's words would likely have resonated with Ruskin, whose arguments in *Modern Painters* and his work as an art critic relied heavily on the empirical world. Ruskin took every critique of the Christian doctrine and church to heart, as he noted that his early 'firm faiths were confused by the continual discovery, day by day, of error or limitation in the doctrines I had been taught'.[10] Some of these errors were spiritual claims on the basis of natural theology, the loss of which undermined the basis of Ruskin's appreciation and celebration of art. MacDonald used the character of Bascombe to stir up the arguments for a materialist world and the conclusions that argued against all that couldn't be proven in the external world. This included the negation of any sense of an interior reality, and MacDonald describes Bascombe's imagination and soul as so bound up that he was unaware of them.

Bascombe insists he argues for truth, and sees truth as a communal, external reality. As MacDonald explains, Bascombe's philosophy lies in the idea that if 'any man knew a truth unknown to another, understood any truth better [...] the truth itself was his commission to apostleship' (p. 56). While he has a seemingly virtuous aim described in religious terms, Bascombe saw only the 'distorted shadow' of the beliefs he was fighting to replace with his own. His reality is one of concrete externals, with no tolerance for imagination which 'was of no higher calling than to amuse him with vagaries' (p. 42). Bascombe's confidence in a shared reality based on logic and natural laws prompts him to engage Wingfold, who 'seem[s] reasonable' (p. 29) and therefore amenable. When seeking to sway Helen to his opinion, he advertises his opinion as liberating men from 'a false and brutal system' of religion. There can be communal lies as well as communal truth. This appeal to a common truth that could be argued from logic and empirical evidence was not unique to Bascombe. Ruskin argued it in *Modern Painters II* (1846), though from a very different perspective, that men may know the truth of God from nature. Obstacles to this sight may be based on cultivation of it: 'that whatever may be the differences of estimate among unpractised or uncultivated tastes, there will be unity of taste among the experienced'.[11] From his early optimism of a common consensus, Ruskin eventually swung to the language of a lone prophet in *Unto This Last* (1860) and *The Stormcloud of the Nineteenth Century* (1884). But MacDonald uses Bascombe's confidence in an easily argued empirical 'truth', to hold up to Ruskin and others the inadequacy of such a simple solution to spiritual questions. As the character's confidence in his rhetorical power prompts him to question a cleric about his beliefs, he is 'chagrined that [his] persuasive eloquence' (p. 47) does not secure Wingfold's quick agreement. From the outset, Bascombe's perceived common consensus does not achieve the results he expects.

MacDonald also pursued the logical conclusions of Bascombe's materialist sentiments for Ruskin and others to whom arguments of fact and empirical evidence held weight. If no life exists outside that which is perceived through the physical senses, as Bascombe asserts, the result is a survivalist mentality and strict adherence to pragmaticism over altruism. Adhering to natural laws to determine the value of a life, Bascombe argues for the strangling of dwarfs at birth as a humane act of natural selection easily performed by man. Bascombe also doesn't scruple at deceiving a dying young man in the novel as he rationalises that the boy will soon be nothing at all. At other times, Bascombe argues for sacrifice of the individual for the good and progress of the whole of society, regardless of circumstance (p. 47). Along with his worldview, Bascombe's physique illustrates Darwinian principles, as he 'looked as fine an instance of natural selection as the world had to show' (p. 39), leaving him with little empathy for the frail or deformed. His selection of Helen as a convert to his philosophy and eventually as a wife affirms his worldview, as MacDonald points out that to 'one who has read Darwin' the couple would appear the ideal – perfectly suited to survival (p. 39). In contrast, he sees Polwarth and Rachel as 'physical failures' nullified of their humanity, as he states, 'monsters ought not to live' (pp. 59f). Through the character of the young atheist, MacDonald presents the moral vacuum that he believed came out of materialist thinking; Ruskin would have agreed, as is evinced in such works as *Unto This Last*, which criticised the pursuit of material profit at the expense of people.

In response to Bascombe's disturbing questions, Wingfold opts for earnest investigation of the claims of the church. This may not have been Bascombe's intent in posing the questions, as Wingfold spurns the easy option that Bascombe holds out to him – that he may retain respectability in representing the church because of its traditional and social significance. Wingfold knows enough of the supernatural claims of the church to reject treating it as simply a social institution. Whether he can believe these claims becomes the crux of the novel. MacDonald from the outset rejects natural theology as a basis for Wingfold's conviction. At the conclusion of his discussion with Bascombe, Wingfold is unsettled enough to make a determined search rather than mildly agree to uncertainty.

MacDonald challenges readers who are content to rely on vague faith, learned traditions, or arguments from books. In the first moments after his discussion with Bascombe, Wingfold ponders what reading he might do to argue for the church, and his mind pauses on Paley and Butler, natural theologians that Ruskin and MacDonald would probably have read at university. The reliance on outside arguments for faith and the vast reading list this requires quickly overwhelms Wingfold. Rather than looking to theology or the doctrines of the church, Wingfold poses for himself the questions, 'if there be a God, how am I to find him?' (p. 79) and could the Jesus of the Bible be he? Under the guidance of a friend, Wingfold approaches his New Testament directly to investigate the internal validity of the claims and the man/God that the story presents.

Here is the crux of MacDonald's argument: Wingfold looks for an internal validity to the good news, independent of natural theology or historical analysis (p. 62). But without asserting the infallibility of the Scriptures, MacDonald gives Wingfold and his friend Polwarth the freedom to investigate the claims of the story without the need for historical verification of the text. Declining to recommend any theological texts, Polwarth urges Wingfold to read the 'New Testament as if [he] had never seen it before, and read – to find out' (p. 90). It is a story to read and evaluate if one is 'drawn to the man there presented' (p. 24). This requires a resonance and interaction with the person the story points to, and the eventual trust in the person of Christ that it engenders in Wingfold. The text itself, its authorship, historicity and dating, and other points of validity drop away as the message it bears resonates with Wingfold's heart. This assertion of an internal validation of truth might have jarred one such as Ruskin, who relied so heavily on external sources. Yet in pointing his protagonist to respond to the story of Christ, MacDonald was also encouraging the readership to try a new basis for faith.

Ruskin's sources are not only external but also communal, as he pointed to nature as the simplest template of truth that could be seen by all his readers.[12] Bascombe's arguments from obvious externals would have appealed to Ruskin, Paley and others who subscribed to natural theology, demanding that all truth must prove itself by the testimony of the senses or by deductive logic (p. 246). But MacDonald uses the character to again push the extreme conclusions of arguing for a truth limited to what all can assent to. While Ruskin appealed to men's logic and sight, Bascombe further denies all inward reality of imagination and only admits to what is 'plain and clear' (p. 42). MacDonald remonstrates against Bascombe's inclination 'to deny what we cannot prove', and uses Helen's musings as a counter-perspective: 'what if the warm hope denied should be the truth after all? What if it was the truth in it that drew the soul towards it by an indwelling reality?' (p. 211). There is a loss of individual arrival at truth when reality is determined by what the masses collectively see. But through Wingfold's and Helen's individual searches and conclusions, MacDonald allows for much more private conclusions than Ruskin advocated. The individualism of faith for Wingfold comes in refusing to rely on traditions or others' words, but instead on his own process and conclusions. His proofs come in testing the words not only against his emotional response but also in the outcome of his obedience. As Wingfold notes, he was challenged to take the dependence spoken of in Scripture and only knew it once he applied it. This experiential certainty allows Wingfold to risk intellectual doubts in the midst of an active faith: 'it is the truth of the God of men to me; I will stand or fall with the story of my Lord; I will take my chance' (p. 497).

Even in his role as a minister, Wingfold asserts that there are no certain facts that may prove the existence of God. In ceasing to ask for proofs but rather testing His word by applying it to his life, Wingfold finds 'a power that holds constant and sweetest relation with the dark and silent world within us; that the same God who is in us, and upon whose tree we are the buds, if not yet the flowers, also is all about us' (p. 415).

MacDonald's proofs of truth are interior. His language of 'constant and sweetest relation' seeks to root the reader amid a fairly subjective idea of a God who is within and all around. The absence of empirical proof must find new comfort in the relationship and the ideal. For the sense of beauty and purpose that empirical facts cannot provide, MacDonald argues for immaterial truth that may sacrifice a social credibility. As Wingfold notes to his listeners:

> Even if there be no hereafter, I would live my time believing in a grand thing that ought to be true if it is not [...] Let me hold by the better than the actual, and fall into nothingness off the same precipice with Jesus and John and Paul and a thousand more, [who ...] with their death make even the nothingness into which they have passed like the garden of the Lord. (p. 377)

In Wingfold's effort to investigate without the benefit of external facts but rather in obedience to and testing of the words of God in his own experience, he finds the reality of the relationship breaking into his life. His journey sparks the interest and investigation of others, and though growth comes through discussion, MacDonald makes it clear the truth is arrived upon individually.

This may be MacDonald's most adamant refutation of Ruskin's reliance on external facts: his curate's spiritual awakening comes through an internal response to the message of the story of Jesus rather than the open testimony of nature, the validation of scientific proof or the testimony of the church. The inescapable fact of a subjective relationship with the author of Scripture provides the story's only basis for faith. It's a more individualistic argument than Ruskin would likely have been comfortable with; as a social critic, he addressed himself to the collective reality of Victorian society rather than the individual experience. But with debates questioning the once 'homogenous and satisfactory natural theology', Ruskin and others probably felt and mourned the tenuousness of a collective reality.[13] MacDonald and his characters offered an alternative of a more individual reality, to be attested by some but not assented to by all.

Here was a new mode of knowing, not through the eye, but the attesting experience of the Holy Spirit. Wingfold voices more personal doubts that Bascombe doesn't address: what if he believes simply because he wants it to be true? MacDonald's response is that an honest search will not allow for deception at the outcome. Domineering and arrogant, Bascombe as a character floats on the periphery of credible conclusions; he is immediately presented to the reader as a gadfly stimulating debate, but not as a sympathetic character to follow. Noting Bascombe is 'a character not the most interesting' (p. 41), MacDonald is also dismissive of any virtuous qualities in him, for though Bascombe may be 'armed in honesty, the rivets were self-satisfaction' (p. 43). While he presses the conclusion to the immoral outcomes of Bascombe's beliefs, MacDonald seems to treat the character's arguments as simply the outermost layer of debate. Bascombe's certainty also distances him from the reader, as the honesty and openness of Wingfold remind the reader that all inquiry demands an acknowledgement of what is not known as much as what is. The issues within the church prove more serious as they come closer to the experience of his protagonist. In addressing the apathy of the church in the novel, MacDonald addressed a concern he and Ruskin shared.

After the publication of *Essays and Reviews* in 1860, in which liberal clergy supported higher criticism and rational explanations for miracles, the centralised Church of England had indeed come under fire as an institution. In his personal correspondence and published journal *Praeterita* (1886), Ruskin himself felt the inadequacy and unwillingness of the church to give any good news to the masses.[14] The final straw that resulted in his rejection of the evangelical faith had come when listening to a minister in Turin commending the righteous few of his congregation. Ruskin's early Calvinist doctrine no longer fitted with his mission as a social critic to turn the nation from their materialist bent. In the decades leading up to his loss of faith, Ruskin had openly supported an evangelical approach to art and society, believing both should serve to glorify God. With his disillusionment in the evangelical faith, Ruskin resorted in 1860 to social critiques of political economy and wrote one of his most well-known works, *Unto This Last*. Immediately controversial, the series of periodicals that made up *Unto This Last* argued for economic dealings that benefitted all classes, that brought regulation of a minimum wage, that tempered consumption with an awareness that the more we consume the fewer resources others have. Concerned about the loss of the individual good in a materialist world, Ruskin created his own pulpit where he believed the church had abdicated it.

Sharing Ruskin's concerns regarding materialism and the lack of an ecclesiastical response, MacDonald's frustration with the stagnation and impotence of the church comes through in his novel. The character of Mrs Ramshorne, Bascombe's aunt, upholds an impersonal, moralistic Christianity that does not aid Wingfold's search for God. Mrs Ramshorne's religion centres on the traditional centrality of the church in respectable society; she herself is the widow of a clergyman and feels some ownership of the church. Concerned with maintaining the respectable appearance of the clergy, she is horrified by the curate's pulpit confessions as not in keeping with the 'dignity of the profession' (p. 567). She falls asleep while her niece sings pious songs, but keeps awake to critique Wingfold's unconventional sermons. Like the hierarchical structure that nourished Wingfold's dispassionate career, Mrs Ramshorne's church relies on tradition and maintaining the social status quo. As MacDonald points out, her reliance on appearances limits her spiritual sensitivity, for 'nothing is so deadening to the divine as the habitual dealing with the outsides of holy things' (p. 487). Like Bascombe, Mrs Ramshorne sits on the periphery of Wingfold's quest to find God and her actions as a character focus the reader on the limits of a religion based on externals rather than personal investigation.

MacDonald uses the novel to challenge the passive assent that many in the nineteenth-century church contented themselves with, apathy Ruskin also abhorred. Wingfold's final sermon targets the self-satisfied Christians of his congregation who never cared enough to doubt (p. 497). They are 'poverty-stricken believers', presenting a 'death's head Christianity' to the world that doesn't come close to the 'mighty-hearted' Jesus (p. 498f). Wingfold urges his audience to repent and believe in a nobler Christ, and Ruskin's loss of allegiance to the church didn't stop him from likewise calling the masses to repent and re-evaluate their beliefs and actions.

By following the doubts of the curate, a trained representative of the church, MacDonald attempts to dispel assumptions of inherent piety that the reader might ascribe to the employees of the institution. Wingfold ironically should be a source of encouragement in the faith, and finds himself initially in a vacuum of belief. MacDonald implies the inadequacy of the professionalisation of the church for fostering faith. Rather than his training as a curate, it is the questions of an atheist that stimulate Wingfold's quest.

The conclusions that the curate, Mr Drew the draper, Helen, and Leopold individually draw about Jesus share the common principle of accepting His deeds and His message as the ultimate good, and therefore true. Certainty in proofs has little do with their new reliance on God; rather Wingfold explains that in dedicating himself to following Jesus means he has 'experienced such a conscious enlargement of mental faculty, such a deepening of moral strength, such an enhancement of ideal, such an increase of faith, hope and charity towards all men' (p. 497). Aware of the demands for more empirical evidence, Wingfold dismisses this precondition, saying 'I am content even to share their delusion, if delusion it be, for it is the truth of the God of men to me' (p. 497). This self-attesting reality of God for the characters extends to the existence of all parts of the spiritual world, and MacDonald explains (with the apostle Paul and later C. S. Lewis) that our discomfort in the world verifies another reality:

> But there is that in us which is not at home in this world [...] To that in us this world is so far strange and unnatural and unfitting, and we need a yet homelier home. Yea, no home at last will do but the home of God's heart. (p. 424)

For the characters in the novel seemingly unaware of the inner testimony to Christ, namely Bascombe, Mrs Ramshorne, and other members of Wingfold's congregation, MacDonald makes provision for their awakening at any time. As in his correspondence with Ruskin, MacDonald notes that his characters all may experience the blessings and benefits of doubts. The dismaying fears that Ruskin found so lethal to his confidence in Christendom drive MacDonald, on the other hand, deeper into investigation and to the resolve of a self-attesting confidence. The internal assent becomes the primary proof. Only these doubts and a personal exploration can foster a true look at the message of Christ. As Wingfold explains to his congregation, he fears more for 'him whose belief is but the absence of doubt, who has never loved enough that which he thinks he believes to have felt a single fear lest it should not be true' (p. 498). Entering into doubt brings proofs unavailable without it.

To eighteenth-century theologians such as Paley, nature was at once a stable proof that MacDonald, in contrast, saw as a prompt to spiritual things. Nature may at times bear witness to the reality of the spiritual world, but it just as readily confounds those who want it for a materialistic talisman. In *Thomas Wingfold, Curate,* MacDonald notes that the winter serves as a time 'when all things remind man that his life is not in them', pointing away from the external answers. In contrast to Ruskin, the undermining of natural theology doesn't seem to have touched MacDonald's confidence in the revealing aspects of nature; nature played a regular role in his writings, but rarely as a communal, empirical proof. In his poem 'Nature A Moral Power' MacDonald illustrates the at times hidden power of nature, which requires a response from the beholder: 'Nature, to him no message dost thou bear/ Who in thy beauty findeth not the power/ To gird himself more strongly for the hour/ Of night and darkness'.[15] In *Modern Painters II* (1846) Ruskin had seen nature as a solution to social spiritual ills, and declared that if men looked to the natural world they would see a 'near, visible, inevitable, but all beneficent Deity, whose presence makes the earth itself a heaven'.[16] In contrast, nature in the novel conveys limited revelation of the Creator but does affirm the truth of the universe once a particular character grasps it. Nature stimulates but does not direct. For Helen, as she ponders the implications of her materialistic philosophy, nature becomes strangely human. Riding out in the dusk, she finds the evening seems to be 'thinking around her' and the wind stirs in her a longing for a peace promised by its gentle touch (p. 159). She is initially described as playing the piano 'woodenly', with precision but without passion and yet her new spiritual life rouses her sensitivity to the world around her and ultimately to the Creator. When she is unable to express the desolation of her brother's death, the mournful colour of the evening sky stirs her repressed emotion. The empathy she feels from her Creator through the colours in the sky place nature in a mediating position but not as a concrete validation. Helen's new sensitivity to the things of God and the vehicle of nature would make no sense to the materialistic Bascombe. For Wingfold, in the first consternation of his search, the evening stars quiet his heart with a message he does not yet understand. Nature does not resolve questions, but encourages those who are searching and stirs up those ready to begin.

Although a prompter to truth, nature is not the consistently reliable source Ruskin alluded to in *Modern Painters.* For MacDonald's story, nature also serves to discourage reliance upon appearances. In terms of outward appearances of the characters, MacDonald belies nature's accurate testimony as the spiritual giant of the book is the dwarf, Joseph Polwarth. The dialogue frequently highlights Polwarth's crooked frame and Bascombe's handsome one, stressing the misrepresentation of each physically. The two dwarves frequently refer to the hardship of life in their physical frames and the longing to be out of it, distancing the reader from Bascombe's satisfaction in the allotment of natural graces. The facts of the eye, that Ruskin took such comfort in, fail to discern all beauty. MacDonald also sees that the limits to our current senses may be temporary, as mere shadows of what heavenly senses offer. As Polwarth declares, 'the spaces all between us [...] may be the home of the multitudes of the heavenly host, yet seemingly empty to all who have our provision of senses' (p. 486). Polwarth expectantly looks to what he does not see to atone for and fullfil what he lacks in the current material world.

MacDonald's novel *Thomas Wingfold* was well received and became the first of a trilogy about the characters in Glaston. Wingfold may well have served as a literary response to discussion MacDonald and Ruskin shared regarding truth. Writing over ten years prior to the publication of the novel, Ruskin noted his persistent cynicism in one of his letters of 1866, saying 'Do not think I dislike what you say – or feel it unkind. But it is merely patting a tortoise's shell.'[17] MacDonald for his part was not dissuaded by Ruskin's shell or other men's scepticism. The doubts pushed the dialogue forward, and nature served as a stimulant if not the proof that it once was. Doubt serves as the stimulant for Thomas Wingfold's journey and is a force that each character must wrestle with in the novel. Wingfold's process modelled MacDonald's own, as he explained to his father: 'My error seems to be always searching for faith in place of contemplating the truths of the gospel which produce faith.'[18] These words, coming fifteen years prior to the publication of *Thomas Wingfold*, indicate MacDonald's own struggle to find faith as his protagonist does. The good he found in the investigation prompted his dialogues with Ruskin. As MacDonald noted in the essay 'The Fantastic Imagination':

> The best thing you can do for your fellow, next to rousing his conscience, is—not to give him things to think about, but to wake things up that are in him; or say, to make him think things for himself. The best Nature does for us is to work in us such moods in which thoughts of high import arise.[19]

Notes

1. Greville MacDonald, *George MacDonald and His Wife* (London: George Allen and Unwin, 1924), p. 373.
2. Gerald Parsons, ed, *Religion in Victorian Britain: Interpretations*, vol IV (Manchester: Manchester UP, 1998), p. 4.
3. Robert M. Young, *Darwin's Metaphor: Nature's Place in Victorian Culture* (Cambridge: Cambridge University Press, 1985), p. 27; William Paley, *Natural Theology: or Evidence of the Existence and Attributes of the Deity, collected from the appearances of nature*, ed Matthew D. Eddy and David Knight (Oxford: Oxford University Press, 2008), p. 104.
4. George Eliot, 'John Ruskin's *Modern Painters*, vol III,' *George Eliot: Selected Critical Writings*, ed Rosemary Ashton, The World's Classics (Oxford: Oxford UP, 1992), p. 248.
5. John Ruskin, *The Works of John Ruskin*, ed E. T. Cook and Alexander Wedderburn, Library Edition, vol 36 (London: George Allen, 1909) in *Internet Archive* http://www.archive.org/stream/worksofjohnruski36ruskiala#page/n5/mode/2up [accessed 15 August 2010].
6. MacDonald, *George MacDonald and His Wife*, p. 366.
7. MacDonald, *George MacDonald and His Wife*, p. 334.
8. John Ruskin, *Praeterita and Dialecta*, vol III (London: George Allen, 1907) in *Internet Archive* http://archive.org/stream/praeterita03rusk#page/38/mode/2up [accessed 18 May 2011], pp. 37f.
9. George MacDonald, *Thomas Wingfold, Curate* (London: K. Paul, Trench, Trubner, 1893), p. 43. Further references in text.
10. John Ruskin, *Praeterita*, vol II (London: George Allen, 1907) in *Internet Archive*, http://www.archive.org/stream/praeterita02rusk#page/n9/mode/2up [accessed December 15 2011], p. 231.
11. John Ruskin, *Modern Painters*, vol II (1843) in *Project Gutenberg*, http://www.gutenberg.org/files/29907/29907-h/29907-h.htm [accessed 27August 2012], p. 25.
12. John Ruskin, *Modern Painters*, vol I (1843) in *Project Gutenberg*, http://www.gutenberg.org/files/29907/29907-h/29907-h.htm [accessed 24 August 2011], pp. 193, 205.
13. Young, pp. 127–28.
14. Ruskin, *Works*, p. 280; *ibid*, *Praeterita*, vol III, pp. 37–38.
15. George MacDonald, *The Poetical Works of George MacDonald* (London: Chatto and Windus, 1893) in http://archive.org/stream/poeticalworksge00macdgoog#page/n6/mode/2up [accessed 10 August 2012].
16. Ruskin, *Modern Painters*, vol II, p. 104.
17. Quoted in Greville MacDonald, *George MacDonald and His Wife*, p. 334.
18. MacDonald, *George MacDonald and His Wife*, p. 93.
19. George MacDonald, 'The Fantastic Imagination,' *A Dish of Orts* (London: Sampson Low, 1883) in Gaslight Etext http://gaslight.mtroyal.ca/ortsx14.htm [accessed 1 December 2011].

Bibliography

Abrams, M. H., *Natural Supernaturalism: Tradition and Revolution in Romantic Literature* (New York: Norton, 1971).

Bradley, J. L. (ed), *Ruskin: The Critical Heritage* (London: Routledge, 1984).

Brown, Stewart J., *Providence and Empire: Religion, Politics and Society in the United Kingdom, 1815–1914*, Religion, Politics and Society in Britain Series (Harlow: Pearson, 2008).

Eliot, George, 'John Ruskin's *Modern Painters*, vol III', *George Eliot: Selected Critical Writings*, ed Rosemary Ashton (Oxford: Oxford UP, 1992), pp. 247–59.

MacDonald, George, 'The Fantastic Imagination', in *A Dish of Orts* (London: Sampson Low, 1893) in Gaslight Etext http://gaslight.mtroyal.ca/ortsx14.htm [accessed 1 December 2011].

— *Thomas Wingfold, Curate* (London: K. Paul, Trench, Trubner, 1893).

MacDonald, Greville, *George MacDonald and His Wife* (London: George Allen & Unwin, 1924).

Leon, Derrick, *Ruskin: The Great Victorian* (London: Routledge, 1949).

Paley, William, *Natural Theology: or Evidence of the Existence and Attributes of the Deity, collected from the appearances of nature*, ed Matthew D. Eddy and David Knight (Oxford: Oxford UP, 2008).

Parsons, Gerald (ed), *Religion in Victorian Britain: Interpretations*, vol IV (Manchester: Manchester UP, 1998).

Ruskin, John, *Modern Painters*, vol I, (1843) in *Project Gutenberg*, http://www.gutenberg.org/files/29907/29907-h/29907-h.htm [accessed 24 August 2011].

— *Modern Painters*, vol II (1846) in *Project Gutenberg*, http://www.gutenberg.org/files/29906/29906-h/29906-h.htm [accessed 3 September 2011].

— Modern Painters, vol III (1856) in Project Gutenberg, http://www.archive.org/stream/modernpaintersv0030028mbp#page/n5/mode/2up [accessed 15 December 2011].

— *Praeterita*, 3 vols (London: George Allen, 1907) in *Internet Archive*, http://www.archive.org/stream/praeterita01ruskuoft#page/n375/mode/2up, http://www.archive.org/stream/praeterita02rusk#page/n9/mode/2up, http://www.archive.org/stream/praeterita03ruskuoft#page/38/mode/2up [accessed 15 December 2011].

— *The Storm-Cloud of the Nineteenth Century* (London: 1884) in *Project Gutenberg* http://www.gutenberg.org/files/20204/20204-h/20204-h.htm#FNanchor_20_27 [accessed 5 August 2011].

— *Unto This Last and Other Essays*, ed Ernest Rhys (London: Dent, Everyman's Library, 1907, rpt 1938).

— *The Works of John Ruskin*, ed E. T. Cook and Alexander Wedderburn (London: George Allen, 1909), in *Internet Archive* http://www.archive.org/stream/worksofjohnruski36ruskiala#page/n5/mode/2up [accessed 15 August 2010].

Sudduth, Michael, *The Reformed Objection to Natural Theology* (Farnham: Ashgate, 2009)

Wheeler, Michael, *Ruskin's God*, Cambridge Studies in Nineteenth Century Literature and Culture (Cambridge: Cambridge University Press, 1999).

Young, Robert M., *Darwin's Metaphor: Nature's Place in Victorian Culture*, (Cambridge: Cambridge University Press, 1985).

Thomas Wingfold, Curate and the Mid-Nineteenth-Century Eugenics Debate

GINGER STELLE

To twenty-first-century ears, the term *eugenics* is heavily loaded with negative connotations, bringing to mind images of Nazi death camps and the murder of millions. For the Victorians, however, in the wake of Charles Darwin's discoveries, the then-new theory of eugenics offered an opportunity to take control of human evolution and move it forward in the 'right' direction. Though the term itself was not coined until Francis Galton's 1883 *Inquiries into Human Faculty and Its Development*, the theories had been discussed and debated for nearly two decades. This early debate took many forms and involved people all across the scientific, political, literary, and religious sectors of society.[1] As the other chapters in this volume illustrate, George MacDonald was an active participant in the debates of his age, and those surrounding the early theories of eugenics are no exception. His novel *Thomas Wingfold, Curate* (1876), particularly the treatment of the characters George Bascombe and Joseph Polwarth, clearly shows both an awareness of the ongoing debates and MacDonald's strong personal objection to the central ideas that would eventually become the theory of eugenics.

To say that Charles Darwin's *Origin of the Species* (1859) is one of the most influential and far-reaching books of the nineteenth century is a cliché; it is also true. Its effects reached into nearly every aspect of human life, and ultimately changed the way humanity, as a species, viewed itself and its place in the universe. Even before Darwin's book, many in the nineteenth century were concerned with the issue of degeneration, the fear that society was getting, on the whole, worse rather than better. Diane Paul writes: 'Victorian thinkers struggled to explain the apparent descent of so many city dwellers into lives of pauperism, violence, and crime' (Paul, p. 22).

Darwin's theories provided the beginnings of an answer. Overall, Darwin's theory of natural selection was one of generally upward progress. However, though Darwin initially avoided much discussion of how his theories applied to humans, it was clear to many of his contemporaries that 'progress was not guaranteed' for 'the human animal' (Paul, p. 23). An 1868 essay from William Greg titled 'On the Failure of "Natural Selection" in the Case of Man' argued that the 'effect of the state of social progress and culture we have reached is to counteract and suspend the operation of that righteous and salutary law of "natural selection" in virtue of which the best specimens of the race – the strongest, the finest, the worthiest – are those which survive, surmount [...] and propagate an ever improving and perfecting humanity' (quoted in Paul, p. 29). Greg (and others like him) saw many of the social reforms that had been taking place in Britain as antithetical to the process of natural selection; they felt that 'moral sentiments' were 'interfer[ing] with its beneficent culling of the weak' (Paul, p. 23) and the result was that the 'least valuable individuals and classes were now outbreeding the best' (p. 29), leading to the overall decline of the human race. Furthermore, this decline was

> terrifying to the average middle-class Victorian [...] On the one hand, it represented a profound socioeconomic fear of the paupers and lower classes. Individually, it could take on physical or mental forms, as perceived degenerates were considered malformed or grotesque in their features and deficient in their intellects. These factors also fed into a fear of moral regression; certain 'types' of people were believed to be more inclined to criminal lifestyles.[2]

These fears persisted throughout the second half of the nineteenth century and were a primary reason for the eventual spread and popularisation of the eugenics movement across Britain, the United States, and Continental Europe before the end of the century.

The theories that would eventually be labeled 'eugenics' are generally credited to Francis Galton, a cousin of Darwin, who was deeply influenced by his cousin's writings. His 1865 article 'Hereditary Talent and Character' set out to address the question of whether or not mental abilities are transmitted from parent to child, and what that might mean for the future of the human race. He begins his article as follows:

> The power of man over animal life, in producing whatever varieties of form he pleases, is enormously great. It would seem as though

> the physical structure of future generations was almost as plastic as clay, under the control of the breeder's will. It is my desire to show, more pointedly than – so far as I am aware – has been attempted before, that mental qualities are equally under control.[3]

Though he begins with a comparison to animal breeding, Galton quickly switches to a consideration of humanity, writing: 'The breeders of our domestic animals have discovered many rules by experience [...]. But we have not advanced, even to this limited extent, in respect to the human race' (p. 157). By examining the family trees of successful and renowned members of society, Galton concluded that intelligent and talented parents produced intelligent and talented children, who, in turn, produced more intelligent and talented children of their own. Though he acknowledged that very little was known about the mechanics of human heredity (p. 157), he contends that the existence of heredity, and its applicability to mental as well as physical characteristics, was indisputable.

From this contention, Galton extrapolates the potential effect on the future of humanity. According to Galton, 'What an extraordinary effect might be produced on our race if its object was to unite in marriage those who possessed the finest and most suitable natures, mental, moral, and physical!' (p. 165). He elaborates:

> No one, I think, can doubt from the facts and analogies I have brought forward, that, if talented men were mated with talented women, of the same mental and physical characters of themselves, generation after generation, we might produce a highly-bred human race, with no more tendency to revert to meaner ancestral types than is shown by our long-established breeds of race-horses and fox-hounds. (p. 319)

Galton also describes the method by which this overall elevation of humanity could be accomplished:

> For instance, if we divided the rising generation into two castes, A and B, of which A was selected for natural gifts, and B was the refuse, then, supposing marriage was confined within the pale of the caste to which each individual belonged, it might be objected

that we should simply differentiate the race – that we should create a good and a bad caste, but we should not improve the race as a whole. I reply that this is by no means the necessary result. There remains another very important law to be brought into play. Any agency, however indirect, that would somewhat hasten the marriages in caste A, and retard those in caste B, would result in a large proportion of children being born to A than to B, and would end by wholly eliminating B, and replacing it by A. (p. 319)

With this one essay, Galton inaugurated the eugenics movement.

He was not finished. In 1869, he published *Hereditary Genius*, a much expanded version of the ideas in this initial article. Instead of looking at a limited list of 'eminent' men, he looks at 'eminent' men across society as a whole, from a wide variety of professions and fields, including judges, statesmen, military commanders, literary men, painters, divines, and even oarsmen and wrestlers.[4] His conclusions were the same: intelligent and talented people have intelligent and talented children. However, Galton goes further than he did in his initial article. Rather than simply discussing what was *possible*, he argues what he believes is desirable:

> It seems to me most essential to the well-being of future generations, that the average standard of ability of the present time should be raised ... We are in crying want for a greater fund of ability in all stations of life; for neither the classes of statesmen, philosophers, artisans, nor labourers are up to the modern complexity of their several professions. An extended civilisation like ours comprises more interests than the ordinary statesmen or philosophers of our present race are capable of dealing with, and it exacts more intelligent work than our ordinary artisans and labourers are capable of performing. Our race is overweighted, and appears likely to be drudged into degeneracy by demands that exceed its powers. (*Hereditary Genius*, pp. 344–45)

Adding to this 'crying want' was the shifting demographic of society. As discussed above, many Victorians were concerned about the varied birth rates among the different socio-economic classes. Galton shared this concern:

> Again, there is a constant tendency of the best men in the country, to settle in the great cities, where marriages are less prolific and children are less likely to live. Owing to these several causes, there is a steady check in an old civilisation upon the fertility of the abler classes; the improvident and unambitious are those who chiefly keep up the breed. So the race gradually deteriorates, becoming in each successive generation less fitted for a high civilisation, although it retains the external appearances of one, until the time comes when the whole political and social fabric caves in, and a greater or less relapse to barbarism takes place, during the reign of which the race is perhaps able to recover its tone. (*Hereditary Genius*, p. 362)

Galton's answer to the degeneration he saw was to encourage the 'abler classes' to have children earlier and more often, and to dissuade or delay the reproduction of the 'less fitted'.

In 'Hereditary Improvement' (1873), Galton further explored the methods which could bring about the improvement he sought for humanity. First, he claims that 'It is the obvious course of intelligent men – and I venture to say it should be their religious duty – to advance in the direction whither Nature is determined they shall go; that is, towards the improvement of their race'.[5] He further explains:

> If, however, we look around at the course of nature, one authoritative fact becomes distinctly prominent, let us make of it what we may. It is, that the life of the individual is treated as of absolutely no importance, while the race is treated as everything, Nature being wholly careless of the former except as a contributor to the maintenance and evolution of the latter [...] We are naturally apt to think of ourselves and of those around us that, being not senseless chips, but living and suffering beings, we should be of primary importance, whereas it seems perfectly clear that our individual lives are little more than agents towards attaining some great and common end of evolution. We must loyally accept the facts as they are, and solace ourselves with such hypotheses as may seem most credible to us. ('Hereditary Improvement', pp. 119–20).

In other words, Galton argues that the individual should be willing to sacrifice his or her own personal wishes for the general good of humanity, even if the sacrifices might seem extreme. Galton suggests that this privileging of the race over the individual 'may come to be looked upon as one of the chief religious obligations' ('Hereditary Improvement', p. 120). He continues further:

> It is no absurdity to expect, that it may hereafter be preached, that while helpfulness to the weak, and sympathy with the suffering is the natural form of outpouring of a merciful and kindly heart, yet that the highest action of all is to provide a vigorous, national life, and that one practical and effective way in which individuals of feeble constitution can show mercy to their kind is by celibacy, lest they should bring beings into existence whose race is predoomed to destruction by the laws of nature. It may come to be avowed as a paramount duty, to anticipate the slow and stubborn processes of natural selection by endeavouring to breed out feeble constitutions and petty and ignoble instincts and to breed in those which are vigorous and noble and social ('Hereditary Improvement', p. 120).

Galton views and describes his plan of racial improvement as an ultimate duty, which all of mankind must endeavor to bring about, and while he is careful to attest that he did 'not for a moment contemplate coercion as to whom any given person should marry; such an idea would be scouted now-a-days almost as much as that of polygamy or of infanticide' ('Hereditary Improvement', p. 124), he nonetheless suggests that failure to cooperate would bring consequences:

> I do not see why any insolence of caste should prevent the gifted class, when they had the power, from treating their compatriots [the 'non-gifted'] with all kindness, so long as they maintained celibacy. But if these continued to procreate children, inferior in moral, intellectual and physical qualities, it is easy to believe the time may come when such persons would be considered as enemies to the State, and to have forfeited all claims to kindness. ('Hereditary Improvement', p. 129)

Galton does not elaborate on what should happen to these 'enemies to the State,' but it is not difficult to imagine (and indeed history has proven) some of the possibilities contained in Galton's statement.[6]

Galton's books initially met with a 'lukewarm reception' (Paul, p. 31); however, they succeeded in presenting to public view a completely different perspective on human development, and in doing so, stirred up a debate that would rage for decades. Eventually, it would separate into two distinct branches: positive eugenics and negative eugenics. Throughout his career, Galton tended to support positive eugenics, which 'hoped to bring about a change through moral suasion – the ablest and the brightest would be educated and urged to have larger families than the average couple' (Carlson, p. 9). Negative eugenics focused on preventing the so-called 'unfit' from reproducing at all, using segregation, incarceration, forced sterilisation, and even (as in the case of Nazi Germany) 'systematic genocide' to eliminate 'unfit' races.[7] While the idea of negative eugenics is abhorrent to modern sensibilities, in the Victorian period and the early twentieth century, it actually became significantly more popular than the positive alternative (Perry, p. 18).[8] Although these two branches had not yet clearly separated at the time of *Thomas Wingfold*'s publication, the seeds were present, and the ideas were percolating.

Though he never mentions Galton by name, MacDonald's works show that he was aware of the debate surrounding human development and evolution, both past and future. Unlike many of his contemporaries, he seems to have had little trouble incorporating Darwin's theories of evolution into his worldview. MacDonald accepted evolution as the means through which God created and directed human development. In *Robert Falconer* (1868), MacDonald uses evolutionary language to describe the development of an individual human: 'They are in God's hands [...] He hasn't done with them yet. Shall it take less time to make a woman than to make a world? Is not the woman the greater? She may have her ages of chaos, her centuries of crawling slime, yet rise a woman at last'.[9] In *The Princess and the Goblin* (1872), MacDonald explains the origin of the goblins in clearly evolutionary/devolutionary language:

> There was a legend current in the country, that at one time they lived above ground, and were very like other people. But for some reason or other [...] they had all disappeared from the face of the

> country. According to the legend, however, instead of going to some other country they had all taken refuge in the subterranean caverns, whence they never came out but at night [...] they had greatly altered in the course of generations; and no wonder, seeing they lived away from the sun, in cold and wet and dark places [...] They were now, not ordinarily ugly, but either absolutely hideous, or ludicrously grotesque both in face and form [... They] were not so removed from the humans as such a description would imply. And as they grew misshapen in body, they had grown in knowledge and cleverness.[10]

This is clearly a description of the emergence of a new species through generations of adaptation and evolution. In *The Princess and Curdie* (1883), a central plot device features a boy who, by the touch of a hand, can tell what animal a person is growing (or degenerating) into, which shows MacDonald's engagement with Victorian fears of degeneration (Reiter, pp. 217–18). MacDonald definitely seems to have had a 'comfortable attitude toward the ideas of an old earth and creation by evolution'.[11]

That comfortable attitude did not extend to the theories Galton proposed. From MacDonald's perspective, the relationship between the individual human and the God who created him/her is the centrepiece of the universe. He would have viewed Galton's assertion that 'the life of the individual is treated as of absolutely no importance' ('Hereditary Improvement', p. 119) as inherently dangerous. Over and over again, in both fantasy and non-fantasy, in fiction and non-fiction, MacDonald focuses on individual development, on the idea 'that God wants each person to change, to become the particular person that He had in mind in creating each' (Fink, p. 62). Even in his use of evolutionary language in *Robert Falconer*, MacDonald makes it clear that the individual is of supreme importance when he says 'Shall it take less time to make a woman than to make a world? Is not the woman the greater?' (*Robert Falconer*, p. 459). Curdie is cautioned to be careful of judging whether any given individual is growing upwards or downwards based on outward appearance because 'two people may be at the same spot in manners and behaviour, and yet one may be getting better and the other worse, which is just the greatest of all differences that could possibly exist between them' (*The Princess and Curdie,* p. 97). The growth and development of the individual, not the race as a whole, is the focus.

MacDonald makes this clear in his essay 'A Sketch of Individual Development' (1880).[12] In this essay, he follows a 'typical child of man' (p. 48) from birth through the realisation of faith in Christ. At one stage, MacDonald's hypothetical protagonist looks around at 'the unideal of men in whose company he can take no pleasure – men who are as of a lower race, whom he fain would lift, who will not rise' (p. 58). In this idea of lifting his fellow man from the state of a lower race to a higher one MacDonald echoes some of the language of eugenics. However, when viewed in context, it becomes clear that MacDonald is actually doing something very different. At this stage of development, his protagonist revels in the 'indwelling poetry of science' and the wonders of an evolutionary process that culminated in the arrival of 'the kind he calls his own' (p. 56). This is quickly followed by disillusionment and by the realisation that as 'far as he can see or learn, all the motion, all the seeming dance, is but a rush for death, a panic flight into the moveless silence […] He is filled with horror – not so much of the dreary end, as at the weary hopelessness of the path thitherward' (pp. 56–57). He escapes this horror only when the scientific discoveries he makes '[wake] in him the hope of a central Will, which alone can justify one ecstatic throb at any seeming loveliness of the universe' (p. 57). He continues:

> Life without the higher glory of the unspeakable, the atmosphere of a God, is not life, is not worth living. He would rather cease to be, than walk the dull level of the commonplace – than live the unideal of men in whose company he can take no pleasure – men who are as of a lower race, whom he fain would lift, who will not rise, but for whom as for himself he would cherish the hope they do their best to kill. (p. 58)

When MacDonald speaks of raising 'men who are as a lower race' to a higher level, he is not speaking of eugenic improvement, or even of raising the species as a whole. He is speaking of awakening in each individual a belief and hope in a living, present God. MacDonald goes on to assert that 'Oneness with God is the sole truth of humanity […] In proportion as the union is incomplete, the derived life is imperfect' (p. 74). He clings to the belief that at the heart of things and causing them to be, at the centre of monad, of world, of protoplastic mass, of loving dog, and of man most cruel, is an absolute, perfect love; and that in the man Christ Jesus this love is with us men to take us home. To nothing else do I for one owe any grasp upon life. In this I see the setting right of all things. (p. 75)

He concludes the essay by challenging any 'who would rise to the height of his being [...] to test the Truth' of his assertion about Christ. Again, MacDonald echoes the language of eugenics when he talks about perfecting humanity and rising to the height of one's being, but the path to these things is through the growth and development of the individual. For MacDonald, the life of the individual is not a detriment to humanity's improvement; it is the only way that improvement can happen.

This conflict between the eugenics debate and MacDonald's emphasis on the individual reaches its fullest expression in the novel *Thomas Wingfold, Curate*. The plot of the novel is fairly straightforward. Thomas Wingfold is a curate who suddenly realises that he does not know if he actually believes in Christ. The novel depicts the stages of his journey from doubt to belief. Parallel to this is the story of Helen Lingard, who neither believes nor disbelieves because she has never given it much thought. She is forced to confront her apathy when her younger brother, Leopold, to whom she is devoted, commits a murder and runs to her for sanctuary. Both Helen and Wingfold are prompted on their respective journeys by two central figures: George Bascombe, a convinced atheist who considers it his mission in life 'to destroy the beliefs of everybody else,'[13] and Joseph Polwarth, a convinced believer in and follower of Christ. It is through Bascombe and Polwarth that MacDonald challenges the early theories of eugenics.

At first glance, George Bascombe is a eugenist's dream. MacDonald describes him as 'tall and handsome as an Apollo and strong as the young Hercules, dressed in the top of the plainest fashion, self-satisfied, but not offensively so, good-natured, ready to smile, as clean in conscience, apparently, and as large in sympathy, as his shirtfront. Everybody who knew him counted George Bascombe a genuine good fellow' (p. 12). Bascombe embodies everything Galton would have valued in his ideal humans: healthy, good-looking, morally upstanding. He is gifted with 'persuasive eloquence', which promises to make him a success in his chosen profession, the law (p. 27). MacDonald says that 'To one who had read Darwin, [... Bascombe and Helen] must have looked as fine an instance of natural selection as the world had to show' (p. 39). Moreover, Bascombe views himself as 'one of the prophets of a new order of things' and 'a mighty foe to humbug', which he defines as anything beyond a purely materialistic understanding of the universe (p. 33).[14] Many of the ideas espoused by Bascombe are in keeping with the theories put forth by Galton. He privileges Nature as the controlling power of the universe:

> Nature is cruel enough in some of her arrangements, it can't be denied. She don't scruple to carry out her plans. It is nothing to her that for the life of one great monster of a high-priest millions upon millions of submissive little fishes should be sacrificed; and then if anybody come within the teeth of her machinery, don't she mangle him finely – with her fevers and her agues and her convulsions and consumptions and what not? (p. 42)

He is 'severe' about the 'obligation to punish' wrongdoers (and that strictly) on the basis that 'the good of the whole, and not the fate of the individual, was to be regarded' (p. 47).

Furthermore, Bascombe reveals himself to be a believer in eugenics. While walking with Helen, they encounter two dwarves, an uncle and niece. His reaction is 'moral indignation mingled with disgust. The healthy instincts of the elect of his race were offended by the sight of such physical failures, such mockeries of humanity as those' (p. 45). He tells Helen that 'It is shameful! [...] Such creatures have no right to existence' (p. 45). He continues:

> She [Rachel Polwarth] ought to have been strangled the moment she was born – for the sake of humanity. Monsters ought not to live [...] Don't mistake me, dear Helen. I would neither starve nor drown them after they had reached the faculty of resenting such treatment – of the justice of which [...] I am afraid it would be hard to convince them. But such people actually marry – I have known cases – and that ought to be provided against by suitable enactments and penalties. (p. 46)

When Helen protests against his cruelty in 'heap[ing] unhappiness upon' those who 'are unhappy already', Bascombe replies: 'It is the good of the many I seek, and surely that is better than the good of the few' (p. 46). Not only does Bascombe espouse eugenic principles, he espouses *negative* eugenic principles, actually arguing for the legally enforced celibacy or outright termination of someone he sees as 'hav[ing] no right to existence' (p. 45). It seems there can be no reasonable doubt that MacDonald was drawing on the theories of eugenics being debated in Victorian society when he developed the character of Bascombe.

What MacDonald thought of those attitudes becomes clear over the course of the novel. MacDonald refers to Bascombe and Helen as 'two such perfect specimens of the race' (p. 47), but it is clear he intended this ironically. Bascombe is far from a 'perfect specimen'. He is much more closely akin to those described in 'Sketch of Individual Development' as 'of a lower race' (p. 58) because, like those people, Bascombe has rejected any belief in God, and with it, any belief in anything other than a strictly material existence. MacDonald writes that the 'region of a man's nature which has to do with the unknown was in Bascombe shut off by a wall without chink or cranny; he was unaware of its existence [...] He could not present to himself the idea of a man who found it impossible to live without some dealings with the supernal' (*Thomas Wingfold*, p. 32). MacDonald viewed the existence of the supernal as incontrovertible; Bascombe's refusal to even acknowledge the possibility indicates that he is incomplete. He has consciously closed off a part of his fundamental humanity. Furthermore, Bascombe's principles abandon him at a crucial juncture. Faced with irrefutable proof that Helen's brother is guilty of murder, rather than insist on Leopold's punishment (as his principles dictated), Bascombe goes to France to avoid becoming entangled in a messy situation (pp. 358–59). In the end, MacDonald's ultimate judgment on Bascombe is revealed when Bascombe is rejected by Helen. Having spent the entire book trying to convince Helen that there is no God or life after this one, Helen utterly rejects both Bascombe and his principles, saying 'You need no God [...] therefore you seek none [...] But I need a God – oh, I cannot tell how I need him, if he be to be found! and by the same reasoning I will give my life to the search for him' (p. 504). Bascombe is dumbstruck, and eventually the only thing he can say is 'Well, I'm damned!' to which MacDonald responds 'And so he was

– for the time – and a very good thing too, for he required it' (p. 505). In both the descriptions of Bascombe and in the outcome of the plot, MacDonald's disapprobation of Bascombe and his principles is clear.

That this disapprobation was specifically directed at the theories of eugenics Bascombe proclaimed, and not just at Bascombe's rejection of God, is clearly reflected in the juxtaposition of Bascombe with Joseph Polwarth. Polwarth is one of the dwarves in the park, whose very right to existence Bascombe challenged (p. 47). Nor is Bascombe the only character to make assumptions about Polwarth based on his physical appearance; Helen's aunt claims that 'People that are crooked in body are always crooked in mind too' (p. 438). However, MacDonald immediately begins to oppose Bascombe's words with an entirely different understanding of Polwarth. When Wingfold meets the Polwarths, he comes away 'with the feeling that their faces were refined and intelligent, and their speech was good' (p. 57). As his character becomes more and more prominent in the novel, it becomes clear that Polwarth is Bascombe's almost-complete opposite. Bascombe has the flawless outside, but is spiritually bereft. Polwarth has a 'soul [...] as grand and beautiful and patient as his body is insignificant and troubled' (p. 286). Wingfold calls him 'the wisest and best man I have ever known' (p. 286).

Indeed, Polwarth is the spiritual centre of the novel. He serves as a mentor to Wingfold on his spiritual journey, and helps him through some of the worst of his doubts:

> My dear sir, no conviction can be got, or if it could be got, would be of any sufficing value, through that dealer in second-hand goods, the intellect. If by it we could prove there is a God, it would be of small avail indeed: we must see him and know him, to know that he was not a demon. But I know no other way of knowing that there is a God but that which reveals *what* he is – the only idea that could be God – shows him in his own self-proving existence – and that way is Jesus Christ as he revealed himself on earth, and as he is revealed afresh to every heart that seeks to know the truth concerning him. (p. 88)

As this excerpt (one of many) shows, Polwarth is the character who embodies and speaks MacDonald's core religious principles.[15] While his physical condition would suggest to a eugenist like Bascombe that Polwarth's life was essentially valueless, that the world would be better off without him, MacDonald portrays a man of limitless value, without whom the world, and especially the lives of Wingfold, Helen, and Leopold, would be a colder, darker, more joyless place. Polwarth is directly involved in Leopold's repentance and salvation, as well as Helen's eventual decision to search for God. Had he been strangled at birth as Bascombe suggested, none of that might have happened. The world is a richer place for his presence in it.

MacDonald goes still further, however. Not only is Polwarth an asset to humanity in spite of his disability, but MacDonald also suggests a direct link between Polwarth's physical struggles and his spiritual victories. Polwarth describes his childhood:

> The isolation that belonged to my condition wrought indeed to the intensifying of my individuality [...] The sole triumph I coveted over my persecutors was to know that they could not find me – that I had a friend stronger than they. It is no wonder I should not remember when I began to pray, and hope that God heard me. I used to fancy to myself that I lay in his hand and peeped through his fingers at my foes. (p. 83)

In another place, he comments that 'just because God made me so I have been compelled to think about things I might otherwise have forgotten' (p. 306). His physical disability has helped him grow closer to God. His niece Rachel is similar. Though her face shows 'lines of past and shadows of present suffering', Wingfold nonetheless considers it 'one of the sweetest he had ever seen' because of its 'prevailing expression of [...] placidity' and contentment (p. 68). She tells Wingfold, 'You don't know how happy I am as I lie here, knowing my uncle is in the next room, and will come the moment I call him – and that there is one nearer still [...] whom I haven't to call. I am his, and he shall do with me just as he likes' (p. 202). Her suffering has brought her closer to God.

This is a common theme in MacDonald's writing, and indeed, the Polwarths are hardly the only characters in MacDonald's *oeuvre* that fit this pattern. A number of these characters date from this period of his writing, including the Mad Laird Stephen Stewart and the blind piper

Duncan MacPhail in *Malcolm* (1875), as well as mute Sir Gibbie (1879). In addition, MacDonald created a number of characters in this period who would have been judged as 'undesirable' by the eugenists: the wild gypsy child Theodora in *The Seaboard Parish* (1868), the street child Poppie in *Guild Court* (1868), and even Little Diamond in *At the Back of the North Wind* (1871), who is (wrongly) considered feeble-minded by the people around him. Richard Reis calls these characters MacDonald's 'handicapped saints' and considers them 'the most characteristic and effective of MacDonald's people'.[16] In the context of the eugenics debate, this takes on an even greater significance as MacDonald clearly cautions against assigning value based on artificial, human-defined standards of 'fitness'.

MacDonald underscores this by presenting a couple of direct comparisons between Bascombe and Helen and the Polwarths. Helen comes upon Rachel, working and singing. The sound 'went to [Helen's] heart like a sting, making the tall, handsome, rich lady envy the poor distorted atom who, through all the fogs of her winter, had yet something in her that sought such utterance […] For the being of Helen to that of Rachel was as a single, untwined primary cell to a finished brain' (p. 121). Later MacDonald writes: 'If we are but the creatures of a day, yet surely were the shadow-joys of this miserable pair [the Polwarths] not merely nobler in their essence, but finer to the soul's palate than the shadow-joys of young Hercules Bascombe' (p. 171). In both instances, MacDonald affirms his view that true value lies in the relation of the individual human soul to the creator-God at the centre of the universe.

Early in *Thomas Wingfold*, when describing the garden belonging to Helen's family, MacDonald complains:

> A large garden of any sort is valuable, but an ancient garden is invaluable […] Yet not one of the family had ever cared for it on the ground of its old-fashionedness; its preservation was owing merely to the fact that their gardener was blessed with a wholesome stupidity rendering him incapable of unlearning what his father, who had been gardener there before him, had had marvellous difficulty in teaching him. We do not half appreciate the benefits to the race that spring from honest dulness. The *clever* people are the ruin of everything. (p. 35)

MacDonald was writing at a time when the value of 'honest dulness' was unappreciated and the 'clever people' were trying to redefine human value in terms of racial improvement. MacDonald viewed the eugenic ideal being debated by Francis Galton and others as inherently dangerous, because it devalued the individual in the hope of improving the species. For MacDonald, the only hope for improvement to the species was in the improvement of each individual through a closer relationship with God. *Thomas Wingfold, Curate* represents his most direct argument against the theories of eugenics and serves as a reminder to us all never to forget where true human value lies.

Notes

1. Diane B. Paul, *Controlling Human Heredity: 1865 to the Present* (Amherst, NY: Humanity Books, 1998), p. 31. Further references in text.
2. Geoffrey Reiter, '"Travelling Beastward": George MacDonald's Princess Books and Late Victorian Supernatural Degeneration Fiction' in *George MacDonald: Literary Heritage and Heirs*, ed Roderick McGillis (Wayne, PA: Zossima, 2008) 217–26, p. 218. Further references in text.
3. Francis Galton, 'Hereditary Talent and Character', *MacMillan's Magazine* 12 (1865), p. 157. Further references in text.
4. Francis Galton, *Hereditary Genius: An Inquiry into its Laws and Consequences* (London: MacMillan, 1869), p. xxix. Further references in text.
5. Francis Galton, 'Hereditary Improvement', *Fraser's Magazine* 7 (1873), p. 119. Further references in text.
6. It is worth quoting Galton at this length both because he was the first to really set eugenics forth and also because it can be difficult to separate the early eugenics movement from the extremes reached in the mid-twentieth century. Seeing the actual language being used by the movement at the time of MacDonald's writing helps to understand the actual state of the debate in 1876, without superimposing twenty-first century sensibilities.
7. Elof Axel Carlson, *The Unfit: A History of a Bad Idea* (Cold Spring Harbor, NY: Cold Spring Harbor Laboratory Press, 2001), pp. 10–11.
8. Michael W. Perry (ed), *Lady Eugenist: Feminist Eugenics in the Speeches and Writings of Victoria Woodhull* (Seattle, WA: Inkling Books, 2005), p. 18. This was more true of the United States than of Britain (Carlson, pp. 9–10); however, negative eugenics took hold in Britain as well. G. K. Chesterton, who campaigned against eugenics, notes in *Eugenics and Other Evils* (1922) that a bill espousing negative eugenics had already 'passed with the applause of both parties through the dominant House of Parliament' (p. 19).
9. MacDonald, *Robert Falconer*, p. 459. Further references in text.
10. George MacDonald, *The Princess and the Goblin* (1872; Whitethorn, CA: Johannesen, 2002), p. 13.
11. Larry Fink, '"Natural History – The Heavenly Sort": George MacDonald's Integration of Faith and Reason' in *'A Noble Unrest': Contemporary Essays on the Work of George*

rises to the status of hero by working towards the spiritual and physical welfare of the community. Indeed, Marion may have been modelled after Hill, but the Hill that MacDonald portrays in *The Vicar's Daughter* has been perfected to exemplify not only social reform but divine reform, targeting the souls of the poor as well as their physical needs.

In the mid-1870s, using their adeptness for higher art, most likely due to John Ruskin's primary influence, both Octavia Hill and her sister, Miranda, constructed an organisation of artists and writers to bring beauty to the communities of the poor. The organisation was called the Kyrle Society and MacDonald, as well as his family, played an active role in its initial stages.[5] The Society was supported by various sub-committees or branches (Decorative, Open Spaces, Musical, and Literature Distribution), each responsible for 'diffusing' beauty to the poor in various manners. William Morris fervently supported the Kyrle Society and he, along with Walter Crane, Lord Leighton, Arthur Rackham, and other artists, worked actively through the Decorative branch. MacDonald's talents were used in the Musical branch. It was also during this time that Hill obtained Barrett's Court, a dilapidated housing complex which was eventually rebuilt and named St Christopher's Place. After establishing the new place, Hill began to use it for providing a variety of 'wholesome entertainments' for her tenants. In a letter to her friend Mary Harris, Hill points out that the MacDonald family initiated the first of the entertainments: 'Last night the season opened with a capital play by the MacDonalds, the room was crowded to overflowing.'[6] William Raeper relates that, at Barrett's Court, 'Grace would play Beethoven on her piano, and Greville would scratch on his violin. Their speciality was Carols at Christmas time, punctuated by MacDonald's dramatic renderings of specially composed nativity verses'; in *Reminiscences of a Specialist* (1932), Greville MacDonald remarks that Grace's fine interpretations of Beethoven, Chopin, and Schumann were an especial draw for these social gatherings.[7] Not only did these gatherings become a significant outlet for MacDonald's ministry, but also they provided ample opportunities to work with Hill and to observe her ideals of a more personal and effective social reform which he recreated within his literature.

By the time MacDonald wrote and published *The Vicar's Daughter*, he had lived at the Retreat in Hammersmith for about five years and was continuing to cultivate his friendship with Hill. Both MacDonald and his family were active volunteers for Hill and her fellow-workers and he often opened his aptly-named house to receive her tenants as his personal guests. As well, broader knowledge of Hill's activism was steadily increasing. She produced several reports regarding her work and the need for housing reform in London in the latter part of the 1860s. These would eventually be collected together and published as *Homes of the London Poor* (1875).[8] Hill's housing schemes had a theological impact on the development of MacDonald's social concerns and Hill's articles compiled in *Homes of the London Poor* were directly mirrored in *The Vicar's Daughter*. This is dramatically illustrated in that MacDonald incorporated Hill's and Ruskin's housing reform as one of the key activities of Marion Clare.

That MacDonald used Lady Byron as the prototype for Lady Bernard was apparent at the time of the novel's publication. Lady Byron was instrumental in MacDonald's relocation to London and served as his patroness until her death in 1860. However, a point not yet discussed is that Lady Bernard was the result of a fusion between both Lady Byron and Ruskin. Just as Lady Bernard is responsible for funding Marion's housing complex in the novel, so is Ruskin responsible for having funded Hill's controversial housing schemes. In the novel, Marion's concerns for her 'grandchildren' (the families under her care) lead her to establish a housing project for them and other families whose homes have been crushed by the industrial railway. Lady Bernard and Marion formulate an arrangement that both mirrors and idealises Ruskin's and Hill's housing scheme at Paradise Place. MacDonald details the plan as such:

> Each family is to have the same amount of accommodation it has now, only far better, at the same rent it pays now, with the privilege of taking an additional room or rooms at a much lower rate. Marion has undertaken to collect the rents, and believes that she will thus in time gain an additional hold of the people for their good, although the plan may at first expose her to misunderstanding. From thorough calculation she is satisfied she can pay Lady Bernard five per cent for her money, lay out all that is necessary for keeping the property in thorough repair, and accumulate a fund besides to be spent on building more houses, should her expectations of these be answered. The removal of so

> many will also make a little room for the accommodation of the multitudes constantly driven from their homes by the wickedness of those, who, either for the sake of railways or fine streets, pull down crowded houses, and drive into other courts and alleys their poor inhabitants, to double the wretchedness already there from overcrowding. (*VD*, p. 387)

Two points must be addressed here. First, MacDonald is exhibiting concern over the negative effects of industrialism. Second, MacDonald demonstrates his belief that man must work and pay for what he receives. This is one of the essential points given in the novel and is illustrated with Lady Bernard's insistence upon the working poor being made to pay for their housing. Likewise, Ruskin was adamant that Hill's tenants do the same – suggesting the same return figure of five per cent.[9] Ruskin's claim to Hill was that the scheme would be far more advantageous to the poor. She records that Ruskin once told her 'that a working man ought to be able to pay for his own house; that the outlay upon it ought, therefore, to yield a fair percentage on the capital invested' (*Homes*, p. 18).

Though Hill was originally reluctant to enforce payment, she afterwards began to see the good effects of this structure, for, by paying, the working poor were able to earn what would be theirs and no longer feel anchored by charity. Hill writes: 'I have tried to remember, when it seemed hardest, that the fulfilment of their duties was the best education for the tenants in every way. It has given them a dignity and glad feeling of honourable behaviour which has much more than compensated for the apparent harshness of the rule' (*Homes*, 19). In addition to collecting rent, Hill used these opportunities to encourage and cheer her tenants.[10] These occurrences would have been interpreted by MacDonald as displaying the significance of human touch so greatly emphasised by the ministry of Jesus in *The Miracles of Our Lord* (1870). Although the element of mutual trust took some time to be established, Hill eventually began to make a positive change in helping the impoverished families socially progress which, ultimately, provided them with a sense of honour by earning what they were given.

Another key point in *The Vicar's Daughter* that reflects Hill's theories in social reform is the assertion that monetary gifts may actually hinder the progressive growth of the working poor. Each of the novel's main characters had to come to the realisation that, when considering proper aid for an individual, money can do little good, if any. The reason is that more importantly than financial aid, the poor require human recognition. This idea recurs throughout MacDonald's fiction.

In *The Vicar's Daughter*, during a dinner conversation between two vicars, Mr Walton and Mr Blackstone, the subject of almsgiving arises. Mr Blackstone, who lives and works in London, declares how 'alms from any but the hand of a personal friendship tend to evil, and will, in the long run, increase misery' (*VD*, p. 91). Thus, Blackstone implies that what the poor truly need is human compassion and recognition. Marion makes this need explicitly known later in the novel when she mirrors Blackstone's thought that monetary offerings may serve no good. Her defence is:

> When compassion itself is precious to a man, [...] it must be because he loves you, and believes you love him. When that is the case, you may give him any thing you like, and it will do neither you nor him harm. But the man of independent feeling, except he be thus your friend, will not unlikely resent your compassion, while the beggar will accept it chiefly as a pledge for something more to be got from you; and so it will tend to keep him in beggary. (*VD*, p. 163)

Marion adds that 'the true way is to provide them with work, which is itself a good thing, besides what they gain by it' (*VD*, pp. 163–64). With this example, MacDonald is critiquing the impersonal act of handing out monetary tokens. He believed that, although meant with the best of intentions, it would deny the poor the divine right of labour, completely disrupting their journey towards human perfection.

The novel's emphasis upon the ills of monetary aid was greatly influenced by Hill and Ruskin. Already, Hill began to design arguments to persuade the upper classes to help the working-class poor whilst refraining from monetary gifts. Hill's brother-in-law, C. Edmund Maurice, wrote that she

> believed in personal and sympathetic intercourse with the poor, as far more important than any organisation; and that, where co-operation and organisation were necessary, she preferred small

local efforts to great centralised schemes. At the same time, she felt that the giving of money, when dissociated, as it too often is, from real sympathy, does infinite harm, and should be checked by reformers of charity. (p. 257)

Hill's designs culminated in a paper presented to the Social Science Association in 1869, entitled 'The Importance of Aiding the Poor without Almsgiving'. Hill specifies that although systems may be set in place to effect some change for the needy, and may offer some help, the full range of transforming aid will be limited unless each individual or family is targeted, 'the ground of which can be perceived only by sweet subtle human sympathy, and power of human love'.[11] By stepping over the theoretical lines of the then current state of Victorian bureaucracy in social reform, Hill proposes that each case should be given personal precedence according to the situation. Remarking upon Hill's treatise, E. Moberly Bell states that the 'principles here laid down were implicit in all Octavia's work'; and furthers it by emphasising that money given solely to meet the bodily needs would serve to do harm if it did not aid spiritual needs, which was of 'supreme importance'.[12]

It is also important to consider Ruskin's addendum, published as *Supplement to the Report of an Attempt to Raise a Few of the London Poor without Gifts* (1870). Ruskin supported Hill's treatise but he sought to clarify that both the offering of employment and the joint housing scheme (referring to their initial experiment at Paradise Place) were also gifts. MacDonald agrees with Ruskin and echoes this point in his fiction. And so it is in *The Vicar's Daughter* that MacDonald reveals the extent to which he understood Hill's designs and offers his greatest appeal to draw attention towards the need to help the London poor. Though monetary aid may temporarily ease suffering, MacDonald believed that human compassion and encouragement to develop the imagination would have far greater effects for the good of society.

Though *The Vicar's Daughter* addresses the more tangible points of housing reform and the importance of labour, both of which are principal factors in the spiritual well-being of an individual, MacDonald was especially concerned with the spiritual reformation of humanity. In *The Vicar's Daughter*, MacDonald develops his theory of the divine role of the imagination as represented by Marion's unique methods of reforming the individuals under her care. This is a crucial point for MacDonald since he believed that the development of the imagination 'is one of the main ends of the divine education of life with all its efforts and experiences. Therefore the first and essential means for its culture must be an ordering of our life towards harmony with its ideal in the mind of God' (*Orts*, p. 36). Using Marion as the instrument to demonstrate the theory previously described in 'The Imagination', MacDonald illustrates that the working man, when placed in an environment that is responsive to the care of his own imagination, will achieve a far better good for himself than only having the needs of his physical state met. In his essay, MacDonald proposes through this argument that the imagination of man is divinely linked with the imagination of God and that, as God is ever thinking and creating, so does man think and create. God's imagination flows into man's imagination. In addition to this, MacDonald intensifies this theory by proposing that '[m]an is but a thought of God' (*Orts*, p. 4). Therefore, according to MacDonald, all things originate from God. The purpose of man's imagination, then, is to actively pursue the things which bring him closer to God (*Orts*, p. 2).

Marion exemplifies this theory with the poor under her care when she brings them together for her music recitals. Like other characters in MacDonald's fiction, Marion has come to understand that God can be found via the arts, especially in music. In the novel, Marion's music offers a healing power. As Marion is telling her story to Wynnie Percivale, the novel's narrator, she refers to the encouragement given to her by Lady Bernard to use her talents with music by playing the piano for hospitalised children. Marion adds:

> For she [Lady Bernard] had a strong belief that there was in music a great healing power. Her theory was, that all healing energy operates first on the mind, and from it passes to the body, and that medicines render aid only by removing certain physical obstacles to the healing force. She believes that when music operating on the mind has procured the peace of harmony, the peace in its turn operates outward, reducing the vital powers also into the harmonious action of health. (*VD*, pp. 145–46)

The healing power of music is given in many of MacDonald's works and is undoubtedly a by-product of his romantic idealism. Indeed, the belief that music could have healing properties is not surprising, especially since MacDonald supported the practise of homeopathic medicine. Yet, in a deeper, spiritual sense, such a belief demonstrates MacDonald's view of the spiritual significance of music and the divine imagination.

Later in the novel, Lady Bernard purchases a building where Marion can offer wholesome entertainment to the poor. Towards the end of one evening, a clergyman, 'who knew how to be a neighbour to them that had fallen among thieves' (*VD*, p. 159), offers a few words of instruction and encouragement without being dogmatic. Overall, Marion's method of socially reforming the poor is reminiscent of MacDonald's understanding of Jesus. She states her purpose thus:

> My teacher taught me that the way for *me* to help others was not to tell them their duty, but myself to learn of Him who bore our griefs and carried our sorrows. As I learned of him, I should be able to help them. I have never had any theory but just to be their friend,—to do for them the best I can. When I feel I may, I tell them what has done me good, but I never urge any belief of mine upon their acceptance. (*VD*, p. 152)

This confession is later illustrated when Marion encounters a drunken husband who had just struck his wife. Instead of preaching to the wretched man, she invites him up to her room so that he might hear her play the piano. Leaving the stricken wife behind, with a request for her to come up shortly afterwards, Marion begins playing softly for him. Eventually the man falls asleep under her soothing melody and Marion improvises through her music. MacDonald writes:

> She sung and prayed both in one then, and nobody but God heard any thing but the piano. Nor did it impede the flow of her best thoughts, that in a chair beside her slumbered a weary man, the waves of whose evil passions she had stilled, and the sting of whose disappointments she had soothed, with the sweet airs and concords of her own spirit. (*VD*, p. 234)

As Marion 'prays' out her music, the man unconsciously takes it in and wakes with a clearer mind. Marion asks him to consider visiting the National Gallery with his wife and the man consents. Whilst gazing at the art and discussing each painting, the couple begins to reconnect with each other and were never known to quarrel again (*VD*, p. 236).

Thus, music is not the only means by which MacDonald shows that spiritual reform may be given. As the above example has shown, the imagination, when applied to art and natural beauty, has the potential to reach even the working class poor who may have no knowledge of theory or symbolism. For MacDonald, the imagination is all that is needed to turn a developing mind to the inquiry of spiritual truth. This example precedes MacDonald's essay 'The Fantastic Imagination', where he implies that '[t]he best thing you can do for your fellow, next to rousing his conscience, is – not to give him things to think about, but to wake things up that are in him' (*Orts*, p. 319). This is also illustrated with the use of the fine arts in *The Vicar's Daughter*.

MacDonald offers a few in-depth descriptions of the work of Percivale, Wynnie's husband, who is an artist. Early in the novel, Percivale admits that his art is inspired by love for his wife; it is his love 'which enabled him to see not only much deeper into things, but also to see much better the bloom that hangs about every thing, and so to paint much better pictures than before' (*VD*, p. 16). MacDonald's point is direct. It is out of Percivale's love that his art springs; thus, his beauty comes from God. Percivale is able to see more clearly because his imagination has been cultured and tuned by his spiritual self. In 'The Imagination', MacDonald explains this visionary point, stating that a man may perceive the world around him in accordance to his imagination; that 'the world around him is an outward figuration of the condition of his mind' and that this world serves mankind (*Orts*, p. 5). MacDonald clarifies this point by adding later: '[f]or the world is [...] the human being turned inside out. All that moves in the mind is symbolised in Nature' (*Orts*, p. 9), that '[t]he forms of Nature are the representations of human thought in virtue of their being the embodiment of God's thought' (*Orts*, p. 18). By emphasising that all things are derived from God's imagination, MacDonald then draws attention to the point that it is man's duty to seek out and find the source from whence his ideas have sprung. MacDonald writes: '[t]he man, then, who, in harmony with nature, attempts the discovery of more of her meanings, is just searching out the things of God' (*Orts*, p. 18).

Incorporating this theory into *The Vicar's Daughter*, MacDonald displays a unique interpretation of social reform, introducing the request that the poor be given aid to help develop their imaginations. Doing so would instil in them a desire and passion to seek out that which inspires beauty. This is the key to understanding MacDonald's idea that '[t]o inquire into what God has made is the main function of the imagination' (*Orts*, p. 2). Marion refrains from rebuking the drunken husband and offering dogmatic sermons to the people under her care; instead, she uses the tools that inspire imaginative development to encourage the people to think for themselves and seek out the source from whence their passions originate: God.

To help develop their perception of beauty, Marion suggests that, in lieu of money, a more beneficial solution for the poorer in society would be to offer them natural beauty such as flowers, stating '[a]ll the finer instincts of their being are drawn to the surface at the sight of them. [...] A gift of that sort can only do them good' (*VD*, p. 163). She insists that the poor need to experience beauty, for in beauty they may develop their perceptions of God's work in their lives. This point is echoed throughout MacDonald's works; for example, Lucy Burton, the female 'social worker' in *Guild Court* (1868), proposes a similar idea and actually takes her subjects out of London and into the country, believing that fresh, clean air and open, green spaces were necessary for spiritual reformation.[13]

The spiritual benefit of Nature to the poor was an idea continuously proposed by Hill. Though she eventually served as a co-founder of the National Trust in 1895, she began her environmental campaigns much earlier and used the Kyrle Society to help accomplish these ideals. In the publication of *Our Common Land* (1877), Hill attacks a proposed bill to enclose open land and presents a vision of how ample green space, freely provided for the common welfare, is needed for the moral betterment of the poor. Early in her text, Hill claims:

> To us the Common or forest looks indeed crowded with people, but to them [the poor] the feeling is one of sufficient space, free air, green grass, and colour, with a life without which they may think the place dull. Every atom of open space you have left to

these people is needed; take care you lose none of it; it is becoming yearly of more vital importance to save or increase it.[14]

MacDonald mirrors Hill's environmental ideals in several of his poetical works leading up to the publication of *The Vicar's Daughter*. The strongest example is 'A Manchester Poem' (1871), where MacDonald presents a city that has become scarred by the ills of industrialism.[15] The poem begins with MacDonald's typical view of industrialism:

> Slave engines utter again their ugly growl,
> And soon the iron bands and blocks of stone
> That prison them to their task, will strain and quiver
> Until the city tremble. The clamour of bells,
> Importunate, keeps calling pale-faced forms
> To gather and feed those Samsons' groaning strength
> With labour; [...]. (*PW1*, ll. 7–13)

The shabby housing conditions of the poor, where home is portrayed as 'a dreary place!', are described:

> Unfinished walls,
> Earth-heaps, and broken bricks, and muddy pools
> Lie round it like a rampart against the spring,
> The summer, and all sieges of the year. (*PW1*, ll. 37–40)

The single source of hope displayed within their shabby dwellings is a Bible. Though the scene is Dickensian, with the hard-working but poverty-stricken family hovering around a meek fireplace and a Bible, MacDonald is not content. Even though he believed that true life and all hope can only be found in Jesus, he still turns to Nature. Thus, the impoverished family depicted in this poem is unable to obtain spiritual comfort while they remain in this setting. Rather than only consulting the Bible, they must go directly to Nature to find spiritual truths. However, in the poem, MacDonald's Manchester does not offer parks or other green spaces where locals may encounter Nature. Instead, poor and destitute families must forsake the city and find spiritual refuge in the surrounding countryside. Once there, they are free from their factory prisons and can experience life as God had intended they should. MacDonald states that here, in the midst of Nature:

> the humble man of heart
> Will revel in the grass beneath his foot,
> And from the lea lift his glad eye to heaven,
> God's palette, where his careless painter-hand
> Sweeps comet-clouds that net the gazing soul;
> Sweeps endless stairs, and blots half-sculptured blocks;
> Curves filmy pallors; heaps huge mountain-crags;
> Nor touches where it leaves not beauty's mark. (*PW1*,
> ll. 108–15)

Nature awakens a sense of hope within the poor family and ignites their imaginations to ponder the origin of all things, leading them to God. MacDonald continues:

> Then wakes an unknown want, which asks and looks
> As for some thing forgot – loved long ago,
> But on the hither verge of childhood dropt:
> 'Tis but home-sickness roused in the soul by Spring!
> Fresh birth and eager growth, reviving life,
> Which *is* because it *would be* […] (*PW1*, ll. 120–25)

As they continue upon their excursion, they find a snowdrop flower (always a symbol of hope in MacDonald's writing). They gently uproot it, bring it home with them, replant it in a pot, and set it in place of the family Bible: 'Bearing all heaven into a common house,/ It brings in with it field and sky and air' (*PW1*, ll. 190–191). MacDonald's point here is explicitly stated. The hope that the flower inspires within the family offers a greater source of comfort than whatever message they may otherwise read in the Bible. Articles from Nature, such as flowers, are given a special honour, replacing religious dogma and biblical tracts in MacDonald's fiction.

The greatest example of Marion's talent for developing a divinely inspired imagination amongst the poor comes from the way in which she presents the Bible to her tenants. During one occasion, Wynnie makes an appearance at one of Marion's 'conversation-sermons'. At first, she is surprised at what Marion is reading aloud to the poor. Instead of the New Testament, which would have been the obvious choice, Marion takes her reading from 'The First Gospel of the Infancy of Jesus Christ', an early Gnostic gospel. Surprisingly, the reading serves a creative purpose, generating discussion among the listeners. Problems with miracles, existentialism, evil and the 'Historical Jesus' are discussed. Marion's way of presenting biblical stories was indeed creative and full of psychological insight, encouraging her listeners to seek out the truth of the stories in relation to their own imaginations. Like her author, Marion did not merely offer lessons with an expected moral added at the conclusion; rather, if the listener could be brought to feel the truth of the story from within, it would have a greater impact.

In 'The Imagination', MacDonald writes that God's art is in all things, whether it is discovered in Shakespeare's dramas, art, music or even the mere observation of the human race (*Orts*, pp. 3–5, 22); additionally, to be at one with God is to develop the perception that all things are in motion and are progressing towards what God had originally intended them to be. MacDonald writes:

> For the end of imagination is *harmony*. A right imagination, being the reflex of the creation, will fall in with the divine order of things as the highest form of its own operation; 'will tune its instrument here at the door' to the divine harmonies within; will be content alone with growth towards the divine idea, which includes all that is beautiful in the imperfect imaginations of men; will know that every deviation from that growth is downward; and will therefore send man forth from its loftiest representations to do the commonest duty of the most wearisome calling in hearty and hopeful spirit. This is the work of the right imagination; and towards this work every imagination, in proportion to the rightness that is in it, will tend. The reveries even of the wise man will make him stronger for his work; his dreaming as well as his thinking will render him sorry for past failure, and hopeful of future success. (*Orts*, p. 35)

For MacDonald, '[o]neness with God is the sole truth of humanity. Life parted from its causative life would be no life; it would at best be but a barrack of corruption, and outpost of annihilation. In proportion as the union is incomplete, the derived life is imperfect' (*Orts*, p. 74). In his essay on the imagination and in works such as *The Vicar's Daughter*, MacDonald offers a theory suggesting that the connection between God and man is able to, and indeed must be, obtained by way of the properly developed imagination.

Like many other socially conscious characters in MacDonald's novels, Marion Clare learned that, in order to fully help those within her reach, she had to come to an understanding of their humanity and their need for compassion. For Marion, the best way to aid the social progress of the poor was to target their souls instead of offering them monetary gifts. This was accomplished by providing them with exposure to natural beauty, music and other fine arts, thereby initiating imaginative growth. MacDonald represented the social efforts of Octavia Hill by demonstrating these unique methods of social reform throughout *The Vicar's Daughter*.

Notes

1. George MacDonald, *The Vicar's Daughter* (London: Tinsley Brothers, 1872; reprinted by Whitethorn, CA: Johannesen, 1998); further references to this edition will be given in the text identified by the abbreviation VD.
2. George MacDonald, *A Dish of Orts* (London: Sampson Low, Marston, 1893; reprinted by Whitethorn, CA: Johannesen, 2009); further references to this and other essays from this edition will be given in the text identified by the abbreviation *Orts*.
3. Robert Lee Wolff, *The Golden Key: A Study of the Fiction of George MacDonald* (New Haven: Yale UP, 1961), p. 296.
4. See Ginger Stelle's article, 'The Exemplary Deviant: Wynnie as a Symbol of Victorian Womanhood in *The Vicar's Daughter*' in *North Wind: A Journal of George MacDonald Studies*, 24 (2005), pp. 51–60, highlighting MacDonald's challenge to the stereotypical role of women through his portrayal of Wynnie Percivale.
5. The original title for the organisation, as proposed by Miranda Hill, was 'The Society for the Diffusion of Beauty'. However, the society's namesake was John Kyrle (1637–1724), an early philanthropist who planted trees and constructed a public park in Ross-on-Wye. For a thorough history of the society, see Anne Hoole Anderson's 'Bringing Beauty Home to the People: The Kyrle Society, 1877–1917' in *Octavia Hill's Letters to Fellow-Workers, 1872–1911: Together with an Account of the Walmer Street Industrial Experiment*, ed Robert Whelan (London: Kyrle Books, 2005), pp. 703–33.
6. '1 November 1874', quoted in C. Edmund Maurice (ed), *Life of Octavia Hill as Told in Her Letters* (London: Macmillan, 1913), p. 310.
7. William Raeper, *George MacDonald* (Tring: Lion, 1987), p. 265; Greville MacDonald, *Reminiscences of a Specialist* (London: George Allen & Unwin, 1932), p. 34. MacDonald's daughter, Grace, later marred Kingsbury Jameson and named their first child, Octavia

Grace, after Octavia Hill. Unfortunately, Grace died two years later in 1884 and this was followed by her daughter's death in 1891.
8. Octavia Hill, *Homes of the London Poor* (London: Macmillan, 1875; reprinted with Andrew Mearns' *The Bitter Cry of the Outcast London: An Inquiry into the Condition of the Abject Poor*, London: Frank Cass, 1970); further references to this edition will be given in the text identified by the abbreviation *Homes*.
9. See *Homes*, p. 18, for a detailed description of Ruskin's financial plan.
10. See M. J. Daunton's *House and Home in the Victorian City: Working Class Housing, 1850-1914* (London: Edward Arnold, 1983), pp. 140-41, for Hill's approach to her tenants.
11. Maurice, pp. 257-58.
12. E. Moberly Bell, *Octavia Hill: A Biography* (London: Constable, 1942), p. 108.
13. George MacDonald, *Guild Court: A London Story* (London: Hurst & Blackett, 1868; reprinted by Whitethorn, CA: Johannesen, 1999), pp. 195-205.
14. Octavia Hill, *Our Common Land and Other Short Essays* (London: Macmillan, 1877), pp. 4-5. In addition to this text, see Hill's later work, *Colour, Space, and Music for the People*, reprinted from *Nineteenth Century*, May 1884 (London: Kegan Paul, Trench, 1884), pp. 7-11.
15. George MacDonald, *Poetical Works*, 2 vols (London: Chatto & Windus, 1893; reprinted by Whitethorn, CA: Johannesen, 1996), I, 422-29; further references to this edition will be given in the text identified by the abbreviation *PW1*.

Bibliography

Anderson, Anne Hoole, 'Bringing Beauty Home to the People: The Kyrle Society, 1877-1917' in *Octavia Hill's Letters to Fellow-Workers, 1872-1911: Together with an Account of the Walmer Street Industrial Experiment*, ed by Robert Whelan (London: Kyrle Books, 2005), pp. 703-33.
Bell, E. Moberly, *Octavia Hill: A Biography* (London: Constable, 1942).
Daunton, M. J., *House and Home in the Victorian City: Working Class Housing, 1850-1914* (London: Edward Arnold, 1983).
Hill, Octavia, *Colour, Space, and Music for the People*, reprinted from *Nineteenth Century*, May 1884 (London: Kegan Paul, Trench, 1884).
— *Our Common Land and Other Short Essays* (London: Macmillan, 1877).
Hill, Octavia and Andrew Mearns, *Homes of the London Poor and The Bitter Cry of Outcast London: An Inquiry into the Condition of the Abject Poor* (London: Frank Cass, 1970).
MacDonald, George, *A Dish of Orts* (1893) (Whitethorn, CA: Johannesen, 2009).
— *Guild Court: A London Story* (1868) (Whitethorn, CA: Johannesen, 1999).
— *Poetical Works* (1893), 2 vols (Whitethorn, CA: Johannesen, 1996).
— *The Vicar's Daughter* (1872) (Whitethorn, CA: Johannesen, 1998).
MacDonald, Greville, *Reminiscences of a Specialist* (London: George Allen & Unwin, 1932).
Maurice, C. Edmund (ed), *Life of Octavia Hill as Told in Her Letters* (London: Macmillan & Co, 1913).
Raeper, William, *George MacDonald* (Tring: Lion, 1987).
Ruskin, John, *Supplement to the Report of an Attempt to Raise a Few of the London Poor without Gifts* (London: G. Meyers, 1870).
Stelle, Ginger, 'The Exemplary Deviant: Wynnie as a Symbol of Victorian Womanhood in *The Vicar's Daughter*', *North Wind: A Journal of George MacDonald Studies*, 24 (2005), pp. 51-60.
Wolff, Robert Lee, *The Golden Key: A Study of the Fiction of George MacDonald* (New Haven: Yale UP, 1961).

Military Bodies and Masculinity in 'The Broken Swords'

JENNY NEOPHYTOU

When George MacDonald wrote to his father in June 1853, he reminisced about the field he and his brothers had played in as children, now strange 'with the iron nerves run through it, which makes the dear, rugged North one body with the warm, rich, more indolent South'.[1] In this image, railway technology separates the field from MacDonald's memories of his childhood home, while simultaneously creating a conduit through which the perceived characteristics (both moral and physical) of North and South can pass. The body, overlaid by artificial iron nerves, becomes an intimate yet profoundly externalised metaphor that unites the personal and social fears generated by the transport revolution.

In a similar way, when MacDonald's mentor Alexander John Scott gave lectures on socialism in 1841 he argued that the image of the human body demonstrated in microcosm the mechanisms of the social machine, emphasising the role of the individual worker in the external society. In so doing, he championed the cause of social obedience on the grounds that 'if there be incapacity in the hands or in any other region rightly to discharge their proper function, the whole body suffers with it'.[2] The human body as a social metaphor is frequently seen in Victorian literature, unavoidably uniting cultural change with its impact upon the individual. In *The Body and Social Theory*, Shilling argues that 'the study of social mobility, of racism, the formation of the "underclass", social inequalities in health and schooling, and globalisation, are all concerned implicitly with the movement, location, care, and education of bodies'.[3] In doing so, he effectively argues that the social development of a nation is founded upon, and in turn reflected by, the animation and construction of the human body. Application of this theory allows us access to the political subtext of MacDonald's narratives, illuminating the ways in which the physical bodies of his protagonists reflect the aspirations embraced by his political and religious ideologies and, more subtly, the changing social pressures of his era.

Over the years of MacDonald's literary career, the physical body became a political territory claimed by numerous factions debating issues of class, empire, gender, and religion in the British national media. MacDonald was himself a member of the Christian Socialist Movement, whose number also included close friends such as F. D. Maurice and A. J. Scott. The Christian Socialists were known for their prolific conflation of body and society. Indeed, Charles Kingsley's continued association of physical masculinity and morality was soon dubbed 'Muscular Christianity'. MacDonald, along with many Christian Socialists, was wary of the term. In *David Elginbrod* (1863) Mr Arnold uses the term 'Muscular Christian' to mock the physically strong protagonist, while Ralph Armstrong (*Adela Cathcart,* 1864) concedes that many laugh at 'what, by a happy hit, they have called Muscular Christianity'.[4] Still, while MacDonald may claim that 'the true Christian muscle' is the heart, his narratives frequently oppose effeminate bodies, foreign bodies, monster bodies, and manly bodies in a literary resolution of political anxieties.[5] In this he was not unique: Kingsley's *The Water-Babies* (1863) and Thomas Hughes' *The Manliness of Christ* (1880) both use physicality to reflect morality, and both writers were undoubtedly great stalwarts of the Christian Socialist movement. However, MacDonald's unique social nexus together with his economic situation makes him of interest to academic study. Following his move to London in 1859, MacDonald came to be surrounded by some of the most influential social reformers of the Victorian era, including John Ruskin, Octavia Hill, Josephine Butler, the Leigh-Smiths and Russell Gurney. Greville MacDonald recalls the impact of some of the consequent debates in the biography *George MacDonald and His Wife*, where he admits that 'thanks to the frequent talk of women's rights [...] I am still crushed at times by the conviction [...] that I, as a male, am still a worm'.[6] However, friendship did not necessarily lead to agreement, and MacDonald's political stance on many of the issues that concerned his friends – particularly as regards women's rights – appears deeply ambiguous. While respect and intimacy eventually developed between the MacDonald family and the Miss Leigh-Smiths, George MacDonald's first reaction was to name them 'rather fast, devil-may-care sort of girls [!] not altogether to our taste', and although they all seemed 'to draw and paint well' it was only the poorly Anna who redeemed herself by being 'more sweet and womanly'.⁷ Of course, this type of conflict was far from uncommon among the Christian Socialists and their affiliates. Octavia Hill and F. D. Maurice were known to have regular disagreements over matters of feminine propriety, while Charles Kingsley had no difficulty in supporting the controversial Contagious Diseases Acts during Josephine Butler's campaigns.⁸ However, MacDonald's position as a writer navigating the tenuous bridge between middle-class status and poverty made controversial narrative economically unsafe, leading to the sometimes startling differences in narrative style and political engagement found within his work.

Although best remembered today for his fairy tales, MacDonald's fame as a contemporary writer was founded upon his prolific publication of conventional novels infused with theology and an element of realism. While MacDonald himself could work up little enthusiasm for some of his novels (describing them as 'work undone that snarls at my heels') his financial situation was constrained enough to force him, where it did not conflict with his religious beliefs, to appease the literary market.⁹ In 1876 Henry Cecil emphasised the extent to which some of MacDonald's narratives were influenced by his relative poverty, defending what he called 'the perfervid penny dreadful element' in the novel *Thomas Wingfold, Curate* on the grounds that 'a story to him is not simply art but *bread*'.¹⁰ Unusual or controversial styles – such as those employed in *Phantastes* and *Lilith* – gave way to more marketable forms. Despite being regarded today as a pioneering work of fantasy literature, MacDonald's 1858 *Phantastes* met with mixed reviews and initially failed to sell. In contrast, the more conventional 1863 novel *David Elginbrod* received general approbation and became the foundation of a successful literary career. Alexander Strahan's letters in particular demonstrate the pressure on MacDonald to write for the popular market. In an 1870 letter to MacDonald, Strahan goes so far as to beg him to write 'a series of letters from the Vicarage of Marshmallows', commenting that '[a]nything of the Vicarage tone would do'.¹¹ The formulaic nature and commercial success of such novels allows us to view them as a reflection of the social codes and aspirations of MacDonald's expansive customer base. While until recently many critics chose to ignore these novels, focusing instead on MacDonald as a revolutionary writer of fantasy and theology, I argue that within these more traditional novels MacDonald's use of body-imagery (encoding the appropriate performance of social roles within the political context) is inherently conservative, propounding the ideals of Christian Socialism while simultaneously trying to appease his predominantly middle-class readership.

Although MacDonald's writings appeared in print as early as 1846, it is perhaps fair to say that the political environment of the 1850s provided the spur for MacDonald to launch his literary career.[12] Like many of his contemporaries, MacDonald was concerned by the growth of political instability between Russia and Turkey – the more so after diplomatic efforts failed, leaving his brother John trapped in Moscow and the object of an assassination attempt.[13] The politics of the Crimean War were broadcast and extensively debated in the British national media, polarising opinion between those of the Peace Party (supported by Richard Cobden and John Bright) and the Whig government. Despite Greville MacDonald's claims that his father was no politician, MacDonald entered the argument with 'The Broken Swords', a short story published in the October 1854 issue of *The Christian Spectator*.[14] In this short story, MacDonald describes the structure of what he terms 'Christian tragedies', which forms the basis of many of MacDonald's future novels: 'the heart [...] seeks knowledge and manhood as a thing denied by the maker [...] so sets forth alone to climb the heavens, and instead of climbing falls therefore into the abyss'.[15] MacDonald concludes the narrative pattern with the protagonist realising 'I have sinned against my *Maker* – I will arise and go to my *Father*' (p. 635). This reclassification of God from 'maker' to 'father' is a key feature of MacDonald's work (notably seen in 'The Castle: A Parable' and *Unspoken Sermons*), situating domesticity at the centre of both the masculine and the spiritual, and marking fatherhood as the final stage of the developmental journey from boy to man. Implicitly concerned with the development of spirituality and social responsibility in young men, 'The Broken Swords' contextualises a familiar narrative pattern, using the politics of the Crimean War to debate the qualities contributing to social masculinity. In doing so, MacDonald positioned manliness within a contemporary military environment, establishing a connection between martial activity and social masculinity that can be found throughout MacDonald's *oeuvre*.

In 1854, *The Christian Spectator* was a periodical with a strong focus on the juxtaposition of Christian teachings and political events. Topics as diverse as Ragged Schools, the 1851 census, cholera, and parliamentary reform were hotly debated alongside detailed political analyses of the Crimean War. When 'The Broken Swords' was republished ten years later as part of the 1864 *Adela Cathcart*, the political edge of the story appears deliberately blunted – due in part to narrative changes, and in part to its altered position within the body of the work. I argue that the male body plays a different role in each text, delineating contrasts in a continually evolving political morality. As a result, issues of class conflict, citizenship, urbanisation and foreign policy become fluid themes in an overarching debate that carries social masculinity from a periodical concerned with politics and the wartime environment into an era of domestic reform.

The nature of manliness was extensively debated in *The Christian Spectator*, which in 1854 published a trilogy of essays on the mental, moral and domestic claims of young men. The importance of the subject is communicated by the consideration that 'the national boyhood moves in constant subordination to [young men], considers them its standard, courts their company, defers to them as superiors, receives their opinions without examination, and copies their peculiarities'.[16] The influence of young men as social instigators and role-models was a topic of great anxiety during the 1850s, and particularly so after the outbreak of war. Walton argues that the newly martial environment prompted a cultural redefinition of masculinity, in response to media complaints that 'luxury and wealth, together with a long period of peace, had made the stock quality of Englishmen deteriorate'.[17] In retaliation against Romantic ideals of effeminate men, Walton notes how the increasingly popular 'Beard and Moustache Movement' asserted the pre-eminence of masculinity. However, cultural associations between facial hair, animalistic impulses, poverty and military violence acted to polarise opinions on desirable masculine qualities in a time of war. Directly engaging with this debate, the bearded MacDonald opens the narrative of 'The Broken Swords' by displacing a childlike, Romantic protagonist into the heart of a martial conflict. In doing so, he draws attention to the pervasive feeling that a society which cloisters masculinity within Evangelical and Romantic ideals is unprepared for the harsh necessities (and moral complexities) of the Crimean War.

Prefacing the 1854 edition of 'The Broken Swords', MacDonald published the following poem:

> Of the poor bird that cannot fly
> Kindly you think and mournfully;
> For prisoners and for exiles all
> You let the tear of pity fall;
> And very true the grief should be
> That mourns the bondage of the free.
> The soul, she has a father land;
> Binds her not many a tyrant's hand?
> And the winged spirit has a home,
> But can she always homeward come?
> Poor souls, with all their wounds and foes,
> Will you not also pity those? (ll. 1–12)[18]

Within this poem (which is missing from the 1864 version), the presence of victim, tyrant and soldier mimics contemporary representations of the main agitators in the Crimean War, descriptions of whom often conflated morality and physicality. Like 'the poor bird that cannot fly', Turkey was described as the 'sick man of Europe' – an ineffective and unmanly invalid needing protection from an aggressive and tyrannical Russia.[19] Even MacDonald, in an 1854 letter to his father, argued that '[i]t seems base to help the Turks instead of the Poles or Hungarians – one of whom is worth 100,000,000 of the other'.[20] While acknowledging Turkey's right to sympathy, the poem focuses attention on a single soldier sustaining physical and spiritual wounds for a morally questionable cause.

'The Broken Swords' is the story of this nameless protagonist as he moves from a position of effeminate uncertainty to one of masculine strength, a change that parallels his developing recognition of social duty within the martial, work, and domestic environments. When he leaves home for a commission in the army, the young man is presented as a diminutive, physically dependent and sheltered 'pet', whose 'conscience, tender and not strong' transfers 'slowness of determination into irresolution' (p. 634). This prompts the narrator to argue that the conjugation of delicate nature and martial livelihood contains 'elements of strife sufficient to reduce that fair kingdom' – whether body or country – 'to utter anarchy and madness' (p. 634). Commanded to lead an attack on a 'poor disabled town', the protagonist hesitates, asking 'was the war a just one?' (p. 635). Unable to answer his own question, he is haunted by a dream in which he sees 'the body of his father, with his face to the earth; [...] the rough, bloody hand of a soldier twisted in the loose hair of his elder sister, and the younger fainting in the arms of a scoundrel belonging to his own regiment' (p. 636). Within this dream, the regiment rebels against the control of the officers – an act of disobedience that results in the murder of the father and the rape of the sisters. Together, these images predict not only the destruction of the domestic ideal, but also a denial of specific masculine social duties – those of patriarchal obedience and domestic defence. The murder of the father therefore becomes a symbolic rejection of all fathers, whether physical or spiritual, creating a parallel between rebellion, lack of faith and domestic devastation. While in microcosm this dream describes the potential consequences of a failure of control within the regiment, in macrocosm MacDonald associates the death of homeland moral values (encompassed in the domestic ideal) with the pursuit of a morally questionable war. This parallel is emphasised when the protagonist reads a newspaper article on the war that exclaims '[a]lready crying women are to be met in the streets' (p. 635). Faced with a situation in which two concepts of masculinity, martial courage and moral duty, are opposed, the protagonist becomes intensely agitated. When the Colonel notices this anxiety the protagonist is discharged for cowardice, and his sword broken as an example to the army. The symbolic breaking of the sword is synonymous with the fracturing of one aspect of the protagonist's masculine identity – that of martial courage. However, MacDonald asks 'how many men are there who are dependent on ignorance and a low state of the moral feeling for a courage, which a further and incomplete development of the higher nature would [...] entirely overthrow!' (p. 636). In doing so, he engages with the question that stood at the heart of mid-Victorian debates on masculinity: if a moral ideal of masculinity must be abandoned in wartime for the sake of martial victory, does it follow that martial success is dependent upon the recruitment of men who are physically strong and courageous, but morally weak? In an 1854 letter to his father, MacDonald separates moral doubt from accusations of pacifism and cowardice. He writes 'I quite agree with you that there are far worse things than any amount of war and bloodshed; but I am not politician enough to be able to apply my principles to the settling of the question of this war'.[21] Despite upholding the liberalism of Cobden and Bright, MacDonald followed the lead of *The Christian Spectator* in abjuring the Peace Party, criticisms of whom were 'heavily weighted with the language of gender and accusations of effeminacy'.[22] He goes on to argue that manliness is not revealed by a willingness to act or abstain regardless of circumstance, asserting that 'most external manifestations of manhood are dependent on a right condition of heart'.[23]

In a physical expression of his fractured masculine image, the protagonist's body (prevented from developing fully by 'an over-activity of the inward life') is contrasted with that of a 'great, broad-shouldered lieutenant' whose 'firm-set lips [...] and the fire of his eye, showed a concentrated resolution' (pp. 634, 636). However, although the protagonist's sword is broken, the other soldiers also lack the 'right condition of heart' for MacDonald's dual construction of masculinity. Possessed of muscular strength and courage, they are yet willing to attack an apparently defenceless opponent (p. 636).[24] While we are never told that their swords are broken, the protagonist later hears that the entire regiment died in the attack. In contrast, when the protagonist carries away the shards of his broken sword, MacDonald compares the act to the way 'the friends of a so-called traitor may bear away his mutilated body from the wheel' (p. 637). Like his sword, the protagonist's masculine self-image has been broken on the wheel of conflict between two different constructions of manliness; between internal morality, and the external display of martial courage. However, his retention of the two shards offers the reader hope that the young soldier's masculine identity, like his sword, can be re-forged.

MacDonald's use of the moral ambiguity of the Crimean War allows him to express the masculine body as a stage of development between the animal (lacking morality) and the effeminate (lacking strength). We are left in no doubt regarding the worse of the two offences. The protagonist's decision to keep the two shards of his sword confirms that masculine strength can develop in time, while the moral lack demonstrated by the other soldiers is irreparable. However, closer analysis reveals another layer supporting the apparent moral divide between masculine success and failure. Prior to the protagonist's dismissal, the regiment exists under the control of officers (the General having issued commands against 'disorder and pillage'), yet this does not prevent the protagonist from fearing 'what might follow in the triumph of enraged and victorious foes' (p. 636). It is therefore implied that the outcome of the battle is caused by regimental disobedience, with the external moral control of the officers being abrogated in the heat of battle. This assertion of moral awareness on the part of the officers is interesting, since they too are complicit in the dawn attack. However, by equating the external control of officers with a moral 'leash', MacDonald marks a clear distinction between the qualities expected of officers (frequently drawn from the more wealthy families able to purchase commissions) and those expected of mere soldiers (more usually drawn from the lower or working classes). While on one hand the officers are portrayed as soldiers who have gained status through courage and obedience (see for example the 'resolution' and 'animal life' of the Lieutenant), one of the protagonist's first acts is to accept his commission as a gift from his uncle (p. 636). As such, the moral framework that dictates masculinity appears to be imbued with a class dynamic, being derived specifically from the aristocratic or middle-class officers in order to maintain control over the potentially disobedient poor.

The industrialised Manchester in which MacDonald lived while he wrote 'The Broken Swords' is vividly depicted in 'A Manchester Poem' as a hub of Chartism, but an earlier version of the poem is both more brutal, and more sympathetic, in its depiction of the suffering factory workers. Published in his 1857 *Poems*, 'A Dream Within A Dream' tells the story of a poet watching a couple in Paradise dream of life in a Manchester factory. Within the 'chimneyed city', cotton-labourers are put to work by growling 'slave engines'.[25] The dreaming couple enter the factory

> amid the jar,
> And clash, and shudder of the awful force
> That, conquering force, still vibrates on, as if
> With an excess of power, hungry for work.
> (ll. 217–20)[26]

MacDonald's use of language – 'the jar', 'the clash', 'awful force', 'excess of power' – suggests disquiet over the rapid technological advances within the factory. Perhaps this is not surprising. In 1856, MacDonald devoted much time to preaching, and his congregation frequently included cotton-labourers with 'Chartist passions still surging in their bosoms and the Peterloo massacre keeping alive their indignation against mill owners'.[27] MacDonald's familiarity with his subject is evident in 'A Dream Within

'A Dream' when the protagonists, represented as a working-class husband and wife, adapt their 'differing strength' to work. With disturbing imagery, MacDonald echoes the merciless force of the machines by depicting the man's body as a composite of 'wheels,/ And cranks, and belts, and levers, pinions, screws—' showing industrial machinery and flesh as '[o]ne body all, pervaded still with life'.[28] Just as 'The Broken Swords' encompasses a young soldier's physical masculinity in the image of his shattered sword, so 'A Dream Within A Dream' expresses a cotton-labourer's body through the machines of his trade. However, by internalising the machine's relentless activity and demand for power, MacDonald also encapsulates the anger and political unrest of the Chartist movement. In 'A Dream Within A Dream', the threat of this anger is muted in tragedy as the man and woman die, choking on the cotton dust that floats from the looms in a 'heaving tide of death'.[29] However, when the story reappears in 'A Manchester Poem', MacDonald's treatment of the issue appears more decisive.

In 'A Manchester Poem', the behaviour of the man and woman is sharply distinguished from that of the other factory workers. At once more vibrant and more threatening than 'A Dream within a Dream', 'A Manchester Poem' further blurs the boundaries between machines and workers, describing both alike as straining against the 'iron bands and blocks of stone / That prison them to their task'.[30] Despite expressing vague admiration for the 'grandeur' and 'peaceful disposition' of the Chartists in 1841, in 'A Manchester Poem' MacDonald moves beyond characterising workers as 'a conquering force [...] with an excess of power'.[31] Instead, he raises concerns that the fetters of factory work 'will strain and quiver/ Until the city tremble'.[32] As with the animalistic soldiers of 'The Broken Swords', who are killed in battle when they run out of control, 'A Manchester Poem' shows the factory workers on the brink of destroying themselves and the city in their struggle for social reform.

The class politics underlying the political bodies of 'A Manchester Poem' echoes a number of the social principles articulated by Alexander John Scott in *Discourses* (a collection of lectures published after his death in 1866). Although MacDonald had seen Scott lecture many times while at Highbury (1848–1850), they did not become intimate friends until MacDonald moved to Manchester in 1853.[33] Still reeling from his failure as a Congregationalist minister in Arundel, and with charges of unorthodoxy hanging over him, MacDonald could not help being profoundly influenced by Scott, who had himself had his licence to preach revoked under a charge of heresy in 1831.[34] Scott was one of the founding members of the Christian Socialist movement, alongside F. D. Maurice and Thomas Erskine. Like his better-known friends, Scott advocated a vision of social reform that was inherently conservative, relying on obedience and acquiescence to maintain social harmony. His rejection of systemic reform in favour of individual spiritual rehabilitation echoes Maurice's distaste for social systems, and these combined influences were upheld by both MacDonald and Octavia Hill, with MacDonald passionately asserting that no good could be 'effected save through individual contact'.[35] Implicitly, this puts the impetus to change on the individual rather than society, and assumes the responsibility of the individual in social conflict. According to Scott, the influence of individual spiritual re-education would allow harmony to exist between the different parts of the social body, so that individuals would be able to 'look upon the body of man as one', despite 'how strangely multifarious are the portions of which it is composed'.[36] Where a part of the social body fails to act according to its 'right function', Scott describes a dystopia in which '[t]he body acts upon it precisely like a foreign substance, and it acts upon the body precisely like a foreign substance'.[37] Scott's description of rebellion as a 'poison' acting on the social body is reflected in 'The Broken Swords', as well as in 'A Manchester Poem' and 'A Dream Within a Dream'. MacDonald's construction of social masculinity, being driven by collaborating themes of class and conflict, implicitly creates parallels between images of bestial soldiers and monstrous machine-bodied Chartists. In each case, the failure of hierarchical control/obedience results in a conflict that has the potential to spread beyond the immediate disturbance. Before the soldiers are killed in 'The Broken Swords', they commit atrocities that cause a surviving officer to weep, recognising the justification for the protagonist's earlier emotional collapse and declaring that the so-called coward is 'nobler than I' (p. 646). Likewise, the rebelling workers of 'A Manchester Poem' threaten to destroy the entire city in their struggle for power. Within these polarised conflicts, MacDonald's protagonists demonstrate that resolution can only be reached by individuals who are neither masters nor monsters – by factory workers who are willing to walk 'with bended neck/ Submissive to the rain', and by officers who refuse immoral conflict, yet re-enlist as anonymous recruits when conflict becomes justifiable.[38] Through passive resistance against the destructive actions of the rebels, MacDonald's protagonists form a line of defence between social order and disorder – between encroaching 'foreign' values, and a middle-class vision of homeland morality.

This attempt to resolve class tensions is further confirmed in 'A Manchester Poem', when MacDonald uses the male dreamer's bodily submission to transform Manchester into a spiritual testing ground '[d]earer than Eden-groves'.[39] This echoes the sentiment expressed in an 1856 letter to Henry Sutton (then deeply involved in social reform through temperance societies) where MacDonald asserts that 'our holy ideal will be perfected by much that is odious & nauseous in its immediate neighbourhood'.[40] While he appears to suggest that such hardship is beneficial to spiritual development, this message is sharply contrasted by his novels on urban reform (primarily written in Hammersmith between 1867 and 1875). Following the lead of Octavia Hill, novels such as *Robert Falconer* and *The Vicar's Daughter* cite housing reform as a means to spiritual development, under the assumption that spirituality is stifled when it is denied access to beauty. Indeed, in a letter to her sister Miranda in 1865, Hill quotes MacDonald as saying that 'when we have seen the perfectly beautiful [...] it helps us to see all that is lovely in less beautiful things'.[41] However, MacDonald's letter to Henry Sutton demonstrates that it is not *all individuals* who will benefit from the hardship, but rather their development towards the 'holy ideal' exemplified in the bodies of submissive workers and domestic defenders. Like Miss Clare in *The Vicar's Daughter* (1872), a middle-class woman who lives in a violent working-class estate, the dreaming man and woman of 'A Manchester Poem' embody values that are described as alien to their collective. Just as Miss Clare by birth belongs to the middle classes, so do the dreaming couple belong in Heaven rather than the Manchester factory. Miss Clare's middle-class values help her to reform her working-class neighbours, while the dreaming man and woman articulate apparently 'heavenly' values of submission, quiescence and obedience in the midst of a Chartist rebellion. In a similar way, the disgraced officer of 'The Broken Swords' takes on factory work during a strike, before returning anonymously to the army. Existing in a state of disguise, these characters endorse the social practices and values of their natural locus, whether the middle class or Heaven, yet appear to belong to the working class. As such, they promote unity through a seemingly disinterested obedience to the social hierarchy, which is nevertheless associated with the morality of a 'superior' social state.

Within their class disguises, the bodies of those exemplifying the 'holy ideal' act as signposts to their social and spiritual origin. In 'The Broken Swords', the physical appearance of the young soldier's body alienates him from both the military and factory societies, articulating a combined moral and social status that is foreign to either environment. While his slight build externalises a moral delicacy during military action, in the factory he finds that the 'whiteness of his hands and the tone of his voice not merely suggested unfitness for labour', but also generated 'suspicion as to the character of one who had evidently dropped from a rank so much higher' (p. 639). By inscribing his social status on his body, MacDonald naturalises the protagonist's 'white hands', making them appear to be attributes of birth rather than class. Similarly, while his hands may develop the calluses of factory labour, the 'educated accent of his speech' remains unchanged, with the result that his perceived status remains static regardless of employment or living conditions (p. 642). Alienated from his regiment by moral delicacy, he is equally alienated from the workplace by the hands and speech that denote his social position. Even after he has 'approximated in appearance to those amongst whom he laboured' MacDonald informs us that there remain signs that 'would have distinguished him to an observer' (p. 642). One of these is the way in which he reacts to women.

In *Hidden Hands*, Johnson quotes an 1842 report that demonstrates the extensive conflation of womanhood and the Victorian national identity, stating that 'The estimation of the sex has ever been held a test of the civilisation of a people'.[42] Within this report, which used the rhetoric of female sexuality to protest against the employment of women in the mines, the 'estimation' of womanhood becomes the standard by which to measure moral behaviour. MacDonald's narratives demonstrate the pervasive nature of this assumption. In 'The Broken Swords' the action of rape articulates a breakdown in civil order, yet is symptomatic of a wider disregard for the domestic ideal of womanhood. More overtly, in *Donal Grant* (1883), MacDonald writes that 'Every man has to be his brother's keeper; and if our western notions concerning women be true, a man is yet more bound to be his sister's keeper'.[43] This allusion to Genesis 4:9 describes a social and spiritual imperative for a man to defend women, so long as they adhere to what he terms the 'western notions concerning women'. Throughout MacDonald's narratives, this construction of womanhood is upheld as a contrast to masculinity: intangible, emotive, and defenceless where masculinity is physical, action-driven, and combative. The polarity is most frequently articulated through references to Pygmalion, epitomising a conflict between an apparently masculine duty to defend the untouchable feminine ideal, and a man's desire to possess (and therefore destroy) her. This narrative is most literally retold in the 1858 romance *Phantastes*, when Anodos falls in love with a marble statue. While he tries to obey an order from the Faerie Queen to 'Touch Not!', he soon loses self-control.[44] By touching and awakening the statue, Anodos transforms her from amorphous 'Woman' to an individual woman, who runs away crying. In contrast, 'The Broken Swords' describes an inverted Pygmalion narrative, wherein the protagonist maintains self-control. Rather than idolising a marble statue, the disgraced officer falls in love with an unconscious, plague-afflicted woman. As she begins to regain consciousness he discovers a letter from her soldier-lover, and exercises 'painful self-denial' by choosing to leave rather than compel her affection.[45] Unlike either Pygmalion or Anodos, the disgraced soldier proves his masculinity by refusing to 'forcibly' claim the object of his desire, and therefore leaves her in a state of idealised, immobile womanhood.

The protagonist emerges from his 'spiritual trial' in the manufacturing town having proved his masculine worth. Now possessed of a healthy and masculine body, he decides to re-enlist in the army in an attempt to regain his lost honour. This is made possible by MacDonald's decision to recast the war in a positive moral light, with the protagonist assigned to a defensive rather than offensive position, and able to defend a young girl against an attempted rape.

The scene of the soldier's re-enlistment is full of parallels to his earlier dismissal. He is clearly no longer the boy who wore military dress, yet was alienated from his regiment by a delicate appearance. Instead, he returns to find that 'his dress indicated a mode of life unsuitable as the antecedent to a soldier's', while 'his appearance, and the necessity of recruits combined, led to his easy acceptance' (p. 645). In the comparison, MacDonald informs us that the protagonist's new masculinity is an internal reality, rather than an external display. However, he is soon distinguished by his commander as an individual of 'reckless bravery' with 'precision in the discharge of duties bringing only commendation and no exalted honour' (p. 646). His final victory also contains parallels to his earlier martial disgrace. When he acts alone to protect the girl from her aggressors, he prevents the re-enactment of his nightmare of domestic destruction, in which he had been powerless to prevent the rape of his sisters by his own regiment. Moreover, the reader is reminded of the protagonist's earlier assertion that 'the girl alone, weeping scorching tears over her degradation' could approximate his shame at the dishonourable discharge (p. 641). His ability to defend the girl, therefore, brings the narrative full-circle, allowing him to regain his masculine honour while still retaining his moral position. In a physical confirmation of this fact, we are told that '[h]is stature rose, his chest dilated'. even as his actions allow the girl to escape by throwing herself off a cliff (p. 648). Emphasising the parallel between the two bodies, the protagonist is killed by the attacking soldiers, while the girl's body lies 'a broken, empty, but undesecrated temple, at the foot of the rock' (p. 648). Having fulfilled this final stage in his physical and moral growth, we witness a recursion of the scene in which his sword was broken, marking the conclusion of his developmental journey. As he dies, his spirit rises 'triumphant, free, strong, and calm, above the stormy world, which at length lay vanquished beneath him', reinforcing the collusion of spiritual and physical muscularity within a vision of martial success (p. 648).

Under the guise of communicating a narrative concerning the development of the first failing, then triumphant martial body, in 'The Broken Swords' MacDonald indirectly criticises the moral basis of Britain's participation in the Crimean War. In the death of the protagonist's first regiment, MacDonald asserts that mere physical strength is insufficient – that military victory depends on the combination of physical prowess and internal moral strength, which cannot exist in combat without a moral justification. The concluding vision of muscular morality resolves contemporary fears that moral strength may be synonymous with martial inefficacy, yet simultaneously upholds a middle-class construction of masculinity as the literal and metaphorical saviour of the homeland. From 'The Broken Swords' onwards, MacDonald continues this theme of military masculinity, while the point of conflict shifts to position manliness against new social or domestic threats, whether foreign invasion, Chartism, or urbanisation. Examples of this can be seen in texts from the 1864 novel *The Portent* (where a wound taken in battle allows Duncan to rescue Lady Alice and her property from the predatory interests of her family) to the numerous poems dedicated to General Gordon following his death in Khartoum. Transformed from a military commander into 'the black sheep's faithful shepherd', Gordon is styled as a religious hero who, from 'love of life', refused to obey the order to stand down.[46] However, the shift in masculine focus is perhaps most apparent when we compare 'The Broken Swords' in the *Christian Spectator* to the same narrative in *Adela Cathcart*.

While the text of the two versions remains broadly consistent (other than a few rephrasings and clarifications), when 'The Broken Swords' was republished as part of *Adela Cathcart* in 1864 the contextualising framework of the 1854 *Christian Spectator* was removed. The omission of the poetic preface (referencing the Crimean War) allows MacDonald to transform the story into a metaphorical account of Ralph Armstrong's crisis of faith within his curacy. Although the curate claims that the story is based on an overheard conversation, the narrator, John Smith, believes that Ralph Armstrong has instead 'embodied the story of his own life in other more striking forms'.[47] This allows MacDonald to overlay 'The Broken Swords' with a contemporary reversion in which the young Ralph Armstrong leaves home for university, rather than for military service. While studying, he falls into debt under the influence of a Jewish money-lender. Desperate to pay off his creditor, Ralph enters the clergy just as the protagonist of 'The Broken Swords' enters the factory, only to be alienated from his role by 'a feeling of hypocrisy in the knowledge that I, the dispenser of sacred things to the people, was myself the slave of a money-lending Jew'.[48] Moreover, he begins to ask whether it is 'a manly kind of work, to put on a white gown once a week, and read out of a book'.[49]

This notion of manly work was of great interest to many followers of the Christian Socialist movement, whose ideological and theological labour did not conform to the vision of 'muscular Christianity' which they themselves advocated. In *Dandies and Desert Saints*, James Eli Adams highlights Ford Madox Brown's painting *Work* (1852–1865) in which manual labourers form a point of visual communication between the idle or uninterested rich, and the figures of Thomas Carlyle and F. D. Maurice, who stand to one side watching the workmen labour. Despite Brown's description of intellectual labourers as those who 'seeming to be idle, work', a discomforting incongruity is observable between the depictions of the labourers and the ideologists. Brown's labourers are shown intermingled with women, children and animals, in the midst of a chaotic disorder that strikingly contrasts with the complacent neatness of Carlyle and Maurice. In doing so, Brown effectively devalues the masculinity of the labourers, making it synonymous with disorder, the breakdown of boundaries. While Adams describes the popular 'feminisation of intellectual labour' in the media of the 1850s and 1860s, both the curate's tale in *Adela Cathcart* and Brown's portrayal of 'work' assert the manliness of intellectual labour as a stage beyond that of manual labour.[50] When Ralph Armstrong holds out 'a brawny right arm, with muscles like that of a prize-fighter's' he asks whether clerical work is 'fit for a man to whom God has given an arm like that?'.[51] However, he resolves the question by stating his willingness to undertake 'real spiritual instead of corporeal work' and to 'sacrifice my thews on the altar of my faith'.[52] He goes on to assert that a clergyman who doesn't perform real spiritual work is 'less of a man than any other man who does honestly the work he has to do'.[53] Ashamed of the hypocrisy of his predicament, the young Ralph Armstrong leaves the clergy to work as an accountant in London until his debts are repaid. He lives in cheap lodgings, exposed, again like the protagonist of 'The Broken Swords', to companions 'of all births and breedings' who use 'language which disgusted me to the back-bone'.[54] However, in this environment Ralph Armstrong regains both his masculinity and his faith. As he begins to understand these 'outcasts of the social order', he finds himself able to perform 'the work of the Church' by providing both charitable and spiritual assistance.[55] At last, having repaid his debts and discovered a way to render clerical work 'masculine', he returns to his position as curate and marries Lizzie, a lieutenant's daughter from his erstwhile congregation.

In this reversion of 'The Broken Swords', alleged cowardice is replaced by avarice and lack of faith, culminating in Ralph Armstrong's position as a curate indebted to a Jewish money-lender. In an attempt to regain his masculine honour, he embraces life amongst the working-classes of London. Imitating the development of work epitomised by Brown's painting, Armstrong is transformed from being a gentleman without 'manly work' to being a financial worker living amongst the labouring classes. As he rediscovers his faith, he assumes his position alongside Carlyle and Maurice, performing ideological labour to aid the spiritual development of the poor. Although Ralph Armstrong's autobiographical account has no military context, the martial theme continues to link the two narratives by association. Lizzie's status as a lieutenant's daughter distances Ralph's account from the immediate context of the Crimean War, while Adela Cathcart's father, Colonel Cathcart, periodically refers to the military in an anecdotal fashion, commending the actions of the young officer in 'The Broken Swords', and by implication Ralph Armstrong's actions in London, by saying 'you should not have killed him. You should have made a general of him. By heaven! he deserved it.'[56] Translating 'The Broken Swords' from a debate on the nature of masculinity within a literal military environment, the context of *Adela Cathcart* uses the narrative framework of 'The Broken Swords' to recast the argument into a domestic setting, in which the battlefield is transformed into the spiritual temptations of the city environment, and in which the musculature of the protagonist becomes the spur to prompt the development of masculinity within the context of corporeal and spiritual 'work'.

Notes
1. George MacDonald, letter to George MacDonald Snr, 3 June 1853, in Glenn E. Sadler (ed), *An Expression of Character: The Letters of George MacDonald* (Grand Rapids, MI: Eerdmans, 1994), p. 61.
2. Alexander J. Scott, 'On Schism' in *Discourses* (London: Macmillan, 1866, pp. 251–80), p. 266.
3. Chris Shilling, *The Body and Social Theory*, 2nd edn (London: Sage, 2003), p. 18.
4. George MacDonald, *Adela Cathcart*, 3 vols (London: Hurst and Blackett, 1864), II, 21.
5. George MacDonald, *Adela Cathcart*, 3 vols (Whitefish, MT: Kessinger Publishing, 2004), III, 121.
6. Greville MacDonald, *George MacDonald and His Wife*, 2nd edn (Whitethorn, CA: Johannesen, 2005), p. 300.
7. Greville MacDonald, *George MacDonald and His Wife*, p. 270.
8. Charles Kingsley, letter to Josephine Butler [nd], The Josephine Butler Letters Collection, The Women's Library Special Collections, London Metropolitan University, Article Reference 3JBL/03/03; Gillian Darley, *Octavia Hill: Social reformer and founder of the National Trust* (London: Francis Boutle, 2010), p. 78.
9. Greville MacDonald, *George MacDonald and His Wife*, p. 414.
10. Henry Cecil, letter to his brother, 1876, quoted in Cecil, R., 'A tale of two families', *North Wind*, 7 (1988, pp. 15–21), p. 2.

11. Alexander Strahan, letter to George MacDonald, 27 August 1870, George MacDonald Collection, General Collection, Beinecke Rare Book and Manuscript Library, Yale University, Series 1: Correspondence, Box 3, Folder 135.
12. The poem 'David' was published anonymously in *The Scottish Congregational Magazine*, February, 1846.
13. Greville MacDonald, *George MacDonald and His Wife*, p. 167. This story is also retold in the novel *What's Mine's Mine* as the experience of the character Ian Macruadh.
14. Greville MacDonald, *George MacDonald and His Wife*, p. 192.
15. George MacDonald, 'The Broken Swords', *The Monthly Christian Spectator*, January-December (London: William Freeman, 1854, IV, pp. 633–48), p. 635. Further references in the text.
16. 'The Mental Claims of Young Men', *The Monthly Christian Spectator* (London: William Freeman, 1854, IV, January-December, pp. 129–37), p. 133.
17. Susan Walton, 'From Squalid Impropriety to Manly Respectability: The Revival of Beards, Moustaches and Martial Values in the 1850s in England', *Nineteenth-Century Contexts*, 30 (2008), pp. 229–45.
18. George MacDonald, 'The Broken Swords', p. 633.
19. Asli Çirakman, *From the 'Terror of the World' to the 'Sick Man of Europe': European Images of Ottoman Empire and Society from the Sixteenth Century to the Nineteenth* (New York; Peter Lang, 2002), p. 164.
20. George MacDonald, letter to George MacDonald Snr, September 1854 in Glenn E. Sadler (ed), *An Expression of Character: The Letters of George MacDonald*, p. 82.
21. George MacDonald, letter to George MacDonald Snr, September 1854 in Glenn E. Sadler (ed), *An Expression of Character: The Letters of George MacDonald*, p. 82.
22. Greville MacDonald, *George MacDonald and His Wife*, p. 192; Susan Walton, 'From Squalid Impropriety to Manly Respectability: The Revival of Beards, Moustaches and Martial Values in the 1850s in England', p. 234.
23. George MacDonald, letter to George MacDonald Snr, September 1854 in Glenn E. Sadler (ed), *An Expression of Character: The Letters of George MacDonald*, p. 82.
24. The attack in question is on a 'poor defenceless town' and takes place at dawn 'without sound of trumpet or drum'.
25. George MacDonald, 'A Dream Within a Dream', in *Poems* (London: Longman, Brown, Green, Longmans & Roberts, 1857, pp. 165–89), p. 173, line 207.
26. George MacDonald, 'A Dream Within a Dream', p. 173.
27. Greville MacDonald, *George MacDonald and His Wife*, p. 252.
28. George MacDonald, 'A Dream Within a Dream', p. 173, line 225.
29. George MacDonald, 'A Dream Within a Dream', p. 174, line 235.
30. George MacDonald, 'A Manchester Poem', *MacDonald's Poetical Works*, 2 vols (London: Chatto & Windus, 1893, I, 422–29), p. 422, line 8.
31. George MacDonald, Letter to George MacDonald Snr 28 October 1841 in Glenn E. Sadler (ed), *An Expression of Character: The Letters of George MacDonald*, p. 10; George MacDonald, 'A Dream Within a Dream', p. 173, line 217.
32. George MacDonald, 'A Manchester Poem', p. 422, line 9.
33. William Raeper, *George MacDonald: Novelist and Victorian Visionary*, paperback edition (Tring: Lion, 1988), p. 67.
34. J. Philip Newell, 'The Other Christian Socialist: Alexander John Scott', *The Heythrop Journal*, 24 (1983), pp. 278–89), p. 278.
35. George MacDonald, *Robert Falconer* (London: Hurst & Blacket [nd ?1891]), p. 372.

36. Alexander J. Scott, 'On Schism' in *Discourses*, p. 270.
37. Alexander J. Scott, 'On Schism', p. 271.
38. George MacDonald, 'A Manchester Poem', p. 422, line 15.
39. George MacDonald, 'A Manchester Poem', p. 429, line 242.
40. Joseph Johnson, *George MacDonald, a Biographical and Critical Appreciation* (London: Pitman, 1906), p. 40; George MacDonald, letter to Henry Sutton 5 June 1856 in Glenn E. Sadler (ed), *An Expression of Character: The Letters of George MacDonald*, p. 110.
41. Octavia Hill, letter to Miranda Hill, 21 May 1865, quoted in Emily Southwood Maurice, *Octavia Hill: Early Ideals* (London: George Allen & Unwin, 1928), p. 82.
42. Patricia E. Johnson, *Hidden Hands: Working-Class Woman and Victorian Social-Problem Fiction* (Athens, OH: Ohio University Press, 2001), p. 73.
43. George MacDonald, *Donal Grant* (London: Kegan Paul, Trench, Trübner, 1900), p. 123.
44. George MacDonald, *Phantastes* (Woodbridge: The Boydell Press, 1982), p. 94.
45. George MacDonald, letter to George MacDonald Snr, September 1854, in Glenn E. Sadler (ed), *An Expression of Character: The Letters of George MacDonald*, p. 82.
46. George MacDonald, 'Song of the Saints and Angels', in *MacDonald's Poetical Works*, 2 vols (London: Chatto & Windus, 1893), I, 445, line 10; George MacDonald, 'To Gordon, Leaving Khartoum', in *MacDonald's Poetical Works*, I, p. 444, line 26.
47. George MacDonald, *Adela Cathcart*, 2 vols (London: Hurst and Blackett, 1864), II, 261.
48. George MacDonald, *Adela Cathcart*, p. 19.
49. George MacDonald, *Adela Cathcart*, p. 20.
50. James Eli Adams, *Dandies and Desert Saints: Styles of Victorian Manhood* (Ithaca, NY: Cornell University Press, 1995), p. 2.
51. George MacDonald, *Adela Cathcart*, II, p. 21.
52. George MacDonald, *Adela Cathcart*, p. 22.
53. George MacDonald, *Adela Cathcart*, p. 23.
54. George MacDonald, *Adela Cathcart*, p. 48.
55. George MacDonald, *Adela Cathcart*, p. 61.
56. George MacDonald, *Adela Cathcart*, p. 260.

Bibliography

Adams, James Eli, *Dandies and Desert Saints: Styles of Victorian Manhood* (Ithaca, NY: Cornell University Press, 1995).

Cecil, Robert, 'A tale of two families', *North Wind, A Journal of George MacDonald Studies*, 7 (1988), pp. 15–21.

Çirakman, Asli, *From the 'Terror of the World' to the 'Sick Man of Europe': European Images of Ottoman Empire and Society from the Sixteenth Century to the Nineteenth* (New York; Peter Lang, 2002).

Darley, Gillian, *Octavia Hill: Social reformer and founder of the National Trust* (London: Francis Boutle, 2010).

Johnson, Joseph, *George MacDonald, a Biographical and Critical Appreciation* (London: Pitman, 1906).

Johnson, Patricia E., *Hidden Hands: Working-Class Woman and Victorian Social-Problem Fiction* (Athens, OH: Ohio University Press, 2001).

Kingsley, Charles, Letter to Josephine Butler [nd], The Josephine Butler Letters Collection, The Women's Library Special Collections, London Metropolitan University, Article Reference 3JBL/03/03.

MacDonald, George, *Adela Cathcart*, 2 vols (London: Hurst and Blackett, 1864).
— *Adela Cathcart*, 3 vols (Whitefish, MT: Kessinger Publishing, 2004).
— 'A Dream within a Dream' in *Poems* (London: Longman, Brown, Green, Longmans & Roberts, 1857).
— 'A Manchester Poem' in *MacDonald's Poetical Works*, 2 vols (London: Chatto & Windus, 1893), I, 422–429.
— *Donal Grant* (London: Kegan Paul, Trench, Trübner, 1900).
— *Phantastes* (Woodbridge: The Boydell Press, 1982).
— *Robert Falconer* (London: Hurst & Blackett [nd ?1891]).
— 'Song of the Saints and Angels' in *MacDonald's Poetical Works*, 2 vols (London: Chatto & Windus, 1893), I, pp. 445.
— 'The Broken Swords' in *The Monthly Christian Spectator, January–December* (London: William Freeman, 1854), IV, pp. 633–48.
— 'To Gordon, Leaving Khartoum' in *MacDonald's Poetical Works*, 2 vols (London: Chatto & Windus, 1893), I, pp. 444.
MacDonald, Greville, *George MacDonald and His Wife*, 2nd edn (Whitethorn, CA: Johannesen Publishing, 2005).
Newell, J. Philip, 'The Other Christian Socialist: Alexander John Scott', *The Heythrop Journal*, 24 (1983), pp. 278–89.
Raeper, William, *George MacDonald: Novelist and Victorian Visionary*, paperback edition, (Tring: Lion Publishing, 1988).
Sadler, Glenn E. (ed), *An Expression of Character: The Letters of George MacDonald* (Grand Rapids, MI: Eerdmans, 1994).
Scott, Alexander J., *Discourses* (London: Macmillan, 1866).
Shilling, Chris, *The Body and Social Theory*, 2nd edn (London: Sage, 2003).
Southwood Maurice, Emily, *Octavia Hill: Early Ideals* (London: George Allen & Unwin, 1928).
Strahan, A., Letter to George MacDonald, 27 August 1870, George MacDonald Collection, General Collection, Beinecke Rare Book and Manuscript Library, Yale University. Series 1: Correspondence, Box 3, Folder 135.
'The Mental Claims of Young Men' in *The Monthly Christian Spectator, January-December*, (London: William Freeman, 1854), IV, pp. 129–37.
Walton, Susan, 'From Squalid Impropriety to Manly Respectability: The Revival of Beards, Moustaches and Martial Values in the 1850s in England', *Nineteenth-Century Contexts*, 30 (2008), pp. 229–45.

God and Gender in *Robert Falconer*: Deifying the Feminine

PHILIP HICKOK

Rolland Hein has argued that 'George MacDonald was first of all a Christian; secondly an artist'.[1] Hein supports this claim with Ronald MacDonald's assertion that his father turned to writing novels as a means of communicating his religious message after losing his pulpit at Arundel. Ronald MacDonald relates:

> Once I asked him why he did not, for a change of variety, write a story of mere human passion and artistic plot. He replied that he would like to write it. I asked him then further whether his highest literary quality was not in a measure injured by what must to many seem the monotony of his theme – referring to the novels alone. He admitted that this was possible; and went on to tell me that, having begun to do his work as a Congregational minister, and having been driven […] into giving up that professional pulpit, he was no less impelled than compelled to use unceasingly the new platform whence he had found that his voice could carry so far.[2]

Richard Reis reiterates Ronald's statement, saying of MacDonald as a novelist 'he wanted to spread his essentially religious message to as many readers as possible'.[3]

It can hardly be surprising that religion is such a major aspect of MacDonald's novels both because of the importance that religion was to MacDonald personally and the prominent role that it played in Great Britain in the nineteenth century. Greville MacDonald wrote in 1924: '[t]o-day we hardly realise how large a factor in daily life were matters of religion' in the mid-nineteenth century.[4] Greville wrote this in an English context, but religion was of even greater significance in Scotland, which had 'defended a variant of the state church sufficiently different from Anglicanism for its Clergy to defy the British government in the early 1840s'.[5] The Established Church in Scotland played such an important role in Scottish culture that the Disruption of 1843 not only split the church in two, but also fractured Scotland's national identity. Andrew Drummond and James Bulloch write: '[b]efore the Disruption Scotland had a national history; afterwards she had not',[6] implying that the ceding of power to Westminster in the Union of 1707 did little to shatter the national consciousness in comparison. This is largely due to the heavy influence of Calvinism, spearheaded in Scotland in the sixteenth century by John Knox, in Scotland's history. Previous to the Disruption was the 'historic Calvinist standpoint that the Christian Church, the Household of Faith, could so impress itself upon the surrounding community that the standards of the Gospel became the rule of life for society at large',[7] turning Christian discipline into 'a matter of the public punishment of offenders for sexual misconduct'.[8] For MacDonald, working in the realm of realist fiction, it was imperative to both portray and discuss religion in his Scottish novels.

Modern readers appear to have a complicated relationship with the religious aspect of MacDonald's novels, being both drawn in by his message and yet put off by his method of expression. His novels are seen as having been infected with bad pulpit traditions,[9] making it necessary for them to be heavily edited. This is precisely the excuse that Michael Phillips has given for redacting eighteen of MacDonald's novels. On his website (macdonaldphillips.com) Phillips states that there are two problems that modern readers encounter with MacDonald's writing style: the use of Scots in the Scottish novels and his 'tendency toward preaching and rambling [that] often erupts without warning, and he lapses into off-the-subject discourses which slow up the story line considerably'.[10] Paradoxically, Phillips has redacted the novels in order to lessen the preaching and yet to highlight and clarify MacDonald's spiritual vision.

Robert Lee Wolff claims that modern readers of Victorian literature read without truly understanding the literature they are reading. Wolff writes:

> Innocently we read Victorian fiction for enjoyment, and fail to realise that often we are not understanding it. Though not very remote from our time, the Victorian novelist wrote – in language that appears misleadingly like our own – for an audience who automatically understood his allusions, who did not need the

explanations that we in fact need but usually do not know we need.¹¹

Such is certainly true for readers of MacDonald's fiction, though they more readily accept the need for explanations in his Scottish novels largely due to his incorporation of Scots in his characters' dialogue, rather than think they need a better understanding of the religious background. Yet the need to have a better understanding of the religious background is apparent, for, in 1906, a year after MacDonald's death, Louise Willcox said of him '[h]e was to his own age shockingly liberal, and to ours he is amazingly orthodox'.¹² Phillips agrees that MacDonald looks very orthodox in our age, saying '[i]n fact, the totality of George MacDonald's theology demonstrates how very orthodox he was', noting that so many of his sermons could have been preached in many an evangelical pulpit,¹³ though according to MacDonald's son Ronald, they were more commonly preached from a Unitarian pulpit.¹⁴ The volume of MacDonald redactions demonstrates an inherent misunderstanding of MacDonald's works, for he was incredibly concerned about the meaning in his works. Ronald MacDonald maintains that his father was forever revising his works, 'until lovers of the old, not always without reason, have prayed him to have done with polishing'.¹⁵ MacDonald's focus in 'polishing' his works was an effort to bring the greatest clarity to his message. He criticises Percy Shelley's poetry for its focus on the '*utterance*, instead of the *conveyance* of thought',¹⁶ showing that his highest literary ideal was not the sound of his writing, but the meaning he meant to convey.

In 'A "Wolff" in Sheep's Clothing: The George MacDonald Industry and the Difficult Rehabilitation of a Reputation', John Pennington shows that the MacDonald redactors Michael Phillips, Dan Hamilton and Kathryn Lindskoog have redacted his novels to make him more readable to a fundamentalist Christian readership, rather than maintaining the liberalism that he showed in his own age. It is quite common for readers to encounter MacDonald through the religious lens of other writers. Many find MacDonald through an interest in C. S. Lewis. Pennington writes that for these readers, '[t]o align MacDonald with Lewis [...] is to find another religious voice, another writer whose works are safe for fundamentalist Christians'.¹⁷ This implies that the majority of MacDonald's current readers are themselves religious, and are reading his novels through the lens of their own faith. But many readers are not reading MacDonald as MacDonald, but reading him as Phillips would have him.

Essentially, the majority of MacDonald readers do not understand his novels in the most appropriate context. By looking at the depiction of gender in the un-redacted versions of MacDonald's novels, readers can gain a new insight into MacDonald's works. It is certainly not inaccurate to read MacDonald in a religious context, but it is important to understand the religious setting of the novels and compare that to what MacDonald appears to advocate. Readers can often find two narrative strains in MacDonald's fiction, a realist narrative and an idealist narrative. In other words, there is a difference between what MacDonald portrays and what he advocates.

Gender is largely an underdeveloped area of study in the works of George MacDonald. Very few scholars have looked closely at the issue, with the notable exceptions of Ginger Stelle, David Neuhouser, David Holbrook, and William Raeper. Holbrook and Raeper take a psychoanalytic approach to gender, tending to look at the depiction of women in MacDonald's works as revealing aspects of MacDonald's psyche, exposing his inner anxieties about women.[18] Stelle argues that MacDonald's novels discuss important issues in Victorian society, particularly addressing the 'Woman Question'. She sees the 'betterment of women and children' as 'an issue he repeatedly addressed in his novels'.[19] He does so in ways that 'are often so subtle that critics miss them altogether [...] In reality, his female characters continually challenge, albeit subtly, standard Victorian ideas about women'.[20] As a means of challenging Victorian gender ideology Stelle claims that MacDonald 'attacks the standard view of women with its own stereotypes',[21] showing that the public display of ideal femininity does not mean that the woman in question is morally or spiritually ideal. Neuhouser's work shows MacDonald's interaction with social issues in Victorian Britain, looking particularly at the role of women and how MacDonald transgressed some gender norms in his novels.[22]

Douglas Gifford argues that MacDonald's novels are 'deliberate attempts to argue a Scottish-based moral regeneration for Victorian Britain',[23] and in the process of arguing for the moral regeneration of Britain MacDonald's Scottish fiction subtly challenges and reconstructs gender identity. MacDonald largely argues for the moral regeneration of Britain by both challenging and attacking religious ideology. 'He made no war upon the Church as he knew it [...] his war was upon the faithlessness of the officially faithful, and, incidentally only, upon one or two Calvinistic and Augustinian dogmas exaggerated out of all proportion to their service'.²⁴ In *Robert Falconer*, as in many of MacDonald's novels, the attack is specifically against Calvinism. The challenge to Calvinism comes ultimately through the disassociation of God from the traditional masculine identity prescribed by religion.

MacDonald's familiarity with Calvinism comes from growing up attending a church known in Huntly as the Missionar Kirk. The church originated in the eighteenth century as an Anti-Burgher church, belonging to the nearby Presbytery of Elgin. The church itself had been theologically governed by the Westminster Confession and the Shorter Catechism, while a member of the Anti-Burgher denomination. Though the Missionar Kirk of Huntly split from the Anti-Burgher denomination in 1800 when its minister Mr Cowie was excommunicated by the Synod in Edinburgh for allowing and listening to sermons preached in his church by preachers from other denominations, it still maintained its strict Calvinism as it became a Congregationalist church, retaining the framework of thought found in the Westminster Confession even though it had discarded the document.²⁵ The congregation in MacDonald's childhood

> comprised the most energetic men in the locality – men remarkable alike for religious zeal and activity in business. Although not a numerous body, they exercised greater influence on the community than did any other of the religious denominations. This may be accounted for partly by their strict observance of their religious duties. They were ultra-Sabbatarian; so much so that the sending out of a bairn to fetch milk on Sunday morning was condemned as wrong. And while Sunday walking may have been disapproved of by other Churches, among the *Missionars* it was absolutely condemned and reprobated. Balls and card-playing were also anathematised. Moreover, the free use of intoxicants, although it may have been tolerated or winked at in some of the other congregations, met here with unqualified reprobation. They were also very exclusive in regard to membership. It will thus be seen that they were a select body, and such will always have an influence on all around.²⁶

The minister of the Missionar Kirk in MacDonald's childhood, Mr John Hill, was a staunch Calvinist. Robert Troup, MacDonald's college friend at Aberdeen, fellow student at Highbury in London, and for a number of years, the pastor at the Missionar Kirk of Huntly, notes that Hill's Calvinism was indeed significant:

> Mr Hill, like most preachers of his time in Scotland, was a Calvinist. He began his work as such, and so he continued, conservative, all but unchanged, from the first day of his ministry to the last. He had no sympathy with those who in his later years were earnestly proclaiming the universal love of the Father, the universal influence of the Holy Spirit, nor probably those moderate Calvinists who preached the universal atonement of Christ [...] No doubt he held and proclaimed one universal, the free, unlimited, universal invitation of the gospel; but behind it lay a limited divine love, a limited divine influence, and, perhaps, a limited divine atonement [...] But there was one point in which Mr Hill's Calvinism broke down. He came to believe in the universal salvation of those who die in infancy. A man of tender feelings and loving heart and strong family affections, such as he was, could scarcely cling to the old doctrine in that point of elect and non-elect infants, with four of his own children away in the unseen world. To think that any or all of these were enduring eternal misery would have been a constant torture to him and utterly broken the good man's heart.[27]

Hill's adherence to the Calvinist doctrines of atonement and election was at least tempered by a paternal love, but only towards those too undeveloped to be deemed capable of accepting the call of the Gospel. So strongly did he follow Calvinist doctrines that when, as William McNaughton notes, 'a few of the church's young people adopted the *"New Views"*, Hill had occasion strongly to denounce them',[28] MacDonald being one of those young men.

So, the Scotland that MacDonald wrote about, Scotland of the 1820s to the 1840s,[29] contained a similarly patriarchal religious structure to America's conservative evangelicalism. The Established Church, the Secession Church, the Free Church of Scotland, and the many Congregational

Churches were all structured around a masculine hierarchy, women being excluded from positions of leadership or authority within the church's governing body. In a fundamentalist biblical perspective

> at the heart of male-female relationships is a divinely decreed order of rule or sanction, the principle of 'masculine headship'. Variously interpreted as having operative jurisdiction throughout the whole of creation, or only in marriages, family and church relationships, this is the difference which underlies all other differences between men and women.[30]

The visibility of this ideology in the religious institutions depicted in MacDonald's novels is in the noticeable absence of women from positions of leadership in churches.

The notion of masculine headship and feminine subordination originates in the Book of Genesis, citing the order of creation: first Adam, *then* Eve.[31] But I do not mean to tackle the issue of primogeniture. Instead, my focus is on the depiction of God. God has traditionally been viewed in a masculine perspective, given a masculine identity: God as the Father of Jesus Christ, and Christ himself as a man, the Son of God. This makes God, the author and perfecter of the Christian faith, both the centre of truth and the basis of masculine authority.

God's fatherhood has been extended from the begetting of Christ to the begetting of all things. The act of creating has come to be seen in a Western perspective as an act of fathering, which is likely what causes the Victorian poet and Jesuit priest Gerard Manley Hopkins to declare 'The male quality is the creative gift'.[32] Hopkins is not merely ascribing creativity to the male sex, it not being a specific anatomical function of the male species, but to the male gender, inferring that it is a masculine characteristic. Creativity was, in nineteenth-century minds, an important aspect of masculinity, though not for MacDonald. MacDonald sees creativity, or imagination, as something akin to the Divine. He writes, 'The imagination of man is made in the image of the imagination of God'.[33] Imagination itself is given a feminine identity, in contrast to Hopkins. MacDonald writes that the perfect work of the imagination is 'that, namely of full-globed humanity, operating in which she gives birth to poetry – truth in beauty'.[34]

Creating is an active process, and through this association masculinity became linked to activity itself. Feminist scholar Helen E. Longino notes that there is and has been in Western society a 'cultural identification of the male with activity and of the female with passivity',[35] the cultural implication being that for men to be men they must exhibit activity, and for women to be feminine they must be passive. God, in a Calvinist tradition, is therefore masculine since he is the active, creative, begetting father of all things. His fatherhood is not just a male function, but also a masculine characteristic, specifically as God is conceived as being asexual. Raeper writes: 'MacDonald's theology, like that of those who influenced him, celebrated the rediscovery of God as Father',[36] implying a cultural definition of fatherhood that exceeds a biological definition. As the natural father of eleven children and adoptive father to two more, MacDonald 'felt that his own fatherhood had to be a reflection of God's Fatherhood, and he looked back to his own father as someone who had taught him that "fatherhood is at the great world's core"',[37] suggesting a phallogocentric ideology. But for MacDonald, the fatherhood of God is a masculine authority tempered by feminine love. MacDonald sees that God as Father 'looks down lovingly' for '[l]ove is all. And God is all in all'.[38] MacDonald writes that the kingdom of Christ is 'a rule of love, of truth – a rule of service'.[39] Love is the highest ideal, the only enduring thing. He writes: 'Nothing is inexorable but love'.[40] Whereas MacDonald sees Calvinism ultimately conceiving of God as 'a great King on a grand throne, thinking how grand he is, and making it the business of his being and the end of his universe to keep up his glory, wielding bolts of a Jupiter against them that take his name in vain', he claims the more accurate image is '[t]he simplest peasant who loves his children and his sheep were – no, not a truer, for the other is false, but – a true type of our God beside that monstrosity of a monarch'.[41] God, for MacDonald, is not just the Calvinist masculine 'Trinity of Father, Son and Holy Spirit, but of Father, Mother and Child'.[42] Femininity is just as much a vital part of God as is masculinity.

It cannot be overstated that in Calvinist Scotland God is masculine. Going back to early Scottish Calvinism there is a pervasive misogynist view of women. John Knox believed that women were by nature 'weak, frail, impatient, feeble and foolish, and experience hath declared them to be unconstant, variable, cruel and lacking the spirit of counsel and regiment'.⁴³ Unlike men, who are created in the image of God, women are made in the image of man to be his subordinate.⁴⁴ Scottish Calvinism sees women as bringing evil into the world, thereby placing them under further subjugation to masculine authority.⁴⁵

The masculine God of Calvinism is a punitive authoritarian. Under Calvinism 'the role of God was conceived in the mode of a trial judge who exacted the penalty demanded by the law, or as the prosecuting attorney who charged sinners with violating the law'.⁴⁶ Such a penal authoritarianism finds its place in *Alec Forbes of Howglen* where it was 'the God of a corrupt Calvinism [...] that ruled the world, and not the God revealed in the man of Christ Jesus'.⁴⁷

MacDonald's Scottish novels show a particular concern to bring the reader closer to his understanding of God as revealed in Christ, largely by having his characters discover this version of God. While many of the novels show this discovery at a distance, chronicling the events leading up to an awareness of what MacDonald sees as the true image of God, in *Robert Falconer* he reveals this discovery on a more personal level, depicting Robert's inner journey to a discovery of God's feminine character.

In *Robert Falconer* MacDonald problematises masculine authority by its absence. Robert Falconer first appeared in MacDonald's first realist novel, *David Elginbrod* (1863). Yet the character was so significant in MacDonald's imagination that he published a novel in 1868 titled simply *Robert Falconer*. The plot is broadly defined by Robert's quest to find his degenerate absent father, meaning that masculine authority is missing from Robert's childhood home, though in a grander sense it is a quest to discover his spiritual Parent. Instead the authoritative figure is Mrs Falconer, his grandmother and matriarch of the Falconer household. She plays a similar role to that of Thomas Crann in *Alec Forbes of Howglen* (1865), the other MacDonald novel in which the landscape of Huntly features so prominently. She is the embodiment of Calvinist doctrine. Her Calvinistic faith is such that she prays for sinners – including her son, Robert's absent father – 'Lord lead them to see the error of their ways [...] Let the rod of thy wrath awake the worm of their conscience that they may know verily that there is a God that ruleth in the earth'.⁴⁸

Calvinism is a corrupting influence on Mrs Falconer, for it alienates her from her son and emotionally strains Robert who grows up without feminine affection. It hardens her to a point where she cannot embrace Robert, making her relation to him seem to be an aspect of duty rather than a relation of love. By connecting Mrs Falconer to both Calvinism and authoritarianism, she being exacting with Robert and vehemently opposed to his pursuit of music, MacDonald is showing that both are unsuited to connect to God. For God is 'simply and altogether our friend, our father – our more than friend, father, and mother – our infinite love-perfect God'.[49]

Mrs Falconer teaches Robert the fundamentals of Calvinist faith so thoroughly that within him rose 'the evil phantasms of a theology which would explain all God's doing by low conceptions [...] of right, and law, and justice, then only taking refuge in the fact of the incapacity of the human understanding when its own inventions are impugned as undivine. In such a system, hell is invariably the deepest truth, and the love of God is not so deep as hell' (p. 77). This masculine God that Robert learns from his grandmother, demanding obedience, love, and worship at the threat of eternal damnation, is ineffective in the exertion of authority, being explicitly unable to hold Robert to Calvinist doctrine.

Robert instead heads away from God and pursues things that are beautiful, learning to love music through the influence of the beautiful and feminine Mary St John, whom Robert first mistakes as an envoy from God, 'an angel come down to comfort his grannie' (p. 46). Mary St John gives him instruction in music and it is this that first makes him aware of beauty. Mary, who is loving, kind, encouraging, helpful and musical, is a strong contrast to Mrs Falconer, who is incapable of showing any physical tenderness to Robert and destroys the fiddle he learns to play.

Beauty and music in the novel are closely associated with femininity, largely because they involve feeling. And it is through femininity that Robert eventually discovers God. In MacDonald's perspective, God calls people to 'himself' through 'his' femininity. He believed, following the German Idealism of Novalis, that Nature was the feminine voice through which God called people to faith. Novalis sees that 'Nature is no longer dead, hostile Matter, but the veil and mysterious Garment of the Unseen; as it were, the Voice with which the Deity proclaims himself to man'.[50] It is precisely through Nature that MacDonald has Robert Falconer come to God. In Robert's spiritual development, the spark that first awakens him to what MacDonald calls 'the greatest need that the human heart possesses' (p. 123) is a new awareness of Nature, and through that an awareness of God. The moment of this awareness occurs in an idyllic setting. Robert, having just enjoyed a swim in a river on a hot Saturday afternoon in late July, 'ascended the higher part of [a] field, and lay down upon a broad web to bask in the sun. In his ears was the hush rather than the rush of the water over the dam, the occasional murmur of a belt of trees that skirted the border of the field, and the dull continuous sound of beatles [sic] at their work below, like the persistent growl of thunder on the horizon' (p. 122). Rather than simply relaxing in this setting and letting his mind wander, Robert is uniquely aware of the natural world around him. He feels the sun, hears the river flowing over the dam, and is even keenly aware of the movement of beetles underneath him. MacDonald points out that had Robert possessed a book such as *Robinson Crusoe* or *The Lady of the Lake* he would likely have been reading it instead of observing Nature, making him 'blind and deaf to the face and voice of Nature, and years might have passed before a response awoke in his heart' (p. 122). The moment when this response awoke in his heart is worth quoting at length:

> He lay gazing up into the depth of the sky, rendered deeper and bluer by the masses of white cloud that hung almost motionless below it until he felt a kind of bodily fear lest he should fall off the face of the round earth into the abyss. A gentle wind, laden with pine odours from the sun-heated trees behind him, flapped its light wing in his face: the humanity of the world smote his heart; the great sky towered up over him, and its divinity entered his soul; a strange longing after something 'he knew not nor could name' awoke within him, followed by the pang of a sudden fear that there was no such thing as that which he sought, that it was all a fancy of his own spirit; and then the voice of Shargar broke the spell [...] But once aroused, the feeling was never stilled; the desire never left him; sometimes growing even to a passion that was relieved only by a flood of tears. (pp. 122f)

This longing that Robert feels for a thing that he could not name is the Divinity that moved the wind and towered over Robert in the expanse of the sky. MacDonald writes, 'Strange as it may sound to those who have never thought of such things save in connection with Sundays and Bibles and churches and sermons, that which was now working in Falconer's mind was the first dull and faint movement of [...] the need of the God-Man' (p. 123). MacDonald clearly points out that there is an intimate connection between God and Nature. According to MacDonald,

> There must be truth in the scent of that pine-wood: some one must mean it. There must be a glory in those heavens that depends not upon our imagination: some power greater than they must dwell in them. Some spirit must move in that wind that haunts us with a kind of human sorrow; some soul must look up to us from the eye of that starry flower. It must be something human, else not to us divine. (p. 123)

God is a God hidden in Nature, 'One whose form was constantly presented' (p. 123) to Robert in Nature.

It must be recognised that Nature has been connected to femininity for centuries. Carolyn Merchant writes that Nature and the earth were identified 'with a nurturing mother: a kindly beneficent female who provided for the needs of mankind in an ordered, planned universe'.[51] Merchant notes that an opposing female identification of Nature was 'wild and uncontrollable nature that could render violence, storm, droughts, and general chaos. Both were identified with the female sex and were projections of human perceptions onto the external world'.[52] MacDonald incorporates the personification of Nature as woman in *Robert Falconer*, referring to Nature with the feminine pronoun, 'she' (p. 325).

After a period of deep grief, Robert Falconer travels throughout Europe. It is in his wanderings on the continent that Robert finally comes to God, but again through the influence of Nature. One Bible verse has been occupying Robert's grief-stricken thoughts: 'My peace I give unto you' (p. 325). At the height of his grief, he cries out 'Lord Christ, give me thy peace' (p. 325). The peace that then arrives for Robert comes through the ministrations of Nature:

> Suddenly he was aware that the earth had begun to live again. The hum of insects arose from the heath around him; the odour of its flowers entered his dulled sense; the wind kissed him on the

forehead; the sky domed up over his head; and the clouds veiled the distant mountain tops like the smoke of incense ascending from the altars of the worshipping earth. All Nature began to minister to one who had begun to lift up his head from the baptism of fire. He had thought that Nature could never more be anything to him; and she was waiting on him like a mother. (p. 325)

While it is feminine Nature that ministers to Robert, MacDonald points out that it is not Nature on its own. It is God who is actually ministering, for God 'is ever uttering himself in the changeful profusion of nature'.[53] MacDonald writes: 'God and not a woman is the heart of the universe'.[54] The personification of Nature as female makes Nature nothing more than God's instrument. In the late seventeenth century Richard Hooker wrote: 'God being the author of Nature, her voice is but his instrument'.[55] This implies a separation of feminine Nature from the dominant and active masculine God. What MacDonald is emphasising is that the feminine characteristics of Nature are part of God. Feminine Nature is simply another side of God.

MacDonald so emphatically believes in God's femininity that he writes in 'A Sketch of Individual Development' that 'There is no type so near the highest idea of relation to a God, as that of the child to his mother. Her face is God, her bosom Nature, her arms Providence – all love – one love – to him an undivided bliss'.[56] What seems clear is that God's authority is historically masculine, but God's love, the all-important aspect of God's character, is divinely feminine.

By approbating God's more feminine characteristics, the novel shifts the balance of power in gender relationships. Masculinity doesn't hold its hegemonic authority any longer, because the basis of that authority, the divine masculine, is not necessarily only masculine. God's power lies in the feminine aspect of love. It is, for lack of a more suitable pronoun, His goodness and love that require humanity's obedience, not His justice and retribution. MacDonald writes: 'Obedience, then, is as divine as Will, Service as divine as Rule. How? Because they are one in their nature; they are both a doing of the truth. The love in them is the same'.[57]

There are extensive possibilities in the study of gender and religion in MacDonald's *oeuvre*, but there is a frequent connection between femininity and the divine. Significantly, the God-figure in MacDonald's *The Princess and the Goblin* and *The Princess and Curdie* is the great-grandmother. Then, in novels such as *David Elginbrod* and *Alec Forbes of Howglen*, the most righteous characters are women, though as, Raeper notes, MacDonald's righteous women have their converse.[58] Further study should also be done on the effeminacy of MacDonald's righteous male characters, such as Eric Ericson. What is evident is that MacDonald's novels value feminine characteristics to a greater extent than his modern-day readers readily recognise. Certainly as gender connects to religion in *Robert Falconer* femininity becomes an aspect of divinity, implying that women are also created in the image of God and are therefore not naturally relegated to be subservient to men.

Notes

1. Rolland Hein, *The Harmony Within: The Spiritual Vision of George MacDonald* (Eureka, CA: Sunrise Books, 1982), p. 113.
2. Ronald MacDonald, 'George MacDonald: A Personal Note', *From a Northern Window: Papers, Critical, Historical and Imaginative* ed Frederick Watson (London: James Nisbet, 1911, pp. 55–113), pp. 66–67.
3. Richard Reis, *George MacDonald's Fiction: A Twentieth-Century View* (Eureka, CA: Sunrise Books, 1972), p. 52.
4. Greville MacDonald, *George MacDonald and His Wife* (London: George Allen & Unwin, 1924), p. 98.
5. Mary Poovey, *Making a Social Body: British Cultural Formation 1830–1864* (Chicago: University of Chicago Press, 1995), p. 2.
6. Andrew L. Drummond and James Bulloch, *The Church in Victorian Scotland 1843–1874* (Edinburgh: Saint Andrew Press, 1975), p. 4.
7. Drummond and Bulloch, *The Church in Victorian Scotland 1843–1874*, p. 1.
8. Andrew L. Drummond and James Bulloch, *The Scottish Church 1688–1843*, (Edinburgh: Saint Andrew Press, 1973), p. 86.
9. See Richard Reis, *George MacDonald's Fiction: A Twentieth-Century View*, pp. 53–55.
10. Michael Phillips, *The Writings, Spiritual Vision and Legacy of George MacDonald* (available online at www.macdonaldphillips.com, updated 2006).
11. Robert Lee Wolff, *Gains and Losses: Novels of Faith and Doubt in Victorian England* (New York: Garland, 1977), p. 1.
12. Quoted in Michael Phillips, *George MacDonald: Scotland's Beloved Storyteller* (Minneapolis: Bethany House, 1987), p. 162.
13. *George MacDonald: Scotland's Beloved Storyteller*, p. 166.
14. Ronald MacDonald, 'George MacDonald: A Personal Note', p. 69.
15. Ronald MacDonald, 'George MacDonald: A Personal Note', p. 66.
16. George MacDonald, 'Shelley' in *A Dish of Orts* (Whitethorn: Johannesen, 2009, pp. 264–81), p. 275.
17. John Pennington, 'A "Wolff" in Sheep's Clothing: The George MacDonald Industry and

the Difficult Rehabilitation of a Reputation' in *George MacDonald: Literary Heritage and Heirs*, ed Roderick McGillis (Wayne: Zossima Press, 2008, pp. 239-58), p. 244.
18. See William Raeper, *George MacDonald* (Tring: Lion, 1987), pp. 201-08; and David Holbrook, *A Study of George MacDonald and the Image of Woman* (Lewiston: Edwin Mellen Press, 2000).
19. Ginger Stelle, 'The Exemplary Deviant: Wynnie as a Symbol of Victorian Womanhood in *The Vicar's Daughter*', *North Wind*, 24 (2005), pp. 51-60 (p. 51).
20. Ginger Stelle, 'The Exemplary Deviant: Wynnie as a Symbol of Victorian Womanhood in *The Vicar's Daughter*', p. 52.
21. Ginger Stelle, 'When Bad Girls Go Good: Stereotype Reversals in George MacDonald's *Alec Forbes of Howglen*', *North Wind*, 25 (2006), pp. 27-39 (p. 27).
22. David L. Neuhouser, 'George MacDonald and Social Issues' in *'A Noble Unrest': Contemporary Essays on the Work of George MacDonald*, ed Jean Webb (Newcastle: Cambridge Scholars, 2007), pp. 6-14.
23. Douglas Gifford, 'Myth, Parody and Dissociation: Scottish Fiction 1814-1914' in Douglas Gifford (ed), *The History of Scottish Literature: Nineteenth Century* (Aberdeen: Aberdeen University Press, 1988, pp. 217-58), p. 227.
24. Ronald MacDonald, 'George MacDonald: A Personal Note', p. 87-88.
25. Drummond and Bulloch, *The Church in Victorian Scotland 1843-1874*, p. 54.
26. George Gray 'Recollections of Huntly as it was Seventy Years Ago', *Huntly: A Scottish Town in Former Days*, ed David Robb (The George MacDonald Society, 1998), pp. 66-67.
27. Robert Troup, *The Missionar Kirk of Huntly* (Edinburgh and Glasgow: John Menzies, 1901), pp. 133-34.
28. William D. McNaughton, *Early Congregational Independency in the Highlands and Islands and the North-East of Scotland* (Tiree: The Trustees of Ruaig Congregational Church, 2003), p. 391.
29. David Robb, 'Realism and Fantasy in the Fiction of George MacDonald' in Douglas Gifford (ed), *The History of Scottish Literature: Nineteenth Century* (Aberdeen: Aberdeen University Press, 1988, pp. 275-90), p. 279.
30. Elaine Storkey, *Created or Constructed? The Great Gender Debate* (Carlisle: Paternoster Press, 2001), p. 88.
31. For an example of this in nineteenth-century Britain see William Landels, *Woman's Sphere and Work Considered in the Light of Scripture* (London: James Nisbet, 1877), pp. 8-9. The Genesis account is alluded to by St Paul in 1 Corinthians 11:7-9.
32. Quoted in Sandra M. Gilbert and Susan Gubar, *The Madwoman in the Attic: The Woman Writer and the Nineteenth-Century Literary Imagination* (New Haven: Yale University Press, 1979), p. 3.
33. George MacDonald, 'The Imagination: Its Functions and Its Culture' in *A Dish of Orts* (Whitethorn: Johannesen, 2009, pp. 1-42), p. 3.
34. George MacDonald, 'The Imagination: Its Functions and Its Culture', pp. 14-15.
35. Helen E. Longino, 'Subjects, Power and Knowledge: Description and Prescription in Feminist Philosophies of Science' in *Feminism and Science*, ed Evelyn Fox Keller and Helen E. Longino (Oxford: Oxford UP, 1996, pp. 264-79), p. 265.
36. William Raeper, *George MacDonald* (Tring: Lion, 1987), p. 242.
37. Raeper, *George MacDonald*, p. 258.
38. George MacDonald, 'The Child in the Midst', *Unspoken Sermons* (London: Alexander Strahan, 1867), p. 20.

39. George MacDonald, 'The Child in the Midst', p. 14.
40. George MacDonald, 'The Consuming Fire', *Unspoken Sermons*, (London: Alexander Strahan, 1867), p. 27.
41. George MacDonald, 'The Child in the Midst', p. 22.
42. Raeper, *George MacDonald*, p. 248.
43. John Knox, 'The First Blast of the Trumpet Against the Monstrous Regiment of Women' in *The Political Writings of John Knox*, ed Marvin A. Breslow (Washington: Associated University Presses, 1985, pp. 37–80), p. 43.
44. See William Landels, *Woman's Sphere and Work Considered in the Light of Scripture*, pp. 8–9.
45. John Knox, 'The First Blast of the Trumpet Against the Monstrous Regiment of Women', p. 46.
46. J. Denny Weaver, *The Nonviolent Atonement*, (Grand Rapids, MI: Eerdmans, 2001), p. 17.
47. George MacDonald, *Alec Forbes of Howglen*, p. 31.
48. George MacDonald, *Robert Falconer* (London: Hurst and Blackett, 1900), pp. 36–37. Further citations given in the text.
49. George MacDonald, 'The Child in the Midst', p. 21.
50. Thomas Carlyle, 'Novalis' in *Critical and Miscellaneous Essays* (Philadelphia: A. Hart, later Cary and Hart, 1852, pp. 167–87), p. 176.
51. Carolyn Merchant, 'Nature as Female' in *The Death of Nature: Women, Ecology, and the Scientific Revolution* (San Francisco: Harper & Row, 1980, pp. 1–41), p. 2.
52. Carolyn Merchant, 'Nature as Female', p. 2.
53. George MacDonald, 'The Child in the Midst', p. 22.
54. *Robert Falconer*, p. 325.
55. Quoted in Carolyn Merchant, 'Nature as Female', pp. 6–7.
56. George MacDonald, 'A Sketch of Individual Development' in *A Dish of Orts* (Whitethorn: Johannesen, 2009, pp. 43–76), p. 44.
57. George MacDonald, 'The Child in the Midst', p. 14.
58. William Raeper, *George MacDonald*, p. 203.

Imagining Reformed Communities: Discussing Social Myths in George MacDonald's *Princess* Novels and Christina Rossetti's 'Goblin Market'

CHRISTINE CHETTLE

Both Christina Rossetti and George MacDonald defended the ability of the imagination to negotiate social boundaries. In an 1865 letter to her brother, Dante Gabriel Rossetti, Christina defends her choice of illegitimacy as a poetic subject on the grounds that her poetic imagination allows her to transcend differences in experience: '[u]nless white could be black and Heaven Hell my experience [...] precludes me from hers, yet I don't see why "the Poet mind" should be less able to construct her from its own inner consciousness than a hundred other unknown quantities'.[1] MacDonald muses on the various effects of the imagination in an 1882 essay, positing it as a way of illuminating social dynamics: 'To construct from a succession of broken images a whole accordant with human nature [...] to approach the scheme of the forces at work [...] this is the province of the imagination'.[2] Reflecting on the use of the imagination to convey an abstract idea in a social setting invites the question of the process of this conveyance: that is, the method of interpretation. Rossetti's 'Goblin Market' (1862) is a text that has inspired many interpretations, with both readers and critics eagerly seeking to attach a specific meaning to her marauding goblins and to create various allegories around her tale of sisterly sacrifice. In his 1882 essay, MacDonald notes that 'no man is capable of seeing for himself the whole of any truth' and he continues this cautioning in a later essay of 1893 ('The Fantastic Imagination'), warning against a hasty attachment of meaning to a particular image: 'Words are live things that may be variously employed to various ends'. His warning comes in the context of a discussion of fairy tales: '[fairy tales are] there not so much to convey a meaning as to wake a meaning [...] And if they can be so used as to convey definite meaning, it does not follow that they ought never to carry anything else'.[3] I wish to explore how both Rossetti and MacDonald use elements of fairy tales in 'Goblin Market' (1862), *The*

Princess and the Goblin (1871–1872) and *The Princess and Curdie* (1881) to create a space of social speculation, rather than of social allegory.

First of all, as Victorian tellers of fairy tales, both can be located in a literary context of complicating nineteenth-century social conflicts through the use of fantasy. Rosemary Jackson speaks of Victorian fantasy by writers like Charles Kingsley and MacDonald as a type of social displacement: 'Their embrace of Platonic idealism was less of a transcendental movement, and more of a displacement of psychological and social issues, for their fantasies betray a dissatisfaction with their own idealism'.[4] Stephen Prickett has expressed the potential of Victorian fantasy to explore contemporary cultural conflicts in a subconscious space, terming the Victorian fantastic an 'underside' of the Victorian imagination.[5] Prickett highlights both Rossetti's and MacDonald's abilities to mediate such conflicts, suggesting that 'Goblin Market' can indicate a society divided by both sexual and mental goblins,[6] and noting that MacDonald sees 'the truth [as] hidden beneath nature, rather than visible in the surface of things; it is the job of the artist to create the hidden pattern afresh in his own work'.[7] Yet Victorian fantasy can operate as a space of active discussion as well as of displacement or of unconscious conflict, and both MacDonald and Rossetti reflect on the transformation of communities in conflict in ways that propel debate on contemporary issues.

Other Victorian writers indicate the potential for discussion in a combination of fairy-tale tropes; in Dickens's *A Christmas Carol*, Scrooge revisits the experience of loneliness as dramatised by a schoolboy surrounded by characters from a mixture of fairy-tale and fantasy traditions (in poignant opposition to human companionship): Ali Baba from the *Arabian Nights* and Valentine and Orson from a French folk-tale meet Daniel Defoe's Robinson Crusoe. After this collage of fantasies, Scrooge is more open to sympathising with deprivation in his fellow men.[8] In George Eliot's *Daniel Deronda*, the Meyrick sisters ponder the adventures of Daniel Deronda and Mirah Lapidoth by terming Daniel 'Prince Camaralzaman' and Mirah 'Queen Budoor' after characters in a tale from the Arabian Nights.[9] This is an interesting choice, because this fairy tale ends with Prince Camaralzaman – as permitted by Islamic law – marrying two wives in order to resolve dissatisfactions,[10] and like Eliot's text, it explores tensions around the expectations of marriage. From the very beginning of the novel, Daniel's name is linked with that of another character, Gwendolen, teasing the reader with the question of whom he will marry, and highlighting the complications around resolution through marriage within the novel.[11] The discussion of Daniel's prospects led one unsatisfied reader to write an unauthorised sequel, in which Daniel and Gwendolen did marry.[12]

MacDonald himself extends this potential for debate in his novel *Adela Cathcart*, in which a storytelling club meets regularly to read and discuss tales, including fairy tales like *The Light Princess* and contemporary accounts of traumatic events like losing a new-born baby. Christina Rossetti's poem 'Goblin Market' (1862)[13] depicts a story-telling context that is descriptive rather than discursive, but the enigmatic nature of the poem sparked plenty of debate on its first publication and, indeed, continues to do so. Contemporary reviewers, confused by Dante Gabriel Rossetti's illustrations, debated whether 'Goblin Market' was a 'moral allegory against the pleasures of sinful love' or 'an immoral narrative celebrating the delights of the flesh'.[14]

Rossetti's poem dramatises the results of two sisters' varying reactions to temptation, telling the story of Lizzie's battle to save her dying sister Laura and rid the land of goblins. George MacDonald's novel *The Princess and the Goblin*[15] introduces the characters of Irene and Curdie, and traces their internal development through encounters with each other and with goblins. The two return in a sequel, *The Princess and Curdie*,[16] in which Curdie goes on a quest to restore a troubled kingdom.

For both writers, goblins represent a type of human–animal hybrid that encodes a social threat. Rossetti describes her goblins as 'merchant men', but men with 'a cat's face' or 'a tail' [...], or who prowl 'like a wombat [...] obtuse and furry' (ll. 70–76). They evoke a world that is external to the lives of the rural sisters and so the delicious but destructive fruit that the goblins sell is particularly tempting to the sisters. MacDonald begins his novel *The Princess and the Goblin* by casting his goblins as socially oppressed: 'At one time they lived above the ground and were very like other people. But for some reason or other [...] the king had begun to treat them with more severity [...] and the consequence was [...] they had all taken refuge in the subterranean caverns' (p. 6). This experience makes them physically ugly: 'They had greatly altered, seeing they lived away from the sun, in cold and wet and dark places. They were now [...]

absolutely hideous' (p. 6). It also makes them emotionally flawed: '[t]hey so heartily cherished the ancestral grudge against those who occupied their former possessions [...] that they sought every opportunity of tormenting them' (p. 7). *The Princess and Curdie* contains another type of human–animal hybrid, although these are not called goblins. This is a spiritual hybrid: creatures who appear human, but whose souls have degenerated into beasts. The figure of the goblin in Rossetti's poem has inspired interpretations outside a fairy-tale context that picture the goblins as pornographic phalluses, producers of industrialised food, or figures of reverse colonisation, just to name a few.[17] Whatever the interpretation, however, the goblins generally operate as a threat to the sisters' social order. MacDonald's goblins share this sense of threat, which critics have also extended beyond a fairy-tale context: Geoffrey Reiter interprets both MacDonald's goblins and his regressed humans in the light of a late-Victorian discourse of degeneration as a threat which reveals darker impulses within society.[18]

The poem and the novels all emphasise the importance of a loving, harmonious society as a contrast to the communal threat of the goblins, with Laura 'joining hands to little hands' and bidding them 'cling together' in Rossetti's poem (ll. 560–61); in *The Princess and Curdie*, a symptom of the problems in the kingdom is the fact that, as Curdie puts it, 'the people keep their gates open, but their houses and their hearts shut' (p. 247). While Rossetti's text nods towards problematic structures of gender and class, she leaves specific identification to others, whereas MacDonald actively alludes to contemporary constructions of class and gender (for example, Irene, 'a true princess', is happy both to kiss a miner boy and to muddy her petticoat and cheerfully picks up stones, but would never dream of telling a lie). In all three texts, experiences of dissonance in the tales of fairy grandmothers, animal–human goblins, and magical juices recall moments of social dissonance in the Victorian period. However, a comparison with MacDonald's texts extends myths in Rossetti's text of renewing a threatened community in developing debate as an initial context for reform, reflecting on the dynamics of rewriting communal structures, and complicating the establishment of lasting change in order to demonstrate the necessary requirements for reform.

The process of change begins with developing a sense of perception; the characters must experience a re-education to prepare them for their resistance to the goblin threat. Lizzie in 'Goblin Market' demonstrates self-education as she revises her strategies for resisting goblins from passive avoidance to discerning confrontation; in *The Princess and the Goblin*, Irene must decipher various educational influences in order to rescue Curdie from the goblins; and in *The Princess and Curdie*, Curdie's interactions with Irene's grandmother extend the importance of self-education that Lizzie shows: he is cultivated so that he can determine his own strategies against hostile townsmen and courtiers. Each educational situation contains a fantastic element (the seductive goblin jingle, a magical thread, and hands that detect the inner nature) that evokes transgressive tensions common to contemporary discourses around education.

The education of women in itself had transgressive connotations, provoking questions about how one might prepare women to work outside a domestic context and whether such preparation or aim was a good idea. The education of the working classes caused similar discussion. Dinah Birch, in discussing Matthew Arnold's programme of education founded in Greek culture, notes that different topics were associated with different groups: an education in the classics denoted an upper-class gentleman, while science was associated with working-class students, and contemporary literature was linked to women.[19] Another question which arose in consideration of women's education was assessment: should education be tested? The educational reformer Emily Davies argued the advantages of formal examination in teaching both men and women: 'The fact of having an examination to work for, would not only be a stimulus to themselves, it would also serve as a defence against idle companions'.[20] In Rossetti's and MacDonald's texts, their characters' training in perception is tested and indeed proves a defence from the attacks that occur when they step outside normative boundaries and associations. In 'Goblin Market', Lizzie prepares herself to examine the goblins' words in order to survive an exchange without giving in to them. She has hitherto chosen to resist temptation by ignoring it, to 'thrust a dimpled finger/ In each ear, shut eyes and r[u]n' (ll. 67–68), when the question of goblins presents itself. Her knowledge of Jeanie's experience with the goblins has taught her that maidens 'should not loiter in the glen/ In the haunts of goblin men' (p. 16). However, her observation of her sister makes her reflect that this education is no longer sufficient and that she must extend her perceptive range:

> Laura dwindling
> Seemed knocking at Death's door:
> Then Lizzie weighed no more
> Better and worse / ... /
> And for the first time in her life
> Began to listen and look (ll. 320–28)

Lizzie pushes herself to use the observational skills she needs to pay particular attention to goblins' words. The price of the goblin fruit is that she stays to eat it; she cannot take it away with her. The goblins tempt her with lists of delicious fruits, but hidden in these lists are the words 'take a seat with us' and 'eat with us'. These words sound delightfully hospitable, but Lizzie, thinking of Laura, responds with 'one waits at home alone for me', extending her former training in resistance into a new context. Lizzie's self-training in observation and resistance allows her to survive both the goblins' seductive jingle and the violent attack that follows, in which the goblins 'scratch', 'kick', and 'maul' her to make her eat their fruit, but she 'would not open lip from lip' (l 431):

> Kicked and knocked her,
> Mauled and mocked her,
> Lizzie uttered not a word [...] (ll. 428–30)

Education as a form of survival served as an inspiration for the founding of schools that would give girls a full education. Frances Buss, who co-founded Cheltenham Ladies' College and was known to the MacDonald family,[21] wrote in 1871 that her reforms had been prompted by a desire to give women 'good elementary training' that would 'lighten [...] the misery of women brought up "to be married and taken care of" and then left in the world destitute'.[22] Lizzie is attacked by goblins rather than by poverty, but the difference which her self-training makes – training which Laura and Jeanie did not pursue – underlines the important role of education in survival for women.

MacDonald gives Irene a similar transformation in education, but points out restrictions in access as well; unlike in Lizzie's case, these are not caused by self-determined ignorance. At the beginning of *The Princess and the Goblin*, he states that her attendants wish to control her movements as they 'were much too afraid of the goblins to let her out of the house', and, although he notes that 'they had good reason', the fact that 'the little princess had never seen the sky at night' dramatises a sense of restriction behind such reasoning (p. 7). However, Irene's interactions with her fairy grandmother train her in reflection and debate. She instructs Irene to tell her nurse about her visit to her fairy grandmother, even though (as she later comments) she knows that Lootie will not believe the princess. Irene is 'astonished and angry' to encounter Lootie's assessment of her experience as being either lies or a dream, which obviously differs from her own view, and she enters into an argument with the nurse on the subject (p. 18). This dialectic experience increases her awareness of differences in perspective and gives her confidence in forming and expressing her own opinion. Irene's new training in balancing perceptions allows her to defend her own point of view against Curdie's by pointing out illogical elements in his words: '[t]hen if you don't know what I mean, what right have you to call it nonsense?' (p. 116). Her reliance on her own point of view allows Irene to bring them both out of danger from the goblins.

Unlike Lizzie, Irene does not confront the goblins directly, but her perception means that both she and Curdie escape them. Irene's education gives her an independence of thought which assists her both in an expected context (with her nurse in the palace) and in unexpected contexts (in a mine, with goblins nearby); it also reflects contemporary comments on the role of independent thought in the aims and methods of education. George Eliot wrote in 1855 that good education prepares its pupils for application in a number of contexts: '[h]e is the most effective educator who aims less at perfecting specific acquirements than at producing that mental condition which renders acquirements easy, and leads to their useful application'.[23] Eliot's views are in contrast with the approach taken by some nineteenth-century educational texts, such as the popular *Mangnall's Questions*. First published in 1823, this text went through at least eighty-four editions and offered its (often female) pupils an education by memorising vast series of questions and answers. These questions emphasised set answers not just to empirical facts ('When was Rome founded? About 752 years BC by Romulus')[24] but also to matters requiring wider interpretation ('What is the abuse of liberty? When the people of a state, no longer regarding the laws, deviate into licentiousness').[25] Irene's re-education has taught her to move beyond memorisation of accepted facts, giving her a 'mental condition' which will allow her to apply her powers of perception in a number of contexts. Surviving the goblins by following the magical thread reimagines some of the tensions between merely accepting facts and developing an interpretative perspective. Irene must first develop a mental condition that will allow her to decide how the thread should be followed; this condition means that she defies Curdie's comprehensive knowledge of the mine. Irene's mental cultivation helps her to make innovative decisions about which facts to accept. Whether it involves a magical thread or not, women's educational reform required a fine balance.

MacDonald extends questions of educational reform still further in *The Princess and Curdie*, in which Curdie's education is taken in hand. The question of widening access to education received much debate throughout the nineteenth century and although the Education Act of 1870 stipulated that every child below ten should attend school, the question of what working-class children should learn, and why, still remained. Alfred Dewes commented in 1868 that '[m]en will still gravely tell us that all should be taught to read (for otherwise how can they read their Bibles?), and perhaps to write; but beyond these, and things like these, they go on with all gravity to ask, What need have the working classes of mental cultivation[?]'.[26] Irene's grandmother, in her desire to cultivate Curdie's spiritual being, also emphasises his (and his father's) mental growth, demonstrating the value of educating a miner both inside and outside his working context. As with Lizzie, Curdie requires help to 'listen and look'; part of his re-training is corrective, instead of merely developmental, as with Irene. The text evokes radical views on educating working men, such as the anti-utilitarian ethos of Dante Gabriel Rossetti and John Ruskin's lecture series on art for a Working-Men's College. Both Ruskin and Rossetti emphasised that their students should learn to draw by observing and reflecting upon nature,[27] and Ruskin blurs the line between metaphysical and utilitarian education in a comment on observational methods: 'nothing distinguishes great men from inferior men more than their always, whether in life or in art, knowing the way things are going [...] your wise man sees the change or changing in them, and draws them so, – the animal in its motion, the tree in its growth, the cloud in its course, the mountain in its wearing away'.[28]

In preparing Curdie for his task of rescuing the royal family and cleansing the kingdom, Irene's grandmother, like Ruskin, underlines the importance of being able to know the changing nature of men, but as a way of surviving monstrosity: '[j]ust so two people may be at the same spot in manners and behaviour, and yet one may be getting better and the other worse, which is just the greatest of all differences that could possibly exist between them' (p. 220). To assist with this, she gives him a special power of touch, that can alert him to when an individual is no longer a 'man' inside, but a 'beast': '[you] will be able always to tell, not only when a man is growing a beast, but what beast he is growing to, for you will know the foot [...] According, then, to your knowledge of that beast will be your knowledge of the man you have to do with' (p. 221). Such knowledge will serve him well in the court of Gwyntystorm, giving him the ability to defeat 'beasts' who masquerade as 'men'. However, Irene's grandmother cultivates an independence of thought in Curdie as well as outfitting him with useful tools. When he asks for particularly specific directions, she comments: '[y]ou must learn to use far less direct directions [...] You have orders enough to start with, and you will find, as you go on, and as you need to know, what you have to do' (p. 224). Rossetti's text depicts a renewal of perception as the beginning of change, but MacDonald develops this concept still further by associating it with groups specific to Victorian educational reform (women, working-class men). The fact that both Irene and Curdie require a change in education may suggest that the education of different groups is complementary and that giving everyone the ability to debate multiple views and to think independently is necessary for a completely reformed society.

Once a process of change has been initiated, existing moral structures need to be renewed. Both Rossetti's and MacDonald's texts combine patterns of rewriting that had contemporary resonance, allowing a Victorian reader to renew a sense of religious, class and gender community. Lizzie gives a new mythology of sisterhood power by her reworking of religious imagery. Not only do her actions of loving sisterly sacrifice invite comparison to Christ, but her own words – not the speaker's – consciously re-construct her body as miraculous salvation. The words 'Suck my juices/ [...] Squeezed from goblin fruits for you/ [...] Eat me, drink me, love me' (ll. 468–71) famously mirror Christ's 'This is my body, broken for you. Take and eat [...] This is my blood, shed for you.'[29] Lizzie's conscious reconstruction mirrors manipulations of language by Victorian feminists. Female appropriations of the divine are a hallmark of Victorian sisterhoods. Victorian feminists like Anna Jameson and Barbara Leigh Smith of the Langham Place Group, the theist feminist Frances Power Cobbe and the Evangelical feminist Josephine Butler, who used the term 'the Great Father-Mother, God', started a trend of feminising the masculine Christian God. Reworkings of the masculine Christian God led to renewals of the symbol of the communion doctrine as a space of equality. Eileen Yeo summarises this new space as 'a "communion of labour" between men and women in all spheres of public and private life'.[30]

Such symbolic communion also extends to the contemporary rewriting and re-interpretation that Victorian women were doing of moral and religious narratives. Julie Melnyk describes how *The Christian Lady's Magazine*, begun in 1834, overcame institutional bans on females conducting theological exegesis by incorporating biblical exegesis in the form of religious fiction: '*The Christian Lady's Magazine* published long-running series of articles on female characters from the Bible [...] [the series cited] the examples of Deborah, Hannah, and Mary, as justifications of women's poetry and prophecy, quoting and analyzing their scriptural songs at some length'.[31] These periodicals – the *Christian Lady* ran for twelve years, but had successors, such as the *Christian World Magazine* – allowed women to decentre religious narratives of female social spheres by reinterpreting and rewriting biblical texts. Rossetti's text combines both trends: Lizzie's actions and words recall the passion of Christ and the words of the communion service, but a reader with biblical knowledge is required in order to make this link explicit.

In *The Princess and the Goblin*, the operation of biblical rewriting implied by Lizzie's words and actions becomes an explicit revision of wider social context. Princess Irene effects a combination of various Victorian archetypes in order to redefine the meaning and abilities of a 'princess'. In his notes in the magazine version of *The Princess and the Goblin*, MacDonald democratises the word princess – 'Every little girl is a princess' – but emphasises the moral requirements of this role: 'I have seen little princesses behave like the children of thieves and lying beggars, and that is why they need to be told they are princesses'.[32] MacDonald sets up a new moral hierarchy: anyone can be a princess, but princesses do not lie and they do not steal. Roderick McGillis, in his notes on MacDonald's text, links this required morality with John Ruskin's definition of queens in *Sesame and Lilies* (1865). Like MacDonald, Ruskin forms a social hierarchy in terms of morality. Ruskin defines queens as 'right-doers' and admonishes 'idle and careless queens' for their rejection of purity in abdicating the 'myrtle crown, and the stainless sceptre, of womanhood'.[33] However, McGillis's linking of Princess Irene solely with Ruskin's lily-queen eludes another Victorian archetype that she embodies: that of the self-made man, which resembles Ruskin's definition of manliness more than his definition of queenliness. Ruskin describes men as 'active, progressive, defensive [...] the doer, the creator, the discoverer, the defender'.[34] As a moral queen as well as a doer and a discoverer, Princess Irene becomes a composite of Victorian gender archetypes and MacDonald celebrates these merged qualities as belonging to a true princess. In his descriptions of Irene's explorations, MacDonald praises her undaunted courage. Irene is temporarily confounded by a maze of passages, but she goes on with her explorations: 'She wiped her eyes with her hands, for princesses don't always have their handkerchiefs in their pockets, any more than some other little girls I know of. Next, like a true princess, she resolved on going wisely to work to find her way back' (p. 9).

The link between morality and courage is not difficult to make, but courageous women were not generally depicted as being explorers. Irene's courage also evokes the true gentlemen in Samuel Smiles' *Self-Help* (1859). Smiles depicts courage as being a male preserve: '[i]t is in misfortune that the character of the upright man shines forth [...] he takes stand upon his integrity and his courage', and he celebrates the lives of, among others, working-class men whose qualities of courage and integrity have allowed them to transcend class boundaries.[35] Princess Irene has the moral heart of Ruskin's queen, but she expands this role by exemplifying Smiles' true gentleman.

Like Lizzie, her transgressive movements represent her love for another. Unlike Lizzie, however, Irene's search is prompted by the trust developed through her love for her grandmother. For Irene, her sacrifice is the discarding of irrelevant restrictions. However, Princess Irene's expanded femininity develops a love for others which allows her to combat such social restrictions. Princess Irene, being a true princess, is determined not to break her word, no matter the social consequence; she resolves to give Curdie a promised kiss, despite her nurse's horrified remonstrations. Lootie is caught up in social artificialities. She says '[t]here's no occasion [to give him a kiss]; he's only a miner-boy', but the princess understands her obligation to brotherly love: 'He's a good boy, and a brave boy, and he has been very kind to us [...] I promised!' (p. 33). Irene learns to rely on her moral instinct for social empathy as developed by her fairy grandmother. This allows her to ignore the restrictions on her movements. When Curdie discovers her in the mine, he is shocked: '"However did Lootie come to let you go into the mountain alone?" he asked' (p. 117). Irene, bolstered by her grandmother's spiritually symbolic thread, has ignored Lootie: 'Lootie knows nothing about it. [I found you] by keeping my finger upon my grandmother's thread' (p. 117). Irene's absorption of differing class archetypes (the moral queen, the self-made gentleman) creates an in-between space around her that allows her to express love most fully. Whereas Lizzie rewrites religious images of love for others, Irene rewrites social conditions for creating a harmonious community.

However, although new systems of meaning may be developed, ideal communities must incorporate permanence as well as initiate renewal. Talking about the past becomes a way of rehabilitating the community; the evocation of contemporary depictions of renewed communities raises the question of how to determine a valid communal myth. At the end of 'Goblin Market', we leave Laura telling tales of the sisters' past in order to bind together their children (who, as she bids them cling together with the words 'There is no friend like a sister' (l. 562), are presumably female). The goblin men still feature, but, stripped of the term goblin, they take on the lesser role of the 'wicked, quaint fruit-merchant men' who serve to illustrate the vivid heroism of her sister who 'stood/ in deadly peril to do her good/ And win the fiery antidote' (ll. 557–59). This sisterly love also has the capability to transform liminal space: sisters are relations as well as friends; sisterly love can manifest in both calm and stormy weather, not just at goblin twilight; sisterly love shines brightest in one's weakest moments, because then one can see how the sister cheers, lifts, and strengthens the sufferer. Laura's tale rehabilitates the seductive goblin jingle that imprisoned her in the goblin world. (l. 27) Now, the repeated goblin jingle keeps children listening, but as educational entertainment, rather than in a destructive way. However, the reader cannot tell what Laura's audience may think of her tale. Their identity has been subsumed in Laura's rhymes, even though these are benign. The ending of 'Goblin Market' leaves many questions open for debate, the silence of Laura's audience aside: the sisters are wives, but who are their husbands? What did these husbands make of the sisters' experience?

MacDonald's text extends the uncertainty latent in Rossetti's ending as past events encode current commands. The legend of the socially oppressed goblins (see introduction) contextualises the rest of the novel, explaining the distaste the palace servants have for the miners, who work in the mountain, and complicating the goblins as quasi-victims, quasi-villains. It implements a spatial coding for the novels: the mountain is associated with the lower classes; the palace is the site of the privileged (which includes royal servants as well as the royal family itself). After Curdie and Irene cross these various spaces, both the mine and the palace are breached and merged through flooding. The text presents a vivid image of social confusion as 'dead goblins were tossing about in the current through the house. They had been caught in their own snare; instead of the mine, they had flooded their own country' (p. 164). After this, the miner boy Curdie gains acknowledgement of his abilities from the king, who commands his servants 'to mind whatever Curdie should say to them' (p. 165). These words also mirror Laura 'bid[ding] them to cling together'; the king binds his servants and Curdie together with the assumption that Curdie can protect them against the goblins given his past actions. The socially coded movements of Irene and Curdie create a new middle class in between the upper class of the palace and the lower class of the mountain.

These coded movements have been seen as evoking psychological tropes,[36] but David Cannadine's examination of ideals of reforming polarised class groups suggests another interpretation to these transgressive movements.[37] Cannadine notes that the middle classes were celebrated as knitting together a society riven between the aristocracy and the peasantry, especially by Whig politicians such as Lord Milton, John Lambton, Lord John Russell, and Sir James Graham, arguing in favour of the Reform Bill, which, finally implemented in 1832, gave new political rights to the middle classes.[38] This vision of the harmonising middle classes carried on throughout the century, past the Chartist campaigns, so that Macaulay could confidently predict that future generations would see Victorian England as a golden age when 'all classes were bound together by brotherly sympathy'.³⁹ But William Cobbett, writing in 1830, argued that discerning action, rather than just sympathy, was necessary for true reform. He complains that 'the "education" canters' increase the spread of crime 'by pretending that it is not want of food and clothing, but want of education, that makes the poor, starving wretches thieves and robbers'. Cobbett points out that reform must represent depth of action: 'To be sure immorality leads to felonies. Who does not know that? But who is to expect morality in a half-starved man, who is whipped if he do not work?'.⁴⁰ The events at the end of *The Princess and the Goblin* mirror this spirit as other characters show changed action, as the flooding of the palace causes social changes beyond the King's democratic words to Curdie and the servants. Irene's nurse, the once-snobbish Lootie, goes to stay with Curdie and his parents, and in the cleansed regime the goblins' hearts soften and they become friendly with the human inhabitants. Where 'Goblin Market' has a single teller talking about communal love to an audience, MacDonald's text contains multiple characters who demonstrate the actions of a cleansed and loving community. The reader leaves Irene and Curdie at the end of *The Princess and the Goblin* with a vision of society transformed by the socially transgressive miner and princess.

The Princess and Curdie emphasises the importance of an ability to determine truth in order to ensure a truly transformed society. It opens with a rude awakening from the previous happy ending, as Irene has disappeared to a distant city and Curdie, summoned by Irene's fairy grandmother, must argue his way into the palace past the snobbish housekeeper who calls him 'an out-of-doors labourer, a nobody' (p. 214). Irene's grandmother refutes this dismissal by telling Curdie and his father that they 'have the blood of the royal family in [their] veins', and mentions that she has been trying to 'cultivate your family tree [...] and I expect Curdie to turn out a blossom on it' (p. 208). This assessment would seem to counter the democratic movements of *The Princess and the Goblin*: Curdie can transgress social codes because he is a prince in disguise. Colin Manlove, describing MacDonald as celebrating compassion to individuals rather than a wider system of rights, suggests that the announcement of Curdie's royal blood is a prerequisite for his marriage to Irene.⁴¹ Curdie's discovery of royal blood affirms his relationship with his parents as he turns to them to discuss this revelation, and in so doing discovers that his mother, a 'true woman', has a hand that is like that 'of the beautiful princess' even though, as she says, it is 'cracked, rheumatic, old [...] and its short nails all worn down to the quick with hard work' (p. 227). The phrase 'true woman' links her to Irene, a 'true princess' who does not mind kissing a miner boy or muddying herself, but would not lie and is brave. Curdie's change in social definition does not mean that he changes his identity as a miner. In MacDonald's sermon on 'Kingship', he outlines a spiritual kingship based on the words of Jesus in the gospels; Jesus describes a kingdom in which 'everyone' can become a king – as long as they tell the truth:

> The Lord's is a kingdom in which no man seeks to be above another: ambition is of the dirt of this world's kingdoms. He says, 'I am king, for I was born for the purpose, I came into the world with the object of bearing witness to the truth. Everyone that is of my kind, that is of the truth, hears my voice. He is a king like me, and makes one of my subjects.'[42]

Like Jesus, Curdie and Irene (the 'true princess' who does not lie) are able to bear witness to the truth because they can see past social ambition and superficialities. Others with the inner qualities of truth can become part of the royal identity: for instance, the child Barbara plays with the king's crown and becomes his constant companion. It is their ability to tell true stories that gives them a royal identity, rather than any type of blood. Curdie and Irene instigate a new social system, which prioritises an inner truthfulness. The condition of the nation becomes an outward manifestation of an inner humanity. So when 'Men and women that had human hands' are brought to court, 'a new and upright government, a new and upright court' forms; inner reform binds the community together (p. 340). However, when the community does not retain this inner identity, society fails. The novel ends with the appearance of a new king who prioritises money and his actions cause the destruction of the city. Reform may depend on myths of loving harmony for inspiration, but these myths cannot remain symbolic and must continue to bear witness to the truth in order to retain any type of power.

MacDonald's texts extend Rossetti's transformed community: reform is not just a matter of sharing inspiration, but of discernment and witness as well. While the fantastic elements in all three texts prevent the enforcement of a particular meaning, the evocation of contemporary debates about education, morality, and idealised communities opens a discussion of the meaning of transformation and of how such possible meanings might threaten nineteenth-century society. These evocations place MacDonald and Rossetti beyond the bounds of genre categorisation as writers who speculate on both textual and social conditions, and by so doing, allow multiple communities to meet in discussion. The fact that both writers have particular identities as writers of fantasy or writers of children's tales or writers of religious texts invites speculation on the ambiguous borders of such genres, particularly in the light of a shared cultural memory within the nineteenth century of imaginative fantasies (like the *Arabian Nights* and Grimm's *Household Tales*), and the potential in crossing these borders. For example, what might Emily Brontë's waif-turned-landlord Heathcliff have to say to MacDonald's goblin prince Harelip, and vice versa?

Notes

1. Christina Rossetti to Dante Gabriel Rossetti, 13 March 1865, in *The Letters of Christina Rossetti*, vol 1, ed Anthony Harrison (Charlottesville: Virginia University Press, 1997), p. 234.
2. George MacDonald, 'The Imagination: Its Functions and its Culture', in *A Dish of Orts* (London: Sampson Low, Maeston, Searle and Rivington, 1882, pp. 1–42), p. 16.
3. George MacDonald, 'The Fantastic Imagination', in *George MacDonald: The Complete Fairy Tales*, ed U. C. Knoepflmacher (Harmondsworth: Penguin, 1999, pp. 5–10), p. 7–8.
4. Rosemary Jackson, *Fantasy: The Literature of Subversion* (London: Methuen, 1981), p. 146.
5. Stephen Prickett, *Victorian Fantasy* (Waco, Texas: Baylor University Press, 2005), p. 11.
6. Prickett, pp. 102–03.
7. Prickett, p. 162.
8. Charles Dickens, *A Christmas Carol and Other Writings*, ed Michael Slater (London: Penguin, 2003), pp. 58–59.
9. George Eliot, *Daniel Deronda* (London: Penguin, 1995), pp. 184, 209.
10. 'The Story of the Amours of Camaralzaman,' *The Arabian Nights' Entertainments* (Philadelphia: L. Johnson, 1832), pp. 215–43.
11. See George Eliot, *Daniel Deronda*, pp. 7, 728.
12. See Anna Clay Beecher, *Gwendolen, or Reclaimed. A Sequel to Daniel Deronda by George Eliot* (Boston: W. F. Gill, 1878).
13. Christina Rossetti, 'Goblin Market', in *The Complete Poems of Christina Rossetti*, ed Rebecca W. Crump (Baton Rouge: Louisiana State University Press, 1979), pp. 11–26. References henceforth in text.
14. Contemporary reviews quoted in Lorraine Kooistra, *Christina Rossetti and Illustration* (Athens, OH: Ohio University Press, 2002), p. 69.

15. George MacDonald, *The Princess and the Goblin* and *The Princess and Curdie*, ed Roderick McGillis (Oxford: Oxford University Press, 1990). References henceforth in text.
16. See previous note.
17. See '"Goblin Market" – Ribald Classic', illustrated by Kinuko Craft, in *Playboy* 20 (September 1973), pp. 115–19; Michael Symons, *A History of Cooks and Cooking* (Illinois: University of Illinois Press, 2004), pp. 323–51; and Margaret Linley, 'Nationhood and Empire', in *A Companion to Victorian Poetry*, ed Richard Cronin, Alison Chapman and Antony H. Harrison (Oxford:Blackwell, 2002, pp. 421–37), pp. 432–33.
18. Geoffrey Reiter, '"Travelling Beastward": George MacDonald's Princess Books And Late Victorian Supernatural Degeneration Fiction', in *George MacDonald: Literary Heritage and Heirs: Essays on the Background and Legacy of His Writing*, ed Roderick McGillis (Wayne, PA: Zossima, 2008, pp. 217–26), p. 222.
19. Dinah Birch, *Our Victorian Education* (Oxford: Blackwell, 2007), p. 29.
20. Emily Davies,*The Higher Education of Women* (London: 1866), p. 142.
21. See William Raeper, *George MacDonald* (Tring: Lion, 1987), p. 165.
22. Annie Ridley, *Frances Mary Buss: Her Life and Works* (London: Longmans, Green, 1895), p. 93.
23. George Eliot, 'Unsigned Review for the *Leader*, 27 October 1855', in *Thomas Carlyle: the Critical Heritage*, ed Julius Paul Seigel (London: Routledge and Kegan Paul, 1971, pp. 409–11), p. 409.
24. Richmal Mangnall, *Historical and Miscellaneous Questions* (London: Longman and Hurst, 1823), p. 7.
25. Mangnall, p. 143.
26. Alfred Dewes, 'Letter to Oliver Heywood, 1868' in *Education and Democracy*, ed A. E. Dyson and Julian Lovelock (London: Routledge and Kegan Paul, 1975), p. 217.
27. Kristin Mahoney, 'Work, Lack, and Longing: Rossetti's "The Blessed Damozel" and the Working Men's College', *Victorian Studies: An Interdisciplinary Journal of Social, Political, and Cultural Studies*, 52 (2010), pp. 219–48 (p. 225).
28. John Ruskin, *The Elements of Drawing* (London: Smith, Elder, 1857), p. 121.
29. Luke 22.19, *The New Oxford Annotated Bible*, ed Michael Coogan (Oxford: OUP, 2001), p. 139.
30. Eileen Yeo, 'Protestant Feminists and Catholic Saints in Victorian London', in *Radical Femininity: Women's Self-Representation in the Public Sphere*, ed Eileen Yeo (Manchester: Manchester University Press,1998, pp. 127–48), p. 129.
31. Melnyk, p. 195.
32. See explanatory notes by Roderick McGillis, p. 343.
33. John Ruskin, *Sesame and Lilies* in *The Works of John Ruskin on CD-ROM*, ed E. T. Cook and Alexander Wedderburn (Cambridge: Cambridge University Press, 1996), p. 90.
34. John Ruskin, *Sesame and Lilies*, p. 68.
35. Samuel Smiles, *Self-Help* (London: John Murray, 1876), p. 42.
36. Ruth Jenkins, '"I am spinning this for you, my child": Voice and Identity Formation in George MacDonald's Princess Books', *The Lion and the Unicorn*, 28 (2004), pp. 325–44.
37. David Cannadine, *Class in Britain* (New Haven: Yale University Press, 1998), pp. 65–66.
38. David Cannadine, *Class in Britain*, p. 70.
39. David Cannadine, *Class in Britain*, p. 98.
40. William Cobbett, *Rural Rides* (London: Thomas Nelson, 1830), p. 275.

41. Colin Manlove, 'The Princess and the Goblin and The Princess and Curdie', North Wind: A Journal of George MacDonald Studies, 26 (2007), pp. 1-36 (p. 1).
42. George MacDonald ,'Kingship' in Creation in Christ: Unspoken Sermons (Vancouver: Regent College Publishing, 2004, pp. 136-42), pp. 138-39.

Bibliography

Primary Texts
MacDonald, George, The Princess and the Gobli and The Princess and Curdie, ed Roderick McGillis (Oxford: Oxford University Press, 1990).
Rossetti, Christina, 'Goblin Market' in The Complete Poems of Christina Rossetti, ed Rebecca W. Crump (Baton Rouge: Louisiana State University Press, 1979), vol 1, 11-26.

Other Texts
Beecher, Anna Clay, Gwendolen, or Reclaimed. A Sequel to Daniel Deronda by George Eliot (Boston: W. F. Gill, 1878).
Birch, Dinah, Our Victorian Education (Oxford: Blackwell, 2007).
Cannadine, David, Class in Britain (New Haven: Yale University Press, 1998).
Carpenter, Mary Wilson, '"Eat Me, Drink Me, Love Me": The Consumable Female Body in Christina Rossetti's "Goblin Market"', Victorian Poetry, 29 (1991), pp. 415-34.
Cobbett, William, Rural Rides (London: Thomas Nelson, 1830).
Coogan, Michael (ed), The New Oxford Annotated Bible (Oxford: OUP, 2001).
Craft, Kinuko, '"Goblin Market" - Ribald Classic', Playboy, 20 (1973), pp. 115-19.
Davies, Emily, The Higher Education of Women (London: 1866).
Dewes, Alfred, 'Letter to Oliver Heywood (1868)' in Education and Democracy, ed A. E. Dyson and Julian Lovelock (London: Routledge and Kegan Paul, 1975).
Dickens, Charles, A Christmas Carol and Other Writings, ed Michael Slater (London: Penguin, 2003).
Eliot, George, 'Unsigned Review for the Leader, 1855', in Thomas Carlyle: the Critical Heritage, ed Julius Paul Seigel (London: Routledge and Kegan Paul, 1971), pp. 409-11.
— Daniel Deronda (London: Penguin, 1995).
Harrison, Antony (ed), The Letters of Christina Rossetti, vol 1 (Charlottesville: Virginia University Press, 1997).
Jenkins, Ruth, '"I am spinning this for you, my child:" Voice and Identity Formation in George MacDonald's Princess Books', The Lion and the Unicorn, 28 (2004), pp. 325-44.
Jackson, Rosemary, Fantasy: The Literature of Subversion (London: Methuen, 1981).
Kooistra, Lorraine, Christina Rossetti and Illustration (Athens: Ohio University Press, 2002).
Kirby, Peter, 'Child labour, public decency and the iconography of the Children's Employment Commission of 1842', Manchester Papers in Economic and Social History, 62 (2007).
Linley, Margaret, 'Nationhood and Empire' in A Companion to Victorian Poetry, ed Richard Cronin, Alison Chapman and Antony H. Harrison (Oxford: Blackwell, 2002), pp. 421-37.
MacDonald, George, Creation in Christ: Unspoken Sermons (Vancouver: Regent College Publishing, 2004).
— 'The Imagination: Its Functions and its Culture' in A Dish of Orts (London: Sampson Low, Maeston, Searle and Rivington, 1882), pp. 1-42.

— 'The Fantastic Imagination' in *The Complete Fairy Tales*, ed U. C. Knoepflmacher (Harmondsworth: Penguin, 1999), pp. 5-10.
Mahoney, Kristin, 'Work, Lack, and Longing: Rossetti's "The Blessed Damozel" and the Working Men's College', *Victorian Studies: An Interdisciplinary Journal of Social, Political, and Cultural Studies*, 52 (2010), pp. 219-48.
Mangnall, Richmal, *Historical and Miscellaneous Questions* (London: Longman and Hurst, 1823).
Marsh, Jan, *Christina Rossetti: A Literary Biography* (London: Cape, 1994).
Manlove, Colin, 'The Princess and the Goblin and The Princess and Curdie', *North Wind: A Journal of George MacDonald Studies*, 26 (2007), pp. 1-36.
Melnyk, Julie, 'Women's Theology and the British Periodical Press' in *Reinventing Christianity*, ed Linda Woodhead (Aldershot: Ashgate, 2010), pp. 191-98.
Prickett, Stephen, *Victorian Fantasy* (Waco, Texas: Baylor University Press, 2005).
Raeper, William, *George MacDonald* (Tring: Lion, 1987).
Reiter, Geoffrey, '"Travelling Beastward": George MacDonald's Princess Books and Late Victorian Supernatural Degeneration Fiction', in *George MacDonald: Literary Heritage and Heirs: Essays on the Background and Legacy of His Writing*, ed Roderick McGillis (Wayne, PA: Zossima, 2008), pp. 217-26.
Ridley, Annie, *Frances Mary Buss: Her Life and Works* (London: Longmans, Green, 1895).
Ruskin, John, *Sesame and Lilies*, in *The Works of John Ruskin on CD-ROM*, ed E. T. Cook and Alexander Wedderburn (Cambridge: Cambridge University Press, 1996).
— *The Elements of Drawing* (London: Smith, Elder, 1857).
Smiles, Samuel, *Self-Help* (London: John Murray, 1876).
'The Story of the Amours of Camaralzaman,' *The Arabian Nights' Entertainments* (Philadelphia: L. Johnson, 1832), pp. 215-43.
Symons, Michael, *A History of Cooks and Cooking* (Illinois: University of Illinois Press, 2004).
Yeo, Eileen, 'Protestant Feminists and Catholic Saints in Victorian London' in *Radical Femininity: Women's Self-Representation in the Public Sphere*, ed Eileen Yeo (Manchester: Manchester University Press, 1998), pp. 127-48.

Sitting on the Doorstep: MacDonald's Aesthetic Fantasy Worlds and the Divine Child-Figure

ALLY CROCKFORD

The mirror has lifted [the room] out of the region of fact into the realm of art [...] But is it not that art [...] reveals Nature in some degrees as she really is, and as she represents herself to the eye of the child?[1]

George MacDonald's theological views of children and childlike qualities are no secret: not only scholars, but casual readers of his work – his fantasy stories and novels in particular – are immediately presented with an unmistakable idealisation of the essence of childhood embodied in his protagonists, child and adult alike, and his vision of the divine. His perspective is stated baldly in the first volume of *Unspoken Sermons*, in the essay entitled 'The Child in the Midst': 'For the *childlike* is the divine, and the very word "marshals me the way that I was going"'.[2] As a result it seems to have been unconsciously, and almost unanimously, accepted that the child in MacDonald's fantasies constitutes nothing more than – to quote one example from Glenn Edward Sadler – 'a redemptive figure [that] participates in and exemplifies universal love and immortality'.[3]

However, to reduce the child to such limited importance denies the role that the child plays in MacDonald's creation of fantasy worlds and his often overlooked aestheticism. By exploring MacDonald's union of aestheticism and spirituality, we can uncover a greater understanding of the fantastic worlds for which he is remembered and the nature of the child-figure's central role in two of his major fantasy novels. I am particularly interested in *At the Back of the North Wind* (1871) and *Lilith* (1895), and in the way their child-figures interact with, even intertwine with, their fantastic worlds. I will analyse the nature of these worlds, attempting to uncover the significance of their aestheticism and its relationship with the divine. MacDonald's location of his child-figures within fantastic aesthetic worlds seems to result from a tortured duality of feeling towards his own theology which Colin Manlove suggests is carried throughout both his fantastic and realistic fiction.[4] The child-figure's divine aestheticism becomes a way for MacDonald to work through his own theological anxieties regarding the reality of everyday life and the promise of a heavenly life after death. Envisioning the child as an idealised union of humanity and divinity, MacDonald attempts to capitalise on the child's potential to mediate the gap between life and death.

Due to his place in the development of modern fantasy literature and the influence of early interpretations by G. K. Chesterton and C. S. Lewis, MacDonald has often been confined within the category of a 'fantasy' or a 'mythopoeic' writer. Such a definition has led to the near exclusion of considerations of his work in relation to the many other literary and artistic movements with which he would have come into contact during his many decades of writing, and there have been few attempts to explore the extent to which MacDonald was influenced by or engaged with such movements. Yuri Cowan associates MacDonald's work with aestheticism, while Adelheid Kegler asserts his potential ties to symbolism. These two perspectives aside, however, most MacDonald criticism is interested in his work as it engages with the fantasy genre or Christian theology.

Cowan is convinced that such exclusionary approaches have had a detrimental effect on a more nuanced understanding of MacDonald's work: 'To see MacDonald as a shaper of Christian myths is to ignore both the non-dogmatic nature of his views on moral and social renewal and the emphasis on individual interpretation that colours his views on art, both of which are characteristic of the concerns of the Aesthetic movement in general'.[5] I would qualify this statement by saying that to read MacDonald *purely* in light of his relationship to the genre of British fantasy literature or his development of Christian myths is to undermine, even to negate, the elements of his fiction that engage with other literary and theological influences. To overlook these influences is to approach these stories from a narrow position profoundly opposite to MacDonald's own. George MacDonald, despite the strength of his religious convictions, was a man whose experience of the world around him was constantly being influenced by different facets of society, of religion, of life. It therefore stands to reason that, just as his spiritual beliefs were influenced by his experiences[6] – to such an extent that his own theology often came into conflict with Calvinist dogma[7] – so his literary efforts might similarly exhibit the imprint of those movements in literature around him.

In any scholarly discussion of literary aestheticism, MacDonald's work is not likely to be given much, if any, consideration. Yet, while MacDonald would never be classified an aesthete, he was certainly touching on aspects of aestheticism's fundamental beliefs. 'The Aesthetic project', according to Cowan,

> is one of continuing to receive impressions of art and to create new forms from them, and of absorbing them into one's life on a daily basis, thereby making one's character more refined and individual. If there is one agreement among the diverse writings of the Aesthetic movement, it lies in their desire to maintain the tension (or harmony) between the fictional and the actual, the real and the ideal, life and art. It is not 'the Truth' that will make us free, it is Art.[8]

While critics like Walter Pater, Vernon Lee, or John Ruskin[9] wrote extensively on the nature of aesthetics, attempting, in Pater's words, to 'distinguish, to analyse, and separate from its adjuncts, the virtue by which a picture, a landscape, a fair personality in life or in a book, produces this special impression of beauty or pleasure, to indicate what the source of that impression is, and under what conditions it is experienced',[10] MacDonald's non-fiction prose more often took the form of spiritual sermons than traditional or aesthetic criticism. And yet, those sermons as well as his fiction are laden with evidence that he, too, bore the trademark quality of the aesthetic critic: 'not that [they] should possess a correct abstract definition of beauty for the intellect, but a certain kind of temperament, the power of being deeply moved by the presence of beautiful objects'.[11]

There is, of course, a division between Pater's and Lee's art-for-art's-sake aestheticism and Ruskin's aesthetic. It is true that Ruskin's relationship to British aestheticism is a complicated one. The question becomes, as Freedman suggests, 'of whom […] do we speak when we refer to the "aesthetic movement?"'.[12] He goes on to concede that 'aestheticism […] represents primarily an angle of vision that aims at [a] purification of vision […] but which increasingly discovers the impossibility of such preternatural clarity of sight; it privileges art not as an end in and of itself, but as a focusing or sharpening of the contradictions one thereby faces'.[13] It is within this more general conceptualisation of nineteenth-century British aestheticism that I aim to situate MacDonald. Certainly MacDonald's prose, fictional and non-fictional alike, offers a reflection of the author as a man who cultivated a deeply sensitive appreciation for, even adoration of, beauty. But beyond this simplistic association, MacDonald demonstrates an affinity with Pater's description of the aesthetic critic, and his prose is characterised by the 'focusing or sharpening of [...] contradictions' which Freedman describes as an essential defining quality of British aestheticism.

In contrast to Pater and Lee's aestheticism, which sought to divorce artistic from moral evaluation, MacDonald's is predicated on the necessity of a close relationship between the aesthetic and the spiritual. In fact, Rolland Hein's description of MacDonald's belief system describes them as intrinsically linked:

> Today, many people who think about the relation of Christianity to art discern an incompatibility between them. They see art, by its very nature, as having to be free and unconstrained by dogma, and Christianity as arbitrary and confining. Such people would be quick to see MacDonald as a man torn between two worlds [...] [But] in MacDonald's system of belief nothing is more compatible, nothing is more unified in nature, intent, and purpose, than art and faith. As he states [...] 'Beauty is the only stuff in which Truth can be clothed'.[14]

The emphasis on a relationship between Christianity and art that Hein describes brings to mind Ruskin's aesthetic theory. MacDonald's son Greville offers a glimpse of his father's close relationship with John Ruskin, against whose description of the moral value of art and beauty Lee was so strongly opposed. The younger MacDonald takes pains to emphasise 'how strong was the two men's sympathy'.[15] As Roderick McGillis points out, MacDonald's letters to Ruskin reveal the extent of their personal relationship, but little of MacDonald's perspectives on – or relation to – his friend's intellectual or aesthetic position.[16] That said, despite their stark differences in religious beliefs, MacDonald's fiction reveals some reflection of aesthetic theories regarding the relationship between art and moral value not unlike Ruskin's own. Ruskin specifically identified a distinction between the aesthetics of form and the expression of morality within art, outlined clearly in his description of the 'three great branches of architectural virtue':

> (1.) That [art] act well, and do the things it was intended to do in the best way. (2.) That it speak well, and say the things it was intended to say in the best words. (3.) That it look well, and please us by its presence, whatever it has to do or say.[17]

In MacDonald's aesthetic philosophy, however, art does not serve spiritual causes by inspiring its audience to observe doctrine, and neither does spirituality imbue art or beauty with a value it might otherwise have lacked. They are, to repeat Hein's phrasing, intrinsically 'unified in nature, intent, and purpose'.

It could be argued, therefore, that MacDonald's aestheticism and that of canonical aesthetes like Pater or Lee are as two sides of the same coin – where Pater and, in particular, Lee idealise art for art's sake rather than its moral or spiritual value, MacDonald's vision is of a purity of art and beauty in which no such valuation exists because art *is* spirituality. Lee reacts against Ruskin's evaluation of art based on its moral value, its service to a particularly religious morality; MacDonald might react against the same method of evaluation, but because the very essence, the nature, of all art – of beauty itself – is divine. It is this aestheticism which colours his fantasies, specifically his creation of fantastic worlds. Drawing from the German Romanticism by which he was so inspired, MacDonald explores and articulates his spiritual vision, but also sculpts a world made wonderful by his own unique aestheticism, the locus of which is the child-figure and the divinity of its childlike essence.

Although I do not wish to focus on *Phantastes* (1858) in this paper, its affinity with *Lilith* offers some insight into MacDonald's aesthetic worlds. In considering Mr Vane's journey through his attic mirror into a world of fantasy, it is helpful to turn to Cosmo von Wehrstahl: 'What a strange thing a mirror is! [...] The mirror has lifted [my room] out of the region of fact into the realm of art [...] But is it not that art [...] reveals Nature in some degrees as she really is, and as she represents herself to the eye of the child [...]?' (*Phantastes*, pp. 154–55). Although there is no similar passage in *Lilith* exploring the role of mirrors in the transition between the mundane world and the realm of art, Mr Vane's reaction to his situation after passing through the mirror in the garret echoes MacDonald's earlier sentiment in *Phantastes*. Vane wonders whether he may have 'wandered into a region where both the material and psychical relations of our world had ceased to hold? Might a man at any moment step beyond the realm of order' (*Lilith*, p. 11), the 'realm of order' which he has left behind being no different from the 'region of fact' which was transformed in the mirror in *Phantastes*. The world in which Vane now finds himself may not be similarly termed a realm of art, but the role that mirrors play in Vane's transition between reality and a place 'so little correspondent with the ways and modes of this world – which we are apt to think the only world' (p. 12) suggests an affinity with the mirror world in *Phantastes*. The similarities hint at *Lilith*'s construction of a fantasy world which is imprinted with MacDonald's aestheticism, as I shall explore below. In both worlds, Nature is unveiled 'as she really is', and, crucially, 'as she represents herself to the eye of the child'. This seeming truth of Nature is little correspondent with the mundane world constructed through the eyes of the adult, a world that is greyed and dulled by greed, ignorance, and cynicism. MacDonald's vision of an aesthetic world essentially defined by its accessibility to the eyes of a child characterises the fantasy world in *At the Back of the North Wind* in particular.

When Diamond steps through North Wind to visit the land at her back, the narrator is quick to note the difficulty inherent in describing what he saw: 'I have now come to the most difficult part of my story. [...] For of course I could know nothing about the story except Diamond had told it; and [...] what he did remember was very hard to tell' (p. 93). It is interesting to note that the narrator does not make it clear whether it is Diamond who finds what he remembers difficult to tell, or whether it is the narrator who has trouble transcribing Diamond's memories. The suggestion of a struggle faced by the adult mediators in relating a true likeness of the country at the back of the north wind paints the image of a land characterised by an extra-linguistic quality to which children are sensitive, but which is denied adults. Indeed, the first thing we are told about the country at the back of the north wind is that 'the people there do not speak the same language for one thing. Indeed, Diamond insisted that they do not speak at all' (p. 93). Although the narrator scoffs at this particular example of what he implies is childish fancy, throughout the story Diamond rarely 'insists' unless what he is insisting upon is in fact so. In the end, despite the narrator's protestations, the description of inhabitants communicating to each other by silent nods suggests that it is a space in which communication exists outside of language. It is not surprising, therefore, that language offers such an inadequate means of accurately depicting such a place. This extra-linguistic, even non-verbal, quality of the country is intimately tied in with its definition as an aesthetic realm, an association best relayed in *At the Back of the North Wind* through song.

According to Diamond's account, as well as those of 'Durante' and 'Kilmeny', the country at the north wind's back is defined by the river flowing through it. However, the focus of these references is invariably not the river itself, but the tunes which it sang. These songs are entirely non-verbal; never sung aloud, they simply envelop the minds of the inhabitants, and yet the implication is always that they are sung, never played. They are not instrumental songs, as Diamond makes clear, for they are 'the tunes the river at the back of the north wind *sung*' (p. 96, my emphasis), yet they are not necessarily verbal, either. Later, a glimpse of these songs is offered in the book of 'nonsense' verses Diamond discovers on the beach shortly after his journey, which he declares to be almost the very tune that the river sang.[18] The poems are characterised by their cyclical nature and steady rhythm – 'the sweetest wind/ that blows by the river/ flowing for ever/ and over the shallows/ where dip the swallows/ above it blows/ the life as it goes/ awake or asleep/ into the river/ that sings as it flows' (117) – one reading these verses might be struck by the seeming monotony, repetition and precise, fragmented structure of each line.

Roderick McGillis indicates that the verse, in so far as it functions as a 'nursery rhyme', 'warn[s] us that form is as important as content'.[19] Yet this poem so clearly differs from the revised versions of 'Little Boy Blue', 'The Cat and the Fiddle', and 'Little Bo Peep' that the extent to which it is supposed to work as a nursery rhyme, epithet aside, is questionable. So, too, is the assumption that form is 'as important' as content; although McGillis sees the metaphors as the key to the poem's importance,[20] the intrusive form of the poem suggests otherwise. The lack of clear rhythmic structure or rhyme scheme in the poem forces the technical devices to the fore so that the focus is on the verse's musical components rather than its content. The chaotic metrical pattern varies frequently, reasserting the presence of the poem's rhythm, but not so drastically as to upset the progression of the poem entirely. The effect calls to mind musical notation, as if the poem was structured according to a single time signature. The fragmented lines are suggestive of measures on a score, musical phrases which correspond to the time signature without necessarily following a consistent rhythmic pattern. The form, what McGillis describes as 'language drawing attention to itself',[21] works to defer meaning in the words themselves: they are privileged not so much for their ability to carry meaning as for their musicality.

Given their friendship, it is interesting to consider Ruskin's description of the relationship between language and art in relation to MacDonald's poetry in *At the Back of the North Wind*. Ruskin writes that

> It is not [...] always easy, either in painting or literature, to determine where the influence of language stops, and where that of thought begins. Many thoughts are so dependent upon the language in which they are clothed, that they would lose half their beauty if otherwise expressed. But the highest thoughts are those which are least dependent on language, and the dignity of any composition and praise to which it is entitled, are in exact proportion to its independency of language or expression.[22]

It seems that MacDonald similarly saw language, at least, if not literature itself, as an important and yet intrinsically flawed method of artistic creation. His representation of language in both *At the Back of the North Wind* and *Lilith* questions the linguistic function of words while the power of song threads throughout the very fantastic spheres in which language is reconstructed.

MacDonald thus reconstructs words themselves as extra-linguistic, aesthetic elements akin to music, and weaves them into his creation of fantastic literary worlds. As with Diamond, the Lovers in *Lilith* are more sensitive to this aesthetic language. Lona's conversations with Vane undermine his linguistic authority – in one instance in particular his attempts to communicate are reduced to meaningless mouth-sounds: 'I do not know about *world*. What is it? What more but a word in your beautiful big mouth? – That makes it something!' (p. 63). Of course, the fantastic space that MacDonald creates in *Lilith* is not itself characterised by silence and non-verbal communication. The importance of the extra-linguistic aesthetic and its relationship to the child is instead made clear primarily by the waters which flow hidden beneath this world, so that the land is quite literally steeped in it. The river in *At the Back of the North Wind* was clearly intricately bound up with music of a kind of purely aesthetic nature; likewise when the underground waters in *Lilith* are first mentioned, they seem to exist almost entirely as music rather than as any kind of physical matter. The water itself is not seen – it is the 'sweet watery noise [...] the veiled melody of molten music' (p. 53) which permeates the soil and twice heals Vane.

The importance of water in George MacDonald's work, Hein points out, is typically associated with 'the biblical image of the Living Water: the life of God that scripture indicates He bestows upon those who believe' (p. 92). Yet the water upon which MacDonald's fantasy land is built is music, a current that is clearly equally influenced by the author's aestheticism as it is by his divinity. Once again, the two are inextricably linked for MacDonald, and water plays an integral part in this union; in his unspoken sermon, 'The Truth', he describes water as that which 'dances, and sings, and slakes the wonderful thirst [...] Let a man go to the hillside and let the brook sing to him till he loves it, and he will find himself far nearer the fountain of truth' (p. 68). Water is here associated once again with music, with singing; the correlation is not unique to *At the Back of the North Wind* or *Lilith*. Most importantly, water, for MacDonald, is associated with an elemental beauty that carries the truth of God.

MacDonald's description of water, perhaps more than any other aspect of his fantasies, evokes Oscar Wilde's description of aestheticism as 'a search after the signs of the beautiful. It is the science of the beautiful through which men seek the correlation of the arts. It is, to speak more exactly, the search after the secret of life'.[23] As with the river in *At the Back of the North Wind*, water in *Lilith* is often equated with song: 'river[s] of water made vocal by its rocks' (*Lilith*, p. 232), and thickets which 'gave birth to a rivulet, and every rivulet to its water song' (p. 233). The duality of water's significance in both *Lilith* and *At the Back of the North Wind* clarifies MacDonald's fusion of spirituality and aesthetic within the child-figure. Water in *Lilith* seems almost to centre around the

Lovers – themselves the very essence of the childlike which MacDonald so admired. Mara and Adam both identify the Lovers' growth as ultimately tied to their access to water: Mara enigmatically suggests that 'when they are thirsty enough, they will have water, and when they have water, they will grow [...] beneath, it is flowing still' (p. 73), and Adam chastises Vane for failing to provide wells for the children in order that they might grow. Furthermore, the appearance of the Lovers is frequently announced by a 'burst of bell-like laughter' or 'laughter clear and sweet as the music of a brook', and their communication with Vane consists of stories 'often seeming to mean hardly anything', and on one occasion 'a strange crooning song, with a refrain so pathetic that, although unintelligible to me, it caused tears to run down my face' (p. 61).

It is interesting to note that when the water finally returns to the land it becomes itself essentially childlike – the Lovers imagine it flowing in rivers, 'merry and loud, like thousands and thousands of happy children' (pp. 197–98) – because the comparison, which is here most explicit, occurs in *At the Back of the North Wind* as well. In Diamond's dream, he is guided by 'the gurgling and plashing of a little stream' which had a voice 'like the laughter he had heard from the sky' (p. 199) – the laughter of small children. Thus the voice of the river in Diamond's dream is, like the river in *Lilith*, the voice of laughing children, its 'merry tune' composed once again of their childlike non-verbal expression. In fact, Diamond's own engagement with verbal and non-verbal forms of communication, and with a reconsideration of language, forms a key element of one of the novel's major plot segments. The story of Diamond's time in London in *At the Back of the North Wind* is marked in part by his attempts to learn how to read – his entry into the world of rational, communicative language.[24] His transition, however, is never completed; dying before he can be fully inducted into the dreary, colourless world of adult language, Diamond returns to the non-verbal aesthetic paradise at the back of the north wind.

Diamond's interactions with the adults around him are characterised by his inability to properly engage with them using their own language; one conversation with his mother in particular stands out. In it, the elements of adult discussion which Diamond takes note of and considers cause his mother some anxiety, and reveal his precarious position within discourse:

> 'Really, Diamond, a body would need to mind what they say to you.'
> 'Why?' said Diamond. 'I only think about it.'
> 'That's just why,' said his mother.
> 'Why is that why?' persisted Diamond [...] After various attempts to understand [...] resumed and resumed again in spite of invading sleep, he was conquered at last, and gave in, murmuring over and over to himself, 'Why is why?' (p. 146)

The tension in this interaction demonstrates the way in which Diamond's attempts to communicate with the adults in his life nearly always fail in some way. Entering into their world of rational language from one that privileges musicality over functionality, Diamond's ability to see beyond what is communicated causes a sense of anxiety which is compounded by his persistent undermining of linguistic convention. Simply by thinking about the language used around him, Diamond eventually reaches the unanswerable question of 'Why is why?', forcing a breakdown in communication with his mother. And yet it is this failure which marks him as 'God's baby', which brings him closer to the divine, occupying a position denied the adults whose ties to language keep them firmly shackled to reality.

As the novel closes, Diamond is permitted a return to his interaction with North Wind. Just as his initial stay in the country at North Wind's back takes place while Diamond has been ill and comatose, his later encounters with her coincide with supposed returns of his illness; he has not, we learn, truly been to the land at the back of the north wind – he has seen but a shadow of it. In order to reach the realm itself Diamond must die, relinquishing his hold on symbolic reality in order to pass through the North Wind and travel to the paradise at her back. These transitional states in which Diamond is permitted access to that world create a further link between the child-figure and MacDonald's divine aesthetic paradises. Sally Shuttleworth considers the way in which the study of the child's mind evolved throughout the nineteenth century. In exploring the distinction between the child's mind and the adult's, such studies and discussions reveal a deep-seated anxiety raised by the prospect of the child's unknowability, and thus its potential freedom from adult boundaries.

In her exploration of studies and representations of the child mind in the nineteenth century, Shuttleworth turns to Robert Macnish's *The Philosophy of Sleep* (1830), noting that it 'establishe[d] an important continuum between childhood and the dream state'.[25] For Macnish the relationship between the child mind and the dream state is based on the idea that during childhood, as in dreams, judgement is weakened, according to Shuttleworth. But there is another connection which neither Macnish nor Shuttleworth address directly, namely that both states are defined largely by their essential unknowability. The comparison of childhood to the state of dreaming did not end with Macnish in 1830; Shuttleworth points out that 'the dream state as defined by Macnish and others, where intellectual control is in abeyance, has become a defining characteristic of the child mind, and by extension, of a state of insanity' (p. 50). By aligning childhood with dreams, and further with madness, such conceptualisations emphasise the child mind as a state of seeming non-existence, one which exists in a conceptual blind spot which is difficult, if not impossible, to re-create or articulate within rational discourse.

This impossibility of conceptual reconstruction of the child-mind is similarly one of the clearest defining features of MacDonald's fantastic worlds: in both *Lilith* and *At the Back of the North Wind* these worlds defy description. The narrators in both texts find themselves facing inevitable failure attempting to capture that which cannot be captured, and both visibly respond to the anxiety inherent in their position. To clarify, I am not suggesting that MacDonald was aware of either Macnish's work or similar studies; despite their popularity, there is no direct evidence linking the two. However, as Shuttleworth makes clear, both literary and scientific accounts of the child mind shed light on anxieties which surrounded questions about the state of mind which the child inhabits, that it may prove a world utterly and permanently undefinable. MacDonald's fantasy worlds are constructed in line with such anxieties and the theories of the child mind which they inspired, offering a similar vision of childhood as a state existing on a continuum with dreams, madness, and even death.

By constructing fantasy worlds in *Lilith* and *At the Back of the North Wind* as literary experiences of the child-mind, marking them with a unique relationship with the aesthetic as well as the divine which is predicated on the child's place outside of rational adult discourse, MacDonald deliberately distances his adult characters, and his adult readers, from these spaces. The child's mind becomes a paradise, but it is one which the adult characters in both novels can only glimpse. Vane is kept at a distance, and his narrative is distanced likewise, resulting – through his own admission – from his frustrating reliance on the inadequacies of language. Interrupting his narrative to emphasise his struggle as writer, he laments that 'I am indeed often driven to set down what I know to be but a clumsy and doubtful representation of the mere feeling aimed at, none of the communicating media of this world being fit to convey it, in its peculiar strangeness, with even an approach to clearness or certainty' (*Lilith*, p. 45). The juxtaposition of the fantasy world, the child-figures, and the adult-figures emphasises the seemingly inseparable distance between child-paradise and adult-reality. This distance taps into an anxiety which characterises much of MacDonald's work, if not all of it, and is related to the child's importance to his theological beliefs.

It cannot be denied that, by MacDonald's own admission, divinity is an essential element of MacDonald's child-figures, and in attempting to look beyond this defining characteristic I do not wish to overlook it entirely. Yet if the child-figure's divinity is not the sole reason for its key position in either *At the Back of the North Wind* or *Lilith*, then why this centrality? Certainly it would be easier to create Wordsworthian child characters who embody divine nature and serve simply to inspire adult readers to adopt a new world-view. But Vane's oft-debated rejection from Mount Paradiso and abrupt return to the doldrums of 'real life' seems to disallow such a reductive interpretation. Vane's relationship with the Lovers would seem to have almost exactly that influence: it is during his time spent with the Lovers that he comes closest to understanding, and certainly takes great strides towards appreciating, the fantastic world in which he finds himself. Vane becomes, at least to his mind, 'like a child, constantly wondering, and surprised at nothing' (p. 90). The text, of course, does not end with Vane following the children to the true Heaven of Mount Paradiso; he, like the reader, is thrust harshly back into a sudden reality. One thing which this ending does make clear, to me at least, is that the role of the child, and the importance of the childlike to spiritual salvation, is not limited to its ability to enable a return to the child's way of seeing the world. Vane's final disappointment is also perhaps the most jarring and blatant instance in which MacDonald's fantasies force the adult-figures – and the reader with them – away from the child-paradises which lie at their core. The instability of the child's unique vision in the face of its envelopment within communicative, symbolic language and the struggle faced by adult narrators in articulating the stories they are trying to recount suggest that such a return is not possible. MacDonald thus seems to reject Reinhard Kuhn's theory that 'as long as the adult can recover, through the intellect, the imagination, or the involuntary memory, the mental set of the child [...] then he can relive the profound reality of his erstwhile condition and can even retranslate it into terms comprehensible to other adults'.[26] For MacDonald none but the child – not just any child but an *ideal* child – can attain more than a glimpse of paradise until the moment of their own death.

Through its complex place in MacDonald's aesthetic theology, the child also becomes part of a means by which he attempts to work through the spiritual tensions which present themselves in his work. The extent to which MacDonald's faith pervades his writing and his life left him with the appearance of one who welcomes this transition from living death to life after death; his son's recollections offer the image of a man who faced death fearlessly, the result of 'his personal embodiment of the sixth beatitude'. [27] Yet Manlove identifies a trend stretching 'across MacDonald's writing as a whole, between his fantasy fiction on the one hand and his many novels of "real life" on the other',[28] namely the 'continual oscillation between a longed-for heaven and the all-too-earthly present, between hope and doubt, rapture and happiness'.[29] MacDonald may have faced death without fear, but his work suggests that his ecstatic expectation of the paradise after which his fantastic worlds are built was tempered with a 'world of doubt'.[30]

The distance highlighted by placing the child-figure and its heavenly aesthetic fantasy world so tantalisingly out of reach is also the distance between humanity and the divine which seems to have tortured MacDonald. Manlove goes on to describe that for MacDonald, 'between these two there could be no resolution, only the continued desire that one would give away to the other, and the mingling acceptance and resignation in their not yet doing so, yearned for joy and lived doubt'.[31] This torture characterises the duality of MacDonald's fiction as a whole, and is also found in the tensions crafted within his fantasies surrounding the child-figure and its tenuous position within 'real life'. By constructing his fantastic realms, themselves shades of the Heaven he anticipated, as childlike spaces, mirroring the aesthetic, non-verbal, undefinable state of childhood itself, MacDonald mediates these tensions. In its union with the spiritual, the child-figure offers a bridge between divinity and humanity, and the position that it occupies between the two worlds – not just its investment with the divine – is essential to MacDonald's fantasy literature. The child is swathed in the possibility of a reconciliation of these two otherwise divergent spheres. Although in both novels he abstains, leaving the adult stranded in the everyday world, the child still represents *a union of humanity and divinity*, if one that can only ever be defined by its unrealisable potential. The conclusions of both *Lilith* and *At the Back of the North Wind* indicate that lingering potential; the loss of the child leaves a path for the adult to follow. Thus, Vane concludes that 'when I wake at last into that life which, as a mother her child, carries this life in its bosom, I shall know that I wake, and shall doubt no more' (p. 238).

Notes

1. George MacDonald, *Phantastes: A Faerie Romance for Men and Women*, special edn (London: Paternoster, 2008), p. 154–55.
2. MacDonald, 'The Child in the Midst', in *Unspoken Sermons* (London: Alexander Strahan, 1867), p. 3.
3. Glenn Edward Sadler, 'Defining Death as "More Life": Unpublished Letters by George MacDonald', *North Wind*, 3 (1984), p. 5.
4. Colin Manlove, 'The Logic of Fantasy and the Crisis of Closure in *Lilith*', in *Lilith in a New Light: Essays on the George MacDonald Fantasy Novel*, ed Lucas H. Harriman (London: McFarland, 2008), p. 56.
5. Yuri Cowan, 'Allegory and Aestheticism in the Fantasies of George MacDonald', *North Wind*, 25 (2006), p. 39.
6. See Richard Reis, *George MacDonald* (New York: Twayne Publishers, Inc, 1972) pp. 31–51; see also Greville MacDonald's *George MacDonald and His Wife* (London: Allan & Unwin, 1924), and William Raeper's *George MacDonald* (Tring, Herts: Lion, 1987), which both explore the ties between MacDonald's experiences and influences and his theological development through his own letters.
7. Greville MacDonald, in *George MacDonald and His Wife*, describes his father's dismissal from the congregation at Arundel as stemming from such conflict; one of the charges raised against him on this matter Greville suspects 'probably originated in his *Songs of Novalis*: he was tainted with German Theology' (pp. 178–79); see also David Robb, *God's Fiction: Symbolism and Allegory in the Works of George MacDonald* (Eureka, CA: Sunrise Books, 1989) pp. 6–7, 11–13, 17.
8. Cowan, 'Allegory and Aestheticism', p. 54.
9. For a more specific discussion of Ruskin's relationship to British aestheticism, see Kenneth Daley, 'From the Theoretic to the Practical', *Prose Studies: History, Theory,*

Criticism, 20.2 (1997) pp. 90–107. Wolfgang Iser also explores Pater's connection to Ruskin in *Walter Pater: The Aesthetic Moment*, trans David Henry Wilson (Cambridge: Cambridge University Press, 1987) pp. 11–14, 26, 33–35, 47, and 63.
10. Walter Pater, *Studies in the History of the Renaissance* (London: MacMillan, 1873), p. ix.
11. Pater, *Studies*, p. x.
12. Jonathan Freedman, *Professions of Taste: Henry James, British Aestheticism, and Commodity Culture* (Stanford, CA: Stanford University Press, 1986), p. 3.
13. Freedman, *Professions*, p. 10.
14. Rolland Hein, *The Harmony Within* (Grand Rapids, MI: Christian University Press, 1982), pp. 148–49.
15. Greville MacDonald, *George MacDonald and His Wife*, p. 330.
16. Roderick McGillis, 'What's Missing: Lacunae in the Life and Letters of George MacDonald', *The Lion and the Unicorn*, 19. 2 (1995), p. 283.
17. John Ruskin, *The Stones of Venice, Volume I: The Foundations* (London: George Allen, 1903), p. 60.
18. Although the Narrator points out that he '[does] not exactly know what the mother read, but this is what Diamond heard, or thought afterwards that he had heard [...] when he thought he understood the verses he may have been only dreaming better ones' (p. 114), the relationship between the verses and the songs from the back of the north wind lies in Diamond's declaration of their similarity. The verses that we are given are those that Diamond heard, and they are the verses that are, he states, akin to the songs from the back of the north wind.
19. McGillis, 'Language and Secret Knowledge in *At the Back of the North Wind*', in *For the Childlike*, ed Roderick McGillis (London: The Scarecrow Press, 1992), p. 146.
20. McGillis, 'Language and Secret Knowledge', p. 146.
21. McGillis, 'Language and Secret Knowledge', p. 146.
22. Ruskin, *Modern Painters, Volume I* (London: Smith, Elder, 1873), p. 8–9.
23. 'Oscar Wilde's Arrival', *New York World*, 3 January 1882, p. 1, in *Oscar Wilde in America: The Interviews*, ed Matthew Hofer and Gary Scharnhorst (Chicago, Il: Illinois University Press, 2010), p. 14.
24. In 'Language and Secret Knowledge', McGillis notes that his time in London also 'mark[s] Diamond's beginning [...] He begins to be a poet' (p. 151), and suggests that North Wind 'is the visiting Muse – MacDonald's version for children of the Romantic anima figure that visits the poet in dreams or visionary moments – bringing intimations of eternity. She is Diamond's poetic genius' (pp. 154–55). It is interesting that Diamond's education – marked by the more meaningful, communicative nursery rhymes – is balanced by his own creation of poetry that emulates the musicality of the river's song.
25. Sally Shuttleworth, *The Mind of the Child: Child Development in Literature, Science, and Medicine, 1840–1900* (Oxford: Oxford University Press, 2010), p. 48.
26. Reinhard Kuhn, *Corruption in Paradise: The Child in Western Literature* (Hanover, NH: Brown University Press, 1982), p. 12.
27. Greville MacDonald, *George MacDonald and His Wife*, p. 200.
28. Manlove, 'Logic', p. 56.
29. Manlove, 'Logic', p. 55.
30. Manlove, 'Logic', p. 56.
31. Manlove, 'Logic', p. 56.

Bibliography

Cowan, Yuri, 'Allegory and Aestheticism in the Fantasies of George MacDonald', *North Wind*, 25 (2006), pp. 39-57. http://www.snc.edu/english/nwarchive.html [Accessed on 13 August 2010].

Ellman, Richard, *Oscar Wilde* (New York: Vintage Books, 1988).

Freedman, Jonathan, *Professions of Taste: Henry James, British Aestheticism, and Commodity Culture* (Stanford, CA: Stanford University Press, 1986).

Hein, Rolland, *The Harmony Within* (Grand Rapids, MI: Christian University Press, 1982).

Kegler, Adelheid, 'Below in the Depths: MacDonald's Symbolic Landscape', *North Wind*, 24 (2005), pp. 29-40. http://www.snc.edu/english/nwarchive.html [Accessed on 13 August 2010].

Kuhn, Reinhard, *Corruption in Paradise: The Child in Western Literature* (Hanover, NH: Brown University Press, 1982).

Lee, Vernon, 'Ruskinism' in *Belcaro: Being Essays on Sundry Aesthetical Questions* (London: T. Fisher Unwin, 1887, 2000), pp. 197-229.

MacDonald, Greville, *George MacDonald and His Wife* (London: Allan & Unwin, 1924).

MacDonald, George, *At the Back of the North Wind* (London: J. M. Dent & Son, 1871, 1973).

— *Lilith* (Mineola, NY: Dover Publications, 1895, 2008).

— *Phantastes: A Faerie Romance for Men and Women*, ed Nick Page, special edition (London: Paternoster, 2008).

— 'The Child in the Midst' in *Unspoken Sermons* (London: Alexander Strahan, 1867), pp. 1-26.

— 'The Truth' in *Unspoken Sermons, Third Series* (London: Longmans, Green, 1889), pp. 56-82.

Manlove, Colin N., 'The Logic of Fantasy and the Crisis of Closure in *Lilith*', in *Lilith in a New Light: Essays on the George MacDonald Fantasy Novel*, ed Lucas H. Harriman (London: McFarland, 2008), pp. 46-58.

McGillis, Roderick, 'What's Missing: Lacunae in the Life and Letters of George MacDonald', *The Lion and the Unicorn*, 19. 2 (1995), pp. 282-87. http://muse.jhu.edu [Accessed on 15 November 2010].

— 'Language and Secret Knowledge in *At the Back of the North Wind*', in *For the Childlike*, ed Roderick McGillis (London: The Scarecrow Press, 1992).

'Oscar Wilde's Arrival', *New York World*, 3 January 1882, p. 1, in *Oscar Wilde in America: The Interviews*, ed Matthew Hofer and Gary Scharnhorst (Chicago, IL: Illinois University Press, 2010).

Pater, Walter, *Studies in the History of the Renaissance* (London: MacMillan, 1873).

Raeper, William, *George MacDonald* (Tring, Herts: Lion, 1987).

Reis, Richard, *George MacDonald* (New York: Twayne, 1972).

Robb, David S., *God's Fiction: Symbolism and Allegory in the Works of George MacDonald* (Eureka, CA: Sunrise Books, 1987, 1989).

Ruskin, John, *Modern Painters*, Volume I (London: Smith, Elder, 1873).

— *The Stones of Venice, Volume I: The Foundations* (London: George Allen, 1903).

Sadler, Glenn Edward, 'Defining Death as "More Life": Unpublished Letters by George MacDonald', *North Wind*, 3 (1984), pp. 4-18. http://www.snc.edu/english/nwarchive.html [Accessed on 13 August 2010].

Shuttleworth, Sally, *The Mind of the Child: Child Development in Literature, Science, and Medicine, 1840-1900* (Oxford: Oxford University Press, 2010).

III. IDEALS AND NIGHTMARES

Stirring the Senses: Identity and Suspense in George MacDonald's *David Elginbrod*

ELIZABETH ANDREWS

Domestic intrigue emerged as a central theme explored by mid-nineteenth-century authors. The British novel evolved from the turn-of-the-century elaborately staged Gothic crimes in works like Matthew Lewis's *Monk* (1796) and Ann Radcliffe's *The Mysteries of Udolpho* (1794) into the historical realism of Walter Scott's *Waverley* novels (1814–1831) and Charles Dickens's narrative social commentary. Writers of mid-century sensation fiction draw upon the titillation present in Gothic narratives while situating their tales in the realistic domestic sphere employed by the latter authors. The sensational subjects of this subgenre of the Victorian novel revolve around the rules that govern the domestic sphere. This preoccupation, illustrated by sensation novelists through the criminalised depiction of shocking and scandalous domestic mysteries, reflects anxieties about these domestic rules that govern social identities and gender delineations. Simultaneously, writers of religious fiction were drawing upon the same heritage of historical realism and fascination with domestic settings.

This essay will address the similarities between mid-Victorian religious fiction and sensation fiction, demonstrating that George MacDonald's deft usage of tropes common to sensation fiction in his novel *David Elginbrod* (1862) achieves a narrative result more closely fitting the didacticism exemplified by novels generally classified as religious fiction. As we will see there is often an overlap between what can be considered sensation fiction and what can be considered religious fiction. Though ostensibly dissimilar, close readings of MacDonald's work and a sampling of sensation fiction reveal common themes of gender and class inequality, constructed within a solution-driven narrative which calls for activism and social change. Ultimately MacDonald's work emerges as both significantly influenced by and contributing to the greater dialogue of mid-Victorian popular novels.

Over the past thirty years, literary critics such as Winifred Hughes, Michael Diamond and Lyn Pykett have established the role of sensation fiction as a genre exploring the intricate strata of social values, written rules and understood expectations governing social behaviour in the Victorian period.[1] More recently, critics like Richard Fantina and Kimberly Harrison have drawn attention to the problematic nature of essentialising the genre. Limiting 'sensation fiction' to a particular time period, a selection of authors, or even a specific list of tropes is fraught with difficulty: some novels that exemplify the characteristics of sensation fiction are written well outside the 1860s, many writers of sensation fiction wrote different kinds of stories, and, significantly, the features of sensation novels are not exclusive, nor are they exhaustive. Harrison and Fantina point to the tradition of mid-Victorian novels, describing sensation fiction as 'a generic hybrid – formally, thematically, and ideologically – sensation fiction is an integral part of Victorian studies'.[2] New approaches to the analysis of these novels will aim to account for the complex interrelationships between previously delineated sub-genres of the Victorian novel, such as sensation fiction and religious fiction, and the narrowly confined 'standard' Victorian novels of writers like the Brontës, Dickens, George Eliot, W. M. Thackeray, and Anthony Trollope.

Sensation novels remain critically notable despite historical academic neglect because they sold remarkably well. 'Despite the outrage of Victorian critics and churchmen', Harrison and Fantina report, 'sensation novels were frequently best sellers'.[3] The publishing market moved from three-decker novels towards serial publication, which required magazines to capture the interest of their audiences quickly in order to secure sales of subsequent issues. Multiple stories and features of a magazine assured a more consistent purchasing audience. Likewise, the more intriguing the plots contained within the magazine were, the more dedicated the readership became. Serialised novels were not unlike television programmes today, dependent upon a complex network of advertisers, writers, and production outlets.

While sensation novelists are usually associated with presenting intriguing material, writers of religious novels were operating within the same publishing market. The influence of the Oxford movement in response to perceived secularisation of the Anglican Church generated many publishing enterprises, printing and distributing pamphlets, magazines and religious fiction to a broad audience. Evangelical novels and sensation novels often appealed to the same audience and sought to influence similar social issues. Like sensation fiction, religious fiction often explores concerns regarding the sanctity of the family and domestic space, yet in religious fiction, mysteries surrounding inheritance, suggestions of bigamy, drug and alcohol abuse, and seemingly supernatural occurrences are generally resolved through demonstrations of faith and conservative behaviour. Margaret Maison notes that 'to the Victorian reader religious novels meant "theological romances".[4] In this way, religious novels are distinguished by their overt didacticism rather than plot structure or significant generic features. Writers of religious fiction adapted their writing styles to the developing market and intrigue sold well.

Religious fiction also provided an opportunity for displaced theologians like George MacDonald to publicly expose their views. By addressing readers in a familiar popular format, adapted to the author's conservative moral views, novelists could impart a lesson to the greater public without the associated drawbacks of close association with the institution of a church:

> Those who had left the churches to interpret the teachings of Christ in a new and unorthodox way seized upon the novel as their most powerful mouthpiece. George Mac[D]onald openly declared that, having been deprived of his pulpit by the Congregational Church, he was using the novel as a substitute medium for the propagation of his religious convictions, and Mrs Humphry Ward, Marie Corelli and many other exponents of new creeds all reached the public in this way.[5]

Here, Maison describes the popular novel as an alternative ministry to that of preaching to a congregation. This view complicates moralistic objections to sensation fiction in the light of the many similarities shared between these two types of novels, and it illuminates both the commercial and cultural aspects of novel publishing during this period. Not only did religious fiction provide an entertaining story intended to impart a moral lesson, but it also provided insight into contemporary theological debate within British churches at this time. Robert Lee Wolff observes that '*David Elginbrod*, even to a reader easily bored with Scotch rural life and too sophisticated for the flummery of mesmerism, in this way incidentally provides a kind of tour of the mid-Victorian Scotch and English religious scene'.[6] As Wolff demonstrates, MacDonald and other writers of religious fiction were contributing to a broader debate about Christianity by utilising a popular secular form for addressing a wide audience.

While George MacDonald is more widely known today for his fantasy novels, the elements of sensation fiction that appear in his career are significant indicators of his engagement with the novel form as it progressed in the Victorian period. Joseph Johnson notes that MacDonald's realist novels established him as an author upon whom publishers could count for book sales:

> The three stories *David Elginbrod*, *Alec Forbes*, and *Robert Falconer* won for themselves a numerous and appreciative audience, and placed the author in the front rank of story-tellers, and among the seers of nature and lovers of all sorts and conditions of human life.[7]

Praise abounds for MacDonald's storytelling ability and his views on education, which are elaborately detailed throughout *David Elginbrod*, yet detractors argue that, as was the case with many writers of religious novels, MacDonald attempted to accomplish too much. Wolff observes that though MacDonald follows the elaborate plotting of the sensation novel format, he falls short of maintaining the suspense common to such novels:

> *David Elginbrod* has many faults. Disjointed, long-winded, didactic, with an elaborate plot whose clumsy mysteries the author himself robs of their effect by flat-footedly explaining them away at once, it understandably frightened the publishers. Yet, with all its irritating qualities, it bears the marks of a struggling original talent, striving within the same novel to combine both the Gothic and the realistic genres.[8]

By giving away significant plot points, such as the coincidence of Margaret Elginbrod working in the same house as Hugh Sutherland or revealing the fact that the white spectral figure is actually physically Euphra

Cameron, MacDonald undermines the mystery he has painstakingly established. Yet these reassurances of logic underscore the irrationality of the sensational aspects of mesmerism that he employs. MacDonald incorporates the Gothic and domestic aspects of previous novels in the same way that writers of sensation fiction build upon them, but he endeavours to explain away the frightening elements of irrationality to create a controlled 'realist' environment in which good is rewarded and evil is punished, thereby furthering his moralist aims.

The principal agenda in *David Elginbrod* involves social responsibility. Through the characters of David himself, Margaret, and Robert Falconer, the novel glorifies practical assistance towards others as Christian service. These Christ-like servants are the characters who provide rational explanations and soothing ministrations to the other characters who are variously confused, ill, and otherwise lost. Maison addresses MacDonald's preoccupation with this agenda, suggesting that it singularly detracts from the success of his realist narratives:

> Thus in his novels he rather regrettably subordinates his delightful poetic imagination, his mystical religious fervour, his dry and subtle Scottish wit and his deep understanding of childhood (so prominent in his verse and his juvenile fiction) to the ends of propaganda for the cause of practical social helpfulness, and busies himself with spiritual biographies of the Christian as social worker that are the most monotonous and the least inspiring of all his creations.[9]

Regardless of the overall success of *David Elginbrod* as a narrative, the notion of 'practical social helpfulness' that it promotes is essential to understanding MacDonald's position as a novelist in the mid-Victorian period. As demonstrated below, many features of the novel fit comfortably with other novels in this era that are considered sensation novels; however, it is the didactic premise of the novel that differentiates the social activism of sensation fiction from that of religious fiction.

Maison notes that despite MacDonald's heavy-handed religious didacticism, the subject matter of a spiritual quest for identity was a relevant and thrilling theme for his audience. She states: 'to the Victorian common reader [...] religion was an intensely exciting and absorbing affair'.[10] This excitement is reflected in the sensationalised elements of the novel. *David Elginbrod* provides examples of the context of fascination with sensationalism that was prevalent during this time. When a police officer unexpectedly calls at Hugh's lodgings, the housemaid, Sally, becomes alarmed on his behalf. She offers to conceal Hugh because a 'pleaceman' has come to call upon him: 'Sally was a great reader of the "Family Herald," and knew that [concealing someone in the house] was an orthodox plan of rescuing a prisoner'.[11] Hugh has in fact invited the police officer and is amused by Sally's dramatic reaction, but the self-referential nature of MacDonald's allusion to sensational elements in the contemporary press, such as 'rescuing a prisoner', draws a connection between Hugh's dramatic struggle with his identity, and subsequent confusion over religious doctrine, and the drama inherent in life-and-death narratives involving prison escapes.

These novels were not merely occupied with complex plotting and melodramatic narrative action to stir the senses. Mid-Victorian novelists relied upon the mystery inherent in unravelling events that appear inexplicable. 'Sensational and fantastic literature confront taboo', Pykett explains; 'they are associated with excess, with the irrational, non-rational or supernatural, and with carnival or misrule'.[12] In sensation novels such as Collins' *The Woman in White* (1859) this excess is generated by a series of unhappy domestic arrangements disrupted by the purported presence of a ghostly lady, who is ultimately revealed to be a real person, around whom the main characters unite in their cause, bringing about an almost Austen-esque traditionally structured 'happy' domestic ending. In Collins' novel, the supernatural elements disrupt the fabric of traditional domesticity, which is reorganised and reinstated by the characters who work together to unearth the secret identity of the purported ghost. MacDonald addresses the supernatural elements of his narrative in a directly religious way. Hugh's faith is tested by his confrontation with the two ghostly figures he encounters. These 'ghosts' are also real people and are actually the two significant women in Hugh's life, elucidating his identity crisis. Once Euphra is physically and emotionally broken, a tidy domestic resolution with Margaret becomes possible. In MacDonald's novel, by contrast to Collins', supernatural elements highlight the protagonist's spiritual quest rather than uniting characters and ultimately the coupling in *David Elginbrod* is driven by rewarding good and punishing evil.

Writers in this era struggle to maintain the balance between Gothic and domestic settings, melodrama and pragmatism, rationalist and supernatural elements. One of the ways writers address taboo is to present a controversial subject, like ghosts or mesmerism, such that characters must engage with it to achieve their goals, and then ultimately the writer explains it away through the revelation of new information. Richard Reis suggests that MacDonald and his peers utilise this method of suspense to include subject matter, like the supernatural, which would otherwise promote censure:

> Another device for the achievement of suspense is the inclusion of apparently supernatural elements in what otherwise seems to be a perfectly realistic story. In the end, of course, what seemed supernatural has a perfectly natural explanation.[13]

While *David Elginbrod* implicitly condemns mesmerism by associating the practise of this questionable 'science' with evil characters instead of good ones, much of the second half of the novel is given over to precise descriptions of practices involving ouija boards, spiritual embodiments, ghosts walking, and physical and spiritual possession. Johnson argues that this is an essential part of the novel's appeal, stating that '[m]uch of the popular interest in the book lies in the complications that arise from the reputed ghost stories, and the evil machinations of Funkelstein, one of the worst types of character that MacDonald has drawn'.[14] So while some critics suggest that MacDonald's social activism detracts from the readability of his narrative, others like Reis and Johnson point out that it is the supernatural elements involved in MacDonald's social and spiritual mission that lend the novel its best-selling intrigue.

MacDonald's implicit condemnation of the irrational provides a comparative point with sensation fiction. Religious novels frequently superimpose 'reason' and morality in such a way as to make sense of cause and effect, whereas sensation novels tend to allow for conflicting and chaotic stimulation, often without providing rational explanation. An example from *David Elginbrod* illustrates MacDonald's didactic demonstration of the importance of providing a superstructure for a child's education:

> Hugh thought for a moment, and seemed to see that the boy, not being strong enough to be a law unto himself, just needed a benign law from without, to lift him from the chaos of feeble and conflicting notions and impulses within, which generated a false sense of slavery. (MacDonald 1872: pp. 115–16)

This excerpt is juxtaposed with the narrative drama of Hugh struggling to comprehend his seemingly irrational experiences with supernatural figures. In this way, MacDonald promotes Harry's education as a metaphor for Hugh's spiritual quest. Christianity is suggested as the 'benign law from without' to free Hugh from 'a false sense of slavery'. There are exceptions to this comparison, of course. Frequently sensation novelists do explain away mysteries involving ghosts and legal quandaries, but sensation novels are characterised by a lingering sense of suspense or irresolution that points to insufficiency in roles or laws or expectations of characters. Collins' *The Woman in White*, for example, conveniently distributes the characters at the conclusion of the novel according to the treatment they presumably deserve, but the inclusion of edited epistolary entries towards the end of the narrative underscores the fact that the story was compiled and edited by Walter, the character who necessarily has a vested interested in how the preceding events are perceived. The reader is left to muse over whether Walter emerging as a hero with everything working out satisfactorily for him is a result of the cause and effect of events as they play out in the novel or as a result of the way in which the narrative is constructed from Walter's viewpoint. The difference between presenting cause and effect as mediated by Christian faith and this alternative method frequently employed in sensation fiction emphasises the different roles that the interplay of rationality and irrationality can play out in mid-Victorian novels.

Both sensation and religious fiction from the mid-nineteenth century share solution-driven narratives that call for activism and social change. This contrasts with widely held views regarding Victorian novels as classic realist texts. Lyn Pykett defines classic realist texts thus: 'a conservative literary form concerned to reinscribe a commonsense view of things as they are, whose formal and ideological characteristics were adumbrated (and frequently castigated) by a host of critics bent on a radical critique of literature and its institutions'.[15] Pykett hints at the problems critics face when approaching subgenres like sensation and religious fiction with the expectation that these novels aim to 'reinscribe' the status quo that they describe. Significantly, sensation and religious novels describe social problems frequently perpetuated by well-meaning but narrow-minded patriarchal figures. For example, the figures of Mr Arnold and Mr Grasford in *David Elginbrod* are each made slightly ridiculous by the extent to which these patriarchs are out of tune with the actual occurrences on their respective estates. Yet the cornerstone of characterisation for both of these men is their unyielding authority. When viewed as a realist novel, concerned with upholding traditional ideologies, this characterisation becomes problematic. Instead, MacDonald, along with many of his contemporaries, relies upon the subtle criticism of revealing the inadequacy of these traditional characters. In this way, Victorian authors frequently subvert the 'commonsense view of things as they are' in order to call into question the validity of a classist and sexist social system.

While it is straightforward to suggest that MacDonald critiques gender and class inequality in *David Elginbrod* through the characterisation of failed patriarchs, it is more revealing to address his heroes and how these figures demonstrate the failure of the contemporary social system to account for the kinds of exemplary social service behaviour he promotes. David is characterised by his simplicity; his life is limited in means and scope and therefore he does not encounter many of the challenges faced by Hugh in the larger world. Hugh combats these challenges by struggling and often failing to live up to the example set by David. Falconer, on the other hand, is presented as the character who lives in London and encounters the daily struggles of truly suffering people and yet manages to serve them and his friends without succumbing to the temptations of immodesty, greed or cruelty. Falconer is the ideal social servant, or so it seems. A contemporary review of MacDonald's subsequent novel *Robert Falconer* (1868), which features this same character, demonstrates the improbability of such a hero:

> What particular end Mr Mac[D]onald proposed to himself in the creation of such a character as his hero, we find it difficult to

> conjecture. Beyond the story of his life, which is more interesting than probable, he seems to be intended to point a moral which we do not find it easy to draw. If it be, as we suspect, that Mr Mac-[D]onald feels sceptical of accomplishing any really good work except by individual effort [...], he seems to us to be elaborating in his own mind and suggesting in his novel a fallacy which a consideration of his own methods with his hero might perhaps show him.[16]

The 'methods' to which this reviewer refers are the improbable means by which Falconer manages to possess a fortune and all the requisite resources to accomplish his 'individual effort'. This reviewer emphasises the recurring point that realist novels are not necessarily 'probable'. In the case of the character of Falconer, MacDonald's didacticism is undermined by his character construction. Falconer just happens to possess the fortune and logistical freedom that enable him rather conveniently to perform acts of service to a broad range of people in need. It does not follow, then, that a different individual without these means would achieve similar results by committing himself to a life dedicated to serving others. A quandary emerges whereby the superficial means of narrative construction, which imbues Falconer with seemingly unlimited resources, defies the logic established by the realistic scenario of the novel. In this way, MacDonald, like sensation novelists, uncovers an uneasy surplus of energy by which social problems are revealed.

One of the kinds of social problems highlighted in *David Elginbrod* is uncertainty about gender roles. Some features demonstrated by various characters are cast as appropriately masculine or feminine and subsequent responsibilities derive from these delineations. For example, when the laird's sons that Hugh teaches create walls of snow to jump through to scare passers-by, this activity is initially signalled as great fun when they are scaring Hugh or other men of the house. The situation changes, however, when Hugh observes the boys frightening women:

> It was rare fun to them; but not to the women of the house, who moved from place to place in a state of chronic alarm, scared by the fear of being scared; till one of them going into hysterics, real or pretended, it was found necessary to put a stop to the practice. (MacDonald 1863: p. 78)

In this one sentence MacDonald characterises women, in contrast to men, as easily frightened, as well as indicating that the boys have a responsibility not to frighten the women. Additionally, the women respond to this fear by 'going into hysterics'. MacDonald qualifies this response by indicating that the fear reaction may be 'real or pretended', predicated upon 'the fear of being scared'. From this excerpt it is possible to assert two feasible interpretations: firstly, that the women are more easily frightened than men, or secondly, that the women are feigning hysterics in response to the activity that was meant to frighten them. Regardless of interpretation, this passage offers insight into the problematic nature of generalising and delineating gendered responses to the boys' antics. MacDonald does not take on the taboo of gender inequality by stating that the women are feigning hysterics, but the information is presented in such a way that the reader is meant to interpret the scenario for himself or herself.

Another way in which MacDonald addresses gender issues in *David Elginbrod* is through the feminisation of Harry's undesirable features. This is established when Mr Arnold says to Hugh that he fears the boy may become a 'milksop' (MacDonald 1872: p. 98). Later, when the little boy turns his nose up at the pigs and notes their 'nasty noise', the scene plays out almost like a courtship (MacDonald 1872: p. 103). Hugh is described as accompanying Harry to the barn as he would escort a woman, but instead of accepting this feminised behaviour, Hugh observes that Harry has been 'dreadfully [...] mismanaged' (*ibid.*). Hugh immediately vows to institute changes in Harry's routine:

> Thought Hugh: 'Here are several things to be righted at once. The boy must not have wine, and he must have only one dinner a day; especially if he is ordered to bed so early. I must make a man of him if I can.' (MacDonald 1872: p. 114)

Significantly, Hugh's commitment to his pupil is to masculinise him through structure, routine, and temperance. Temperance with children is a recurrent theme in novels of this period. It is the premise of the opening scene in Ellen (Price) Wood's *Danesbury House* (1860), where Mrs Danesbury attends a dinner party and respectfully negotiates her hosts' criticisms about serving the children wine. Mrs Danesbury tragically dies on her way home from this dinner party and the ensuing narrative action is punctuated by her children recalling her last admonition regarding temperance. In *David Elginbrod*, temperance is associated with masculinity, or with raising a child to exemplify his role as a patriarch. Later, Hugh's praise of Harry is similarly dominated by masculinity. 'You will be glad', Hugh says, 'to hear that Harry has ridden like a man' (MacDonald 1872: p. 136). By riding his horse 'like a man' Harry has begun to achieve the kind of behaviour acceptable for a boy of his status and Hugh's efforts to 'manage' him better are rewarded.

The source of Harry's mismanagement is unsurprisingly traced to Euphra. Though she is the boy's distant cousin and not intended to fill the role of governess or teacher, she was formerly the only person in the house of a suitable status to instruct him. Hugh considers 'that the boy was quite dependent upon her, seeming of himself scarcely capable of the simplest actions' (MacDonald 1872: p. 110). Harry looks to Euphra for approbation and action, which further feminises him, as the behaviours her guidance has perpetuated represent mismanagement of the youth. Once Hugh is installed as a role model for Harry the situation immediately shifts and Harry begins to become masculinised as noted above. Hugh analyses his progress thus: 'The boy's spirit was evidently reviving. Euphra must have managed him ill. Yet she was not in the least effeminate herself' (MacDonald 1872: p. 139). Hugh's reflection that Euphra is responsible for Harry's shortcomings follows from her being responsible for the boy, but the passage continues with his observation that she is not 'effeminate', an observation that appears to baffle Hugh. Regardless of whether Euphra's inability to govern the boy derives from her presumed masculinity or whether Hugh is surprised at this because Harry has taken on inappropriate feminised characteristics despite her masculinity, this scenario exemplifies MacDonald's presentation of problematised gender roles.

In addition to the feminisation of Harry's undesirable features, MacDonald also provides examples of contrasting gender roles. Hugh is consistently compared to Margaret. While he is portrayed as superior in experience and knowledge, it is Margaret who possesses the inner peace Hugh strives to attain. Throughout the novel, Margaret has a capacity to integrate her experiences of the world with her faith in a way that Hugh, until the end of the narrative, does not. Hugh does not see the 'divine in poetry nor the human in God', but Margaret does (MacDonald 1872: p. 49). Yet when Margaret begins to feel dazed in her studies of Euclid, Hugh instructs her to 'just try to keep the things altogether apart' (*ibid.*). Margaret demurs: '"But I canna help it," she replied. "I suppose you can, sir, because ye're a man"' (*ibid.*). Despite narrative reassurances that Margaret is on the right path, in the 'reality' of the novel, authority figures like Hugh who possess experience and knowledge are assumed to possess understanding also. Thus the incongruity in Margaret's characterisation highlights uncertainty regarding gender roles.

Gender inequality frequently parallels class inequality in *David Elginbrod*. As a poor descendant of a 'family of historic distinction and considerable wealth', Hugh struggles with his role in society and often reflects upon the relative values of status and integrity (MacDonald 1872: p. 9). After experiencing the anaemic society of the laird's family at mealtimes, he joins the Elginbrods for a meal of potatoes and milk:

> Hugh thought he had never supped more pleasantly, and could not help observing how far real good-breeding is independent of the forms and refinements of what has assumed to itself the name of *society*. (MacDonald 1872: p. 20)[17]

Hugh consistently observes the qualities of good company that are found in his friends the Elginbrods. He notes the attributes of 'good-breeding' through living amongst a variety of upper class families and preferring the emphasis on character and kindness he experiences with David's family. Ultimately Hugh concludes in his own identity crisis that he would prefer to be associated with integrity than wealth and status. Yet he does not afford this same value observation towards Margaret, perhaps because she is a woman. Hugh's 'pride' makes an alliance with Margaret seem an 'inconceivable absurdity' (MacDonald 1872: p. 28). While he does not see Margaret as of the same class as the field workers, a description of her purity and beauty is also marred by her domestic and agricultural experience: 'The only parts about her which Hugh disliked were her hands and feet' (MacDonald 1872: pp. 55, 77). Despite the fact that Hugh has not actually seen her feet at this point in the story, what is beautiful for a woman in Hugh's eyes is clearly status. This plays out through his infatuation with Euphra, the elegant embodiment of what Hugh presumably believes beauty to be. By establishing Margaret's worn hands and feet as her least desirable feature, MacDonald utilises the later emphasis on Euphra's delicate ankles and feet to underscore the economic and social division between these two women.

Lady Emily provides an alternative upper-class female figure to Euphra. She is meek, agreeable, and frequently ill. The ultimate solace that she receives comes from Margaret's loving ministrations when she is ill. When Lady Emily's faith in God begins to waver, Margaret dramatically testifies to her:

> As Margaret spoke, she seemed to have forgotten Lady Emily's presence, and to be actually praying. Those who cannot receive such words from the lips of a lady's-maid must be reminded what her father was, and that she had lost him. (MacDonald 1872: p. 234)

This passage not only justifies the sensational climax of Margaret's fervent declaration of faith, but MacDonald further reminds his readers of Margaret's social status and the implicit impropriety of a servant speaking to a lady thus. In this way MacDonald presents the shared faith of the two women as a bridge across the economic and social gap between them. No such bond exists between Margaret and less spiritually sympathetic characters such as Mrs Glasford, who looks Margaret over 'as if critically examining the appearance of an animal she thought of purchasing' (MacDonald 1872: p. 92). In addition to utilising features common to sensation fiction to build suspense towards the spiritual crises that his characters experience, MacDonald further demonstrates both the gulf that exists between characters of different classes and the sympathies that can exist between them.

Margaret also prays over Euphra, who receives Margaret's attention with surprise. MacDonald explains that Euphra 'had never received any tenderness from a woman before' (MacDonald 1872: p. 386). Lack of a maternal figure appears commonly in novels of this period, particularly in stories that feature a 'fallen' woman. Maison explains that '[t]he story of the "fallen woman" and her punishment was a favourite theme of mid- and late Victorian fiction, and the novels that punished the most sold the best, as the success of *East Lynne* showed'.[18] Euphra, like Lady Isabel in

Ellen (Price) Wood's *East Lynne* (1861), suffers physically in direct consequence of her emotional and spiritual shortcomings. However, both of these women also repent and ask forgiveness from the characters whom they have directly wronged before they die, leaving readers reassured of their salvation. Euphra is established as an exotic figure: haughty, spoiled, and dark-featured. Her involvement with the bohemian Funkelstein and knowledgeable manipulation of Hugh's affections imply Euphra's 'fallen' status and, as a result, her physical punishment is almost assured.

MacDonald capitalises on the moment of Euphra's conversion to demonstrate the recurrent theme of acts of service. Margaret's superior (spiritual) beauty has heretofore been lost on Euphra, but in her illness she glimpses Margaret's authenticity and loves her. It is this love that delivers her as she has at last experienced the sensation that can convey her from the thrills of involvement with Funkelstein's pseudo-spiritual thievery and criminal activity. This scene is a perfect balance of sensation and religious fiction and is further underscored by class commentary. 'It would have been unendurable to Euphra, a little while before', MacDonald explains, 'to find that she had a rival in a servant. Now she scarcely regarded that aspect of her position' (MacDonald 1872: p. 394). Spiritual delivery for Euphra also includes rising above social rank to observe genuine beauty in others. Like Falconer's wealth that allows him to perform significant charitable deeds, Euphra's sudden disregard for socio-economic distinctions seems unlikely. Yet Euphra goes so far as to ask Margaret to call her by her given name rather than 'Miss Cameron' and the love triangle with Hugh is tidily resolved in Margaret's favour (MacDonald 1872: p. 407). In this way the spiritual mysteries that play out in the novel serve as a backdrop for the anxieties about the domestic rules that govern social identities and gender delineations.

One of the ways in which mid-Victorian sensation and religious fiction highlight the need for social change is through introducing a helpful detective. Richard Reis acknowledges MacDonald's connection to the sensation fiction genre on the grounds of such a figure:

> Perhaps, in fact, he could be included in the school of Victorian sensation novelists (a term customarily applied to three of MacDonald's contemporaries: Dickens, Charles Reade, and Wilkie Collins). Several MacDonald novels include a quite fascinating

detective-story element, usually involved with the discovery of somebody's mysterious ancestry.[19]

In *David Elginbrod* MacDonald utilises Falconer, the detective-figure, not only to help Hugh make intellectual connections regarding the mysterious whereabouts of Funkelstein, but also to provide spiritual guidance and emphasise the importance of charitable acts. Hugh is suddenly able to make sense of the events that have occurred once he has the benefit of Falconer's insight: 'Hugh went home, full of his new friend. With the clue he had given him, he was able to follow all the windings of Euphra's [behaviour], and to account for almost everything that had taken place' (MacDonald 1872: p. 380). Though Falconer only appears towards the end of the novel, he is a central character and essential for driving the narrative towards a solution that not only solves the mystery but also indicates a need for activism and social change.

The solution-driven narrative in *David Elginbrod* calls for activism and social change in much the same way as contemporary mid-Victorian sensation novels. MacDonald distinguishes Christian activism in his novel as acts of service for which God will provide the resources. David summarises this philosophy when explaining to Hugh that the timber to build his sitting room will be provided by the laird's forest: 'That's the way 'at the Maker does wi' oorsels; he gies us the wa's an' the material, an' a whole lifetime, maybe mair, to furnish the hoose' (MacDonald 1872: p. 65). In this unique combination of sensation and religious fiction, MacDonald demonstrates his ability to incorporate contemporary features of fiction writing in order to reach a broad popular audience.

Victorian religious fiction is notable for its didactic vision. MacDonald and his peers recognised the opportunity to employ current narrative features like those present in sensation fiction in order to achieve a popular narrative that would impart his particular lessons regarding moral identity. Maison notes that '[e]vangelicals held the religious field and counteracted the "penny dreadfuls" by at least half-a-dozen pious periodicals containing "healthful moral stories" calculated to encourage conversion, virtue, thrift and self-help among the working classes'.[20] It was among these periodicals that *David Elginbrod* was released, incorporating popular suspenseful features in a plot-driven narrative with a backdrop of domestic anxiety. MacDonald's novel echoes the identity quest explored within many sensation novels. As Harrison and Fantina explain, '[a]t the heart of many sensation novels lies the recognition of the fluidity of identity. Rather than embracing essentialist notions of class, gender, race, and religion, the sensation novelists often complicate and at times defy them'.[21] By reading novels like *David Elginbrod* in the context of contemporary sensation novels the hybridity of subgenres of the Victorian realist novel, such as religious fiction and sensation fiction, become more readily apparent. MacDonald's depiction of domestic mysteries reflects anxieties about the domestic rules that govern social identities and gender delineations, while offering a religious explanation to express the imperative need for social responsibility. MacDonald's *David Elginbrod* can be read as simultaneously religious and sensation fiction thereby illuminating significant socio-cultural issues explored by popular fiction that frequently contrast with the domestic depictions of more mainstream Victorian novelists.

Notes

1. See Winifred Hughes, *The Maniac in the Cellar: Sensation Novels of the 1860s* (Princeton: Princeton UP, 1980); Michael Diamond, *Victorian Sensation: Or, the Spectacular, the Shocking and the Scandalous in Nineteenth-Century Britain* (London: Anthem, 2003); and Lyn Pykett, *The Improper Feminine: The Women's Sensation Novel and the New Woman Writing* (London: Routledge, 1992). For a comprehensive overview of sensation fiction criticism, see Mark Knight, 'Figuring Out The Fascination: Recent Trends in Criticism on Victorian Sensation and Crime Fiction', *Victorian Literature and Culture* 37.1 (2009) and Andrew Radford, *Victorian Sensation Fiction: A reader's guide to essential criticism* (London: Palgrave Macmillan, 2009).
2. *Victorian Sensations: Essays on a Scandalous Genre*, ed Kimberly Harrison and Richard Fantina (Columbus, OH: The Ohio University Press, 2006), p. xxii.
3. Harrison and Fantina, p. ix.
4. Maison, Margaret M., *The Victorian Vision: Studies in the Religious Novel* (New York: Sheed and Ward, 1961), p. 1.
5. Maison, p. 5.
6. Wolff, Robert Lee, *The Golden Key: A Study of the Fiction of George MacDonald* (New Haven: Yale UP, 1961), p. 206.
7. Johnson, Joseph, *George MacDonald: A Biographical and Critical Appreciation* (London: Pitman and Sons, 1906), p. 52.
8. Wolff, p. 182.
9. Maison, p. 313.
10. Maison, pp. 340–41.
11. MacDonald, George, *David Elginbrod* (Boston: Loring Publisher, 1872: reproduced from the 1900 edition of Mackay, Philadelphia), p. 338. Further references to *David Elginbrod* are taken from this edition and given in the text.
12. Pykett, Lyn, 'Sensation and the fantastic in the Victorian novel' in *Cambridge Companion*

to the *Victorian Novel*, ed Deirdre David (Cambridge: Cambridge University Press, 2000, pp. 192–211), p. 194.
13. Reis, Richard H., *George MacDonald* (New York: Twayne Publishers, 1972), p. 58.
14. Johnson, p. 226.
15. Pykett, p. 192.
16. 'Review: *Robert Falconer*', *The Nation*, 27 October 1870, 278, p. 284. While this review pertains to *Robert Falconer* and not *David Elginbrod*, the characterisation of Falconer in the review draws upon the character's description and action in the novel *David Elginbrod* and is therefore pertinent to this discussion.
17. Original italics.
18. Maison, p. 154.
19. Reis, p. 58.
20. Maison, pp. 89–90.
21. Harrison and Fantina, p. xxi.

Bibliography

[Anon], 'Review: *Robert Falconer*', *The Nation*, 27 October 1870, 278, p. 284.
Eliot, Simon, 'The Business of Victorian Publishing', in *Cambridge Companion to the Victorian Novel*, ed Deirdre David (Cambridge: Cambridge University Press, 2000), pp. 37–60.
Johnson, Joseph, *George MacDonald: A Biographical and Critical Appreciation* (London: Pitman and Sons, 1906).
Harrison, Kimberly, and Richard Fantina (eds), *Victorian Sensations: Essays on a Scandalous Genre* (Columbus, OH: Ohio University Press, 2006).
Maison, Margaret M., *The Victorian Vision: Studies in the Religious Novel* (New York: Sheed and Ward, 1961).
MacDonald, George, *David Elginbrod* (Boston: Loring Publisher, 1872; Philadelphia: Mackay, 1900).
Pykett, Lyn, 'Sensation and the fantastic in the Victorian novel', in *Cambridge Companion to the Victorian Novel*, ed Deirdre David (Cambridge: Cambridge University Press, 2000), pp. 192–211.
Reis, Richard H., *George MacDonald* (New York: Twayne Publishers, 1972).
Wolff, Robert Lee, *The Golden Key: A Study of the Fiction of George MacDonald* (New Haven: Yale UP, 1961).

'La Belle Dame' – *Lilith* and the Romantic Vampire Tradition

DAVID MELVILLE WINGROVE

Kiss and Bite are as one ... and one who loves with the whole heart might easily mistake the one for the other.
(Heinrich von Kleist, *Penthesilea*)[1]

Published in 1895 as its author was entering the last decade of his life, *Lilith* is the culmination of George MacDonald's career as a fantasy writer and perhaps the most dazzlingly inventive fantastic novel of the 1890s. (A decade, let's not forget, that includes such 'also-rans' as *The Picture of Dorian Gray*, *Dracula* and *The Turn of the Screw*.) A tale of a young man's journey through a mirror into a parallel world – one populated by mythic archetypes, and ruled over by an evil yet eternally seductive vampire princess – *Lilith* offers the supreme embodiment of the blood-sucking Romantic *femme fatale*, a figure that haunted Goethe, Coleridge, Tieck, Gautier, Keats, Poe, Baudelaire, Le Fanu, Stevenson, and Stoker (to name only a few) and survives to this day in the ruthless vampire divas of *True Blood* and *Twilight*.

Yet oddly enough *Lilith* features rarely if at all in anthologies of vampire fiction, and has been resoundingly overlooked by scholars and historians of the genre. In the same way that MacDonald, an ordained Congregationalist minister and a devoutly religious man, was unable to secure a living due to his unorthodox spiritual views, so *Lilith* has been persistently ignored and omitted by 'gatekeepers' of the canon of Gothic fiction. This novel, perhaps, is simply too strange even for those who revel in the notion of 'strangeness' – or who like their books to be 'strange' in a prescribed and predictable way. At the dawn of the twenty-first century, a Gothic author, and practising if unorthodox Roman Catholic, such as Anne Rice has resisted calls from fans for a Christian vampire novel. Maybe she finds it an impossible feat to pull off. That book, ironically, has already been written. Its author was a seventy-year-old Scottish clergyman of the late Victorian era, and *Lilith* is its title.

1.

You thrill as his pulses dwindle,
You brighten and warm as he bleeds,
With insatiable eyes that kindle
And insatiable mouth that feeds.
(Algernon Charles Swinburne, 'Satia de Sanguine',
ll. 65–68)[2]

The name and character of Lilith spring all too obviously from MacDonald's background as a clergyman and biblical scholar. In the Talmud, Lilith was the first wife of Adam who refused to be subservient to her husband, and insisted, in more graphic versions of the story, in playing the dominant or 'top' role in sexual intercourse. Cast off for her insubordination, Lilith re-entered Middle Eastern mythology as a blood-drinking demon who threatened all mothers and their children. Diane Purkiss paints a clear picture of this mythical Lilith in her study of the supernatural tradition, *Troublesome Things*:

> One story illustrates Lilith's dark and malevolent power: the prophet Elijah meets Lilith, and says, 'O wicked Lilith, where are you going with your foul unclean host?' Lilith's reply freezes to the marrow with its frankness:
> 'My Lord Elijah, I am going to that woman who has given birth to a child, to give her the sleep of death, to take her newborn child, to drink its blood, to suck the marrow of its bones, but to leave its flesh untouched.'[3]

Lilith was also thought to 'drain' the energy of young men through sexual fantasies and nocturnal emissions. In either case, Purkiss makes it clear that 'Lilith works in the dark; by leaving the child's flesh untouched, by refraining from abducting it, she adds mystery to her crimes'.[4] Yet even the lady's name lies shrouded in swathes of ambiguous myth. According to Montague Summers, the leading vampire scholar of the last century,

> The Hebrew Lilith is undoubtedly borrowed from the Babylonian demon Lilîtu, a night spirit, although it is not probable that the Lilith has any connection with the Hebrew Laîlah, 'night'. It was

perhaps inevitable that the Rabbis should assume some such derivation, and it must be allowed that the comparison seemed plausible enough, although it has been shown, on the evidence of the Assyrian word *Lilû*, that the old theory must no longer be maintained, and Lilith is almost certainly to be referred to *lalû*, 'luxuriousness', and *lulti*, 'lasciviousness, lechery'.[5]

Whatever the derivation and meaning of her name, the Talmudic Lilith was clearly a 'lady of the evening' in the truest sense – one who controlled the forbidden night world of sexuality and dreams. She was the mythic embodiment of woman as taboo. In our own time, she has been memorably incarnated by Marianne Faithfull in Kenneth Anger's 1981 film *Lucifer Rising*. Other screen variants have included Maria Casarès as Death in *Orphée* (Jean Cocteau, 1950) and Martine Beswick as the Queen of Evil in *Seizure* (Oliver Stone, 1974).

Yet artistically speaking, Lilith was at the peak of her popularity in the literature and painting of the late Victorian era. One of the most sublimely eccentric of the Decadent writers, Count Stanislaus Eric Stenbock, gave the name Lilith to the beautiful wolf-woman in his 1891 story 'The Other Side'. Armed with her 'strange blue eyes full of tenderness and passion and sadness beyond the sadness of things human',[6] this Lilith lures the pubescent hero away from his devoutly Christian village, and into a forbidden pagan dreamworld that lies on the far side of the river.

In her study of Lilith as a motif in Pre-Raphaelite painting (notably Dante Gabriel Rossetti's 1868 canvas, *The Lady Lilith*), Camille Paglia identifies this renegade pagan goddess explicitly with the Romantic nineteenth-century vampire:

> The Rossetti woman rebels against Victorian convention, her unpinned hair and unstructured medieval gown flowing with lyrical freedom. The heavy head sways on a serpentine neck. Her long thick hair is La Belle Dame Sans Merci's net of entrapment. Her swollen lips are to become a universal motif of Decadent art, thanks to Burne-Jones and Beardsley. The Rossetti vampire mouth cannot speak, but it has a life of its own. It is gorged with the blood of victims.[7]

For decades before MacDonald brought her to life in his novel, Lilith – as rebel, as seductress, as vampire – was already well-established as a literary and visual icon of the Victorian Age.

Nor was the narrative form of the novel in any way unusual for its time. Although it has vastly more literary merit, *Lilith* follows essentially the same plot as two other classics of late Victorian fantasy: *She* (1886) by H. Rider Haggard and *Dracula* (1897) by Bram Stoker. In all three novels, a representative Victorian hero journeys into a 'forbidden' realm ruled over by a malevolent mythical being. At first, the hero falls prey to this being and his/her seductive, and destructive, powers. In the end, however, the evil being is destroyed and virtue triumphs. As even a cursory glance will show, MacDonald's treatment of this theme is far more equivocal and, indeed, problematic, than the bestselling yarns of Rider Haggard and Stoker. In *She*, three British male explorers in Africa subdue an autocratic and seemingly immortal white goddess. In *Dracula*, the virtuous characters (who are largely, though not exclusively, British and middle-class) join forces to hunt down a blood-drinking foreign aristocrat who threatens the purity of their women. In both novels, the core values of Victorian society – hard work, patriarchy, imperialism, and a sexual imagination at once prurient and puritanical – are aggressively and unambiguously affirmed. In *Lilith*, by contrast, the vampire queen is swept from power by a hapless dreamer, the aptly named hero Mr Vane, and a troop of half-wild children, the Little Ones, who are akin to the Lost Boys of James Barrie's *Peter Pan* (1902). Interestingly, the Little Ones share not only the perpetual childhood of the Lost Boys, but also their darker overtones as described by Diane Purkiss: 'The only way to avoid death, Barrie seemed to say, is to be dead already [...] This is also the only way not to grow up.'[8] The Little Ones are mortal children exiled from Lilith's realm – and into an unnaturally prolonged childhood – solely because Lilith sought their annihilation.

Thus, it is not imperial might or moral rectitude that defeat Lilith. It is gentleness, innocence and a dreamy, even fey spirituality that was as alien to MacDonald's time as it is to our own. By the end of the novel, one mystery has been dispelled, only for another – deeper, stranger and more puzzling – to rise and take its place.

> **2.**
> *From the house, so silent now, are driven*
> *All the gods who reign'd supreme of yore;*
> *One Invisible now rules in heaven,*
> *On the cross a Saviour they adore.*
> *Victims slay they here,*
> *Neither lamb nor steer,*
> *But the altars reek with human gore.*
> (Johann Wolfgang von Goethe, 'The Bride of Corinth',
> ll. 57–63)[9]

The Lilith of MacDonald's novel defines herself, first and foremost, through her opposition to the Christian God and her refusal to submit to divine authority. Denying even the existence of a Creator, she proclaims: 'No one ever made me. I defy that power to unmake me from a free woman!'.[10] Her defiance of God and her defiance of Adam, her former husband, are – given the sexual politics of the Victorians, to which MacDonald at least nominally subscribes – two sides of one and the same sin. She can be read as both a harbinger of the late-Victorian and Edwardian suffragette movement, and its legacy of feminism in the twentieth century and beyond, and a relic of the paganism of Antiquity, with its roots in matriarchal societies and worship of a Nature Goddess.

Authors throughout the Romantic vampire tradition have made this connection with unrepentant paganism. In his narrative poem 'The Bride of Corinth' (1797), Johann Wolfgang von Goethe makes his vampire a young girl who died after being forced into a convent when her family converted to Christianity. Still proclaiming the old faith and despising the new, she rises from her tomb and drinks the blood of the young pagan to whom she once was betrothed:

> *From my grave to wander I am forc'd,*
> *Still to seek The Good's long-sever'd link,*
> *Still to love the bridegroom I have lost,*
> *And the life-blood of his heart to drink [...]*
> (ll. 175–78)[11]

In a fascinating if heretical twist, this young woman has turned to blood-drinking not simply as an act of rebellion against the Christian God but as a direct consequence of His enforced reign on earth. Her sexual desires, suppressed and demonised by the new faith, return in pathological form as vampire lust.

A similar transformation takes place in a story by Théophile Gautier, one of the first French authors to follow the lead of Goethe and other German Romantics. 'La morte amoureuse' (1843) has been translated variously as 'The Deathly Lover' or 'The Beautiful Dead' although its nearest English equivalent may actually be 'The Corpse in Love'. It tells the story of Romuald, a young priest who spurns the love of a beautiful courtesan, Clarimonde, to take his vow of chastity. She dies shortly thereafter and comes back to haunt him in vampire form. Still wrapped in her burial shroud, she shows Romuald the scars that mark her transition from life to death and back again:

> What efforts I had to make before I could push up the tombstone with which they had covered me! See! The palms of my hands are all bruised. Kiss them and cure them, my dear love.[12]

The tombstone pushed aside, the body resurrected from the dead, the wounded palms displayed to the incredulous but adoring disciple, Clarimonde is not simply the enemy of Christ but a feminised and sexualised *alter ego* of Christ Himself. She offers eternal life, not through the soul but through the senses, not through the ritual drinking of sacramental wine but through the literal consumption of human blood. Her reward to her followers is tangible and immediate, unlike the nebulous Christian promise of a better life to come: 'For I love you and mean to take you away from your God, before whom so many youthful hearts pour out floods of love that never reach him.'[13]

Despite being an avowedly Christian author, which Gautier emphatically was not, MacDonald too gives his female vampire the physical qualities of the resurrected Christ. Lilith, like Clarimonde, is portrayed as having a wounded hand – or, at any rate, some deformity which makes her unable to unclench it. Even in her final, and not wholly convincing, scene of repentance, she laments: 'I am trying hard, but the fingers have grown together and into the palm.'[14] It remains to Adam, her former husband, to cut the hand off and send her, at last, into the sanctified sleep of death. Mutilations of this sort – in the name of Christian virtue and love – are standard practice in dealing with the vampire woman and this one, as we shall see, is far less brutal than most.

In a further parallel between the undead vampire and the resurrected Christ, MacDonald portrays Lilith as suffering a fatal injury to her side. This seems to alter in size and shape throughout the novel, but generally takes the form of a dark spot or shadow. When the hero first glimpses Lilith in the desert, he remarks: 'on her left side was a dark spot, against which she would now and then press her hand, as if to stifle pain or sickness'.[15] Towards the end of the book, as Lilith sits in a hall of black marble awaiting her downfall, this spot has grown in size to cover a large expanse of skin: 'alas her whiteness! the spot covered half her side, and was black as the marble around her!'.[16]

Similar deformities show up in female vampires before and during the nineteenth century. In Part 1 of his poem 'Christabel' (1797), Samuel Taylor Coleridge describes an encounter between his innocent heroine and Geraldine, a darkly beautiful demoness she meets in the woods at night. As Geraldine undresses to share Christabel's bed, the text hints at her deathly nature:

> Behold! Her bosom and half her side—
> A sight to dream of, not to tell!
> O shield her! shield sweet Christabel!
> (Part 1, ll. 252–54)[17]

Like so much of the poem, this moment is teasingly ambiguous, but I personally concur with Camille Paglia's notion that 'Geraldine must be a classic vampire of great age, her breast withered only when she hungers. After she has sated herself, whether by drinking blood or somehow draining her victim's life-energy, her breasts recover sensual fullness'.[18]

A more graphic and visceral treatment of the same theme occurs in a later poem, 'Les Métamorphoses du Vampire', from Charles Baudelaire's 1857 volume *Les fleurs du mal* ('Flowers of Evil'). In this sonnet, the poet anti-hero copulates enthusiastically with a mysterious and sinister woman. Turning towards her for a post-coital embrace, he rapidly gets a shock:

> She had drunk up my marrow, and sucked my bones dry,
> And as I turned back softly to kiss her, my eye
> Saw nothing but a corpse, where I had spent my lust,
> Its limbs decomposing and swollen white with pus!
> (ll. 17–20)[19]

This vampire's thirst for blood (and other bodily fluids) is identified within a single stanza with the rot and degeneration of her own body. Much of MacDonald's achievement lies in investing this physical taint with spiritual, rather than medical and gynaecological, overtones.

Before moving on to explore other aspects of *Lilith*, I must mention a couple of tantalising footnotes to these parallels between Christ and the vampire. In one fleeting episode that is never followed up, MacDonald locates the physical deformities of Christ and the vampire in the sleeping bodies of Mr Vane's own dead parents. On his first visit to Adam and Eve in the House of the Dead, the hero sees a woman 'with her palm upwards, in its centre a dark spot' and beside her a man 'with his strong hand almost closed, as if clenched on the grip of a sword'.[20] These turn out later to be his mother and father – lending the story an Oedipal dimension that is never fully explored.

To see Christian parallels pushed to their extreme, we must journey almost a century forward in time – to a flamboyant film version of Oscar Wilde's play *Salomé* (1972) by the Italian director Carmelo Bene. Christ Himself appears in this film as a fully fledged vampire (fangs and all) crowned in a wreath of thorns and roses, and feasting on the blood of naked virgins. Such an image would have been deeply shocking to MacDonald, and is inconceivable in the context of *Lilith*, but its underlying symbolism is visible (as we have seen) in much of nineteenth-century vampire writing.

3.

> *Was it my own excited imagination – or the misty influence of the atmosphere – or the uncertain twilight of the chamber – or the grey draperies which fell around her figure – that caused in it so vacillating and indistinct an outline? I could not tell.*
> (Edgar Allan Poe, 'Berenice')[21]

As if to reinforce Lilith's credentials as a pagan goddess – existing in opposition to (but also, oddly, in parallel with) the figure of Jesus Christ – MacDonald stresses throughout the book her connection to moonlight and lunar imagery. This not only relates her to such pre-Christian female deities as Astartë, the Babylonian moon goddess, but also builds on a symbolic juxtaposition dating back to pagan times. In most cosmologies of the ancient world, the sun was the male-identified source of divine power and authority. The moon, by contrast, was typically identified as female – signifying a realm of negation, of chaos and mystery and night.

While lunar imagery is prevalent throughout MacDonald's work, the moon is seen most often as a benign and protective force – closely associated with figures like the grandmother in his 1872 children's fantasy *The Princess and the Goblin*:

> The princess opened the door and entered. There was the moonlight streaming in at the window, and in the middle of the moonlight sat the old lady in her black dress with the white lace, and her silvery hair mingling with the moonlight, so that you could not have told which was which.[22]

This all-loving 'fairy godmother' figure is the polar opposite of Lilith – shielding her grandchild against dark forces, and nurturing her until she is ready to marry Curdie, the young hero. Yet in *Phantastes* – his earlier adult fantasy novel from 1858 – MacDonald already hints at darker aspects of the moon. It is by moonlight that Anodos (a dreamer-hero only slightly less inept than Mr Vane) first glimpses the demonic and predatory Ash, an (unsettlingly) male tree spirit that 'reminded me of what I had heard of vampires'.[23] Feeling a strange presence stalking him through a moonlit wood, Anodos relates:

> I turned my eyes towards the moon. Good heavens! What did I see? [...] I saw the strangest figure; vague, shadowy, almost transparent, in the central parts, and gradually deepening in substance towards the outside, until it ended in extremities capable of casting such a shadow as fell from the hand, through the awful fingers of which I now saw the moon.[24]

The moon, unlike the sun, is not constant. With its dark, hidden aspects and ever-changing multiplicity of phases, it can embrace both Good and Evil, Light and Dark. *Lilith* stands out in MacDonald's writing for its exploration of the moon's dark side. Thus, Mr Vane has his first glimpse of Lilith as she wanders in the desert by moonlight: 'A white mist floated about her, now assuming, now losing to reassume the shape of a garment, as it gathered to her or was blown from her by a wind that dogged her steps'.[25] She is not only coloured like the moon, but also constantly shifting and changing in shape – as the moon does – swathed in a veil that seems a part of her own body. Not simply illuminated by moonlight, she seems to be born and to emanate from it.

Later on in the book, following her dethronement and capture by Mr Vane and the Little Ones, it is the moon that reveals Lilith unequivocally as a vampire. Standing watch over her in the desert, Mr Vane is attacked in a spectacular lunar tableau:

> The moon was half-way down the west, a pale thoughtful moon, mottling the desert with shadows. Of a sudden she was eclipsed, remaining visible, but sending forth no light: a thick, diaphanous film covered her patient beauty, and she looked troubled. The film swept a little aside, and I saw the edge of it against her clearness – the jagged outline of a bat-like wing, torn and hooked. Came a cold wind like a burning sting – and Lilith was upon me.[26]

Struggling for his life as her teeth sink into his flesh, the hero, who has been more than half in love with Lilith up to this point, is able to save himself only by striking at her wounded hand. He then confronts directly, for the first time, the true nature of the temptress he has loved: 'the moon shone out clear, and I saw her face – gaunt and ghastly, besmeared with red'. The face of the moon and the face of Lilith are revealed at one and the same moment. To know one, it seems, is to know the other.

This correlation between the moon and the vampire (female, in particular) seems to run throughout the Romantic and Victorian eras. Hence the innocent Christabel's first glimpse of Geraldine in a moonlit forest glade:

> There she sees a damsel bright,
> Drest in a silken robe of white,
> That shadowy in the moonlight shone:
> The neck that made that white robe wan.
> (Part 1, ll. 58–61)²⁷

Not only revealed by the moon and coloured like the moon in her own person, the vampire woman even dresses to complement the effect. In a German Romantic author such as Johann Ludwig Tieck, this lunar influence extends even to her jewellery. His story 'Wake Not the Dead' (first published in English in 1823) introduces us to a truly discriminating vampire lady named Brunhilda. Tieck relates that 'no ornaments of gold ever decked her person; all that others were wont to wear of this metal, she had formed of silver: no richly coloured and sparkling jewels glittered upon her; pearls alone, lent their pale lustre to adorn her bosom'.²⁸ This marks perhaps the first literary instance of Goth fashion.

Later on in the century, Sheridan Le Fanu allows his lesbian vampire 'Carmilla' (1871) to enter the life of the hapless Laura on a night of dazzling moonlight. Just in case we miss the point, he has a superstitious governess on hand to point out that

> when the moon shone with a light so intense it was well known that it indicated a special spiritual activity. The effect of the full moon in such a state of brilliancy was manifold. It acted on dreams, it acted on lunacy, it acted on nervous people; it had marvelous physical influences connected with life.²⁹

A page or so later, a carriage breaks down as if on cue outside the girl's ancestral *schloss*. Its occupant, Carmilla, insinuates her way into Laura's home and affections. 'How beautiful she looked in the moonlight!',³⁰ the girl enthuses, blithely unaware that Carmilla is feasting on her blood.

In Bram Stoker's novel *Dracula*, which appeared in 1897, two years after *Lilith*, the vampire women seem, once again, to be born of moonlight. The hero, Jonathan Harker – a character even more hapless than Mr Vane – is spending a troubled night in the Transylvanian castle of Count Dracula. He has already encountered, on a previous moonlit night, three spectral women who tried to drink his blood. Saved by the Count for some unspecified purpose of his own by the marvellously cryptic line 'This man belongs to me!'.[31] Harker now becomes entranced by some motes of dust dancing in a moonbeam in one corner of the room:

> Quicker and quicker danced the dust, and the moonbeams seemed to quiver as they went by me into the mass of gloom beyond. More and more they gathered until they seemed to take dim phantom shapes. And then I started, broad awake and in full possession of my senses, and ran screaming from the place. The phantom shapes, which were becoming gradually materialised from the moonbeams, were those of the three ghostly women to whom I was doomed.[32]

One of the more spectacular moments in a novel whose power rests largely on 'lighting' effects (which explains, at least in part, its continued appeal to film makers), this passage presents the female vampire unambiguously as a creature formed of moonlight. She is not simply lit up by the moon for maximum dramatic effect, as Count Dracula so often is, but is part of the very substance of the moon itself. Her life seems tied to the moon, like that of Lord Ruthven in Heinrich Marschner's 1828 opera *Der Vampyr*, who 'is killed, but revives supernaturally in the moonlight'[33] to cause more mayhem.

This proliferation of white lunar imagery extends well beyond the supernatural vampire narrative and into a 'realistic' study of psychological vampirism, 'The Glass of Blood' by the French Decadent author Jean Lorrain. In this twisted tale from the 1890s, the actress La Barnarina has insinuated herself (*á la* Carmilla) into the home of an aristocrat, driven by love for his daughter Rosaria. She goes so far as to give up her career, marry the man and become the girl's stepmother. As the two women grow suspiciously close, the younger grows steadily paler and more anaemic, until she has to go daily to an abattoir to drink fresh blood. La Barnarina is described in terms fitting a classic 'lunar' vampire. Not only is she blonde and pale-skinned, and dressed in white velvet, she also extends her colour scheme into the décor that surrounds her:

> All the flowers are white: white irises, white tulips, white narcissi. Only the textures are different, some as glossy as pearls, others

sparkling like frost, others as smooth as drifting snow; the petals seem as delicate as translucent porcelain, glazed with a chimerical beauty. The only hint of colour is the pale gold at the heart of each narcissus.[34]

Much as Tieck's predatory Brunhilda does with her jewels, this woman transmutes her vampire nature into a style statement – a visual symphony of whiteness and lunar tones. The story ends in a kiss, as La Barnarina tastes the blood 'upon the warm lips of her beloved Rosaria'.[35] The child transmits the blood to her adoptive mother, in an eroticised primal act of moon-worship.

4.

[...] *while I knew that to love such a woman were to sign and seal one's own sentence of degeneration, I still knew that, if she were alive, I should love her.*
(Robert Louis Stevenson, 'Olalla')[36]

For all the spiritual and cosmological richness of *Lilith*, what drives its plot is not the Christian and lunar imagery that MacDonald lavishes upon it. Rather, it is Lilith's role in the cosmic family drama that the myth represents. Her primal identity is as the evil first wife of Adam. Alongside her sexual dominance, the mythic Lilith shows an unwillingness to fulfil her divinely appointed role as a mother. In varying versions of the story, she refuses to bear children, preys on the newborn infants of other women or (in the extreme scenario imagined by MacDonald) hunts down and annihilates her own child. Whatever her incarnation, the existence of Lilith poses a radical living challenge to woman's socially sanctioned role.

MacDonald's novel tells us relatively little about that catastrophic first marriage of Lilith and Adam, although her predatory subjugation of Mr Vane, and his obsessive and even masochistic pursuit of her, give us a taste of what it must have been like. Yet other authors in the Romantic vampire tradition are more than happy to fill in the gaps. Tieck's villainous Brunhilda in 'Wake Not the Dead' is the first wife of the feckless hero Walter, who shares with her an intensely sexual but childless union, 'a passion that rendered them reckless of aught besides'.[37] After her death, he marries the pallid but virtuous Swanhilda, who bears him two children. Still besotted with his dead first wife, he brings her back to life through black magic. Reborn as a vampire, Brunhilda drives her rival into exile and feeds on the blood of all the children in Walter's castle, up to and including his own:

> Whenever she beheld some innocent child, whose lovely face denoted the exuberance of infantine health and vigour, she would entice it by soothing words and fond caresses into her most secret apartment, where, lulling it to sleep in her arms, she would suck from its bosom the warm, purple tide of life.[38]

The blood of children is also the preferred diet of MacDonald's Lilith. Indeed, she dines off Mr Vane only when she is marooned in the desert, with no younger and fresher blood to be had. Taking the form of a white leopard, Lilith prowls about drinking the blood of newborn infants. As one mother explains: 'If the princess hears of a baby, she sends her immediately to suck its blood, and then it either dies or grows up an idiot'.[39] This is what drives mothers to abandon their babies in a wood, where they grow to become the army of the Little Ones – led by Lilith's own cast-off daughter, Lona.

This subversion of the maternal role – whereby woman becomes the taker and devourer of a child's life, not its nurturer and provider – is perhaps the central horror in the myth of Lilith as vampire. It finds its way, symbolically, even as far as *Dracula*. No sooner has the Count arrived in England than he seduces the sweet and virginal Lucy, a girl flawed only by her immoderate romantic and sexual fantasies: 'Why can't they let a girl marry three men, or as many as want her, and save all this trouble?'.[40] Lucy dies and rises again, not simply as a vampire, but as a 'bloofer lady' who lures unsuspecting children and drinks their blood. Her three suitors, together with the vampire-hunter Van Helsing, track her down and catch her in the act:

> With a careless motion, she flung to the ground, callous as a devil, the child that up to now she had clutched strenuously to her breast, growling over it as a dog growls over a bone. The child gave a sharp cry and lay there moaning. There was a cold-bloodedness

in the act that wrung a groan from Arthur; when she advanced to him with outstretched arms and a wanton smile, he fell back and hid his face in his hands.[41]

This wondrously lurid tableau sums up the subversive power of the vampire woman. Cradling an infant in her arms, she not only drinks its blood – rather than allowing it to drink from her, as God and nature have decreed – but she also flings it brutally to one side once it is no longer of use, symbolically rejecting her assigned role as a mother. Cast in the person of the once-virginal Lucy, the Virgin Mother of Christian iconography now throws aside her veil, and stands revealed as a ravening harlot.

Throughout the vampire fiction of the nineteenth century, an evil woman from the past rises to threaten and destroy the virtuous woman of the present. The pagan Bride of Corinth seduces the hero and supplants her Christian sister. In Edgar Allan Poe's story 'Ligeia' (1838), the ghost of the first wife murders her successor with 'three or four large drops of a brilliant and ruby-coloured fluid'[42] and then takes possession of her corpse, transmuting it into her own dark image. Even the ghostly vampire brides in *Dracula* can be seen as 'first wives' who foreshadow the dark fates of the two Victorian heroines, Mina and Lucy.

Still other vampire women – notably Geraldine, Carmilla and La Barnarina – carry out a lesbian seduction of a young girl whose mother has died. This particular victim is vulnerable because she has been doubly deprived – firstly, of maternal nurturing and protection and, secondly, of an all-important role model of virtuous female behaviour. Often seducing the girl's father to consolidate her power, the vampire in these stories can be seen as a 'dark' mother supplanting the good mother, Lilith rising out of her tomb to replace Eve. Such a tradition continues to the present day in such neo-Gothic tales as *Coraline* (2002) by Neil Gaiman. Here a demonic 'other mother' imprisons and supplants the true mother so she can drain the child heroine, vampirically, of her soul. As another child victim warns:

> She will take your life and all you are and all you care'st for, and she will leave you with nothing but mist and fog. She'll take your joy. And one day you'll awake and your heart and soul will have gone.[43]

In line with the Lilith tradition outlined by Purkiss, such a vampire drains her victim of life but leaves the body intact.

Faced with the prospect of a 'false mother' attacking her offspring, the real mother may even return from the grave to defend her. In 'Christabel' the mother's ghost intervenes to try and save her daughter, but Geraldine soon gains the upper hand:

> And why with hollow voice cries she,
> 'Off, woman, off! This hour is mine—
> Though thou her guardian spirit be,
> Off, woman, off! 'tis given to me.' (Part 1, ll. 210–14)[44]

Invariably, in these narratives, the virtuous woman from the past is replaced by a stronger and more sinister *alter ego*, who then threatens to corrupt the virtuous young girl of the present.

In one of the strangest of all such tales, 'Olalla' (1885) by Robert Louis Stevenson, the heroine, who is not a vampire but fears she will become one, is haunted by the portrait of an evil, blood-drinking ancestor. This woman, with her 'cruel, sullen and sensual expression'[45] is the painted image both of Olalla's fears, and of her probable fate. The hero/narrator, of course, falls for the portrait on sight, despite knowing she is the embodiment of evil. 'And yet I had a half-lingering terror that she might not be dead after all, but re-arisen in the body of some descendant.'[46] His love for Olalla is very much the fulfilment of that fantasy. Much as he claims to fear the vampire curse that looms over her, it also gives him a secret thrill. It is debatable throughout the story which of the two women he in fact desires.

In MacDonald's novel, Lilith not only tries to supplant her daughter, Lona, in the affections of Mr Vane, she also slays her daughter in full view of the other characters, moving from spiritual to physical annihilation and pushing the myth to its logical extremes. Once the army of the Little Ones has overrun Lilith's city, Lona embraces her mother, desperate for her to behave as a mother should:

> 'Mother! mother!' cried Lona again, as she leaped on the daïs, and flung her arms around the princess. An instant more and I should have reached them! – in that instant I saw Lona lifted high, and

dashed on the marble floor. Oh, the horrible sound of her fall! At my feet she fell, and lay still. The princess sat down with the smile of a demoness.[47]

In a gesture that mirrors that of Lucy two years later, Lilith replaces maternal care and nurturing with cold-blooded murder. Herein lies the heart of *Lilith* and her myth.

5.

> *I saw pale kings and princes too,*
> *Pale warriors, death-pale were they all;*
> *They cried – 'La Belle Dame sans Merci*
> *Hath thee in thrall!'*
> (John Keats, 'La Belle Dame Sans Merci', ll. 37–40)[48]

The greatest oddity of MacDonald's novel – and the reason, perhaps, for its exclusion from the vampire canon – lies in the fate that is meted out to Lilith at the book's climax. While the end of Lilith has a great deal of imagery in common with other texts, its final purpose is directly at odds with the overall trend of vampire fiction, which seemed to demand ever greater and crueller punishment as the nineteenth century wore on. Nothing marks out the uniqueness of MacDonald as a writer more sharply than the benign fate (by Victorian standards) to which Lilith finally succumbs.

At the dawn of the Romantic Age, the female vampire could get away with no punishment at all. In fact, as Goethe's poem draws to a close, the Bride of Corinth triumphantly dictates the terms of her own funeral. Her body must be burned, in true pagan fashion, and that of her lover/victim along with it:

> *When ascends the fire*
> *From the glowing pyre,*
> *To the gods of old we'll hasten, blest.* (ll. 195–97)[49]

Her end is not destruction or exorcism, but deliverance into a better or, at any rate, a more congenial otherworld. Gautier in 'La morte amoureuse' allows Clarimonde to dissolve with just a sprinkle of holy water: 'The holy dew no sooner touched poor Clarimonda than her lovely body fell into dust and became only a hideous mass of ashes and half-calcined bones'.[50] Even though Christian values are seen to triumph at this point, the tone of the passage reinforces our sympathy with the vampire, and leaves us to wonder if her annihilation was actually such a bright idea.

By the time the Victorian Age was at its height, only a fully fledged ritual slaying would do to expunge the female vampire from the text. It must be carried out, not by the infants or young girls who were her victims, but by the forces of male authority. In this way Laura, the beleaguered heroine of 'Carmilla', is denied access to the denouement of her own story. She relates it to us from second-hand accounts, and Le Fanu's narrative falls flat as a result:

> The body, therefore, in accordance with the ancient practice, was raised, and a sharp stake driven through the heart of the vampire, who uttered a piercing shriek at the moment, in all respects such as might escape from a living person in the last agony. Then the head was struck off, and a torrent of blood flowed from the severed neck.[51]

This scene, with its overtones of penetration and bleeding, is in many ways analogous to the deflowering of a young wife on her bridal night. No wonder the virginal heroine must, of necessity, be excluded from it. The male executioners are not merely removing the vampire as a threat; they are also reinforcing the traditional woman's role she has hitherto scorned to play.

The ultimate scene of this sort is, of course, the staking and decapitation of Lucy in *Dracula*. This is carried out by all three of her suitors, under the watchful – indeed, voyeuristic – eye of Dr Van Helsing. It may strike a modern reader as infinitely more sadistic and depraved than anything Lucy herself actually does:

> The Thing in the coffin writhed; and a hideous blood-curdling screech came from the open red lips. The body shook and quivered and twisted in wild contortions; the sharp white teeth champed together till the lips were cut, and the mouth was smeared with a crimson foam. But Arthur never faltered. He looked like a figure

of Thor as his untrembling arm rose and fell, driving deeper and deeper the mercy-bearing stake, whilst the blood from the pierced heart welled and spurted up around it.[52]

This frankly nauseating scene, with its unmistakable overtones of gang rape, is only incidentally about vampires and vampire-hunting. At its heart lies the collective male impulse to subdue the renegade woman, to subjugate her and put her in her 'rightful' place, which is, of course, on her back, with a large phallic object stuck inside her.

Following her capture by the Little Ones and her brutal murder of her daughter, Lilith too is made to lie supine and undergo a form of penetration, not by a dead stake but by a live serpent, a thing that is 'white-hot, vivid as incandescent silver, the live heart of essential fire'.[53] On a first reading, the scene appears to have punitive, erotic overtones similar to those in Stoker's *Dracula*: 'The princess gave one writhing, contorted shudder, and I knew the worm was in her secret chamber'.[54] Yet its purpose, when viewed in the wider context of MacDonald's writing, is overhelmngly redemptive and spiritual. The penetration of Lilith is that evoked in his sermon 'The Consuming Fire' – one 'which pierces to the dividing line between the man and the evil, which will slay the sin and give life to the sinner'.[55]

The aim of this penetration is not punishment or annihilation, but self-knowledge, as Mara, the teasingly ambiguous 'cat woman', informs a bewildered Mr Vane:

> 'You cannot go near her,' she said. 'She is far away from us, in the hell of her self-consciousness. The central fire of the universe is radiating into her the knowledge of good and evil, the knowledge of what she is. She sees at last the good she is not, the evil she is. She knows that she is herself the fire in which she is burning, but she does not know that the Light of Life is the heart of that fire.'[56]

This reference to fire connects the scene directly to MacDonald's sermon, which insists that any suffering God inflicts is not a punishment for sin, but a means of deliverance from it. It is through suffering that man (or, in this case, woman) may achieve true unity with God: 'It is not that the fire will burn us if we do not worship thus, but that the fire will burn us until we worship thus; yea, will go on burning within us after all that is foreign has yielded to its force'.[57] Lest we should still feel uneasy about what we are reading, Mara even admonishes Mr Vane: 'Do not fear for her; she is not forsaken. No gentler way to help her was left'.[58] Adam, her former husband, cuts off the wounded hand that torments her, with 'one little gush of blood' – a benign substitute for the savage decapitations of Le Fanu and Stoker. Mara then promptly assures Mr Vane: 'Where the dead deformity clung [...] the true, lovely hand is already growing'.[59]

Inconceivable in any other vampire text of its time, the outcome of *Lilith* points the genre in an entirely new direction – one that no later author has adequately explored. The aim is not to be seduced by evil, as Mr Vane admittedly is, albeit temporarily, or to hunt it down and stamp it out, in typically prurient Victorian fashion. Rather, it is to understand evil and redeem it, to return it to God and His all-loving embrace. As MacDonald states in 'The Consuming Fire':

> When that which is immortal buries itself in the destructible [...] it cannot, though immortal still, know its own immortality. The destructible must be burned out of it, or begin to be burned out of it, before it can partake of eternal life.[60]

If MacDonald can show that Lilith is redeemable, then how much more so must we be as readers? Is she not, after all, the incarnation of our own darkest and most unspoken desires? As Mr Vane reflects towards the end of the novel: 'The darkness knows neither the light nor itself; only the light knows itself and the darkness also. None but God hates evil and understands it'.[61]

Unlike the vampire story in its classic form, *Lilith* is not a tale of horror, but a tale of hope. A classic whose time, perhaps, has not yet come. The female vampire of nineteenth-century Romantic fiction is a dark and inexorable force for whom redemption is not an option. She will devour and destroy any victim who is not prepared to rival her in ruthlessness or brutality – to become, however unwillingly, a killer in his own right. *Lilith*, alone among the vampire stories of its time, is a triumph of love over hate – an echo of the central tenet in George MacDonald's life and work: 'Nothing is inexorable but love'.[62]

Notes

1. Quoted in Christopher Frayling, *The Vampyre – Lord Ruthven to Count Dracula* (London: Victor Gollancz, 1978), p. 299.
2. Algernon Charles Swinburne, 'Satia de Sanguine' in *The Dedalus Book of Decadence (Moral Ruins)*, ed Brian Stableford (London: Dedalus, 1990), pp. 181–83.
3. Diane Purkiss, *Troublesome Things: A History of Fairies and Fairy Stories* (London: Allen Lane, 2000), p. 33.
4. Purkiss, *Troublesome Things*, p. 33.
5. Montague Summers, *The Vampire* (London: Studio, 1995), p. 226.
6. Count Eric Ladislaus Stenbock, 'The Other Side' in *The Dedalus Book of Decadence (Moral Ruins)*, pp. 209–24 (p. 215).
7. Camille Paglia, *Sexual Personae – Art and Decadence from Nefertiti to Emily Dickinson* (London: Penguin, 1991), p. 491.
8. Purkiss, *Troublesome Things*, p. 275.
9. Johann Wolfgang von Goethe, 'The Bride of Corinth' (trans John Anster) in *The Vampire Archive*, ed Otto Penzler (London: Quercus, 2009, pp. 747–52), p. 749.
10. George MacDonald, *Lilith: A Romance* (Grand Rapids MI: Eerdmans, 1988), p. 200.
11. Goethe, 'The Bride of Corinth', p. 752.
12. Théophile Gautier, 'The Deathly Lover', in *Dracula's Guest – A Connoisseur's Collection of Victorian Vampire Stories*, ed Michael Sims (New York: Walker, 2010, pp. 101–32), p. 123.
13. Gautier, 'The Deathly Lover', p. 108.
14. MacDonald, *Lilith*, p. 218.
15. MacDonald, *Lilith*, p. 50.
16. MacDonald, *Lilith*, p. 183.
17. Samuel Taylor Coleridge, 'Christabel', in *Supernatural Poetry*, ed Michael Hayes (London: John Calder, 1978, pp. 53–72), p. 60.
18. Paglia, *Sexual Personae*, p. 336.
19. Charles Baudelaire, 'Les Métamorphoses du Vampire' in *Les fleurs du mal*, Le Livre de Poche (Paris: Librairie Générale Française, 1988), p. 135. Author's own translation.
20. MacDonald, *Lilith*, p. 34.
21. Edgar Allan Poe, 'Berenice' in *The Complete Illustrated Stories and Poems of Edgar Allan Poe* (London: Chancellor Press, 1988), pp. 186–92 (p. 192).
22. George MacDonald, *The Princess and the Goblin* (Edinburgh: Canongate, 1989), pp. 81–82.
23. George MacDonald, *Phantastes: A Faerie Romance for Men and Women* (London: Paternoster, 2008), p. 71.
24. MacDonald, *Phantastes*, p. 70.
25. MacDonald, *Lilith*, p. 50.
26. MacDonald, *Lilith*, p. 192.
27. Coleridge, 'Christabel', p. 55.
28. Johann Ludwig Tieck, 'Wake Not the Dead' in *Dracula's Guest* (pp. 69–100), p. 83.
29. Joseph Sheridan Le Fanu, 'Carmilla', in *Vampire Archive* (pp. 603–54), p. 609.
30. Le Fanu, 'Carmilla', p. 624.
31. Bram Stoker, *Dracula*, ed Maurice Hindle (London: Penguin Classics, 1993), p. 55.
32. Stoker, *Dracula*, p. 63.
33. John Warrack and Ewan West, *The Concise Oxford Dictionary of Opera* (Oxford: Oxford University Press, 1996), p. 530.

34. Jean Lorrain, 'The Glass of Blood', in *The Dedalus Book of Decadence (Moral Ruins)*, (pp. 86–94), p. 86.
35. Lorrain, 'The Glass of Blood', p. 94.
36. Robert Louis Stevenson, 'Olalla', in *The Strange Case of Dr Jekyll and Mr Hyde and Other Tales of Terror*, ed. Robert Mighall (London: Penguin Classics, 2002, pp. 93–134), pp. 101–02.
37. Tieck, 'Wake Not the Dead', p. 72.
38. Tieck, 'Wake Not the Dead', p. 85.
39. MacDonald, *Lilith*, p. 114.
40. Stoker, *Dracula*, p. 81.
41. Stoker, *Dracula*, pp. 271–72.
42. Poe, 'Ligeia' in *Complete Stories* (pp. 167–80), p. 178.
43. Neil Gaiman, *Coraline* (London: Bloomsbury, 2009), pp. 101–02.
44. Coleridge, 'Christabel', p. 59.
45. Stevenson, 'Olalla', p. 101.
46. Stevenson, 'Olalla', p. 102.
47. MacDonald, *Lilith*, p. 184.
48. John Keats, 'La Belle Dame Sans Merci' in *Supernatural Poetry* (pp. 109–10), p. 110.
49. Goethe, 'The Bride of Corinth', p. 752.
50. Gautier, 'The Deathly Lover', pp. 131–32.
51. Le Fanu, 'Carmilla', p. 652.
52. Stoker, *Dracula*, p. 277.
53. MacDonald, *Lilith*, p. 201.
54. MacDonald, *Lilith*, p. 201.
55. George MacDonald, 'The Consuming Fire', in *Unspoken Sermons* (London: Alexander Strahan, 1867), p. 38.
56. MacDonald, *Lilith*, pp. 201–02.
57. MacDonald, *Unspoken Sermons*, p. 31.
58. MacDonald, *Lilith*, p. 202.
59. MacDonald, *Lilith*, p. 219.
60. MacDonald, 'The Consuming Fire', p. 45.
61. MacDonald, *Lilith*, p. 206.
62. MacDonald, *Unspoken Sermons*, p. 27.

Bibliography

Baudelaire, Charles, *Les fleurs du mal* (Paris: Librairie Générale Française, 1988).
Frayling, Christopher (ed), *The Vampyre – Lord Ruthven to Count Dracula* (London: Victor Gollancz, 1978).
Gaiman, Neil, *Coraline* (London: Bloomsbury, 2009).
Hayes, Michael (ed), *Supernatural Poetry: A Selection, Sixteenth Century to the Twentieth Century*, (London: John Calder, 1978).
MacDonald, George, *Lilith: A Romance* (Grand Rapids MI: Eerdmans, 1988).
— *Phantastes: A Faerie Romance for Men and Women*, ed Nick Page (London: Paternoster, 2008).
— *The Princess and the Goblin* (Edinburgh: Canongate, 1989).
— *Unspoken Sermons* (London: Alexander Strahan, 1867).
Paglia, Camille, *Sexual Personae – Art and Decadence from Nefertiti to Emily Dickinson* (London: Penguin Books, 1991).

Penzler, Otto (ed), *The Vampire Archive* (London: Quercus, 2009).
Poe, Edgar Allan, *The Complete Illustrated Stories and Poems of Edgar Allan Poe* (London: Chancellor Press, 1988).
Purkiss, Diane, *Troublesome Things: A History of Fairies and Fairy Stories* (London: Allen Lane, The Penguin Press, 2000).
Sims, Michael (ed), *Dracula's Guest – A Connoisseur's Collection of Victorian Vampire Stories* (New York: Walker & Company, 2010).
Stableford, Brian (ed), *The Dedalus Book of Decadence (Moral Ruins)* (London: Dedalus, 1990).
Stevenson, Robert Louis, *The Strange Case of Dr Jekyll and Mr Hyde and Other Tales of Terror*, ed Robert Mighall (London: Penguin Classics, 2002).
Stoker, Bram, *Dracula*, ed Maurice Hindle (London: Penguin Classics, 1993).
Summers, Montague, *The Vampire* (London: Senate Studio Editions, 1995).
Warrack, John and Ewan West, *The Concise Oxford Dictionary of Opera*, third edition (Oxford: Oxford University Press, 1996).

Gothic Degeneration and Romantic Rebirth in *Donal Grant*

JENNIFER KOOPMAN

Scholars have tended to overlook *Donal Grant*, MacDonald's 1883 sequel to *Sir Gibbie* (1879). Frequently mentioned but seldom discussed in detail, *Donal Grant* never achieved the success that *Sir Gibbie* did, and has not fared well critically. Robert Lee Wolff nominates it 'one of the worst' of MacDonald's novels, one that offers 'a mere farrago of worn-out themes from MacDonald's earlier books: somnambulism, irrationally brutal noblemen, preposterous machinery'.[1] Early reviewers made similar remarks about the book's derivativeness, *The Spectator* identifying the titular protagonist as an 'almost odious' copy of David Elginbrod (who appeared in the 1863 novel of the same name), and *The Dial* calling the story a 'mere imitation' of *Malcolm* (published in 1875). The book's relentless preaching also fell under fire: *The Dial* admired MacDonald's 'pure and lovely doctrine', but conceded that his fiction is best read 'solely as sermons'; in a similar frame of mind, *The Spectator* wondered whether it be 'too late to hope that Dr MacDonald may give us a Scotch story the characters in which will refrain from preaching, and from wearing their ethical theories on their sleeves'.[2] More recently, Richard Reis has identified the 'didactic precepts' of *Donal Grant* and other novels as 'the root of MacDonald's general inferiority as a realistic novelist'.[3] William Raeper offers a more nuanced response, positioning the book as a 'pure romance', a work that characterises the shift in MacDonald's prose from earlier realist stories 'where romance and reality jostle side by side' to later works in which 'romance appears to take over reality'.[4]

Certainly, the novel is a romance, a Gothic romance, the fanciful and at times gruesome trappings of which recall the works of Walpole, Radcliffe, Lewis, the Shelleys, and Polidori, among others.[5] It recounts how Donal, a former cowherd, recent college graduate, and aspiring poet, finds work at a mysterious castle as tutor to Davie, the youngest son of the earl. Davie's father, Lord Morven, a secretive, vampiric shell of a man, suffers from ill-health and opium addiction, and is given to wandering the corridors at night in fits of insanity brought on by eerie music that wafts through the castle on windy nights. Lord Morven does not own the castle, but looks after it on behalf of his orphaned niece Arctura, whom he intends to marry to his elder son Percy, a dissolute aristocrat with a penchant for beating his horse, flouting his father's wishes, and corrupting local girls. Tensions mount between Donal and Percy when it becomes obvious that Arctura prefers the poor tutor to her rich cousin, and also because Donal keeps interfering with Percy's attempts to seduce Eppy Comin, a village maid. In the meantime Lord Morven conducts clandestine drug experiments on Donal and Arctura, which cause them to experience nightmarish visions.

Determined to locate the source of the music that inspires Lord Morven's madness, Donal searches the castle and uncovers the secret: the music comes from an Aeolian harp hidden in an air shaft. This leads to a secret chapel at the heart of the castle, long sealed off, where he discovers the decomposed corpse of a woman chained to a bed and her dead infant on the altar. In the adjacent vestry he unearths a more recent relic, a letter by Davie and Percy's late mother. Written in the blood from her own wounded hand, it records the earl's cruelty to her and her anguish following the death of their infant daughter. Meanwhile, Lord Morven lets slip that he was never married to the boys' mother. Hoping to conceal their illegitimacy so that Percy may inherit the title, Morven next attempts to murder Arctura by shackling her to the same bed in the chapel tomb on which her anonymous ancestor perished. Donal arrives in time to rescue her, whereupon Morven confesses his guilt, overcomes his drug habit, and dies, leaving Arctura undisputed heir. She renovates the castle, opening up the chapel, and falls in love with Donal, whom she marries on her deathbed. Thus Donal, instead of the bastard Percy, inherits the castle, which he passes on to relatives of Arctura, preferring instead to establish a school so that he can further educate young men in Christian ways.

MacDonald's critics are correct: the story is derivative. But it is derivative in interesting ways, and I believe deliberately so. For all its artistic imperfections, I would argue that *Donal Grant* offers one of the most conceptually ambitious of MacDonald's books. While flawed as a novel, as a narrative about literary history it testifies to the breadth of his vision. Its conventional Gothic apparatus – the haunted castle, drug addiction, vampirism, madness, murder, live burial, and all the rest – reflect certain preoccupations that MacDonald had as a literary critic, namely with correcting the spiritual flaws of a literary tradition gone astray.

MacDonald's twentieth-century admirers have tended to underplay his historical role as a literary critic, portraying him instead as an ahistorical myth-maker – think of C. S. Lewis's depiction of him as 'an enthroned and shining God',[6] or G. K. Chesterton's vision of him as 'an elemental figure, a man unconnected with any particular age, a character in one of his own fairy tales'.[7] Yet for all these idealising portraits, MacDonald was a man very much connected to a particular age. As a Victorian critic, he was deeply concerned with the literary tradition that preceded him, particularly its spiritual implications. His 1868 anthology *England's Antiphon*, a literary genealogy that traces the divine spirit of English poetry from the thirteenth century down through the nineteenth, demonstrates MacDonald's attempt to establish his own place in this literary tradition. As the narrator of the anthology, he strikes an audacious position vis à vis the poets who came before him. He does not – or dares not – situate himself within the ranks of such literary giants as Shakespeare, Milton, and Chaucer, whom he envisions, along with others, as making up a holy cathedral choir. Yet neither does he position himself below them, as their humble amanuensis. Instead, he asserts the role of *Kapellmeister*, in charge of directing the entire show, as he adopts 'the name of Choragus, or leader of the chorus', whose job is 'to order who shall sing, when he shall sing, and which of his songs he shall sing'.[8] Certainly, in terms of words on the page, MacDonald's presence dominates the anthology, with his introductions and commentaries occupying as much space on the page as the poems themselves. This model of literary history, in which MacDonald is the leader, will work its way into his fiction, so that many of his stories offer fables about literary history, a history that MacDonald appears eager to direct.

No mere literary textbook, the *Antiphon* follows a trajectory similar to the Bible's, beginning with the genesis of poetic song, and ending with revelation and transcendence, as the volume concludes with the promise that the authors entombed (or entomed) within the 'gray glooms of the cathedral arches' of the book will reawaken 'to sing on to him that hath ears to hear' whenever a reader opens 'the shadowy door' of its cover.[9] This pattern of death and resurrection – so widespread in MacDonald's work that it may constitute the ur-plot of virtually all his writing – applies to literary history as well, as the *Antiphon* depicts poetry itself as being in need of redemption and rebirth, particularly during the eighteenth century, which he portrays as a fallen age. Characterised by a 'flatness of spirit, arising from the evanishment of the mystical element', the Augustan period marks the flooding of divine mystery with the bright lights of human reason, as 'the poets of England, with John Dryden at their head, ceased almost for a time to deal with the truths of humanity, and gave themselves to the facts and relations of society'.[10] Its devolution involves a slipping back to the 'swampy level of the time', until the final low point is reached in the French Revolution, when the 'supreme regard for science', joined with 'the worship of power', broke out 'in its crude form [...] as brute force'.[11] Fortunately, deliverance arrives with the emergence of William Wordsworth, England's spiritual saviour, who cures the rationalist blight by redirecting attention from human affairs to God's power in nature. MacDonald reads the redemption of poetry through Wordsworth's personal transformation: from high hopes at the outset of the French uprising, to 'the terrible disappointment that followed', consequent disillusionment – 'for a time, he believed nothing' – and finally, to revelation and reawakening.[12] He credits divine inspiration for Wordsworth's post-revolutionary poetry – '[b]ut the power of God came upon Wordsworth' – as God revealed himself to Wordsworth through 'the benignities of nature'. This spiritual rebirth, which 'restored peace and calmness and hope', had not just a personal effect, but broader implications for English literature, as '[t]he divine expressions of Nature, that is, the face of the Father therein visible, began to heal the place which the [Enlightenment] worship of knowledge had bred'.[13]

The idea that Romanticism revived a world exhausted by Enlightenment is a central Romantic myth that MacDonald firmly believed. For MacDonald, the dark night of the soul is a necessary part of the progress toward transcendence, as it sets the conditions for spiritual rebirth. As his character Ian explains in *What's Mine's Mine*: 'It was Wordsworth's bitter disappointment in the outcome of the French revolution [...] that opened the door for him'.[14] I want to argue that this pattern becomes the dominant mode of historical progress, as MacDonald envisions literary history as requiring salvation not once, but multiple times. Wordsworth's redemption of literature is not the final event, but rather a type to be repeated, and which would be repeated by MacDonald as he positions himself as the next saviour of literature. Much as the Enlightenment was redeemed by Wordsworth's Romantic poetry, so Romanticism is redeemed by the MacDonaldian hero of *Donal Grant*, a novel that depicts Romanticism as a glorious but fallen tradition, led astray from Wordsworthian ideals by the flaws of Coleridge, Shelley, and especially the incorrigible Byron.

In its capacity as literary fable about the fall and redemption of romance at the hands of nineteenth-century writers, *Donal Grant*, while nominally the sequel to *Sir Gibbie*, also functions as a mythological companion to the history begun in *England's Antiphon*. It continues the *Antiphon's* historical saga, albeit in fictional form, as it investigates the dark side of Romanticism, the savage, violent, untamed impulses of Romanticism that *England's Antiphon* did not discuss. *Donal Grant* recounts how English romance, the age-old form associated with Arthurian myth that was reborn through the labours of the Romantic poets, took a dangerous turn away from Wordsworthian nature worship and toward the corrupting influences (in MacDonald's mind) of Coleridgean drug addiction, Byronic perversity, and Shelleyean atheism. In this novelised critique of English Romanticism, MacDonald – who strove throughout his career to channel the Romantic poets' visionary ardour – attempts to correct their flaws via Donal. The castle becomes a radical participant in this discussion: wrapped in a devilish past, concealing dens of horror, haunted by the strains of a lost Aeolian harp, and run by the mad, vampiric, opium-addicted Lord Morven, the castle is romance, stalwart and grim amid the abominations committed by its inhabitants, functioning simultaneously as subject of and setting for debates about the revival of its ancient form. *Donal Grant* is both a Gothic novel and an anti-Gothic fable, as MacDonald sees transformative possibilities in the mode he wishes to purge.[15]

Veiled in a cloak of Arthurian lore, *Donal Grant* enacts a rescue fantasy in which the spirit of romance – embodied in the gentle but frail maiden Arctura – appears as the victim to be saved. With her power usurped by her uncle and marriage to her illegitimate cousin pending, Arctura, her name a feminised form of Arthur, suggests a noble tradition that has gone awry. Her location within the castle reflects her precarious condition: her oubliette-like chamber, which 'looked an afterthought, the utilisation of space accidentally defined by rejection, as if every one of its sides were the wall of a distinct building', suggests her exile from the castle's formal rooms.[16] Its function as the anteroom to the desecrated chapel – her wardrobe conceals the hidden door[17] – implies the estate's corruption of and alienation from its spiritual source. The immurement of her chamber hints at the extent to which Arctura is trapped, walled in by the past – a condition echoed in her dream of being pulled into the grave by her uncle, and which is literalised when her uncle attempts to entomb her alive.

The Arthurian resonances continue with Arctura's uncle Morven, whose name evokes the Latin *mors*, or 'death,' as well as Morgan LeFay, King Arthur's conniving half-sibling, and Mordred, the product of Arthur and Morgan Le Fay's incestuous union.[18] As with Arctura, the architecture of the castle reflects his degraded spiritual condition. The castle reminds Donal of a 'self, with no God to protect from it, a self unrulable, insatiable, [that] makes of existence [...] the hell called madness' – a description that anticipates later portrayals of the earl's insanity and apostasy.[19] In its defensive position vis à vis the landscape, the castle suggests his alienation from the natural–supernatural power of God. Unlike many of MacDonald's castles, cottages, and cathedrals, which tend to merge in harmonious union with the earth, Graham's Grip stands on guard against nature: rising up on the hillside like a soldier ready for battle, 'like a helmet the gray mass of the fortress', the castle appears as 'an athlete stripped for the fight' as it soars above surrounding trees, which 'seemed climbing up to attack the fortress above'.[20] Like the secretive Morven, its hulking form is impenetrable and heavily fortified, its sole entrance a 'small door' concealed in a 'deep recess' between sections of the bulwarks. The entrance hall, 'a mere entry, a cell in huge walls, with [...] a low, round-headed door, like the entrance to a prison', further suggests the inaccessibility of Morven's soul, and the chapel, its horrors hidden in the heart of the building, implies his spiritual deficiency.[21]

Besides being a conventional Gothic villain, Morven embodies several of the more notorious vices of the Romantic poets. The excesses of his villainy hint especially at Lord Byron, whose influence on Gothic romance was solidified during the nineteenth century as he himself became a figure in Romantic fiction. MacDonald's Lord Morven continues this tradition of fictionalising Byron, as the name *Morven*, in its similarity to *Ruthven*, evokes Lord Ruthven of Polidori's 1819 story 'The Vampyre', whom Polidori modelled on Byron, as well as Caroline Lamb's Ruthven in her 1816 novel *Glenarvon*.[22] Byron figures badly throughout MacDonald's writing, as MacDonald, who befriended Byron's widow Annabella Milbanke in the 1850s, clearly took her side.[23] Morven's cruelty toward Arctura, as well as Percy and Davie's mother, recalls in particular Byron's scandalous family life. Morven's callous disregard for his infant daughter and her mother resembles Byron's brutality toward Annabella in childbirth,[24] and his treatment of Arctura carries a strong whiff of incest, the alleged crime for which Byron was exiled from England.[25] Given MacDonald's preoccupation with hands (as well as feet), which, as Raeper notes, he habitually 'charges [...] with an intense eroticism', Morven's shackling of Arctura to the same mouldering bed on which her imprisoned ancestor died is especially suggestive.[26] The violence with which he thrusts her hand into the manacle leaves 'her hand [...] swollen, and the skin abraded,' leading Donal to exclaim at how the earl 'forced' and 'must [have] hurt' her.[27] Her hand injury, with its overtones of the stigmata, implies at least a metaphorical violation. It also echoes the wound he inflicted on Percy and Davie's mother, whose hand bled uncontrollably. Like the captive woman of yore left to perish on the chapel's 'torture bed', the boys' mother also endured 'sorest humiliations' and 'bodily tortures'.[28] While decorousness would have precluded MacDonald from depicting incest directly, Morven's attempt to replay on his niece the abuses suffered by the two unfortunate mothers hints at the incestuous nature of Byron's wrongdoings, as well as his disastrous marriage more generally.

If Morven's depraved family life recalls Byron, his drug use evokes Coleridge, as the book explores the spiritual ramifications of the Romantic preoccupation with drugs as a means of intensifying imaginative experience. In general, MacDonald approved of Coleridge, with *England's Antiphon* hailing him as Wordsworth's equal – 'Coleridge is a sage, and Wordsworth is a seer' – and even as his superior – 'when the sage sees, [...] when feeling and sight are one and philosophy is in abeyance, the ecstasy is even loftier in Coleridge than in Wordsworth'.[29] His work owes much to Coleridge's idea of the symbol, as Stephen Prickett and others have observed, and certainly he admired 'The Rime of the Ancient Mariner', which appears in at least half a dozen of his novels.[30] That said, during the 1850s MacDonald was dismayed to learn of Coleridge's opium dependency. A 'miserable weakness' he called it in an 1853 letter to Louisa, although he reassured himself that it was only a 'passing madness' for Coleridge, not a permanent state.[31] In *Donal Grant*, Morven, a 'slave to his medicines', explicitly compares his addiction to Coleridge's, describing himself as an innocent beguiled by deception and temptation: 'like poor Coleridge, I was first decoyed, then enticed, from one stage to another'.[32] Like Coleridge's insanity, the earl's is also a passing madness, one that comes and goes with the suggestively Romantic wind blowing through the castle's even more suggestively Romantic Aeolian harp. The book depicts drugs as offering a false form of inspiration that results in spiritual destitution, atheism, and madness. True inspiration, MacDonald argues in his essays, can only come from God. Throughout his writing, he characterises the experience as a Wordsworthian natural-supernatural communion that grants people a glimmer of transcendent promise. In 'Wordsworth's Poetry', for instance, he portrays the poet celebrating God's immanence in nature, which is 'an expression of the thought, the feeling, the heart of God himself'.[33] Donal experiences a similar transport when he looks at nature, a moment that he likens to being inspired with God's breath: 'The wind came round him like the stuff of thought unshaped, and every breath he drew seemed to be like God breathing afresh into his nostrils the breath of life'.[34] Drug-induced vision, by contrast, is a nightmare inversion of divine revelation, offering a grim, godless imitation of holy inspiration. When the earl slips drugs into Donal's wine, his experience follows a trajectory familiar to many Romantic drug narratives, such as Coleridge's 'Kubla Khan' or De Quincey's *Confessions of an English Opium-Eater,* as it begins delightfully, rises to dizzying heights, sinks to perilous depths, and concludes with spiritual remorse, a feeling 'akin to shame' that Donal compares to 'having a lack of faith in God'.[35] Under the influence of drugs, he experiences not unity with God, but a disorienting blurring of self and other.[36] In a nod to Romantic atheism, his drug trip leads him to the edge of the stormy sea, where, in a tragic replaying of Percy Shelley's fate, the body of a drowned man washes ashore.[37]

In keeping with contemporary thought that addiction is 'not a physical disease, but a moral vice',[38] the text characterises drug use as an inner failing that 'undermine[s] the moral nature', leading to 'moral decay' and finally 'moral madness'.[39] Donal's urging the earl to overcome his addiction and consequent madness through the vigorous exercise of his will[40] is also in keeping with the wisdom of the day: as Elaine Showalter observes, 'Whether drunkenness or excitement was the cause, Victorian doctors believed that in most cases insanity was preventable if individuals were prepared to use their willpower to fight off mental disorder and to avoid excess'.[41] *Donal Grant* goes even further to portray it as a *spiritual* failing, one that drives a wedge between humans and God. The spiritual hazard of drugs reaches a devilish apex in Morven's madness and atheism, which the text attributes to his opium dependency. Opium inspires and exacerbates his maniacal rants about his self being the only god he worships. Rejecting God's supremacy, Morven claims allegiance to no one but himself: 'He believed neither like saint nor devil; he believed and did not obey, he believed and did not *yet* tremble'. Instead, Morven worships himself. Like Moloch, to whom the narrator compares Morven in his 'pride of self-love and self-worship', Morven styles himself as 'his own king', one 'who had made himself a god – his own god!'.[42] Morven's narcissism is tainted with an especially Moloch-like destructiveness: like Moloch, who demanded child sacrifice, he stands by heartlessly as his infant daughter dies,[43] and is ready to murder his own niece for the sake of his pride.

A staunch defender of his free will, Morven rejects as 'dreary doctrine' Donal's belief that the only true freedom comes from obeying God: Donal insists that 'the sole way for a man to know he has freedom is to do something he ought to do, which he would rather not do. [...] There is no free will save in resisting what one would like, and doing what the Truth would have him do'. The irony, of course, is that Morven, for all his protestations otherwise, has already lost his free will to drug dependency, becoming, as the butler points out, 'a slave to his medicines'. To right this wrong, Donal urges Morven to recover his personal will by following God's will and confessing his sins, so that he may 'resist the devil [and] give up the evil habit that is dragging [him] lower and lower'. Addiction and rebellious self-worship are part and parcel of the same demonic plot, as Morven eventually realises: 'It was those cursed drugs that wiled the soul out of me, and the devil went in and took its place!'. His megalomania resembles that of Satan, whom Donal characterises as the *ne plus ultra* of self-absorption, fundamentally deranged by extreme narcissism: 'the devil must be mad with self-worship! Hell is the great madhouse of creation!'. Arctura further senses the satanic nature of her uncle's derangement: 'When the wind blows so angrily [causing Morven to fall into fits], I always think of that passage about the prince of the power of the air being the spirit that works in the children of disobedience'.[44] To deny God's supremacy and follow one's own selfish will is, in *Donal Grant*, a form of narcissistic madness, albeit one about which the sufferer has some measure of choice and control.

Morven's vampiric appearance emphasises the destructive quality of his unredeemed condition. In the death-obsessed world of MacDonald's novels, the greatest good is to embrace death and be with God. For Morven, however, who seeks to avoid both God and death, the past, though buried, remains undead. Suppressing history renders him unable to transcend it, with the result that he is caught in an interim state of living death, a condition reflected in his vampiric countenance: his face 'cadaverous', with 'eyes more like those of a corpse than a man among his living fellows' and a voice 'terrible as a voice [...] from an unseen world of sin and suffering', Morven wanders about 'in the anomalous condition of neither ghost nor genuine mortal'. His alchemical experimentation becomes part of this effort to resist death, as the housekeeper portrays his drug use as the Faustian ambition of a Romantic scientist who would overleap the bounds of mortality: 'He's taen a doze o' ane o' thae drogues he's aye potterin' wi' – fain to learn the trade of livin' for ever, I reckon!'. Unwilling to submit to God and put the past to rest, Morven is doomed to repeat it in the frenzied ravings that overcome him every time the 'ghost-music' of the Aeolian harp rings out on stormy nights, and in his compulsive attempt to replay with Arctura the outrages committed on women in the past (such as the injured hand and the live burial). Arctura predicts the latter fate in a dream that emphasises Morven's unredeemed state, as her corpse-like uncle beckons her down into 'the mould of the ancient dead', a fearful vision later made real in her imprisonment in the chapel.[45]

The novel thus features two kinds of burial. Morven's repressive, false form of burial is a bad form of death, as it leads only to ghostly, vampiric reanimation, indicating a failure to truly die. By contrast, godly burial is good death, as it leads to heavenly rebirth. Arctura's handling of her family's ugly history illustrates the difference. After uncovering the remains of the anonymous mother and child in the chapel, Arctura buries her ancestors, confident in the belief that she 'would yet talk, [and] live face to face' with them one day in heaven. Her subsequent dream reinforces this idea, as she envisions a child equipped with the 'gorgeous and great wings' of a butterfly rise out of a hill and thank her 'for taking her off the cold stone and making her a butterfly' – an image that combines the stony image of Christ's entombment and resurrection with the classical image of lepidopteral rebirth. Her dream offers the hope that ghostliness need not be a permanent condition, and that true death can overcome and redeem Morven's efforts to avoid it.[46]

Donal also demonstrates the right relinquishing of one's past to God. At the outset of the novel, as he mulls over recent romantic disappointment (which occurred in *Sir Gibbie*), the temptation to dwell in 'dreary thought of the past' is so strong that he can 'scarce avert his eyes' from the 'world of dreams' behind him. Yet he nevertheless delivers his past back to God, with the expectation of later retrieval – 'His past had but crept, like the dead, back to God who gave it; in better shape it would be his by and by!' – and comforts himself with the idea that 'He who turns his back on the setting sun goes on to meet the rising sun; he who loses his life shall find it'. Seizing on the principle that 'the cure o' a' ill's jist mair life', Donal consoles himself with the promise that the 'hert-brak' of unrequited love will bring transformation, and can be considered a natural part of spiritual development, 'jist ane o' the throes o' my h'avenly birth – in the whilk the bairn has as many o' the pains as the mither'. Donal's determination to start 'a fresh life frae this minute' rejuvenates his vision. Following his decision, he finds that 'the old mysterious loveliness, now for so long vanished from the face of the visible world, had returned to it'. In 'the new childhood of a new world', nature is imbued with greater meaning, reflecting Donal's transformed state:

> The scents that wind brought him [...] seemed sweeter than ever wind-borne scents before. [...] The wind hovered about him as if it would fain have something to do in the matter; the river rippled and shone as if it knew something worth knowing as yet unrevealed. [...] The world, like the angels, was rejoicing [...] over a man that had passed from a lower to a higher condition of life – out of its earth into its air: he was going to live above, and look down on the inferior worlds![47]

The nearness of revelation reflects MacDonald's belief in nature as a seat of divine communion, and indicates Donal's ascendancy to a new plane of existence. Donal's renewal and consequent recovery of meaning and purpose offers a positive model of handling history, one that contrasts to Morven's denial of God and attempt to conceal his past.

Donal Grant's sensational depiction of atheistic rebellion as the delusions of a madman functions as a commentary on a real-life atheist, Percy Shelley. MacDonald, who wrote a glowing essay on Shelley for the 1860 *Encyclopædia Britannica*, and who alludes to Shelley in laudatory terms throughout his fiction, objected to Shelley's atheism but seems to have personally identified with Shelley in other ways.[48] Certainly he admired Shelley's visionary drive. *Donal Grant* splits the figure of Shelley among several characters. Lord Morven is the monstrous projection of Shelleyan atheism amplified to its furthest extent, as his deranged megalomania illustrates the madness of self-worship. Shelley's more carnal improprieties are reserved for Morven's son, appropriately named Percy, whose 'tall and slender form' resembles Shelley's physique, and whose filial disobedience and seduction of Eppy Comin recall Shelley's troubled family life and romantic indiscretions. Percy's clandestine courtship of the village maid further evokes the Shelleys, as their encounters take place in a house once occupied by a monster, a real-life ogre that the text explicitly likens to 'Mrs Shelley's creation in *Frankenstein*'.[49] The drowning of Eppy's suitor Stephen Kennedy, a virtuous fisherman whose body washes up ashore the night after Donal's drug trip, hints at Shelley's death at sea, suggesting a good version of Shelley dying with Kennedy, leaving only the dissolute Percy to triumph.

Fortunately, another, better Shelley lives on in Donal Grant. Donal is a compound figure that unites Shelley's good characteristics with MacDonald's. Like MacDonald, Donal has a university education, but comes from a rural, working class background. Again, like MacDonald, Donal is an aspiring poet, who writes verse tinged 'with a slight flavour of Shelley'.[50] Although Donal sees problems with Shelley's atheism, and admits that he was 'misled in his every notion of Christianity',[51] his readiness to forgive Shelley's spiritual flaws echoes the *Encyclopædia Britannica* entry, in which MacDonald laments:

> how ill he must have been instructed in the priciples of Christianity! [...] So far is he from being an opponent of Christianity properly so called, that one can hardly help feeling what a Christian he would have been, could he but have seen Christianity in any other way than through the traditional and practical misrepresentations of it which surrounded him. [...] Shelley's own feeling toward others, as judged from his poetry, seem to be tinctured with the very essence of Christianity.⁵²

What to do about Percy Shelley becomes the question that frames the novel. The book opens with an explicit discussion of the poet's atheism. In Chapter 2, a clergyman warns Donal that reading Shelley's 'Mask of Anarchy' places him 'on the brink of perdition. That book will poison your very vitals'. Donal leaps to a spirited defence of Shelley that reads practically as a dialogue version of MacDonald's 1860 encyclopaedia entry, as he protests that, while Shelley may have been an infidel, he was 'Not of the worst sort. It's the people who call themselves believers that drive the like of poor Shelley to the mouth of the pit'. Like MacDonald, Donal blames Shelley's misguided educators, insisting that '[i]n spirit Shelley was far nearer the truth than those who made him despise the very name of Christianity without knowing what it really was'.⁵³ Upon rereading, however, he admits that Shelley erred, as Donal 'saw more and more clearly how he [Shelley] was misled in his every notion of Christianity [....] He saw in the poet a boyish nature striving after liberty with scarce a notion of what liberty really was'.⁵⁴ Donal's re-evaluation of Shelley introduces explicitly the theme of flawed Romantic poets that becomes an implicit undercurrent throughout the book, as Donal seeks to excise evil elements from the castle and preserve the good, via the power of godly instruction. His role as teacher becomes significant here, as education, rather than procreation concludes *Donal Grant*. Dispensing with the conventional Victorian conclusion of marriage and reproduction, the book ends with Donal establishing a school on the grounds of the estate, where he produces virtuous young Christian men to people the world. Even knavish Percy admits he might have turned out better, had he had the benefit of a tutor like Donal to guide him.⁵⁵ In the end, Percy's fate remains uncertain – he stalks off in a jealous rage; however, the narrator states outright that Donal could have saved him, declaring that '[i]f he had had any faith in Donal, he might have had help fit to make a man of him, which he would have found something more than an earl [....] It would have been the redemption of his being'.[56]

MacDonald's readiness to forgive Shelley's errors echoes Donal's optimistic assessment of human evil: as Donal reminds Arctura, 'nothing in its immediate root is evil; [and] from best human roots worst things spring'. The object, he stresses, is to minimise human fallenness by maximising God's divine perfection: 'Everyone is born nearer to God than to any ancestor, and it rests with him to cultivate either the *goodness* or the selfness in him, his original or his mere ancestral nature. The fight between the natural and the spiritual man is the history of the world'. Redemption can be attained by subsequent generations: as Donal declares, 'The man who sets right his faults inherited, makes atonement of those who went before him; he is baptised for the dead, not with water, but with fire'.[57] His belief in the capacity of individuals to redeem a fallen ancestral past articulates explicitly the implicit hope behind MacDonald's evocations of Shelley: that in repeating Shelley's work in corrected, revised form, the literary tradition – if not Shelley himself – will be redeemed (or at least move closer to godly perfection).

In revising Shelley and recuperating Romanticism, MacDonald participates in an effort similar to that of Mary Shelley, who strove to salvage her husband's posthumous reputation.[58] We might align him, too, with his fellow Victorians Matthew Arnold and Robert Browning, who demonstrated a comparable desire to Christianise or at least idealise the atheist poet.[59] At the same time, MacDonald is also helping himself by asserting the power of reading and criticism to shape and reshape the past, and by engaging in self-mythologisation as he invents a vision of literary history in which he himself plays a significant role. He understood from the beginning that literature might envision redemption, but only God could realise it. That said, his work suggests the reciprocal nature of literary influence: the past does not simply shape the present; the power of influence runs in both directions, as the present is equally capable of defining and redeeming the past.

Notes

1. Robert Lee Wolff, *The Golden Key: A Study of the Fiction of George MacDonald* (New Haven: Yale UP, 1961), pp. 288, 294.
2. 'Three Novels', Review of *Donal Grant, Annan Water,* and *Loving and Serving, Spectator* 57 (1884), pp. 90-91; Review of *Donal Grant, Dial* 4 (1883), p. 138.
3. Richard Reis, *George MacDonald,* Twayne's English Authors 119 (New York: Twayne, 1972), pp. 288, 294.
4. William Raeper, *George MacDonald* (Tring: Lion, 1987), p. 209. Most recently, Rebecca Thomas Ankeny includes *Donal Grant* in her examination of books, storytelling, and literacy in MacDonald's work; however, she does not offer a full reading of the novel. See *The Story, the Teller, and the Audience in George MacDonald's Fiction,* Studies in British Literature 44 (London: Edwin Mellen, 2000), pp. 87-98.
5. William Raeper observes especially that the abduction of Lady Arctura seems to borrow from Wilkie Collins' sensation novel *The Woman in White,* published in 1860 (*George MacDonald,* p. 197). Though a comprehensive study of *Donal Grant's* literary echoes will not be taken up here, the matter merits further discussion.
6. C. S. Lewis, *The Great Divorce* (1946; reprinted Glasgow: Collins, 1988), p. 59.
7. G. K. Chesterton, 'George MacDonald and His Work', in *George MacDonald in the Pulpit: The 'Spoken' Sermons of George MacDonald,* eds J. Joseph Flynn and David Edwards (Whitethorn, CA: Johannesen), p. 371.
8. George MacDonald, *England's Antiphon* (London: MacMillan, 1868; reprinted Whitethorn, CA: Johannesen, 1996), p. 3.
9. MacDonald, *England's Antiphon,* p. 332.
10. MacDonald, *England's Antiphon,* pp. 277, 267-68.
11. MacDonald, *England's Antiphon,* pp. 277, 303.
12. MacDonald, *England's Antiphon,* pp. 303, 304.
13. MacDonald, *England's Antiphon,* p. 304.
14. George MacDonald, *What's Mine's Mine* (London: Kegan Paul, Trench, 1886; reprinted Whitethorn, CA: Johannesen, 1995), p. 217.
15. cf. Scott McLaren, 'Saving the Monsters? Images of Redemption in the Gothic Tales of George MacDonald', *Christianity and Literature,* 55.2 (2006), pp. 245-269.
16. George MacDonald, *Donal Grant* (London: Kegan Paul, Trench, 1883; reprinted Whitethorn, CA: Johannesen, 1998), pp. 261-62.
17. MacDonald, *Donal Grant,* p. 264.
18. Arthurian resonances also occur in *Sir Gibbie,* a matter I discuss in 'Redeeming Romanticism: George MacDonald, Percy Shelley, and Literary History' (doctoral dissertation, McGill University, 2006), pp. 171-96.
19. MacDonald, *Donal Grant,* p. 37.
20. MacDonald, *Donal Grant,* pp. 44, 36, 52.
21. MacDonald, *Donal Grant,* p. 44.
22. John William Polidori, 'The Vampyre: A Tale' in *Three Vampire Tales,* ed Anne Williams (Boston: Houghton Mifflin, 2003), pp. 68-85; Lady Caroline Lamb, *Glenarvon* (Delmar, NY: 1816; Scholars' Facsimiles & Reprints, 1972).
23. For an overview of Byron's appearances in MacDonald's fiction, see my earlier discussion in 'Redeeming Romanticism', pp. 27-31; see also Greville MacDonald, *George MacDonald and His Wife* (London: George Allen and Unwin, 1924; reprinted Whitethorn, CA: Johannesen, 1998), pp. 300-13.
24. For discussion of Byron's cruelty to Annabella during her pregnancy, see David Crane,

The Kindness of Sisters: Annabella Milbanke and the Destruction of the Byrons (London: Flamingon, 2003), pp. 156-57; and Mario Praz, *The Romantic Agony* (London: Oxford UP, 1933 and 1970), pp. 74-75.
25. See Crane, *The Kindness of Sisters*, pp. 45-54; and Praz, *The Romantic Agony*, pp. 75, 90-91.
26. Raeper, *George MacDonald*, p. 204.
27. MacDonald, *Donal Grant*, p. 355.
28. MacDonald, *Donal Grant*, pp. 270, 296.
29. MacDonald, *England's Antiphon*, p. 307.
30. For discussion of MacDonald's inheritance of the Coleridgean symbol, see Stephen Prickett, *Romanticism and Religion: The Tradition of Coleridge and Wordsworth in the Victorian Church* (London: Cambridge, 1976), pp. 230-231; and Stephen Prickett, 'The Two Worlds of George MacDonald', *North Wind: Journal of the George MacDonald Society*, 2 (1983), 14-23, p.21. See also Rolland Hein, *The Harmony Within: The Spiritual Vision of George MacDonald* (Grand Rapids, Michigan: Christian College Consortium, 1982), pp. 149-150; and William Raeper, *George MacDonald*, pp. 110-12, 238-42. Coleridge also 'acted as a prism through which' were filtered the ideas of the German Romantics Schelling, Schlegel, Fichte, Kant, and Schleiermacher, many of whose works MacDonald had also read (Raeper, *George MacDonald*, pp. 239-40). For discussion of the Ancient Mariner's multiple appearances in MacDonald's work, see Koopman, 'Redeeming Romanticism', pp. 24-27; Prickett, *Romanticism and Religion*, p. 257; and Greville MacDonald, *George MacDonald and His Wife*, p. 540 n 1.
31. George MacDonald, letter to Louisa MacDonald, 12 September 1853, George MacDonald Collection 103.1.3.151, Beinecke Library, Yale University, New Haven, Connecticut.
32. MacDonald, *Donal Grant*, pp. 266, 292.
33. MacDonald, 'Wordsworth's Poetry', in *A Dish of Orts* (London: Sampson Low, Marston, 1893; reprinted Whitethorn, CA: Johannesen, 1996), p. 246. For a more detailed discussion of MacDonald's use of Wordsworth, see Stephen Prickett, *Victorian Fantasy* (Bloomington and London: Indiana UP, 1979), pp. 161-62.
34. MacDonald, *Donal Grant*, p. 13.
35. Samuel Taylor Coleridge, 'Kubla Khan', in *English Romantic Writers*, ed David Perkins (Fort Worth: Harcourt Brace, 1995), pp. 546-57; Thomas De Quincey, *Confessions of an English Opium-Eater*, ed Alethea Hayter (1821; reprinted London: Penguin, 1986); George MacDonald, *Donal Grant*, p. 148. F. Hal Broome suggests that, in contrast to these opium narratives, Donal's visions are caused by hashish, 'which was known to produce a "mental hallucination, with some degree of control over the train of thought – a sort of half-waking dream" according to James Braid's *Observation on Trance; or, Human Hibernation*'; see F. Hal Broome, 'The Scientific Basis of George MacDonald's Dream-Frame', in *The Gold Thread: Essays on George MacDonald*, ed William Raeper (Edinburgh: Edinburgh UP, 1990, pp. 87-108), p. 106, n 59.
36. MacDonald, *Donal Grant*, pp. 147, 154, 155.
37. MacDonald, *Donal Grant*, pp. 155, 254.
38. Virginia Berridge, *Opium and the People: Opiate Use and Drug Control Policy in Nineteenth and Early Twentieth Century England* (rev ed, London and New York: Free Association Books, 1999), p. 155.
39. MacDonald, *Donal Grant*, pp. 294, 370, 372.
40. MacDonald, *Donal Grant*, p. 292.
41. Showalter, *The Female Malady*, p. 30.

42. MacDonald, *Donal Grant*, pp. 227, 296, 191, 192.
43. MacDonald, *Donal Grant*, pp. 376-77.
44. MacDonald, *Donal Grant*, pp. 290, 266, 295, 374, 356, 197.
45. MacDonald, *Donal Grant*, pp. 265, 136, 190, 337, 260, 348, 353, 251.
46. MacDonald, *Donal Grant*, pp. 299, 317.
47. MacDonald, *Donal Grant*, pp. 1-2, 5-7.
48. I discuss the connection between Shelley and MacDonald at length elsewhere; see especially 'The Cruel Painter as a Rewriting of the Shelley-Godwin Triangle', *North Wind*, 26 (2007), pp. 48-76; and 'Redeeming Romanticism'.
49. MacDonald, *Donal Grant*, pp. 37, 229.
50. George MacDonald, *Sir Gibbie* (London: Hurst and Blackett, 1879; reprinted Whitethorn, CA: Johannesen, 2000), p. 410.
51. MacDonald, *Donal Grant*, p. 12.
52. George MacDonald, 'Shelley', *Encyclopædia Britannica*, 8th edn (1860), vol 20, 100-04.
53. MacDonald, *Donal Grant*, pp. 10, 12.
54. MacDonald, *Donal Grant*, p. 12.
55. MacDonald, *Donal Grant*, p. 38.
56. MacDonald, *Donal Grant*, p. 244.
57. MacDonald, *Donal Grant*, pp. 263, 262.
58. See Mary Shelley, Preface, *The Poetical Works of Percy Bysshe Shelley*, ed Mary Shelley (London: Edward Moxon, 1847).
59. See Matthew Arnold, 'Shelley' (1888), in *Essays in Criticism* (New York: A. L. Burt, nd), pp. 385-408; and Robert Browning, 'Essay on Shelley', ed Donald Smalley in *The Complete Works of Robert Browning*, gen ed Roma A. King (Athens, Ohio: Ohio UP and Waco, Texas, Baylor University, 1981), vol 5, 135-51.

Bibliography

Ankeny, Rebecca Thomas, *The Story, the Teller, and the Audience in George MacDonald's Fiction*, Studies in British Literature 44 (London: Edwin Mellen, 2000).

Arnold, Matthew, 'Shelley', 1888, in *Essays in Criticism* (New York: A. L. Burt, nd), pp. 385-408.

Berridge, Virginia, *Opium and the People: Opiate Use and Drug Control Policy in Nineteenth and Early Twentieth Century England* (rev edn, London and New York: Free Association Books, 1999).

Broome, F. Hal, 'The Scientific Basis of George MacDonald's Dream-Frame', in *The Gold Thread: Essays on George MacDonald*, ed William Raeper (Edinburgh: Edinburgh UP, 1990), pp. 87-108.

Browning, Robert, 'Essay on Shelley', ed Donald Smalley, in *The Complete Works of Robert Browning*, vol 5, gen ed Roma A. King (Athens, OH: Ohio UP and Waco, Texas, Baylor University, 1981), pp. 135-151.

Chesterton, G. K., 'George MacDonald and His Work', in *George MacDonald in the Pulpit: The 'Spoken' Sermons of George MacDonald*, eds J. Joseph Flynn and David Edwards (Whitethorn, CA: Johannesen), pp. 369-76.

Coleridge, Samuel Taylor, 'Kubla Khan', in *English Romantic Writers*, ed David Perkins (Fort Worth: Harcourt Brace, 1995), pp. 546-57.

Crane, David, *The Kindness of Sisters: Annabella Milbanke and the Destruction of the Byrons* (London: Flamingo, 2003).

De Quincey, Thomas, *Confessions of an English Opium-Eater,* ed Alethea Hayter (1821; London: Penguin, 1986).
Hein, Rolland, *The Harmony Within: The Spiritual Vision of George MacDonald* (Grand Rapids, Michigan: Christian College Consortium, 1982).
Koopman, Jennifer, 'The Cruel Painter as a Rewriting of the Shelley-Godwin Triangle', *North Wind,* 26 (2007), pp. 48–76.
— 'Redeeming Romanticism: George MacDonald, Percy Shelley, and Literary History' (doctoral dissertation, McGill University, 2006).
Lamb, Lady Caroline, *Glenarvon* (1816; Delmar, NY: Scholars' Facsimiles & Reprints, 1972).
Lewis, C. S., *The Great Divorce* (1946; Glasgow: Collins, 1988).
MacDonald, George, *England's Antiphon* (London: MacMillan, 1868; Whitethorn, CA: Johannesen, 1996).
— *Donal Grant* (London: Kegan Paul, Trench, 1883; Whitethorn, CA: Johannesen, 1998).
— Letter to Louisa MacDonald, 12 Sept 1853, George MacDonald Collection 103.1.3.151, Beinecke Library, Yale University, New Haven, Connecticut.
— 'Shelley', *Encyclopædia Britannica,* 8th edn (1860), vol 20, 100–04.
— *Sir Gibbie* (London: Hurst and Blackett, 1879; Whitethorn, CA: Johannesen, 2000).
— *What's Mine's Mine* (London: Kegan Paul, Trench, 1886; Whitethorn, CA: Johannesen, 1995).
— 'Wordsworth's Poetry', in *A Dish of Orts* (London: Sampson Low, Marston, 1893; Whitethorn, CA: Johannesen, 1996), pp. 245–63.
MacDonald, Greville, *George MacDonald and His Wife* (London: George Allen and Unwin, 1924; Whitethorn, CA: Johannesen, 1998).
McLaren, Scott, 'Saving the Monsters? Images of Redemption in the Gothic Tales of George MacDonald', *Christianity and Literature,* 55.2 (2006), pp. 245–69.
Polidori, John William, 'The Vampyre: A Tale' in *Three Vampire Tales,* ed Anne Williams (Boston: Houghton Mifflin, 2003), pp. 68–85.
Praz, Mario, *The Romantic Agony* (London: Oxford UP, 1933 and 1970).
Prickett, Stephen, *Romanticism and Religion: The Tradition of Coleridge and Wordsworth in the Victorian Church* (London: Cambridge, 1976).
— 'The Two Worlds of George MacDonald', *North Wind: Journal of the George MacDonald Society,* 2 (1983), pp. 14–23.
— *Victorian Fantasy* (Bloomington and London: Indiana UP, 1979).
Raeper, William, *George MacDonald* (Tring: Lion, 1987).
Reis, Richard, *George MacDonald,* Twayne's English Authors Series 119 (New York: Twayne, 1972).
Review of *Donal Grant, Dial* 4 (1883), p. 138.
Shelley, Mary, Preface, *The Poetical Works of Percy Bysshe Shelley,* ed Mary Shelley (London: Edward Moxon, 1847).
Showalter, Elaine, *The Female Malady: Women, Madness, and English Culture 1830–1980* (New York: Penguin, 1980).
'Three Novels', Review of *Donal Grant, Annan Water,* and *Loving and Serving, Spectator,* 57 (1884), pp. 90–91.
Wolff, Robert Lee, *The Golden Key: A Study of the Fiction of George MacDonald* (New Haven: Yale UP, 1961).

George MacDonald and the Visual Arts

HELEN SUTHERLAND

George MacDonald has been ill-served by his most ardent supporters, for G. K. Chesterton's assessment that 'had he confined himself to poetry and purely imaginative story-telling he could not have been almost forgotten'[1] positions him as a liminal figure in the Victorian literary world. This was later entrenched by C. S. Lewis in his view of MacDonald as a writer of fantasy forced into writing realist novels to feed an ever-growing family,[2] and as a result MacDonald is normally seen as a mystic in a world of materialism and a romantic in an age of realism. Nor is this evaluation entirely wide of the mark, for it is his fantasy and especially the fantasy novels, *Phantastes* (1858) and *Lilith* (1895), which differentiate him most clearly from his fellow novelists. To accept this evaluation of MacDonald as an exceptional figure who somehow stood outside the culture in which he lived is, however, to accept an inherently unbalanced and incomplete account of him, both as a man and as a writer, for the evidence suggests he was much more centrally placed than this account can allow.

I wish to argue he was allied to his times in three main ways. Firstly, MacDonald was located firmly within the culture of nineteenth-century Britain thematically: the interest in inheritance and especially in righting a wrongful inheritance which MacDonald explores in *The Portent* (1864) and in *Malcolm* (1875) and its sequel, *The Marquis of Lossie* (1877), for example, finds a counterpart in Charles Dickens's *Oliver Twist* (1837–1838) or Wilkie Collins' *The Woman in White* (1860).

Secondly, one could suggest that MacDonald is tied to the culture of his own times through sharing the concerns of the nineteenth century, and more especially by addressing many of the major social concerns of the day in his fiction. *Robert Falconer* (1868), for example, is taken up with the slum life of the urban poor, while *At the Back of the North Wind* (1871) addresses child poverty, and both these texts also deal with the devastating effects of alcoholism on family life.

Finally, MacDonald held a place within the intellectual and cultural milieu of Victorian Britain, with his circle of friendships including such notable figures as F. D. Maurice and Norman MacLeod from the world of theology; Matthew Arnold, Charles Dodgson, and Tennyson from the literary world; John Ruskin, Sir George Reid and Arthur Hughes from artistic circles; as well as Octavia Hill who worked for the improvement of housing for the poor, Dr Elizabeth Garret, the first woman doctor, and Josephine Butler, the reformer,[3] all of whom practised some sort of social work.

In this chapter, however, I want to focus on MacDonald's place among his contemporaries in the world of the visual arts, and explore some of the aesthetic concerns he held in common with them. I am not necessarily arguing that MacDonald either influenced the visual artists I will be discussing, or was influenced by them, but rather what interests me is that their work has features in common with his. These common traits suggest that although MacDonald's finished works differ quite radically from those of his contemporaries - *Phantastes* and *Lilith* being particularly distinctive - their underlying aesthetic bears a close relationship to that of his contemporaries, and he occupied a central, rather than liminal position in the world of the creative arts. This in turn opens onto a view of MacDonald as being a writer of importance in and for his own society, rather than being merely a source of spiritual guidance, as Lewis's anthology and later redactions by, for example, Michael Phillips, might suggest. It is really upon these shared aesthetic features that I will be concentrating, although more specific influences undoubtedly do exist.

Of all the artistic circles in which MacDonald moved, the most important to him, and the one with which he had most in common, was that of the Pre-Raphaelites, although this is not, perhaps, immediately apparent. What is so striking about William Holman Hunt's *The Hireling Shepherd* (1851–1852, Manchester City Art Gallery),[4] for example, is the multiplicity of detail and the uniform precision with which it is rendered. Hunt himself allied this to a realist aesthetic, suggesting that his object was to 'paint a real shepherd and a real shepherdess and a real landscape in full sunlight with all the colours of luscious summer without the faintest fear of the precedents of any landscape painters who had rendered Nature before'.[5] This seems to move his painting some distance from the numinous quality of MacDonald's best work and his elevated view of nature, both derived from German Romanticism, and especially from the writing of Novalis.

For many viewers, however, there is a wide disparity between the realism of Hunt's painting and the realism they perceive around them, not primarily in subject but in the *way* of seeing. While the human eye can focus sharply on only one point at a time, rendering everything else in the field of vision in softer focus the further each object is from that point, Hunt aimed to represent each object he painted as it existed in and of itself without reference to the laws governing human vision. The result is a painting of strict verisimilitude in which every object is rendered with the same degree of precision, which, when viewed as a whole, seems unrealistic or hyper-realistic, even though for Hunt himself it was essentially a realist work.

Hunt's painting is, however, much more than an accomplished exercise in realism, for the 1852 Royal Academy exhibition catalogue entry for it includes a quotation from Edgar's song in *King Lear*:

> Sleepest or wakest thou, jolly shepherd?
> Thy sheep be in the corn:
> And for one blast of thy minnikin mouth,
> Thy sheep shall take no harm. (III.vi.42–45)

The reference to 'jolly' shepherd, together with the lovers' high colour, was taken to refer to excessive alcohol consumption, making the painting a fairly straightforward and none too subtle moral warning against the dangers of intemperance.

Without wishing to deny this aspect of the painting, Hunt's slippage from 'jolly shepherd' to 'hireling shepherd' (a reference to John 10:12 in which Jesus contrasts the hired shepherd who abandons the flock in the face of danger with the good shepherd who 'giveth his life for the sheep') gives a more specifically religious slant to the interpretation which is then elaborated in Hunt's own explanation, for in a letter of 21 January 1897 to J. E. Pythian, he argues that

> Shakespeare's song represents a shepherd who is neglecting his real duty of guarding the sheep: instead of using his voice in faithfully performing his duty, he is using his 'minnikin mouth' in some idle way. He was a type thus of other muddle-headed pastors who instead of performing their services to their flock – which is

in constant peril – discuss vain opinions of no value to any human soul.[6]

Specific symbols within the painting support a religious interpretation; although the death's-head moth being shown by the shepherd to the shepherdess symbolises superstitious fears, she herself is portrayed as a scarlet woman and as such could stand for the Whore of Babylon or the Roman Catholic Church, whose scarlet-robed hierarchy had just been re-established in Britain in the person of Cardinal Wiseman. The lamb, which will be poisoned by eating the unripe green apples next to it on the shepherdess's lap, suggests the vulnerable youth of the land whose minds can be poisoned by dangerous doctrine, while the sheep straying into the corn, which will kill them if consumed by them, can stand for potential converts to the Church of Rome. If, as is often suggested, Hunt was indeed influenced by John Ruskin's *Notes on the Construction of Sheepfolds* (1851), which he read while he was working on *The Hireling Shepherd*, the painting may have yet wider significance, for Ruskin regarded all Christians, including those who were artists and poets, as priests, with their work – whatever that happened to be – being regarded as a sacred duty, neglect of which is sacrilegious.

The Hireling Shepherd is thus a much more complex work than first appears, for it is an embodiment of Hunt's visual realism, even as it attacks negligent churchmen who fail to protect their flock, either generally or more specifically against the newly re-established Church of Rome, and also satirises painters and poets who neglect what Hunt regarded as their primary function to 'fight the conventional, the blind and the wicked'.[7]

As Judith Bronkhurst notes, the symbolism of *The Hireling Shepherd* was 'not imposed on a naturalistic landscape but was central to the conception of the picture',[8] suggesting a holistic aesthetic in which realism and symbolism are held in fusion. According to Chris Brooks, the 'enterprise of realism is an attempt to capture what the *being* of the real world is like' but that for many Victorian artists 'such an enterprise was co-extensive with an attempt to capture the *meaning* of the real world as well'.[9] The result is what Brooks identifies as 'symbolic realism' and he considers this to be a fundamental mode of the Victorian imagination which – when successful – avoids the overt didacticism of a one-to-one correspondence between symbol and meaning.

This can, perhaps, be compared to George MacDonald's well-known dislike of allegory, which he described as 'a weariness to the spirit',[10] as well as to his use of symbols, exemplary figures, or types within his realist fiction. To give just one example, the mute Gibbie of *Sir Gibbie* is a Christ figure who is shown first in sharply delineated urban poverty and dirt, then in equally precisely described rural poverty in a realist novel which deals with the devastating effects of alcoholism on the lives of a range of individuals and explores the demoralising effects of wrongly used wealth – both aspects of much concern in the nineteenth century. Gibbie is, then, a type embedded within a realist setting, just as the symbolism of *The Hireling Shepherd* is fused with the naturalistic landscape setting. 'Being' and 'meaning', to use Brooks' nomenclature once more, are held in balance in both these works; indeed, 'meaning' is made apparent through the 'being' in a more fluid and responsive symbiosis than that normally found in allegory.

Holman Hunt's concern with the religious dimension of art was one he shared with the Pre-Raphaelite Brotherhood in general, although he possibly laid more emphasis on it than did some of the other artists concerned. It was always, however, tied to a realism in representation, as is made clear by George Frederick Stephens (writing under his *nom de plume*, John Seward) in an article, 'The Purpose and Tendency of Early Italian Painting', published in *The Germ*, the literary journal of the Brotherhood. Here Stephens argues that the object of the PRB was to make

> pure transcripts and faithful studies from nature instead of conventionalities and feeble reminiscences from Old Masters [...] by a determination to represent the thing and the whole of the thing, by training himself to the deepest observation of its fact and detail, enabling himself to reproduce, as far as is possible nature herself, the painter will best evince his share of faith.[11]

Nature is thus given a very high value, and painting or reproducing nature is an act of worship. And this, of course, brings us much closer to MacDonald's high view of nature, which was bound up in and by his conception of God. Although I would identify this intertwining of nature, art and religion as the first and perhaps the fundamental feature shared by MacDonald and his contemporary visual artists, I want to suggest that in MacDonald's view the fusion of nature, art and religion is much more organic, for in his essay 'The Imagination: Its Functions and its Culture' (1867) he asks

> What are the forms by means of which a man may reveal his thoughts? Are they not those of nature? But although he is created in the closest sympathy with these forms, yet even these forms are not born in his mind. What springs there is the perception that this or that form is *already* an expression of this or that phase of thought or of feeling. For the world around him is the outward figuration of the condition of his mind.[12]

And I think we can go further here and argue that the world is a figuration of the condition of a man's mind because God has created both the outer world and the inner mind of the man; or as MacDonald has it, 'the imagination of man is made in the image of the imagination of God'[13] and 'man is but a thought of God'.[14] It is therefore impossible to separate the thoughts of the artist from the forms of nature he uses in creating his art, in what seems to be some sort of anticipation of the late nineteenth-century Symbolist movement, which was stronger on the Continent than in Britain.[15]

MacDonald's writing – indeed, MacDonald's mind – is therefore inherently symbolist, and while this works well in the fantasy fiction, it can create problems in the realist fiction, for his incorporation of symbols and types is often regarded simply as failed realism. Gibbie, as we have seen, is a type embedded in a realist novel, but because he is a type rather than a psychologically convincing individual he strains the illusion of verisimilitude, leading to criticism of the novel as failed realism, just as Hunt's depiction of objects as they exist in and of themselves strains the pictorial realism of his work, leading to criticism because the world outside the viewer's window does not 'look like that'.

MacDonald's belief that the world is the outward figuration of the condition of a man's mind finds a striking parallel in the aesthetic of a major Victorian artist closely associated with, though never part of, the Pre-Raphaelite Brotherhood: Edward Coley Burne-Jones. It is difficult to decide how much MacDonald and Burne-Jones knew of each other's work, but Burne-Jones was an intensely literary artist who often had either his wife or his daughter read to him while he was working and so it is more than possible that he had read MacDonald. Whether or not this is the case, it is certain that Burne-Jones and MacDonald knew each other, for Geogiana Burne-Jones spent six weeks with the MacDonalds in Italy during the 1890s, they were near neighbours in London for many years, and were both close friends of Ruskin. It is, therefore, inconceivable that they were entirely unaware of each other's work or of the aesthetic underlying it.

According to Martin Harrison and Bill Waters, Burne-Jones was primarily 'concerned with the inner landscape of the mind and his use of the outer world was as a symbol of it'.[16] Burne-Jones himself explained:

> I mean by a picture a beautiful, romantic dream of something that never was, never will be – in a light better than any light that ever shone – in a land no one can define or remember, only desire – and the forms divinely beautiful.[17]

Burne-Jones's search to depict the 'light better than any light has ever shone' led him to do a series of paintings of *The Days of Creation* (1870–1876, Harvard University Art Museums);[18] in other words, to a subject which is essentially undepictable: the creation of all that there is. Burne-Jones's approach is an indirect one in which he depicts an angel holding a globe wherein the creation is taking place, suggesting that there is another and greater reality beyond the reality we can perceive; a reality that can be expressed – if expressed at all – only through symbols. The series works cumulatively with the angel of *Day 6* standing in front of the angels of the previous days, each holding a globe containing and symbolising the aspect of creation of that day as outlined in Genesis 1.3–31.

Clearly there are strong parallels with MacDonald's belief that the material world as perceived by the senses of sight, hearing, smell, taste and touch is the least part of reality. As David Robb explains,

> To MacDonald, the world revealed by the senses, and the life men lead in it, are not real. There is a more real world, an eternal dimension of reality which is the reality of God [...] His aim in writing, therefore, is to encourage [readers] to regard the world of

the senses as but an ephemeral part of a vaster, more mysterious totality.[19]

In addition to their awareness that the visible, material world is the least part of reality, and that that 'more mysterious totality' can be portrayed only through symbols, there is a strong kinship between MacDonald's 'perception that this or that form is *already* an expression of this or that phase of thought or of feeling' (*A Dish of Orts*, p. 5, quoted above) and *The Flower Book*[20] pictures which Burne-Jones began in 1882. Far from being depictions of flowers each one of which had a commonly known symbolic meaning, these were essentially private works of pure fantasy which together form some sort of journal, published only posthumously, revealing the artist's nature more fully than did his other work.[21] In each case Burne-Jones began with the name of a flower – usually a traditional name rather than a botanical name – and took it into his inner private world where it generated an image. What was important was not the form of the flower, but its name, for he explained: 'I want the name and the picture to be one soul together, and indissoluble, as if they could not exist apart'.[22] Here there seems to be a parallel with the flower fairies Anodos encounters in *Phantastes*, for 'just what the flower says to you, would the face and form of the fairy say [...] you would see strange resemblance, almost oneness between the flower and the fairy, which you could not describe, but which described itself to you'.[23]

The name of the plant which inspired Burne-Jones's painting of *Scattered Starwort* (*The Flower Book*, no. XXIX) is not known, but it depicts angels casting stars through the sky. Their containment within the circular format suggests a vision seen in a crystal ball, recalling the maiden with the crystal globe which 'wavered as with an inward light' encountered by Anodos in his travels through faerie land.[24] As Gabriele Uerscheln notes, in *The Flower Book* the 'viewer's eye is drawn directly into the picture as into a crystal ball in which the artist's visions appear'[25] and she argues that Burne-Jones uses curved lines to define the pictorial planes within each image. This allows him to manipulate the image in a way which suggests that the laws of time and space have been lifted, emphasising the fantasy nature of these worlds.

Other flower paintings prompt thoughts of other fantasies by MacDonald: *Ladder of Heaven* (*The Flower Book*, no. XII), for example, was prompted by lily of the valley (*Convallaria majalis*) and shows a winged figure climbing a rainbow. Of it Burne-Jones wrote:

> I shouldn't like to be cross-questioned about the person going up the rainbow. Pagans [...] may call it Iris, but Christians like you and me, will have it to be a soul, and it shall go up to the top of the rainbow and never go down the other side.[26]

This, of course, calls to mind MacDonald's 'The Golden Key' with Mossy's vision of the rainbow with 'its lovely, its delicate colours, each distinct, all combining'[27] and beautiful people ascending towards the arch, which itself may owe something to *Jacob's Dream* (c. 1805, pen and watercolour, London, British Museum) by William Blake.

These are not references in the usual sense of the word, for it is not clear whether Burne-Jones had read MacDonald's work or not. They can, however, be taken as evidence that the minds of the two men worked in a similar, essentially symbolic, way, and that for both men the unseen had greater reality and vitality than that which could be seen, touched or tasted.

In addition to this there is another link between George MacDonald and Edward Burne-Jones, for both made extensive and creative use of medievalism and Arthurian legend, with *Phantastes* in particular being suffused with the atmosphere of medieval chivalric romance and replete with allusion to Arthurian legend. While in faerie land, for example, Anodos finds a book which contains 'wondrous tales of Fairy Land, and olden times and the Knights of King Arthur's table,'[28] but rather than merely re-telling these MacDonald embeds them in his own story as part of a narrative strategy, the effect of which is to 'convey a mood and new, intensely felt sensations,'[29] as Colin Duriez notes.

Burne-Jones, too, used Arthurian legend throughout his career, though rarely in a straightforwardly illustrative way. In *The Beguiling of Merlin* (1873–1877, Port Sunlight, Lady Lever Art Gallery),[30] for example, he uses Merlin's sense of entrapment to explore his own feeling of powerlessness in his relationship with Maria Zambaco, the model for Nimuë. As he later explained to a friend,

> [T]he head of Nimuë was [...] painted from the same poor traitor and was very like – all the action is like – the name of her was

Mary. Now isn't that very funny as she was born at the foot of Olympus and looked and was primaeval [...] and I was being turned into a hawthorn bush in the forest of Broceliande.[31]

In this case Burne-Jones fuses Arthurian legend with classical references, for not only is Nimuë depicted as a Gorgon figure with snakes for hair, but the draperies of the figures are clearly influenced by the Elgin Marbles, and their sinuous rhythms weave into the branches of hawthorn rendering Merlin immobile and helpless. Far from creating a mere illustration, in this painting Burne-Jones combines Arthurian legend with classical mythology in a highly individual way to create an exploration of his own state of mind at a period of emotional stress, and simultaneously an expression of society's concerns about the sexual power of women.

A number of Burne-Jones's paintings, however, prompt thoughts not of Arthur and the Round Table, but of *Phantastes*. *Flame Heath* (*The Flower Book*, no. XIX), for example, is the name for heather (*Erica*) which prompted an image of Brynhild sleeping in a devastated landscape with tongues of flame around her, but visually is reminiscent of the medievalism of *Phantastes*, as well as gesturing towards the princess's fire in which she bathed the king of Gwyntystorm in *The Princess and Curdie*.[32]

Of course Burne-Jones also had recourse to more conventional literary resources, including *The Broadstone of Honour, or Rules for the Gentlemen of England* (1822) by Kenelm Digby, and the *Morte d'Arthur*, of which he said

> Nothing was ever like *Morte d'Arthur* – I don't mean any one book or any one poem, something that never can be written, I mean, and can never go out of the heart.[33]

What is clear from this is that Burne-Jones is again reaching for the unreachable and in paintings such as *The Last Sleep of Arthur in Avalon* (c. 1878–1898, Ponce, Puerto Rico, Museo del Arte de Ponce) is attempting to depict the undepictable other world which has more reality for him than 'this' world. The desire to depict that which cannot be depicted accounts for the idealised quality of his figures, for he deliberately rejected realism and argued

> You only want types, symbols, suggestions. The moment you give what people call expression, you destroy the typical character of heads and degrade them into portraits which stand for nothing.[34]

He used as an example of this his *Avalon* painting with the three queens – Queen Morgan le Fay, the Queen of Northgalis and the Queen of the Waste Lands:

> They are queens of an undying mystery and their names are Lamentation and Mourning and Woe. A little more expression and they would be neither queens nor mysteries nor symbols, but just – not to mention baser names in their presence – Augusta, Esmerelda, and Dolores, considerably overcome by a recent domestic bereavement. And that [...] is not what I mean.[35]

Freudian assessments of Burne-Jones's art which interpret the androgyny of his figures as evidence of the artist's fear of, or desire to escape from, sex, miss the point; this is not failed realism, but a symbolist mode of painting which aims to express an unseeable totality using symbols and types, rather than highly particularised individuals seeming to bear a direct correlation to the individuals encountered in the empiric world which figure in realist paintings.

There is a parallel here with MacDonald, for the eponymous heroes of *Malcolm, Donal Grant* and *Sir Gibbie* are all types or exemplary figures. Of the three, Gibbie is the most interesting for he is presented as a 'holy fool' (as also is Diamond in *At the Back of the North Wind*). Gibbie is mute but not deaf and this immediately creates distance between him and the reader, emphasising his set-apartness. His actions have to speak for him so he becomes a cipher or symbol to an unusual extent. As already noted, the inclusion of a type within a realist novel strains verisimilitude, which in turn breaches credibility for some readers at least, and ultimately leads to the devaluation of MacDonald as a novelist. If, however, we accept that the inclusion of romance elements, especially the use of types in preference to psychologically convincing and realistic characters, within a realist novel is an aesthetic choice on the author's part, intended to reveal 'meaning' through 'being', the eternal spiritual realities through the materiality of the everyday world in other words, the novel works rather better.

The artist with whom MacDonald is most closely associated is, of course, Arthur Hughes, another artist involved with the Pre-Raphaelite Brotherhood, though never actually part of it, who illustrated many of MacDonald's works. The Victorian period is noted for celebrated pairings of authors and illustrators – Charles Dickens and 'Phiz' (Hablot Knight Browne) or Lewis Carroll and Sir John Tenniel immediately come to mind – and to those ranks could be added the association between MacDonald and Hughes, which was sufficiently close for it to be regarded as a 'brotherhood' by Greville MacDonald.[36] Given the closeness of this relationship it is hardly surprising that the influence was reciprocal, with Hughes giving visual form to MacDonald's ideas and MacDonald influencing Hughes' choice of subjects and themes, even for paintings which were not directly illustrative.

Hughes' painting *The Heavenly Stair* (1887–1888, Bournemouth, Russell-Cotes Art Gallery and Museum)[37] is a good example of this influence, for the Royal Academy catalogue entry included the lines 'Little one who straight/ has come down the heavenly stair' from 'The Christmas Child' by MacDonald, and the painting itself clearly reflects the importance of the stair motif in MacDonald's writing. This motif had figured in many of Hughes' illustrations of MacDonald's work, including 'I was Dead and Well Content' for the 1905 edition of *Phantastes*. More striking, however, and certainly better known, is Hughes' illustration of Princess Irene beginning to climb the stair to her great-great-grandmother's attic in *The Princess and the Goblin*. Furthermore, the reference to MacDonald is emphasised by the visual relationship between the mother, the child, and the father within the *The Heavenly Stair*, which is reminiscent of the relationship between the members of the holy family in many paintings of the Nativity (especially the reverent attitude of the man who corresponds to St Joseph), making the painting even more appropriate to MacDonald's poem, although the title of it was not included in the catalogue entry.

Other examples of MacDonald's influence on Hughes' art can be suggested, at least tentatively. One of the most interesting is a late painting, *Overthrowing of the Rusty Knight* (?1894; completed 1908; location unknown). In the *Catalogue Raisonné* of Hughes' work, Leonard Roberts identifies the source of this subject as Tennyson's *Gareth and Lynette* (1872), in which the young knight Gareth, who has been masquerading as a scullion, heaves the Knight of the Evening Star over a bridge in his quest to rescue Lynette's sister. Although this may well be the case, it is also possible that Hughes was influenced by the meeting of Sir Galahad

"Here it chaunced that upon their quest Sir Galahad and Sir Percivale rencountered in the depths of a great forest."

Arthur Hughes, 'Sir Galahad and Sir Percivale' (Phantastes, chapter III)

and Sir Percivale, of which Anodos reads in *Phantastes*, for as Roberts notes rusty armour is not mentioned in relation to the Knight of the Evening Star, whereas Sir Percivale's armour is described as 'wondrous rosty to behold'.[38] This likelihood is increased as Hughes was working on the painting from about 1894 until 1908, during which time he also worked on illustrations for a 1905 edition of *Phantastes* which was itself some sort of commemoration of the author/illustrator relationship which MacDonald and Hughes had enjoyed for so long.

This late edition contains some of Hughes' best illustrations, that show to the full his talent for 'hinting at the horrible',[39] as Kate Flint puts it, while simultaneously remaining true to the text. Hughes' illustration of the ash tree being cut down at the moment it was about to seize Anodos,[40] for example, contains within one image both a representation of a malignant old man and a tree with an axe laid to its root; in his illustration of Anodos' shadow coming out of the cupboard in the house of the ogre[41] Hughes has drawn the visual relationship between Anodos and the shadow sufficiently close to suggest the optical relationship between a shadow and the object casting it while retaining sufficient visual disjunction to create an element of shock and a frisson of distaste which belong to the text. This is emphasised by the absence of outline which blurs the distinction between the shadow and what is behind or around it, creating an indeterminacy of form which is truly disturbing and which, as Flint suggests, is a means of suggesting the supernatural much favoured by Hughes.[42] This shadow was also a vital part of the original title page of the 1905 edition,[43] for what we originally read as the shadow of the flying horse is in fact the Shadow which attached itself to Anodos.

However, perhaps one of the most interesting paintings Hughes ever did is also one of the most closely linked to MacDonald without being an illustration of one of his texts; this is *The Knight of the Sun* (c. 1860). There are three versions of this vibrantly coloured and visionary painting which have been located[44] and several more whose whereabouts are unknown, with this proliferation being some measure of the importance of the theme to Hughes, or of its popularity with the art-buying public of the mid-nineteenth century, particularly as there are no major changes between the versions. It has been identified by Richard Altick as the death of Arthur,[45] although neither the landscape nor the iconography accord with Malory's 'Death of Arthur'[46] or Tennyson's 'The Passing of

Arthur'.[47] Robin Gibson suggests that 'no literary reference for the subject can be traced, and it must [...] have grown out of Hughes' imagination'[48]

Arthur Hughes, 'A runner with ghostly feet' (Phantastes, chapter VIII)

while Kathy Triggs notes that 'the story of the picture is not MacDonald's' and argues that it 'probably came about by a process of amalgamation of romantic stories Hughes had read'.[49]

The most immediately apparent link to MacDonald is a visual one, for the head of the knight himself bears a very strong resemblance to MacDonald, whom Hughes had only recently met (although as Triggs notes, it is not known whether MacDonald ever actually modelled for the painting).[50] Even if Hughes was merely subconsciously influenced by MacDonald's features the resemblance is strong enough on its own to suggest a link to him.

However, the frame of the version now in Lord Lloyd Webber's collection was originally inscribed with lines from 'Better Things' by MacDonald: 'Better a death when work is done/ Than earth's most favoured birth'. Although the following lines 'Better a child in God's great house/ Than king of all the earth' suggest the humility associated with knights, the poem itself is not really about knights, knighthood or chivalric ideals, initially suggesting an inexplicable mismatch between image and inscription. However, the title 'The Knight of the Sun' may be a reference to *The Mirrour of Princely Deedes and Knighthood wherin is shewed the worthiness of the Knight of the Sunne*, a romance by Diego Ortúñez de Calahorra translated by Margaret Tyler in about 1580. Certainly the Knight of the Sunne is so outstanding even in his first battle that the onlookers 'thought truely [that] he would proue the best knight of the world, sith in so tender years he was of great vertue'[51] and he lived according to the chivalric ideals of knighthood.

The identification of *The Knight of the Sun* with the Knight of the Sunne in *The Mirrour of Princely Deedes* would be in keeping with the inscription on the frame, and would also accord with what is probably Hughes' own description of the painting as showing 'an aged warrior mortally wounded, being carried by his men-at-arms to the shelter of a religious house'.[52] The best and most evocative commentary on the painting is, however, MacDonald's own explanation that 'The sun's work is done, and he has set in glory, leaving his good name behind him in a lovely harmony of colour. The old knight's work is done too; his day has set in the storm of battle, and he is lying lapt in the coming peace'.[53]

MacDonald's extended description of this painting can be taken as a compliment to, and acknowledgement of, his friend and illustrator,

Arthur Hughes. Certainly this working relationship was especially close, but not essentially different from MacDonald's relationships to the other artists, such as Edward Burne-Jones, whose concern was, in Chris Brooks' terminology, to capture the meaning as well as what the being of the real world was like – a world which was incomparably greater than the world perceived through the senses. The celebrated MacDonald/Hughes relationship is a reminder that MacDonald was not an isolated prophet or seer, but was part of a literary, artistic and cultural milieu. To see him in this context is not to diminish his achievements as a writer but to recover a truer appreciation of his contribution to Victorian art and literature.

Notes
1. G. K. Chesterton, introduction to *George MacDonald and His Wife*, Greville MacDonald (Whitethorn, CA: Johannesen, 2005), p. vi.
2. C. S. Lewis, *George MacDonald: An Anthology* (London: Fount, 1983), p. 34.
3. Greville MacDonald, *George MacDonald and His Wife*, pp. 218, 300–02, 328, 368, 380, 413.
4. High-quality reproductions of this painting are to be found in Julian Treuhertz, *Pre-Raphaelite Paintings in Manchester City Art Galleries* (Manchester: Manchester City Art Gallery, 1993) and Judith Bronkhurst, *William Holman Hunt: A Catalogue Raisonné* (New Haven and London: Yale University Press, 2006), 2 vols, I Paintings.
5. Letter from Hunt to J. E. Pythian, 21 January 1897, MS Manchester City Art Gallery files; quoted in Bronkhurst, p. 12.
6. MS Manchester City Art Gallery files; quoted in Bronkhurst, p. 147.
7. George P. Landow, *William Holman Hunt and Typological Symbolism* (New Haven and London: Yale University Press, 1979), p. 41.
8. Bronkhurst, pp. 147–48.
9. Chris Brooks, *Signs for the Times. Symbolic Realism in the Mid-Victorian World* (London: George Allen and Unwin, 1984), p. 3.
10. George MacDonald, 'The Fantastic Imagination', *A Dish of Orts* (London: Dalton, 1908, pp. 313–22), p. 317.
11. John Seward (*nom de plume* of F. G. Stephens), 'The Purpose and Tendency of Early Italian Painting', *The Germ: Thoughts Toward Nature in Poetry, Literature and Art*, 2, 1850 (February), pp. 58–64 (pp. 58, 59), http://gateway.proquest.com/openurl?url_ver=Z39.88-2004&res_dat=xri:bp:&rft_dat=xri:bp:article:e501-1850-000-02-000030 [accessed 21/02/12].
12. George MacDonald, 'The Imagination: Its Functions and its Culture', *A Dish of Orts* (London: Dalton, 1908), pp. 1–42 (p. 5).
13. MacDonald, 'The Imagination: Its Functions and its Culture', p. 3.
14. MacDonald, 'The Imagination: Its Functions and its Culture', p. 4.
15. Although this aspect of MacDonald's work is under-researched it has received some critical attention: Adelheid Kegler's article, '*Wilfrid Cumbermede*: A Novel in the Context of European Symbolism', *North Wind*, 21 (2002), pp. 71–84, is particularly illuminating.
16. Martin Harrison and Bill Waters, *Burne-Jones* (London: Barrie & Jenkins, 1973), p. 23.

17. Letter to a friend, quoted in Cosmo Monkhouse, *Exhibition of Drawings and Studies by Sir Edward Burne-Jones, Bart* (London: Burlington Fine Arts Club, 1899), p. vii.
18. High-quality reproductions of *Days* 1, 2, 3 and 5 of this series can be found in Christopher Wood, *Burne-Jones: The Life and Works of Edward Burne-Jones 1833–1898*, (London: Weidenfeld & Nicolson, 1998).
19. David Robb, 'The Fiction of George MacDonald', *Literature of the North*, ed David Hewitt and Michael Spiller (Aberdeen: Aberdeen University Press, 1983, pp. 70–82), p. 72.
20. The medium used for these small circular works (6 inches in diameter) is a mixture of pastel and watercolour, allowing a more direct technique than would be the case with the oil paint Burne-Jones more commonly used. Reproductions can be found in Edward Burne-Jones, *The Flower Book*, with commentary by Gabriele Uerscheln (Köln: Taschen, 1999).
21. Georgiana Burne-Jones, *Memorials of Burne-Jones* (London: Macmillan, 1906, 2 vols), II, 118.
22. Georgiana Burne-Jones, *Memorials of Burne-Jones*, II, 119.
23. George MacDonald, *Phantastes, A Faerie Romance for Men and Women* (London: Azure, 2002), p. 36.
24. MacDonald, *Phantastes*, p. 115.
25. Burne-Jones, *The Flower Book*, pp. 13–14.
26. Georgiana Burne-Jones, *Memorials*, II, 119.
27. MacDonald, *The Golden Key and other Stories* (Grand Rapids, MI: Eerdmans, 1980), p. 3.
28. MacDonald, *Phantastes*, p. 34.
29. Colin Duriez, introduction to MacDonald, *Phantastes* (London: Azure, 2002), p. vi.
30. A high-quality reproduction can be found in Christopher Wood, *Burne-Jones: The Life and Works of Sir Edward Burne-Jones (1833–1898)* (London: Weidenfeld & Nicolson, 1998), p. 73.
31. Stephen Wildman and John Christian, *Edward Burne-Jones[,] Victorian Artist-Dreamer* (New York: Metropolitan Museum of Art, 1998), p. 171.
32. MacDonald, *The Princess and the Goblin and The Princess and Curdie*, ed Roderick McGillis (Oxford: Oxford University Press, 1990), p. 326.
33. Georgiana Burne-Jones, *Memorials*, II, 168.
34. Georgiana Burne-Jones, *Memorials*, II, pp. 140–41.
35. Georgiana Burne-Jones, *Memorials*, II, p. 141.
36. MacDonald, *Phantastes*, preface by Greville MacDonald (1905), p. viii.
37. Reproductions of all the works by Hughes discussed here can be found in Leonard Roberts, *Arthur Hughes: His Life and Work: A Catalogue Raisonné* (Woodbridge, Suffolk: Antique Collectors Club, 1997); many can also be viewed at http://www.arthurhughes.org.
38. MacDonald, *Phantastes*, p. 32.
39. Kate Flint, 'Arthur Hughes as Illustrator for Children', *Children and their Books: A Celebration of the Work of Iona and Peter Opie*, ed Gillian Avery and Julia Briggs (Oxford: Oxford University Press, 1990, pp. 201–20), p. 218.
40. 'The Ash Shuddered and Groaned', from *Phantastes*, p. 85.
41. MacDonald, *Phantastes*, p. 105.
42. Flint, p. 203.
43. Unpublished; now in Houghton Library, Harvard University. See Roberts, p. 277.

44. The first is oil on canvas, dated 1859–1860, now in the collection of Lord Lloyd Webber; another is oil on panel, dated 1860 and later retouched, now in the Edmund J. and Suzanne McCormick Collection, Yale Center for British Art; the third is watercolour on paper, dated 1860–1861 and now in the Ashmolean Museum, Oxford. See Roberts, pp. 145–47.
45. Richard D. Altick, *Paintings from Books: Art and Literature in Britain 1760–1900* (Columbus: Ohio State University Press, 1985), p. 455.
46. Thomas Malory, 'The Death of Arthur', *Le Morte d'Arthur*, Winchester Manuscript, ed Helen Cooper (Oxford: Oxford University Press, 1998), pp. 512–15.
47. Tennyson, 'The Passing of Arthur', *Idylls of the King* in *Tennyson's Poetry*, ed Robert W. Hill, Jnr (New York & London: Norton, 1999), pp. 512–19.
48. Robin Gibson, 'Arthur Hughes: Arthurian and Related Subjects of the Early 1860s', *Burlington Magazine*, vol 112, no. 808 (July 1970), pp. 451–56 (p. 452).
49. Kathy Triggs, 'The Knight of the Sun – A Note', *North Wind* 10 (1991), pp. 19–21, p. 20.
50. Triggs, p. 20.
51. Diego Ortúñez de Calahorra, *The first part of the Mirrour of Princely Deedes and Knighthood. Wherin is shewed the worthiness of the Knight of the Sunne*, trans Margaret Tyler (London: Thomas East, 1580), p. 47, in *Early English Books Online* http://gateway.proquest.com/openurl?ctx_ver=Z39.88-003&res_id=xri:eebo&rft_id=xri:eebo:citation:99848742 [accessed 21/02/12].
52. Roberts, *Arthur Hughes: His Life and Work: A Catalogue Raisonné*, pp. 145–46.
53. George MacDonald, *The Seaboard Parish* (London: Strahan, 1869), pp. 614–15.

IV. SCOTLAND

Speaking Matrilineally (and Especially of Uncle Mackintosh MacKay)

KIRSTIN JEFFREY JOHNSON

Such a one will see the customs of his ancestors glorified in the mists of the past; what is noble in them will appeal to all that is best in his nature [...]
(*What's Mine's Mine*)

The general subject of George MacDonald's Scottishness, both how it informs him as a person and how it is manifested in his writing, is vast. That MacDonald considered himself a Celt, not only a Scot, and that this shaped his thinking and his writing, is a point he reiterates time and again. His proud parading in Highland gear, whether as a student in Aberdeen or decades later as an old patriarch in Italy, indicated something deeper than a love of ethnic regalia: 'I am a pure Highlander on both sides, though I have no Gaelic'.[1] That he, a polymath, had failed to acquire the language of his ancestors was a life-long regret of MacDonald's – at least three of his grandparents spoke the tongue, as did his uncles on both sides, probably his mother, and definitely his stepmother. In 1863 he wrote to a former teacher: 'I can never forget the lessons I had from you in Gaelic. I wish I had continued the study of the language. I might have been the minister of a parish in the Highlands of Scotland'.[2] That he would have considered such a venture not only indicates the affinity MacDonald had for the Highland culture, but the influence of one of his Gaelic-speaking uncles in particular – a man named Mackintosh Mackay.

MacDonald's strong sense of 'Celticness' was confirmed by his sons, Ronald claiming that their father was 'radically a Gael' and Greville that MacDonald had 'inherited all the characteristic virtues': 'his devotion to the soil, his love of liberty, his intolerance of injustice, his eloquence and love of learning'.[3] In his biography, Greville declares that MacDonald's 'racial inheritance – one of romance, devotion and piety, of unlettered literature and song, of poverty and freedom – is of first importance in understanding his character and work'.[4] Even MacDonald's fellow countrymen – most specifically and perhaps most importantly Huntly folk themselves – considered MacDonald an 'Aberdeenshire Celt'.[5] Thus Greville's claim that this identity is 'of first importance in understanding [MacDonald's] character and work' deserves more attention than it has hitherto been given.

A limited exploration of MacDonald's paternal lineage has made evident that the author used his own family history to shape some of the stories he wrote, Robert Falconer's grandmother being the most recognised and discussed of such characters. Yet there are many other characters informed by MacDonald's ancestry, and this chapter will focus on a particularly important figure in MacDonald's maternal lineage, the aforementioned Mackintosh Mackay.[6] MacKay is himself a significant character in Scottish history, and this chapter serves merely as an introduction to this maternal uncle whose life not only provided MacDonald with substantial novelistic material, but who greatly influenced MacDonald's own understanding and expression of his Gaelic heritage.

Before introducing Mackintosh Mackay it is worth underscoring MacDonald's explicitly Scottish voice – for it will be seen that its determined usage is not unrelated to his uncle's legacy. Unlike some Scots who moved to England, MacDonald was publicly proud of his Scottishness and he intentionally maintained his Aberdeenshire brogue despite the irritation and even scorn this incurred among some of his English audiences. MacDonald delighted in using Doric vocabulary when he came home to visit, and in doing so he was following an example set by his father, whose letters are sprinkled throughout with Doric words and phrases such as 'geck neek', 'Auld Yeel', and 'jeesty'.[7] Although Greville claims that MacDonald was not allowed to speak 'broad Scotch' at the table or before elders, this was certainly not the rule for MacDonald's sisters, as various letters from his father make evident. It is plausible that this was a rule set by and for MacDonald's paternal grandmother rather than his father – if not, such rules were either not upheld, or not maintained. But it is also worth noting that original material (letters and memoirs) in various archives prove that some documents in Greville's biography have had the 'broad Scotch' and the more earthy phrases and anecdotes removed, including evidence that MacDonald's paternal grandmother spoke broad Scots herself.[8] For example, when explaining his great-grandmother's involvement in her husband's banking business, Greville writes that until a better means was procured for keeping the money safe, she had it placed in the family kist (trunk). At one point she may have done, but Greville's main source of information is a document of memories from his father's brother Charles, which reads:

> I cannot but be reminded of asking my grandmother once if when they had the bank in such premises as they had at the time she was not afraid of robbery, to which she replied 'Na, Na laddie, I aye took gweed care after the chop was closed to gang doon and tak' a' the notes and bills and put them into a second chamber pot aneth oor ain bed, and if onybody cain there they wad get the ane wi something in't afore they got the ither ane, an that wid hae wankened us, an' syne if they wid fecht yer grandfather cud … tee, and I wid hae taen my pairt as weel, ye may be sure, na, na, nae fear!'[9]

In understatement, Charles adds: 'This showed character' (Charles 3; 15). This also showed that her son recalls her speaking in Scots, strongly as she apparently encouraged speaking in English. And, that Greville chose not to relate this.

MacDonald's own employment of Scots in his Scottish novels resulted in a mixed response still evident in readers today: some are delighted by the language, others are continually frustrated by how it impedes their reading.[10] What is perhaps not so readily recognised in recent decades is how unique it was for a mid-nineteenth-century author to write like this – nor how greatly it angered some of MacDonald's English readers. This was not merely because comprehension was a challenge, but because MacDonald's replication of the language was considered low and vulgar, and thus irresponsible to his readership: 'exactly as it sounds in a part of Scotland where it sounds most uncouth' as one review phrased it.[11]

A number of late nineteenth and early twentieth century discussions on the revival in Scottish dialect writers pointed to George MacDonald's early contribution as being far more significant than is typically recognised. For example, in 1897 David Christie Murray wrote that while Walter Scott was accepted *despite* the idiom he employed, after Scott there had been none to carry forth the linguistic banner:

> The Muse of the North was silent, or spoke in ineffectual accents. After a long interregnum came George MacDonald, unconsciously paving the way for the mob of northern gentlemen who now write with ease. He brought to his task an unusual fervour, a more than common scholarship, a more than common richness, purity, and flexibility in style, a truly poetic endowment of imagination, and a truly human endowment of sympathy, intuition and insight.

Murray proceeds to point out how MacDonald was largely unrecognised for doing so, and then continues:

> Such readers as were competent to judge of him ranked him high, but, south of the Tweed, such readers were few and far between, for he employed the idiomatic Scotch in which he chose to work, with a remorseless accuracy, and in this way set up for himself a barrier against the average Englishman.[12]

This reviewer was but one of many Scottish critics (many of whom wrote for English journals) who credited MacDonald with paving the way for the legitimacy of Scotsmen to write in their own language even when a significant portion of the readership was not expected to be Scots.

These Scottish critics also occasionally identified Walter Scott's version of Scotland as gratifying an English romanticism, and MacDonald's as offering informed authenticity. For instance in 1867 an English critic complained at length about the generally Celtic nature of MacDonald's writing, asserting that Walter Scott's representation of the Scottish people was much more accessible.[13] Yet a *Blackwood's* critic differed considerably:

> In a sense Sir Walter Scott made Scotland known to the world. [...] The debt we owe Scott can never be repaid. His great task was in part also aided by Burns, Thomson, and the Ettrick Shepherd. But all these men of genius, with all their remarkable work, yet left some gaps in the delineation of Scottish life. As we have said, Scott dealt mainly with Scottish historic romanticism. [...] But romanticism is a little apt to pass by the homes of the decent, God-fearing middle class; it does not easily find poetry in a small town house

or a shop in the village street. It was in this *milieu* that George MacDonald discovered the true line for his talent. He wrote out of his heart, he wrote from his own experience.[14]

Research into MacDonald's own family reveals that not only did he 'write from his own experience', but that he also drew quite considerably upon the experiences of his family and their communities.

In his own literary criticism MacDonald articulates clearly – perhaps most strongly in the essay 'St George's Day', as well as in his lectures – that he considers not only the environment in which an author is raised to be of critical import to that author's work, but also the author's familial heritage: 'For a child is born into the womb of the time, which indeed enclosed and fed him before he was born'.[15] MacDonald's own Celtic heritage is not entirely overlooked in recent scholarship – in the attention given to his paternal lineage biographers often follow Greville's lead with references to Glencoe and Culloden – but at the expense of MacDonald's maternal history.[16] Ronald confirms that his father barely concealed 'family history' in the novels, but that this is true of more than one novel, and of more than one character, is important to emphasise, especially in light of the biographical weight granted to the grandmother character in *Robert Falconer*.[17] Most critical studies of MacDonald's novels specifically reference this character and her resemblance to MacDonald's paternal grandmother.[18] Greville's biography assisted early readers with that connection, much of his information coming from the reminiscence written by his uncle Charles.

This poor paternal grandmother (represented by Falconer's grandmother) receives much attention as she is seen as an archetype of Scottish Calvinism and is thus blamed by many critics for laying a weight of theological angst and rebellion upon her famous grandson. Greville certainly carries some responsibility for this caricature, and for glossing over the truly admirable qualities of both fictional and factual grandmothers, such as their adoption and education of illegitimate children. Even MacDonald's own very real love and respect for his paternal grandmother is usually bypassed. But at least she is recognised as a familial influence, for ill or for good. What is less often recognised – if at all – in discussions of MacDonald's religious upbringing is the presence of his maternal relatives who manifest a very different type of Scottish Christian faith than that of dour nay-saying. These Mackays were also very present in his life.

After MacDonald's mother Helen died, her sister Christina MacKay lived with his family until his father remarried. MacDonald's childhood summers were spent with other MacKay relatives on the Banffshire coast. He continued to write letters to his maternal uncles into his adulthood, and it was a MacKay cousin who introduced him to his future wife Louisa (and who was married to Louisa's brother). Indeed numerous letters in MacDonald archives indicate his ongoing intimacy with, and knowledge of, this extended MacKay family. The letters chronicle a family strong in Celtic pride, and with a profoundly conscious and practised faith.

The essence of these letters and the histories of the families they represent is reflected in MacDonald's novels: MacDonald's childhood summers give the backdrop to the Lossiemouth books;[19] his grandparents and great-grandparents of Sutherland, locally respected as ministers and as farmers, can be recognised in such biographically similar characters as Sgt David Barclay in *Heather and Snow*. Family names not only appear in the novels (and in the names of MacDonald's children), but are often repeated: Falconer, Forbes, Hugh, Christina, Kirsty, Barbara, Janet, Mary, Donald, Alister, Alec, Ian, MacKay.[20] Among these MacKays of MacDonald's heritage is found a long history of active promotion of literature, preservation of language, a passion for Scottish culture, and a love of the physical Scottish land. There are many ministers throughout the family tree. However warranted the repeated critical attention to his paternal grandmother and a repressive form of Christianity that MacDonald wished to challenge, this attention has eclipsed the positive role of his maternal family, a family whose faith encompassed their love of literature and folklore, increased their value of land and language, and compelled them to social action. These people too shaped his life and career, and his writing – both the material and the very practice.[21] Perhaps the most historically important of these maternal relatives is MacDonald's mother's brother, the aforementioned Mackintosh MacKay – a man whose spectre is found most visibly in *What's Mine's Mine* (1886).

Mackintosh MacKay is a prime example of that 'classic Gael' Greville describes, with 'his devotion to the soil, his love of liberty, his intolerance of injustice, his eloquence and love of learning'.[22] A farmer's son turned academic and minister, MacKay was widely celebrated in his day for his passionate care of Highland culture, and for his active opposition to the Clearances and forced emigration. And just like characters in his nephew's novels, MacKay's love for the people and the land, for language and story, and for social justice and God were inextricably entwined. MacKay's father – MacDonald's maternal grandfather – Lt Alexander MacKay of Duard Beg, was a tenant farmer who leased land from his clansman Lord Reay, in Strathnaver. This was during the period in which most landowners were clearing their land of people, sheep being more profitable than leases. In an active effort to stop land from falling entirely into southern hands for vast sheep farms, these MacKays chose to sublease their land to other locals.[23] The community placed a high value on learning: the parishes that MacKay's family inhabited were commended in the years of his childhood (and that of MacDonald's mother) for being remarkable in their educational interests, a surveyor writing that in no other part of the Highlands had he found youth with 'a quicker genius for learning': 'thirst after knowledge is great. [...] teachers are received with avidity and gratitude, and their schools well attended'.[24] Many of the MacKay men from this area, including Alexander, were members of the Reay and Sutherland Fencibles, and various aspects of this historical relationship as well as the local attitude towards stewardship and education are found in *Heather and Snow*.

Alexander was the son of Christina Brodie (or 'Kirsty' – also the name of the protagonist in *Heather and Snow* and of the housekeeper in *Ranald Bannerman*), a minister's daughter once engaged to the son of the leading family of the area. That family included in their household and patronage the important Gaelic bard, Rob Donn. Donn thought highly of his young master's intended, not only praising Christina in his poetry, but also writing poetry specifically for her.[25] When the fiancé abandoned his promise whilst abroad, marrying another, Donn's poetic response was damning. Years later Christina's grandson Mackintosh MacKay, although born two years after the famous bard's death, became the first scholar to collect Donn's work into print.

Donn's most famous elegy speaks of the hospitality, joy in the face of poverty, and patronage of the arts that he had experienced in the MacKay family of which he was a part.[26] These community values he celebrates are aspects of MacDonald's Mackay family heritage. They are also the distinctive hallmarks of the brothers Alister and Ian MacRuadh in MacDonald's novel set in the same landscape of Strathnaver, *What's Mine's Mine*. Even more specifically, they are hallmarks directly emphasised in the MacRuadhs' relationship with their own clan poet 'Rob of the Angels'. Interestingly, Alister/Alexander and Ian/John were also the names of MacDonald's siblings to whom he was closest, and elements of those persons can also be traced in the MacRuadh brothers. This should not be surprising considering MacDonald's convictions about hereditary traits. The MacRuadh clan poet, 'Rob of the Angels', is an illiterate underforester who is also a skilled hunter of deer – as was Rob Donn. *What's Mine's Mine* is full of MacKay family history, a history already intentionally celebrated in print by Mackintosh MacKay when he published his collection of Donn's work, which included biographic information and a loving portrait of the Strathnaver landscape.

Mackintosh MacKay did not remain in the rural Strathnaver community, but he continued to manifest family characteristics and concerns on a national level – even in the way he continued in patronage of the MacKay clan's poet. He began his university studies at St Andrews in 1815. In 1820 he carried on in Theology at Glasgow. While a student, MacKay completed his work as editor of the important *Highland Society's Gaelic Dictionary* (1828). At the time, London's *Quarterly Review* suggested that he should be made a Professor of a 'Chair of the Celtic languages' because, although 'still a very young man', MacKay was so well versed in all the 'dialects of the Celtic race'. The paper described him as having 'already done more for the language of the Scottish Gael than any other individual of the present or last age'.[27] In an era in which oral tradition – what MacDonald called 'living literature' – was being lost and when the Scots and Gaelic languages were fading, MacKay applied his own academic training with incredible energy into the conservation of both.[28] His published collection of Rob Donn's poems was as admired for its English essay on Donn's life as it was for its introduction to the Gaelic poetry.[29]

That collection of Donn's poems also raised an issue of supposed vulgarity not dissimilar to that later faced by MacDonald, for some of MacKay's critics definitely considered some of the published poems too uncouth for public consumption. And just as for MacDonald, this was not merely a complaint against rural roughness, but also against the sexuality.[30] Although recent critic Ian Grimble suggested a 'smugness' in MacKay's decision to omit some of Donn's racier stanzas, that decision should be judged by the mores of 1829 rather than those prevailing today.[31] MacKay was already pushing the boundaries of what was then considered decent by not being more ruthless in his editing, and thus risked not finding a publisher – let alone the damning of censorial reviews.[32] A review of Gaelic books in 1832 remarks that the popularity of MacKay's book was certainly hindered because 'it is alleged many of the poems are decidedly immoral'.[33] Grimble surmises that the bawdier poems Mackintosh does include slipped by his censorial eye, but MacKay's introduction to Donn's poems clearly states this is not the case. He explains that he has actually omitted 'not more than six or seven short pieces' of the body of Donn's work – 'humorous sallies, which seemed to us of immoral tendency, or at least unworthy of record' – a choice which, having been intimate with the bard's family and friends, and knowing that Donn had expressed dissatisfaction with some of that earlier work, MacKay feels the poet himself would have desired.[34] MacKay acknowledges that nonetheless among the published poems are 'certain liberties of speech which fastidiousness may wish to censure'. He justifies their publication with a discussion of the difference between cultural improprieties and that which is actually immoral – noting the 'phraseological liberties' of Chaucer in his defence.[35] Far from being prudish, Mackay has been daring – especially in light of his occupation as a renowned Church of Scotland minister. It is also notable that Donn himself was a church elder – the fact that he was chosen to be such despite the ribald nature of some of his poetry indicates that the Christianity of his community had little in common with the stereotype of dour Federal Calvinism.

But Donn was not the only such bard that interested MacKay – he was intimate with a number of Celtic Seanachies from whom he garnered Highland histories, and whose work he promoted.[36] MacKay's own gift of telling Celtic fairy tales was such that it drew the attention of Icelandic folklorist, Þorleifur Repp.[37] MacKay was also editor of the Gaelic newspaper *An Fhianuis* ('The Witness'), partner to Hugh Miller's circulation of the same name to which he also contributed.[38] Walter Scott considered MacKay 'one of the foremost scholars of his day' and sought him out for translation help and to learn Highland histories that later appeared in Scott's novels – sometimes with explicit acknowledgement of MacKay (lending some irony to Richard Reis's comment that 'MacDonald did not know much about the Highlands, but Scott certainly did').[39]

MacKay's publications include a work on Scotland's church history and a translation of Cowper and Newton's *Olney Hymns* into Gaelic.[40] MacKay's nephew George MacDonald was very aware of these literary, cultural, and language-oriented efforts, and even as late as the 1870s, with the aid of Matthew Arnold, MacDonald worked to garner support for a Civil Pension annuity for his Uncle MacKay, though MacKay died before the effort came to fruition.[41] As late as 1893 MacDonald was still endeavouring to have his uncle's achievements adequately honoured, indicating his persisting admiration.[42]

In 1829, the University of Glasgow conferred upon MacKay the degree of LlD. In 1831, he was appointed Justice of the Peace for Invernesshire. In addition to pastoral responsibility for his own parish, he was a very popular guest-preacher, and thus travelled incessantly throughout the Highlands and Islands. In 1849, he became Moderator of the recently founded Free Church. His work as Moderator did not distract him from his wider cultural and political concerns: he saw it as part of his theological responsibility to fight for the native language and land of the Highlands. As one of the all-too-few men of influence who did protest the Clearances, not unlike the fictional MacRuadh of *What's Mine's Mine*, MacKay was practical in his concern. When asked about the necessity of emigration, he said that there was 'no necessity whatsoever, the very idea is monstrous'.[43] But though he believed that the lack of national intervention was suicidal, the monstrous was nonetheless happening – and so he did what he could for those affected.[44] As a result, 'various societies for aiding emigration of Highlanders to the Colonies owed their existence largely to [MacKay's] advocacy'.[45] Indeed MacKay was so zealous about keeping alive the language of the Celtic faith, culture, and history that at the late age of sixty he chose to go to Australia for a decade, so that he might minister to the remote Gaelic communities there.[46] This decision is similar to that of his nephew's character Ian MacRuadh in *What's Mine's Mine*, who travels to visit Canadian clansfolk to ensure they are well, and to assess their situation.

While the nineteenth-century collation of the *Carmina Gadelica* bore witness that too many Protestant clergy were contributing to the dissolution of Gaelic language and poetry, MacDonald's uncle was striving to do exactly the opposite.[47] He was passionate about his people being able to continue worshipping God in their own poetic, communal language. Arguably, MacKay did more for the language and culture in this capacity than through his academic scholarship, travelling all over the Highlands and even in Australia, preaching in Gaelic, and attempting to train more Gaelic ministers.[48] In this as much as in his collection of Donn's songs and through the *Dictionary*, he was trying to preserve a largely oral culture that, as communities were being dissolved, was facing erasure. MacKay also took action by teaching Gaelic and by urging the education commissions that Gaelic-speaking children should be taught to read in their own language first, rather than only in the foreign tongue of English.[49] Mackintosh MacKay was a Celt who did not take words, identity, or community lightly. It is no wonder MacDonald remained conscious and proud of this uncle and his work, and that he wove so many of the convictions that MacKay voiced and practised into *What's Mine's Mine*.

Sometimes MacDonald's own political voice is overlooked; the more familiar the reader is with nineteenth-century Britain, the less likely this is to occur. In *What's Mine's Mine* MacDonald takes a very strong stand against the same Clearances that his uncle fought, and that were still occurring as MacDonald's novel was published. The story is a strong condemnation not only of the cultural genocide and evictions, but also of the abuse and misuse of the land by those who did not know or love it, even accurately predicting the loss of certain wildlife species such as the capercaillie.[50]

> Mr Palmer's doing of good to the country consisted in making the land yield more money into the pockets of Mr Brander and himself by feeding [sheep and certain] wild animals instead of men. To tell such land-owners that they are simply running a tilt at the creative energy, can be of no use: they do not believe in God, however much they may protest and imagine they do.[51]

In the novel MacDonald depicts scenes very reminiscent of those historical ones enacted by the infamous Sutherland factor, Patrick Sellar: in particular Palmer's overseeing of the burning of a croft while the elderly female tenant refuses to leave – and, like that old Margaret MacKay who purportedly suffered under Sellar, MacDonald's Mistress Conal dies only days after her home was destroyed.[52]

Weaving throughout this storied protest, MacDonald presents a challenge to the romanticisation of Scotland by her southern neighbours. The 'romantic interests' in the novel, a pair of urban sisters from the south, see the Celtic people and land through Romantic eyes. The implied pun seems to be intentional. The young women idealise the local 'uncivilised' people, and are attracted to the brothers because they are 'semi-savages'.[53] Intelligent and articulate yet also sentimental, the elder struggles with melancholy; quixotic, the younger eagerly glamourises the local ruins: 'I love old things!' – together the sisters embody many Romantic ideals.[54] Yet the way in which they perceive and thus label the Highlands is philosophically challenged by the native Celtic brothers, men who demand that their community, their homeland, be allowed its own voice: although it shares resonances with England and the Continent, and can be explored through dialogue with certain voices of those places, their Highlands cannot be defined by the terms set by outside – by foreign – voices. It is its own ancient Celtic self.[55]

MacDonald's uncle Mackintosh MacKay inspired MacDonald on a broader scale than the characterisation and literary themes found in *What's Mine's Mine* and in other novels.[56] His life's work is an important prism through which to understand MacDonald's heritage and worldview. This uncle and MacDonald corresponded for years, and MacKay also visited MacDonald's young family. Even while struggling to feed himself in his first years in London, a young MacDonald had sent money to his uncle's relief work during the Highland potato famine.[57] In later years, following the lead of his uncle's linguistic practice, MacDonald not only included Doric dialogue in his Scottish novels – despite the aforementioned criticisms for doing so – but he also paraphrased some of Christ's parables into Doric poems. While Greville contends that this Calvinist Uncle MacKay was proud of MacDonald's genius but was disturbed by some supposed 'heresies', the tenor of these differences was obviously insufficient to impede a close relationship and the sharing of many faith-inspired passions.[58] It was also apparently insufficient to impede MacKay's encouragement of MacDonald's writing, for when MacKay died he left to his nephew's family 'quantities of paper', a far more valuable gift in the mid-nineteenth century than might be immediately recognised today.[59]

Mackintosh MacKay's particular Christian worldview demanded he fight for a continued Highland existence. As a linguist and gatherer of tales, he knew that being physically separated from the landmarks to which identity was married meant that both historical and fantastical stories would be lost.[60] Yet MacKay fought not just against the Clearances, but also for those communities already cleared, aware that once they had been divorced from their established relationship with the land, maintaining community would be difficult. He did not want the evicted to lose their identity; as explained by the MacRuadh brothers at the end of *What's Mine's Mine*, he wanted these banished people to somehow find a deeper sense of home. MacRuadh had stopped the piper's lament and cried out over the weeping of the parting exiles:

> 'My friends,' he cried, in Gaelic of course, 'look at me: my eyes are dry! Where Jesus, the Son of God, is – there is my home! He is here, and he is over the sea, and my home is everywhere! I have lost my land and my country, but I take with me my people, and make no moan over my exile! Hearts are more than hills. Farewell Strathruadh of my childhood! Place of my dreams, I shall visit you again in my sleep! And again I shall see you in happier times, please God, with my friends around me!'[61]

To the emigrated Scots in Australia Mackintosh MacKay carried the same Gaelic message. MacDonald's maternal uncle was a pastor, a storykeeper, and a leader who was seeking to preserve community, language, and lore, in defiance of time and space. A paternal grandmother's Federal Calvinistic fiddle-burning was clearly not the only family legacy that shaped George MacDonald.

As MacDonald writes about the Clearances in *What's Mine's Mine*, he is exploring both the particular and the general – truths of his family, truth for the Scots, but also truths far greater and wider than for a single nation. He is writing about a way of life that has shaped him, participating with his uncle Mackintosh MacKay in that inherited Celtic tradition of which Greville writes; one he claims shaped MacDonald's 'devotion to the soil, his love of liberty, his intolerance of injustice, his eloquence and love of learning'. MacDonald's uncle, his mother's brother Mackintosh MacKay, stood as a living link – as well as a worthy model – to a family that treasured that integration of spiritual and cultural heritage. MacKay's life's practice was to combat a failure to steward the language and stories of his people, believing that such a failure would jeopardise their heritage and identity. Although MacDonald never managed to acquire the ancestral Gaelic his uncle was fighting so hard to preserve, he nonetheless proudly honoured the Scottish language of his youth, and he penned the passions of his uncle. As a result, MacDonald's contemporary countrymen expressed delight and pride at recognising their land and themselves in his pages: it is an element of MacDonald's craft that deserves more consideration by his readers today, for not only was it daring, it was critically intentional.

Notes
1. *The Bookman,* vol 6, 95 (p. 95).
2. William Raeper, *George MacDonald* (Tring: Lion, 1987), p. 35.
3. Ronald MacDonald, 'George MacDonald: A Personal Note', in *From a Northern Window: Papers, Critical, Historiacal and Imaginative,* ed Frederick Watson (London: James Nesbit, 1911), p. 77; Greville MacDonald, *George MacDonald and His Wife* (London: Allen & Unwin, 1924), p. 39.
4. Greville MacDonald, p. 45.
5. Huntly Correspondent (Anon), 'Obituary: George MacDonald', in *Banffshire Journal* (19 September 1905), n. p.
6. The spelling of the first name varies on documents, but this is the most common form.
7. Letter of 9 January 1852, Beinecke Archives, Yale University, MacDonald Archives (GEN 103, Box 5, Folder 195); letter of 19 March 1850, King's College Archives, King's University (GEN 1, Box 1, Folder 3).
8. For example, compare letter of 19 March 1850, King's College Archives, King's University (GEN 1, Box 1, Folder 3) with Greville MacDonald's account of the letter in his biography (p. 130).
9. The original document with Charles's information is in the archives in King's College, London. The quotation here has been presented verbatim, but one may assume that 'cam' or 'caim' was intended instead of 'cain', and that 'waukened' (English 'wakened') was intended instead of 'wankened'.
10. MacDonald considered Scots a language distinct from English, and but one of the Scottish languages: 'These words, as all that passed between [the laird and his clanswoman], were spoken neither in Scotch nor English, but in Gaelic – which, were I able to write it down, most of my readers would no more understand than they would Phoenician' (George MacDonald, *What's Mine's Mine* (Eureka: Sunrise Books Publishers, 1994), p. 44). Whether or not Scots is a language in and of its own right is a matter long debated. It is however officially recognised as a minority language of Europe. Doric, still spoken today in some pockets of Aberdeenshire and the North East, and the local language of MacDonald's Strathbogie region, is distinct yet again from 'Lowland Scots', and numerous scholars and practitioners argue that it is itself a distinct language. However it should be noted for scholastic accuracy that while Horsbroch, on the Scots Language Society website, marks the North East as having one of the five main Scots dialects, and the term 'Doric' as sometimes referring to this dialect, he

prefers to consider 'Doric' as 'juist anither name for Scots itsel'. In the context of this chapter, 'Doric' refers solely to the language spoken by Scots in the North East. While Scots dictionaries are very useful tools to have to hand while reading MacDonald's novels, and some of the family letters, a Doric dictionary is even more helpful.

11. Anonymous, '*Marquis of Lossie*: A Review', *The North American Review*, no. 258 (September–October 1877), p. 385.
12. David Christie Murray, *My Contemporaries in Fiction* (London: Chatto & Windus, 1897), p. 114.
13. Quoted in Barbara Amell, 'Portent of Prejudice', *Wingfold* 48 (2004), pp. 42–45 (p. 42). This scathing review is an excellent example of how vastly a cultural expectation of representation has changed in the last hundred and fifty years – while today an accurately replicated accent would be expected, it was then a risky and controversial undertaking. To the English Victorian middle classes – by then voracious readers – the Scots oral tradition itself was seen as impolite and low-class: 'local vulgarism'. To place it before one's readership could be considered an affront.
14. William Clarke, 'A Great Scottish Teacher', *Blackwood's Magazine*, May 1875 (pp. 382–83), p. 383.
15. George MacDonald, 'St. George's Day', *A Dish of Orts* (London: Sampson, Low, Marston, 1893), p. 78.
16. Glenn Sadler's collection of letters includes a MacDonald family tree dating back to the early seventeenth century – but Sadler does not trace the maternal lineage, the MacKays (Glenn Edward Sadler (ed), *An Expression of Character: The Letters of George MacDonald* (Grand Rapids, MI: Eerdmans, 1994), pp. xviii–xix). Greville MacDonald's biography includes numerous pages on MacDonald's paternal heritage, yet when he remarks that the maternal side of the family has members 'renowned in science and travel, in adventure and arms, in piety and politics', it is the fame of MacDonald's mother's cousins rather than of his direct ancestors that Greville then depicts.
17. Ronald MacDonald, 'George MacDonald: A Personal Note', p. 77.
18. Some also briefly note connections in *Malcolm* to MacDonald's paternal great-grandfather who was a piper on the north-east coast, and a survivor of Culloden. Greville MacDonald has also indicated the similarities between David Elginbrod and MacDonald's father.
19. MacDonald's paternal forebear was also a refugee and piper on that coast.
20. One of MacDonald's most treasured books was *History of the House and Clan of Mackay* (1829) by Robert MacKay, which contains a detailed map of the region that is the setting for *What's Mine's Mine*. MacDonald's careful attention to the book included handwritten annotations (Greville MacDonald, p. 48). It follows the family history up to MacDonald's grandfather and his issue, including Mackintosh (Robert MacKay, *History of the House and Clan of Mackay* (Edinburgh: Andrew Jack, 1829), p. 559).
21. Archived letters also show that MacDonald was close to his Highland stepmother and to her family – further Celtic influence that MacDonald made evident in the dedication of *The Portent* to his stepmother's uncle. MacDonald's *Hamlet* was dedicated to another of the McColl Gaels (Greville MacDonald, p. 53).
22. Greville MacDonald does not completely overlook MacKay – in fact he says MacKay must be mentioned 'because of his intimacy' with MacDonald – but the detail given is insufficient for a character so important to Highland history, let alone to MacDonald studies (p. 47). William Raeper also mentions MacKay, but it is basically a reiteration of Greville, without due exploration of the effects upon MacDonald. Considering the

comments in Raeper's last essay before his tragic death, it seems likely this was territory into which he had planned to venture further.

23. Mackintosh MacKay later became very active in promoting this option of leasing, to improve conditions and counter arguments for clearance. See Allan W. MacColl, *Land, Faith And the Crofting Community: Christianity and Social Criticism in the Highlands of Scotland, 1843–1893* (Edinburgh: Edinburgh University Press, 2006), p. 27.
24. *Autobiographical Journal by John MacDonald, Schoolmaster and Soldier 1770–1830*, ed Angus MacKay (Edinburgh: Norman Macleod, 1906), p. 11.
25. Ian Grimble, *The World of Robb Donn* (Edinburgh: The Saltire Society, 1999), pp. 58–62. The man Donn is specifically praising, and lamenting, is Ian MacEachainn (in English, 'John MacKay'), father of Christina's intended.
26. Charles Rogers, *The Modern Scottish Minstrel* (Edinburgh: Adam & Charles Black, North Bridge, 1855), p. 318.
27. Anonymous, 'Book Review of *Orain le Rob Donn, &c. – Songs and Poems in the Gaelic Language by Robert MacKay, the celebrated bard of Lord Reay's country; with a Memoir of the Author* by McIntosh MacKay', in *Quarterly Review* (1831), pp. 358–66 (p. 359).
28. George MacDonald, *Alec Forbes* (London: Hurst & Blackett, 1865), p. 219.
29. *Quarterly Review*, p. 359.
30. For a discussion of how MacDonald was taken to task by Ruskin for including sexually inappropriate material in a fairy tale, see http://research-repository.st-andrews.ac.uk/bitstream/10023/1887/6/KirstinJeffreyJohnsonPhDThesis. Clearly Ruskin – and some London publishers – had a more restrictive sense of what was appropriate for publication than either Reverend MacKay or the minister MacDonald.
31. Ian Grimble, *The World of Robb Donn* (Edinburgh: The Saltire Society, 1999), p. 102.
32. Mackintosh MacKay, *Songs and poems: in the Gaelic language By Rob Donn* (Inverness: R. Douglas, 1829), p. xlviii.
33. John Reid, *Bibliotheca Scoto-celtica; Or, An Account of All the Books Which Have Been Printed in the Gaelic Language* (Glasgow: J. Reid, 1832), p. 71.
34. Mackintosh MacKay, p. xlix.
35. Mackintosh MacKay, p. xlviii.
36. Greville MacDonald, p. 43; George Henderson, *The Poems of John Morison, The Songsmith of Harris* (Glasgow: Norman MacLeod, 1843), p. 12. Seanachies were bearers of old lore, the culture, history, and laws of the people preserved in oral memory, recited by the bards. One such man was John Morison (*Gobha Na Hearadh*), the 'songsmith of Harris', who named a son after MacKay (Henderson, p. 2).
37. Andrew Wawn, *The Anglo Man: Þorleifur Repp, Philology and Nineteenth Century Britain* (Reykjavík: Bókaútgáfa Menningarsjóðs, 1991), p. 114.
38. Henderson, p. 20.
39. Walter Scott, *Journal of Sir Walter Scott* (London: David Douglas, 1891), p. 821; Richard Reis, *George MacDonald* (New York: Twayne Publishers, 1972), p. 70. Scott's *The Two Drovers* explicitly acknowledges MacKay's aid.
40. Hew Scott, *Fasti ecclesiæ scoticanæ; the succession of ministers in the Church of Scotland from the reformation* (Edinburgh: Tweedale Court, 1923), p. 24.
41. Greville MacDonald, p. 412. MacKay died in 1873.
42. King's College Archives, King's College, London, George MacDonald Papers, 1/1/74.
43. MacColl, p. 48.
44. MacColl, p. 24. In an article for Hugh Miller's *The Witness* (17 June 1848) MacKay wrote: 'The depopulation of a country is a matter of national concern. Let the national

councils consider it in time' (MacColl, p. 28). For MacKay the whole clearance and emigration debate was inseparable not only from issues of faith, but also from the responsibilities of the Church. In his 1853 Highland Committee report to the Free Church General Assembly he referred to these two evils as 'a disturbing force upon the social and economic temporal condition of our adhering population'. He suggested that 'with the poor laws on the one hand [...] and the profits, as they are thought to be, of sheep-farming on the other, there seems practically a crusade against the whole population of the Highlands and Islands'. Recognising the legal limitations of the Church, he nonetheless voices the 'strong temptation to enunciate our own judgments upon such points, especially when we see such controversies waged between the rich on one hand, and the poor on the other'. Like the MacRuadh brothers, in 1853 MacKay actively counselled against violent reaction or confrontation: 'Be not overcome with evil, but overcome evil with good'.

45. W. A. Sanderson, *Jubilee History of St Andrew's Presbyterian Church, Carleton (The Gaelic Church)* (Melbourne: Arbuckle, Waddle & Fawkner, 1905), p. 20.
46. During MacKay's time in Australia, MacDonald continued to correspond with his uncle across the great distance. Remarkably, a sermon by MacKay in 1855, published by George Robertson, marks the inception of Australian publishing (see Australian Dictionary of Biography, http://adb.anu.edu.au/biography/robertson-george-4489 – accessed 7 July 2012). Another twenty-three years passed before Cambridge UK published the first Australian book. For further detail of MacKay's biography, see Macpherson's *Glimpses of Church* (1893) and Sanderson's *Jubilee History* (1905).
47. A. W. MacColl has published (2007) a carefully researched challenge to received opinion that few Scottish ministers were interested in preserving Highland culture. He addresses the largely ignored response of Scotland's evangelical church to the land problems of the nineteenth century, their action due in no small part to biblical and cultural notions of identity and economic justice, and which 'drew more and more upon the communitarian notion of the people's right to possess their ancestral land' (p. 5).
48. Knowledge of MacKay's endeavours gives further insight to MacDonald's regretful remark to his former Gaelic teacher, 'I might have been the minister of a parish in the Highlands of Scotland' (Raeper, p. 35).
49. Victor Durkacz, *The Decline of the Celtic Languages* (Edinburgh: J. Donald, 1983), p. 164.
50. *What's Mine's Mine*, p. 339.
51. *What's Mine's Mine*, p. 339.
52. *What's Mine's Mine*, p. 392.
53. *What's Mine's Mine*, p. 76.
54. *What's Mine's Mine*, p. 4.
55. A perspective later reiterated by both Raeper and Colin Manlove. Manlove writes that 'Romanticism itself owes a huge debt' to certain Scottish literatures – indicating that those literatures had (and have) their own intact identity (Colin Manlove (ed), *An Anthology of Scottish Fantasy Literature* (Edinburgh: Polygon, 1996), p. 11).
56. For the many character parallels, see in particular Kennedy's descriptions and photo in *Disruption Worthies of the Northern Highlands* (1877) and MacKay's own article in Hugh Miller's *The Witness* (17 June 1848).
57. Greville MacDonald, p. 107. MacKay worked 'strenuously to alleviate' the suffering in the Highlands caused by the potato famine from 1846 to 1848 (Greville MacDonald, p. 215).

58. Greville MacDonald, p. 47.
59. cf. Beinecke Library, George MacDonald Archives, Box 29, miscellaneous.
60. For example, consider the following: 'Your uncle was the only man to have ever climbed that cliff – do you know the story?' 'Let me tell you why this is called the "Fairie's Ben".'
61. *What's Mine's Mine*, p. 416.

Bibliography

Amell, Barbara, 'Portent of Prejudice', *Wingfold*, Vol 48, Fall 2004, pp. 42-45.
Anonymous, 'An Interview', *The Bookman: a review of books and life*, Volume 6 (1898), p. 95.
Anonymous, 'Book Review of *Orain le Rob Donn, &c. - Songs and Poems in the Gaelic Language by Robert MacKay, the celebrated bard of Lord Reay's country; with a Memoir of the Author* by McIntosh MacKay', *The Quarterly Review* (1831) pp. 358-66.
Anonymous, '*Marquis of Lossie*: A Review', *The North American Review*, no. 258 (September-October 1877), p. 385.
Anonymous, 'New Books: *Malcolm* by George MacDonald', *Wingfold*, vol 42, Spring 2003, pp. 25-26.
Clarke, William, 'A Great Scottish Teacher', *Blackwood's Magazine* (May 1875), pp. 382-83.
Durkacz, Victor Edward, *The Decline of the Celtic Languages: A Study of Linguistic and Cultural Conflict in Scotland, Wales and Ireland from the Reformation to the Twentieth Century* (Edinburgh: J. Donald, 1983).
Grimble, Ian, *The World of Robb Donn* (Edinburgh: The Saltire Society, 1999).
Henderson, George, *The Poems of John Morison, The Songsmith of Harris: Collected and edited with a Memoir* (Glasgow: Norman MacLeod, 1843).
'Huntly Correspondent' (Anon), 'Obituary: George MacDonald', in *Banffshire Journal* (19 September 1905, n.p.).
Kennedy, John, '*Dr McIntosh MacKay (1793-1873)*' Disruption Worthies of the Northern Highlands, 1881, Scalpay Free Church of Scotland, http://www.scalpayfreechurchofscotland.co.uk/rte/files/Dr_Mackay.asp. [accessed 17 February 2007].
MacColl, Allan W., *Land, Faith And the Crofting Community: Christianity and Social Criticism in the Highlands of Scotland, 1843-1893* (Edinburgh: Edinburgh University Press, 2006).
MacDonald, Charles, C. F. MacDonald, June, 1885. MacDonald 6/12 19 SEP 2003 (King's College London Archives).
MacDonald, George, *Alec Forbes* (London: Hurst & Blackett, 1865).
— *Heather and Snow* (Whitefish, Montana: Kessinger Publishing, 2004).
— 'St George's Day', in *A Dish of Orts* (London: Sampson, Low, Marston, 1893), pp. 77-140.
— *What's Mine's Mine* (Eureka, California: Sunrise Books, 1994).
MacDonald, Greville, *George MacDonald and His Wife* (London: Allen & Unwin, 1924).
MacDonald, John, *Autobiographical Journal by John MacDonald, Schoolmaster and Soldier 1770-1830*, ed Angus MacKay (Edinburgh: Norman Macleod, 1906).
MacDonald, Ronald, 'George MacDonald: A Personal Note' in *From A Northern Window: Papers, Critical, Historical and Imaginative*, ed Frederick Watson (London: James Nesbit, 1911), pp. 55-113.
MacKay, Angus MacKay, *The Book of MacKay* (Edinburgh: Norman MacLeod, 1906).
MacKay, Robert, *History of the House and Clan of Mackay* (Edinburgh: Andrew Jack, 1929).

MacKay, Mackintosh, *Songs and poems: in the Gaelic language by Rob Donn* (Inverness: R. Douglas, 1829).
Macpherson, Alexander, *Glimpses of Church and Social Life in the Highlands in Olden Time* (Edinburgh: Blackwood, 1893).
Manlove, Colin N., *Scottish Fantasy Literature: A Critical Survey* (Edinburgh: Canongate Academic, 1994).
Raeper, William, *George MacDonald: Novelist and Victorian Visionary* (Tring: Lion Publishing, 1987).
Reid, John, *Bibliotheca Scoto-celticæ; Or, An Account of All the Books Which Have Been Printed in the Gaelic Language* (Glasgow: J. Reid, 1832).
Reis, Richard R., *George MacDonald* (New York: Twayne Publishers, 1972).
Rogers, Charles, *The Modern Scottish Minstrel; Or, The Songs Of Scotland Of The Past Half Century. With Memoirs Of The Poets, And Sketches And Specimens In English Verse Of The Most Celebrated Modern Gaelic Bards* (Edinburgh: Adam & Charles Black, 1855).
Sadler, Glenn Edward (ed), *An Expression of Character: The Letters of George MacDonald* (Grand Rapids, MI: Eerdmans, 1994).
Sanderson, W. A., *Jubilee History of St Andrew's Presbyterian Church, Carleton (The Gaelic Church)* (Melbourne: Arbuckle, Waddle & Fawkner, 1905).
Scott, Hew, *Fasti ecclesiæ scoticanæ; the succession of ministers in the Church of Scotland from the reformation* (Edinburgh: Tweedale Court, 1923).
Wawn, Andrew, *The Anglo Man: Þorleifur Repp, Philology and Nineteenth Century Britain* (Reykjavík: Bókaútgáfa Menningarsjóðs, 1991).

How the Fairies were not Invited to Court

JOHN PATRICK PAZDZIORA

'The world of novel readers owe a debt of gratitude to Mr George Macdonald [sic], for more than one touching picture of Scottish peasant life, for many refined examples of religious thought, and above all for one of the most moving ballads that ever caused a superstitious shudder'.[1] So Andrew Lang began an unfavourable review of *Thomas Wingfold, Curate* (1876). The quotation is telling, not only because Lang, one of the most influential critics of the nineteenth century,[2] identifies MacDonald first as a novelist, and also as a high-ranking poet. It demonstrates the esteem with which Lang held MacDonald, so much so that in reviewing one of his novels, he felt 'pain and diffidence' at damning it with faint praise.

While I need hardly say that there remains much critical work to be done on George MacDonald, even less critical work has been done on Andrew Lang. Nevertheless, it still comes as a surprise that there is, as far as I can ascertain, no criticism at all comparing these two Scottish men of letters. Nor is it, as is the case with Oscar Wilde, that Lang's connection with MacDonald is invisible or nonexistent. Lang read, reviewed, and enjoyed MacDonald; thus, given Lang's stature as a critic, it seems reasonable to assume that MacDonald was at least aware of him. Both found much of their literary identity within the Scottish tradition, particularly in relation to Scottish folklore. And of the Victorians, perhaps only Joseph Jacobs' name is as firmly linked to fairy tales as Lang and MacDonald. Although there are many places to begin such a comparative study, I wish to begin with what for many readers was surely their first introduction to these complex literary figures: fairy tales.

'To Forget and Omit Nothing'

Lang considered William Makepeace Thackeray's *The Rose and the Ring* (1854) to be the exemplar of the literary fairy tale. Writing in 1905, he said 'The old, old fairy tales *are* the best: it is a very difficult thing to write a good fairy story nowadays, but if I know a really good one, it is *The Rose and the Ring*'.[3] Thackeray himself was among the first of the Victorian literati to recognise MacDonald's genius, accepting the first version of *The Portent* (1860) for publication in the inaugural issue of the *Cornhill Magazine*.[4] In relating Thackeray to MacDonald and Lang, however, it seems that in this instance the students have arguably surpassed the master. *The Rose and the Ring* is a rambunctious sprawling satire written in a cloying, flowery style that mimics Perrault and Madame d'Aulnoy; the fairy tale elements are presented as little more than frame narrative for a barrage of pointed witticism. Uli Knoepflmacher correctly calls the book a thinly veiled 'racy comedy of manners'[5] hung on the plot of *Hamlet* – a literary theft Thackeray himself takes pains to point out.[6]

MacDonald suggested in 'The Fantastic Imagination' (1893) that '[t]o be able to live in an imagined world, we must see the laws of its existence obeyed' – that is, the created literary world must be consistent, however fantastic, an idea J. R. R. Tolkien would later elaborate in 'On Fairy-stories'.[7] If there is such a controlling law in *The Rose and the Ring*, then it must be *inconsistency*. The story is riddled with internal contradictions and anachronisms of which the characters are fully aware. Prince Bulbo, for instance, declares to Rosalba that she is the fairest woman 'in all Europe, Asia, Africa, and America, nay, in Australia, only it is not yet discovered' (p. 84). Despite the sparkle and humour of the prose, the brilliance of the satire, and a few genuinely striking passages, *The Rose and the Ring* never takes itself seriously. Lang is correct when he writes that 'Thackeray burlesques [fairy tale] with kindly mockery'.[8]

The stories by MacDonald and Lang that most obviously follow Thackeray in parodying the French *conte* (the eighteenth-century literary fairy tale form) – *The Light Princess* (1862) and *Prince Prigio* (1889) – are quite different in tone. While Thackeray considered *The Rose and the Ring* to be a pantomime, a literary game that readers could join in, both MacDonald and Lang wrote within a larger theoretical framework of the importance, and even the necessity, of fairy tales; their works demonstrate a deep empathy with the form. In this, they share a common purpose that separates them from Thackeray. However, the difference between their respective uses of fairy tale manifests itself in their stories; *Prince Prigio* and *The Light Princess* both emulate and react against Thackeray, but in different ways. This contrast in tone and effect emerges at least partly because of their authors' distinct approaches to the fairy tale tradition.

Jack Zipes has argued that *The Light Princess* 'reflects MacDonald's disrespectful attitude toward traditional folktales and fairy tales'.[9] Certainly, MacDonald had no qualms about playfully ridiculing the literary fairy tale tradition; he felt no need to preserve the usual structures. The Grimms, Andersen, and Perrault are all conspicuous by their absence in 'The Fantastic Imagination'. But it seems more precise to say not simply that MacDonald disrespected traditional fairy tales, but that he re-appropriated them to his own ends; with his deep understanding of not just literary fairy tales but the folklore behind them, he seems to have seen himself in a living, ongoing storytelling tradition. He could thus be free to manipulate and arrange the traditional materials in ways that pleased him, which, as Zipes says, 'freed him to explore personal and social problems to a degree that fostered his radicalism and innovation'.[10]

Both *The Light Princess* and *Prince Prigio* begin with the same structural motif: the absence of a fairy or magical being at a royal christening (combining the motifs F361.1.1 and V87).[11] Thackeray employs the same motif in chapter IV, 'How Blackstick Was Not Asked to Angelica's Christening'. But here the omission is deliberate, even hostile: 'When Princess Angelica was born, her parents did not only not ask the Fairy Blackstick to the christening party, but gave orders to their porter, absolutely to refuse her if she called' (p. 16). The princess's royal parents are simply being pragmatic. Fairy Blackstick wants to retire from fairy-godmothering, and attends christenings only grudgingly. She has taken to giving her royal godchildren the eminently practical, character-building gift of 'misfortune' instead of 'an invisible jacket, a flying horse, a Fortunatus's purse, or some other valuable token of her favour' (p. 12). This seems to be the motif of a fairy controlling a mortal's destiny (labelled as F312.2) rather than the expected motif of the fairy blessing the child (F312.1). In a gesture typical of the work, Thackeray gives the guests at the christening the role of the audience, expecting the tale to proceed according to a certain formula; they complain bitterly when the tale is changed, even though Fairy Blackstick's malediction has largely do with their own nascent treachery. The characters, like perhaps the reader, prefer a roseate and romantic fairy presence, rather than stoic lessons about life. Princess Angelica's parents, then, have finally realised that Fairy Blackstick's presence is undesirable. And this, of course, is the one christening at which she appears uninvited, to the discomfiture of the porter.

Similarly, Lang begins *Prince Prigio* with the chapter 'How the Fairies were not Invited to Court'.[12] This neglect of invitation is entirely the fault of the Queen of Pantouflia, 'who was clever and learned, and who had hated dolls when she was a child' (p. 5). Even though the king and the queen are not able to have children, Lang tell us, the queen refuses to consult the fairies: 'She did not believe in fairies: she said that they had never existed; and that she maintained, though *The History of the Royal Family* was full of chapters about nothing else' (pp. 5–6). Indeed, the king her husband is the grandson of Cinderella and the great-grandson of Prince Giglio (pp. 5, 73). In the fairyland kingdom of Pantouflia, where fairy tales are sober history, the queen's staunch materialism is ludicrous, itself an incredible act of superstition. She continues to deny the existence of fairies throughout the story. When, at the christening party, the only guests who show up are a hundred fairies, 'the queen, though she saw them distinctly, took no notice of them' (p. 8). The fairies proceed to bless her son, Prince Prigio, with all the presents Fairy Blackstick refused to give Giglio: the purse of Fortunatus, seven-league boots, a magic carpet, and so on (p. 9). But one fairy – not evil, just 'a cross old thing' – curses Prigio to be like his mother: 'My child, you shall be *too* clever!' (p. 9). Prigio's curse and his mother's erudition are one and the same: they are too clever to believe in fairies. Yet folk belief and the fairy tradition, Lang argues, contain a rich cultural heritage which the man of letters should seek to recover. In 1873 he wrote:

> We must remember, what we are so prone to forget, the quite unbroken nature of peasant-life, and peasant-faith. The progressive classes had advanced comparatively but a little way in the evolution of creeds and customs when they left the rural people behind. They have turned their back on these again and again, in moments of spiritual excitement, have compelled them to put on a semblance of new belief, and to call on gods not of their making. But the superstitious instinct has permitted the masses to forget and omit nothing of old cults and old rites. [...] If any of the very earliest myths remain in Europe, they must linger in the quiet places where such peasants tell their fairy tales, by the hearth, or in the olive shade.[13]

Lang's theories inform not only his *Fairy Book* anthologies, but the writing of his own fairy tales as well. Pantouflia is a kingdom that has forgotten none of the 'old cults and old rites'; the queen and Prigio have forgotten them through over-zealousness for the new 'creeds and customs' of Enlightenment rationalism. Lang's fairy tale is Prigio's unwitting quest to rediscover his cultural and imaginative heritage, and find his place in his story.

In *The Light Princess*, MacDonald's handling of fairy magic is quite different. The fault of royal childlessness is not, as in Lang, the queen's. For MacDonald, the fault is the king's. As Knoepflmacher observes, the king seems to be 'so sexually naive that he does not know how to go about begetting the offspring he desires'.[14] Even when this childlessness is remedied, it is not with a son; the king remains unable to produce a male heir. But it is not sufficient to reduce the king's ineptitude simply to sexual terms; he seems generally fumbling and absentminded. The trouble with the christening is not, in fact, with the fairies at all, but with the king's own sister, Princess Makemnoit. The king forgets to invite her to the christening, and when she shows up anyway he forgets he forgot to invite her.[15] MacDonald tells us that the king's father similarly forgot to include Makemnoit in his will, leaving her impoverished, 'and so it was no wonder that her brother forgot her in writing his invitations' (p. 3). With a stinging social criticism underlying his drollery, MacDonald writes: 'poor relations don't do anything to keep you in mind of them. Why don't they? The king could not see into the garret she lived in, could he?' (p. 3). The fairies have nothing to do with it. The king has failed not only his sexual responsibility to father a prince, but also failed his own family and the poor of his realm. His oppressive forgetfulness returns to curse his child; this 'atrocious aunt' is a witch of considerable power, and under the guise of doting-old-auntie curses the child with the loss of gravity, in every sense of the word (p. 5).

Makemnoit is not merely 'cross', she is exceptionally wicked: 'In fact she was a witch; and when she bewitched anybody, he very soon had enough of it; for she beat all the wicked fairies in wickedness and all the clever fairies in cleverness' (p. 3). In the frame story MacDonald built around *The Light Princess* in *Adela Cathcart* (1864), Mr Armstrong, a clergyman, objects to the christening scene as being impossible. He says:

> I think [...] there is a real objection to that scene. It is, that no such charm could have had any effect where holy water was employed as the medium. In fact I doubt if the wickedness could have been wrought in a chapel at all.[16]

Although John Smith, as the Carrollian narrator in *Adela Cathcart*, agrees – 'I hold up the four paws of my mind, and crave indulgence'[17] – MacDonald as the narrator does not; he evades the issue, leaving it haunting the reader's mind. When he reused the christening-curse motifs in 'Little Daylight' (1871), he wrote:

> In all history we find that fairies give their remarkable gifts to prince or princess, or any child of sufficient importance in their eyes, always at the christening. Now this we can understand, because it is an ancient custom among human beings as well; and it is not hard to explain why wicked fairies should choose the same time to do unkind things; but it is difficult to understand how they should be able to do them, for you would fancy all wicked creatures would be powerless on such an occasion. But I never knew of any interference on the part of a wicked fairy that did not turn out a good thing in the end. (*Fairy Tales*, p. 280)

Again, MacDonald refuses to address the question didactically or moralistically; he only hints, letting the rest of the tale play out the conundrum. Little Daylight dwells only in the night, the Light Princess is a trial and a grief to her parents, and yet these afflictions came about at their respective christenings. MacDonald is playing here with the idea of liminal time, which he employed earlier to great effect in 'The Shadows' (1857), the concept that on certain occasions and times of year fairies had greater influence in the world; certainly childbirth was one of those times.[18] MacDonald is concerned with showing not only the playful, pantomime face of Faerie, but its darker, malevolent aspect as well.

Metamorphoses

Even in a form so flippant as the *conte*, fairies remain perilous. The fairies, and the gifts of the fairies, are not to be lightly ignored. On this, the stories maintain a tacit agreement. The impetus for the crisis in all three narratives is the neglect of the fairies and a dismissal of their gifts. The result in each case is bodily metamorphosis and estrangement of the recipient from normal human society. In *The Rose and the Ring*, the trials of Prince Giglio and Princess Rosalba are the substance of Fairy Blackstick's gift, and it would not have suited Thackeray's purposes of plot to have any curse placed directly on Princess Angelica. So it is the porter, Gruffanuff, who incurs Fairy Blackstick's revenge. Thackeray makes quite clear that Gruffanuff deserves his punishment: not only does he say the royal family is not at home when they obviously are, he 'made the most *odious vulgar sign* as he was going to slam the door in the Fairy's face' and, when she still refuses to leave, asks her '"whether she thought he was a-going to stay at that there door hall [sic] day?"' (p. 16, emphasis in original). Fairy Blackstick turns his mockery against him, letting his taunt become his punishment. The passage recalls Ovid's *Metamorphoses*:

> as the Fairy waved her wand over him, he felt himself rising off the ground, and fluttering up against the door, and then, as if a screw ran into his stomach, he felt a dreadful pain there, and was pinned to the door; and then his arms flew up over his head; and his legs, after writhing about wildly, twisted under his body; and then he felt cold, cold, growing over him, as if he was turning into metal, and he said: "O—o—H'm!" and could say no more, because he was dumb. (pp. 17–18)

The description drips with malicious glee. Thackeray seems to have created the character specifically to inflict this punishment on him. Gruffanuff is described as being a strong and physically imposing man; he got his job as a porter by being so good at intimidating tradesmen (p. 16). Accordingly, his punishment is diminution and distortion of his body, and loss of speech. Gruffanuff exists only in one dimension; he is a caricature of a particular vice – or perhaps, more accurately, a caricature of a caricature of vice. Certainly, the sequence appears to be a predecessor to Belloc's *Cautionary Tales for Children* (1908). But if the character is deliberately monochromatic, the punishment is polyvalent. Gruffanuff, big, loud, and physical, is reduced to helplessness through the sensible and intellectual fairy. As fairy tale punishments go, this exhibits an inventive cruelty comparable to the Grimms' most grotesque executions:

> He *was* turned into metal! He was from being *brazen, brass!* He was neither more nor less than a knocker. And there he was, nailed to the door in the blazing summer day, till he burned almost red-hot; and there he was, nailed to the door all the bitter winter nights, till his brass nose was dropping with icicles. And the postman came and rapped at him, and the vulgarest boy with a letter came and hit him up against the door. (p. 18, emphasis in original)

Significantly, as Gruffanuff is exposed to the elements and humiliated by people he would ordinarily despise, he retains full consciousness and physical sensation. In other words, he remains present, but unnoticed. His wife and employers eventually decide he has run off to Australia – which has of course not been discovered yet – and he is eventually completely forgotten (p. 19). The physical distortion precludes a complete erasure of his identity, and he is forced to watch his own demise. The substance of Gruffanuff's punishment may be akin to that of Scrooge in Dickens's *A Christmas Carol* (1843): to watch unseen as people scorn and forget him after his death.

Strikingly, Prince Prigio undergoes a similar experience at the hands of the fairies: to be present but absent, unseen and thus nonexistent. His mother the queen shoved all his magical gifts into the lumber room.[19] Now a young man, and disowned by his family for being too clever, Prigio discovers the gifts; he does not know their powers, but considers them more appropriate to wear in the rain than his other clothes. A series of chaotic and hysterical encounters follow, as Prigio utterly fails to realise he's wearing the cap of darkness and seven-league boots. He goes into a tavern but not only can he get no service, a burly soldier even sits on top of him (pp. 31–33). Nor do things improve when Prigio storms out of the tavern in a huff:

> He was not put in a better temper by the way in which people hustled him in the street. They ran against him exactly as if they did not see him, and then staggered back in the greatest surprise, looking in every direction for the person they had jostled. In one

> of these encounters, the prince pushed so hard against a poor old beggar woman that she fell down. As he was usually most polite, he pulled off his cap to beg her pardon, when, behold, the beggar woman gave one dreadful scream, and fainted! (p. 33)

Prigio is frustrated still more when he puts his cap back on and the bystanders 'rushed away in every direction, with cries of terror, declaring that there was a magician in town, and a fellow who could appear and disappear at pleasure!' (p. 34). He sees the reaction to his invisibility as a personal affront. From his own perspective he is continually present and visible; his sense of identity and importance remains unaltered. But the other characters behave as if he isn't there; nor are their reactions to him anything other than happenstance brought about by his own ignorance. The problem, the narrator explains, is that Prigio does not realise that he is the hero of a fairy tale. He has fallen into the story without knowing it:

> By this time, you or I, or anyone who was not so extremely clever as Prince Prigio, would have understood what was the matter. [...] But the prince was so extremely wise, and learned, and scientific, that he did not believe in fairies, nor in fairy gifts.
> 'It is indigestion,' he said to himself: 'those sausages were not of the best; and that Burgundy was extremely strong. Things are not as they appear.' [...]
> Here, as he was arguing with himself, he was nearly run over by a splendid carriage and six, the driver of which never took the slightest notice of him. (pp. 34–36)

Because Prigio's brilliant intellectualism does not allow for fairy gifts, he forces the conclusion that what is happening to him cannot be happening.

Here Lang is almost certainly evoking Dickens's *A Christmas Carol*, specifically the scene when, as Lang puts it, 'Mr Scrooge vainly pleads the popular theory of the origin of hallucinations: "You may be an undigested bit of beef, a blot of mustard, a crumb of cheese, a fragment of an underdone potato"'.[20] This 'popular theory' serves Prigio rather worse than it does Scrooge; in fact, it almost kills him. Writing a 1900 introduction to Dickens's *Christmas Stories*, Lang says, 'We are in a world "not realised", and common sense has long bullied us out of any serious attempt to realise some of its phenomena'.[21] The result of not appreciating the fairies' gifts is a highly intellectual, brilliantly educated ignorance; if Prigio had not been so learned, Lang says, he would have recognised the fairy gifts for what they were. By educating himself out of knowledge of the fairies, he winds up ostracised from the real world, in which fairies and fairy gifts do exist. Lang almost seems to be bullying Prigio back into realisation.

Thackeray and Lang use the bodily transformation and invisibility to touch on a theme which seems to have been reasonably common in Victorian fantasy: the relationship between individuality and presence, whether one can retain one's identity when one cannot be perceived. Scrooge's unseen journeys into assorted Christmases have already been mentioned; but invisibility, and invisible witness of everyday life, also occurs in the writings of Lewis Carroll and Edward Lear.[22] Prigio, of course, does not undergo any grotesque metamorphosis, but like Gruffanuff he suffers the loss of bodily presence and personal dignity. Deprived of physical presence, and the attendant politeness people show him because of his royalty, he overhears unguarded conversation about himself. Whereas Gruffanuff's punishment is meant as humiliation, Prigio's is educational. He learns to see the monstrous pun of the entire story: he is in fact an insufferable prig. The self-awareness afforded to him by his unwitting encounter with fairy-tale phenomena is what allows him to assume his role as the hero of the story, as the fairy-tale prince. Prigio has been living in a world of story and wonder, yet he needs to be partly removed from it in order to see it. Thus enlightened, he can combine his profound intellectual knowledge with the rules and magic of his fairy tale.

So it is all the more striking that the device of invisibility does *not* appear alongside the bodily transformation in *The Light Princess*. Thackeray takes some trouble to make Gruffanuff deserving of his painful metamorphosis; Prigio's discomfiture is ultimately benign. MacDonald, however, places the bodily transformation of the princess at the beginning of the tale, and accentuates the innocence of the victim. Whereas Thackeray and Lang have used metamorphosis as an incidental plot device, MacDonald hangs his entire narrative on it. The transformation of the princess occurs at the christening, as the witch's curse. The passage seems dissonant with the rest of the opening; MacDonald creates the disjointed effect of unease in the midst of merriment. Makemnoit mutters her curse:

> They all thought she had lost her wits, and was repeating some foolish nursery rhyme; but a shudder went through the whole of them notwithstanding. The baby, on the contrary, began to laugh and crow; while the nurse gave a start and a smothered cry, for she thought she was struck with paralysis: she could not feel the baby in her arms. But she clasped it tight and said nothing.
> The mischief was done. (p. 4)

MacDonald's depth of knowledge in folklore and the fairy tradition is in evidence throughout his fiction, and seems to inform this scene. As mentioned above, childbirth was considered to be a particularly dangerous time, with both mother and child at risk of being taken by the fairies.[23] Sir Walter Scott reported that 'in the period intervening between birth and baptism [...] children were believed to be particularly liable to abstraction by the fairies, and mothers chiefly dreaded the substitution of changelings in the place of their own offspring'.[24] Witches, too, were feared during this time, and were considered more wantonly cruel than fairies.[25] Beneath the levity of the narrative, the actual events of the story seem all the more sinister. Happenings which are hilarious to the reader are fearful and terrifying to the characters. Notice that the nurse reacts with fear and protection, even though 'she could not feel the baby in her arms' (p. 4). It is as if the child is suddenly gone, as if the nurse clutches her to keep her from reaching hands. When the princess begins floating and laughing, despite the humour of the scene her nurse reacts with 'terror', and is '[t]rembling in every limb' (p. 5). And when the king sees his daughter laughing and floating, he is 'trembling' and says to his 'horror-struck' wife: 'She *can't* be ours, queen!' (p. 6, emphasis in original). Distressingly, the next chapter bears the title: 'Where Is She?' (p. 6). This is not a comic scenario. Something truly terrifying has happened. Significantly, Sir Walter Scott recorded a case in which a changeling was recognised by uncanny, delighted laughter; the changeling also could not walk correctly.[26] The king, certainly, seems to believe that his daughter might be a changeling; when his wise men advise him that the princess must be made to cry, but not even a professional beggar can move her to tears, the king 'put himself in a rage one day, and, rushing up to her room, gave her an awful whipping' (p. 28). The cause of the king's rage is not specified. Whipping, however, is a historically attested means of banishing a changeling (classified as F321.1.1.7, cf. F321.1.4.6).[27] The theories of his counsellors having failed, the king seems to resort to the violence and cruelty of folk wisdom. This troubling scene seems perhaps to be his last desperate attempt to find and reclaim his daughter.

Makemnoit has taken the princess's gravity. The princess is no longer held to the earth; more forcibly than either Gruffanuff or Prigio, she lives in liminality, neither fully in Middle Earth nor Otherworld. Insofar as body is mass, the princess can be said to have become bodiless. The transformation has rendered her other, estranged from her parents and normal emotion, absent despite her presence. The question can even be asked – if not answered conclusively – whether the princess of the story is the same child born to the king and queen, or whether she is perhaps a fairy child and the real princess was taken away. Where, indeed, is the princess?

'Deeper Spirit'

It seems clear that there is a tangible difference between *The Rose and the Ring* and the stories of Lang and MacDonald. Perhaps because of their shared Scottishness and love of Scottish folklore, Lang and MacDonald have taken a more serious approach even to the frivolity of the *conte*. Lang, however, retains a more whimsical touch, perhaps derived from his admiration for Thackeray, or perhaps from a greater unease in re-appropriating the material, whilst MacDonald draws on the darker, grimmer depths of fairy lore.

Tolkien, despite his cordial dislike of *Prince Prigio*, nevertheless admitted that 'the joy [in the tale] has a little of that strange mythical fairy-story quality';[28] he saw the tension between the mythic joy and the 'half-mocking smile'[29] of the story as being central to Lang's writings:

> This is characteristic of Lang's wavering balance. On the surface, the story is a follower of the 'courtly' French *conte* with a satirical twist, and of Thackeray's *Rose and the Ring* in particular – a kind which being superficial, even frivolous, by nature, does not

produce or aim at a producing anything so profound; but underneath lies the deeper spirit of the romantic Lang.[30]

It is this 'deeper spirit' that appears at the tale's climax – the twist of fate when Prigio learns to believe in fairies and magic, and thus steps into his true identity. After his singular misfortunes with the cap of darkness, Prigio follows the carriage to a palace, and finds himself invisibly gate-crashing a ball. Mingling with the guests unseen, for the first time he hears everyone complaining about how annoying he is – except for one beautiful young lady: 'she declared that it was his *misfortune*, not his fault, to be so clever' (p. 37, emphasis in original). Lang seems here to be alluding to the misfortune which was the unwanted gift of Fairy Blackstick; Prigio has undergone a training apparently deliberately patterned after Thackeray. Hearing the beautiful maiden defend him, Prince Prigio realises that he has, indeed, been undeserving of her defence, and promptly falls in love.

> Now, at this very moment – when the prince, all of a sudden, was as deep in love as if he had been the stupidest officer in the room – an extraordinary thing happened! Something seemed to give a whirr! in his brain, and in one instant *he knew all about it!* He believed in fairies and fairy gifts, and understood that his cap was the cap of darkness, and his shoes the seven-league boots, and his purse the purse of Fortunatus! He had read about those things in historical books: but now he believed in them.[31]

It is only *after* this Romantic awakening that Prigio can vanquish the Firedrake and win the fair maiden's hand. The magic of fairy tales, Lang argues, is in their expression of the non-rational elements of human life, like falling in love, for instance. There is a sort of magic in the world, he suggests, that makes fairy tales necessary. Roger Lancelyn Green says that *Prince Prigio* and its sequels 'go contrary to Lang's own ideals in that they are burlesques, however kindly, of the old tales'.[32] But this seems to miss the deeper meaning which Green himself suggests is there.[33] In the introduction to *The Red Fairy Book* (1890), Lang writes:

> If [these stories] waken, even in a few little boys and girls, the love of reading, if they open the door into a fairyland, not of science

but of fancy, they have reached their proper aim and end. Stories like these will live, or will revive, when, in the changes of human fortunes, science has been lost, when electricity, and steam, and chemistry are buried with their engines and their crucibles beneath the ruins of a world and under the accumulations of innumerable earthworms. Faiths, and Empires, and Philosophies have crumbled and faded, and left the fairy folk happy still in their kingdom beyond the river that runs knee-deep in blood.[34]

Lang seems to be reaching toward the conclusions put forward by later theorists such as Bruno Bettelheim and Jack Zipes that fairy tales are needful for childhood development and social formation. The fairy tales themselves, this cultural heritage 'not of science but of fancy', appear in *Prince Prigio* through metonymy of the fairy gifts – ancient historical artefacts handed down to be treasured and used. In *Prince Ricardo* (1892), Lang would make a stronger case for both fancy *and* reason. But *Prince Prigio* ranks with his most poignant polemics for the necessity of fairy tales.

MacDonald does something different yet again. In 'The Fantastic Imagination', he writes:

> If a writer's aim be logical conviction, he must spare no logical pains, not merely to be understood, but to escape being misunderstood; where his object is to move by suggestion, to cause to imagine, then let him assail the soul of his reader as the wind assails an Aeolian harp.[35]

Note that the imagery and patterns of the tale, the 'mood-engendering, thought-provoking'[36] music and texture of the tale, *assail* the reader. MacDonald understood a symbolic, mythic force inherent in the telling of tales; a tale was to affect the imagination musically, not by explanation.

Critics are often puzzled by the combination of erotic and Eucharist imagery at the climax of what, at least on the surface, is a frivolous burlesque in the manner of Thackeray.[37] I suggest this is because MacDonald's explanations of his own tales are not meant to instruct, but to divert attention away from didactic meaning, and that the *form* itself of *The Light Princess* is such an occlusion; there is a far darker and more primal story underneath the veil of Thackerayan whimsy. When Makemnoit binds the waters, and the lake where the princess swims and gains gravity begins to dry up, the princess herself withers and fades: 'she, like a true Nereid, was wasting away with her lake, sinking as it sank, withering as it dried' (p. 47). The prince 'could not tell whether the lake was dying because the lady had forsaken it; or whether the lady would not come because the lake had begun to sink' (p. 48). The princess and the lake are mystically united, and their symbiotic health or illness affects the kingdom. Beneath the frivolity and physical estrangement of the *conte* are older folk motifs.[38] The princess is again aligned with the fairies, and the fairy realm; she finds selfhood not in human society but in elemental relationship with the lake. If the real princess was changed, then the entwinement of her life with the lake indicates that she would seem to have been changed into a water-spirit. More likely, however, is it that the metamorphosis and loss of gravity that the princess underwent made her akin to the fairy folk. Diving into a lake is often used as a means for entering the otherworld (F153); by diving and floating, the princess retains her liminality, finding peace by existing in an environment that is neither submerged beneath the water (otherworld) nor in the air (her experience of earth).[39] She seems more natural here because she is herself liminal.

A simplistic reading of the story would see the prince as the hero of the tale. He heroically offers to save the princess by stopping the snakebite in the lake bottom with his own body; MacDonald pointedly suggests spiritual imagery when he titles the chapter 'Here I Am', echoing the usual answer of biblical prophets when called by God.[40] The prince is thus a sort of Christ figure, as suggested by the Eucharistic imagery of the biscuits and wine that the princess feeds the prince while the lake fills and he begins drowning. But this is too reductive. The heroic, Christ-like prince becomes increasingly problematic in relation to the story. The golden plate which relates how the lake and thus the kingdom can be saved is specific that the sacrificial hero must come from the kingdom itself: 'If the nation could not provide one hero, it was time it should perish' (p. 50). But the prince is from another kingdom, a thousand miles away. Nor, as the golden plate also insists, does he even die; that he remains alive and well should, according to MacDonald's own rules of internal consistency, result in the nation's death.

In fact, MacDonald's story is much more subtle. Zipes notes that the prince 'is self-sacrificing and tender in the mould of traditional fairy-tale females', but points out that MacDonald does not simply employ gender inversion: '[t]here is a more sensitive interaction between two unique individuals than traditional role-playing at the end of the tale, a special configuration that MacDonald was to develop in all his narratives'.[41] Like 'Cross Purposes' or 'The Day Boy and the Night Girl', *The Light Princess* might be best understood as the story of two individuals learning to love and respect one another by crossing into liminality and the borders of the otherworld. In this context, the true fairy-tale hero is not the prince at all; it is the princess. The story is hers. The prince's sacrifice and courage serve only to awaken within her simultaneous knowledge of love and death, which the golden plate claims are the same thing. The princess pulls the prince out of the hole and out of the lake, despite knowing that the lake will sink again and she will perish. The princess, not the prince, dispenses the Eucharist, filling the priestly role of mediator between God and man. And it is the princess, not the prince, who undergoes the quest. It is her sacrifice of herself, as the kingdom's hero, that frees the waters both in the land and in herself, and breaks her dependence on the external show of gravity she found in the lake: 'But the princess did not heed the lake. She lay on the floor and wept' (p. 63).[42] Her dive into the lake is the culmination of her relationship with the otherworld. She dives not just for her own pleasure but to descend and reclaim her beloved; it is not too much to read it as katabasis, a burial and resurrection. Daniel Gabelman correctly suggests that 'her weight is restored not through a crude awareness of gravity but through an experience of true lightness', and that she has found 'a better, more holistic levity'.[43] More precisely, she has found equilibrium between her conflicting elements of air and water, of her human nature and her fairy nature; this allows her to experience both the laughter of the elves and the tears of men. Her action frees not only the waters of the kingdom, but her own tears; her identity, which was lost in her curse, is given back. She is realigned to understand and inhabit both her own world and the other.

What is, I hope, clear, is that MacDonald has attempted and achieved something very different from both Thackeray and Lang. Whereas Thackeray simply saw the literary fairy tale as an elaborate joke, and Lang as a Romantic cultural inheritance to be preserved and enjoyed,

MacDonald continued the spiritual and mystical tradition of symbolic fantasy; he wrote with a serious purpose, and the work continues his confrontation with death through children's literature. The inscription in the lake says, disturbingly, 'Love is death' (p. 49). It is surely central to MacDonald's tale, and one of the word-plays in the story, that for the princess to be freed, she must embrace her sorrow, and grow grave.

Notes
1. Andrew Lang, 'Three New Novels', *Fortnightly Review* 21:121 (January 1877), p. 93.
2. Marysa Demoor, 'Andrew Lang's "Causeries" 1874–1912', *Victorian Periodicals Review* 21:1 (Spring, 1988), p. 15.
3. Quoted in Roger Lancelyn Green, *Andrew Lang: A Critical Biography* (Leicester: Edmund Ward, 1946), p. 89.
4. U. C. Knoepflmacher, *Ventures into Childland: Victorians, Fairy Tales, and Femininity* (Chicago: University of Chicago Press, 1998), pp. 117–18, 124; William Raeper, *George MacDonald* (Tring: Lion, 1987), pp. 194.
5. Knoepflmacher, p. 102.
6. M. A. Titmarsh [W. M. Thackeray], *The Rose and the Ring, or, The history of Prince Giglio and Prince Bulbo: A fireside pantomime for great and small children* (London: Smith, Elder, and Co, 1855), p. 93. Further citations given in the text.
7. George MacDonald, *A Dish of Orts: Chiefly Papers on the Imagination, and on Shakspere*, 2nd edn (London: Sampson Low Marson, 1893); J. R. R. Tolkien, *Tolkien On Fairy-stories: Expanded Edition, with Commentary and Notes*, ed Verlyn Flieger and Douglas A. Anderson (London: HarperCollins, 2008), p. 52.
8. Andrew Lang, 'Literary Fairy Tales', in F. Von Eeden, *Little Johannes*, trans Clara Bell (London: W. Heinemann, 1895), p. viii.
9. Jack Zipes, *Fairy Tales and the Art of Subversion*, 2nd edn (London: Routledge, 2006), p. 113.
10. Zipes, p. 111.
11. The reference here is to Stith Thompson's six-volume *Motif Index of Folk Literature* (1955–1958), an authoritative classification system for common themes and repeated patterns throughout much of oral folk literature, that provides a standard reference point for discussion of the structural composition of folktale variants.
12. Andrew Lang, *My Own Fairy Book* (Bristol and New York: Arrowsmith and Longmans, Green, 1895), p. 5. Further citations given in the text.
13. Andrew Lang, 'Mythology and Fairy Tales', *Fortnightly Review* 13:77 (May 1873), p. 619.
14. Knoepflmacher, p. 132.
15. George MacDonald, *The Light Princess and Other Fairy Tales*, 1890 (Whitethorn, CA: Johannesen, 1997), p. 4. Further citations given in the text.
16. George MacDonald, *Adela Cathcart*, 1864 (Whitethorn, CA: Johannesen, 2000), p. 60; cf. Daniel Gabelman, *'Divine Carelessness': The Fairytale Levity of George MacDonald* (unpublished doctoral thesis, University of St Andrews, 2011), pp. 130–31.
17. MacDonald, *Adela Cathcart*, p. 61.
18. Lizanne Henderson and Edward J. Cowan, *Scottish Fairy Belief: A History* (East Lothian, Scotland: Tuckwell, 2001), pp. 79–80, 82–83; Diane Purkiss, *Troublesome Things: A History of Fairies and Fairy Stories* (London: Allen Lane, 2000), pp. 52, 56–61.

19. Tolkien would later appropriate this image for a key argument in 'On Fairy-Stories', p. 51.
20. Charles Dickens, *Christmas Books*, ed Andrew Lang, *The Works of Charles Dickens*, 18 (New York: Charles Scribner's, 1899), p. vii. Nor does the reference to Dickens seem accidental; Lang specifically invites comparison between Dickens's Christmas books and Thackeray's, of course including *The Rose and the Ring* (Dickens, *Christmas Books*, p. ix).
21. Charles Dickens, *Christmas Stories from "Household words" and "All the year round"*, ed Andrew Lang, *The Works of Charles Dickens*, 31 (New York: Charles Scribner's, 1900), p. vii.
22. Stephen Prickett, *Victorian Fantasy*, 2nd edn (Waco, TX: Baylor University Press, 2005), pp. 120–22, 137. Examples could be further multiplied, but a full discussion of invisibility and identity in Victorian fiction is beyond the scope of this paper.
23. Henderson and Cowan, pp. 94–95.
24. Sir Walter Scott, *The Minstrelsy of the Scottish Border*, 4 vols (Edinburgh and London: Robert Cadell and Houlston & Stonemason, 1849), II, 319.
25. Henderson and Cowan, p. 137; Purkiss, p. 109.
26. Scott, II, 321.
27. Purkiss, pp. 57, 95–96.
28. Tolkien, p. 76.
29. Tolkien, p. 76.
30. Tolkien, p. 76n.
31. Lang, p. 37, emphasis in original.
32. Roger Lancelyn Green, 'Andrew Lang and the Fairy Tale', *Review of English Studies* 20 (July 1944), p. 231.
33. Green, 'Fairy Tale', p. 231; 'In their own kind, however, they are excellent, and occasional touches of the "melancholy soul" behind the "gay mind", besides the habitual cleverness of the "gay mind", raise them far above the ordinary run of such stories, causing them to retain their freshness and charm unimpaired – qualities that are never more perfectly displayed throughout all Lang's writings than here.'
34. Andrew Lang, *The Red Fairy Book*, Large Paper Edition (London: Longmans, Green, 1890), pp. xv–xvi.
35. MacDonald, *A Dish of Orts*, p. 321.
36. MacDonald, *A Dish of Orts*, p. 320.
37. cf. Raeper, *George MacDonald*, p. 317; Michael Mendelson, 'The Fairy Tales of George MacDonald and the Evolution of a Genre' in *For the Childlike: George MacDonald's Fantasies for Children*, ed Roderick McGillis (Metuchen, NJ and London: The Children's Literature Association and Scarecrow Press, 1992), pp. 36–38.
38. In particular interest to this study, see D1542.3.4, F421.1, M477, N715.
39. *Pace* Gabelman, p. 177, who suggests that the princess's re-transformation begins when the prince attempts to rescue her from the lake. Rather, it is her first encounter with the water – the nearest she has been to the otherworld, in other words – that begins the process that culminates in her katabasis and rebirth; cf Zipes, p. 114.
40. cf. Isaiah 6.8, *et al*.
41. Zipes, p. 114.
42. cf. Gabelman, pp. 197–99: 'the restoration of the princess' lake is best seen as a polyvalent miracle, revealing the harmony at the heart of creation: the interconnectedness of man and nature, inner and outer, spiritual and physical.'
43. Gabelman, p. 146.

Bibliography

Demoor, Marysa, 'Andrew Lang's "Causeries" 1874–1912', *Victorian Periodicals Review* 21:1 (Spring, 1988), pp. 15–22.

Dickens, Charles, *Christmas Books*, ed Andrew Lang, *The Works of Charles Dickens*, 18 (New York: Charles Scribner's, 1899).

— *Christmas Stories from 'Household words' and 'All the year round'*, ed Andrew Lang, *The Works of Charles Dickens*, 31 (New York: Charles Scribner's, 1900).

Gabelman, Daniel, *'Divine Carelessness': The Fairytale Levity of George MacDonald* (unpublished doctoral thesis, University of St Andrews, 2011).

Green, Roger Lancelyn, *Andrew Lang: A Critical Biography* (Leicester: Edmund Ward, 1946).

— 'Andrew Lang and the Fairy Tale', *Review of English Studies* 20 (July 1944), pp. 227–31.

Henderson, Lizanne, and Edward J. Cowan, *Scottish Fairy Belief: A History* (East Lothian, Scotland: Tuckwell, 2001).

Lang, Andrew, 'Literary Fairy Tales', in F. Von Eeden, *Little Johannes*, trans Clara Bell (London: W. Heinemann, 1895), pp. v–xix.

— *My Own Fairy Book* (Bristol and New York: Arrowsmith and Longmans, Green, 1895).

— 'Mythology and Fairy Tales', *Fortnightly Review* 13:77 (May 1873), pp. 618–31.

— *The Red Fairy Book*, Large Paper Edition (London: Longmans, Green, 1890).

— 'Three New Novels', *Fortnightly Review* 21:121 (January 1877), pp. 88–96.

MacDonald, George, *Adela Cathcart*, 1864 (Whitethorn, CA: Johannesen, 2000).

— *A Dish of Orts: Chiefly Papers on the Imagination, and on Shakspere*, 2nd edn (London: Sampson Low Marson & Co, Ltd., 1893).

— *The Light Princess and Other Fairy Tales*, 1890 (Whitethorn, CA: Johannesen, 1997).

Mendelson, Michael, 'The Fairy Tales of George MacDonald and the Evolution of a Genre' in *For the Childlike: George MacDonald's Fantasies for Children*, ed Roderick McGillis (Metuchen, NJ and London: The Children's Literature Association and Scarecrow Press, 1992), pp. 31–49.

Prickett, Stephen, *Victorian Fantasy*, 2nd edn (Waco, TX: Baylor University Press, 2005).

Purkiss, Diane, *Troublesome Things: A History of Fairies and Fairy Stories* (London: Allen Lane, 2000).

Raeper, William, *George MacDonald* (Tring: Lion, 1987).

Scott, Sir Walter, *The Minstrelsy of the Scottish Border*, 4 vols (Edinburgh and London: Robert Cadell and Houlston & Stonemason, 1849).

Thompson, Stith, *Motif-Index of Folk-Literature: a classification of narrative elements in folktales, ballads, myths, fables, mediaeval romances, exempla, fabliaux, jest-books and local legends*, 4 vols (Copenhagen: Roskilde & Bagger, 1955–1958).

Titmarsh, M. A. [W. M. Thackeray], *The Rose and the Ring, or, The history of Prince Giglio and Prince Bulbo: A fireside pantomime for great and small children* (London: Smith, Elder, 1855).

Tolkien, J. R. R., *Tolkien On Fairy-stories: Expanded Edition, with Commentary and Notes*, ed Verlyn Flieger and Douglas A. Anderson (London: HarperCollins, 2008).

Zipes, Jack, *Fairy Tales and the Art of Subversion*, 2nd edn (London: Routledge, 2006).

George MacDonald and the Grave Livers of Scotland

DAVID S. ROBB

MacDonald's first novel, *David Elginbrod* (1863), implies that it is a great advantage to be Scottish if one hopes to improve the world. In the opening 'Turriepuffit' section, the young Scottish hero, Hugh Sutherland, initially callow and conscious of his own social and educational advantages over David and his peasant family, settles in England to take up his appointment at Arnstead as tutor; he instantly shows an instinctive sureness of touch in handling his neurotic young pupil, in contrast to the benighted educational regime which had been hitherto employed. When Hugh moves to London, he encounters the mysterious Robert Falconer, another expatriate Scot who is as streetwise as he is masterful in overcoming every challenge. Falconer emerges as a kind of divinely inspired action-man, a capeless crusader, equally at home in checkmating Funkelstein the evil mesmerist as in chatting in homely Doric speech with an Aberdeen-born London policeman. Hugh's eventual beloved, Margaret Elginbrod, also moves from Scotland to become the principal means of saving that troubled slave of Funkelstein's will, Euphrasia Cameron (a half-Scot in need of rescuing from the evil down south). And underlying it all is the spiritual strength of the now dead David Elginbrod, who may never have left (at least in body) his confined Scottish plot of land but whose natural holiness is a force for good even for troubled souls who have never met him. Readers could be forgiven for thinking, 'Where would the English be without the Scots?'

The pattern recurs in various later novels, particularly when Scottish characters have an opportunity to make their mark on the English scene, especially when that scene is London itself. Thus, in *Robert Falconer* (1868), Robert's Rothieden childhood – one of the strongest portions of MacDonald's entire Scottish fiction – precedes an adult career as force for good in the mean streets of London, while he seeks his lost father (another Scot to be rescued). The connection between Scottish origins and improvement of life in England is clear.

Nor is this the last instance of the sort. In *The Marquis of Lossie* (1877), Malcolm MacPhail, previously revealed at the end of *Malcolm* (1875) as the next Marquis, conceals his real identity and follows his flighty half-sister to London in order to rescue her from, once again, the perils of the city. There, he encounters his old schoolmaster, Alexander Graham, banished from his northern schoolhouse and striving to earn a living amongst the community of English dissenters. MacDonald's portrayal of the world of these dissenters is satiric, but Graham finds a new vocation in preaching from the heart, giving voice to the truth of things as MacDonald himself perceived it. Both characters offer, once more, decisive Scottish interventions amidst the perils and failings of Victorian London.

Even in novels not set in England, such as *Alec Forbes of Howglen* or *What's Mine's Mine*, the pattern of conflict between right and wrong involves, as often as not, a contrast of British nationalities. The conflict, admittedly, also usually involves class divisions as well as national ones – sometimes, too, the opposition is between pastoral truth and flawed urban sophistication: humble Scottish heroes and heroines overcome the sins and mistakes of upper-class, even aristocratic, semi-villains who, even if Scottish by birth, are anglified in speech and outlook. The power to triumph over wrong seems to be peculiarly the province of characters with the good fortune to be born into obscure Scottish circumstances. MacDonald apparently perceives them as specially chosen to embody God's truth and to make it prevail.

How might we explain this repeated pattern? What might it signify? Repeated patterns, of course, are a marked feature of MacDonald's writing. Character-types, events, images, and motifs weave their way meaningfully through his work. Yet one wonders: where might the particular motif of these impressively righteous Scots have come from? To paraphrase Burns's Holy Willie, what was it about the Scots, that they should get such exaltation? One obvious answer is to assume a kind of autobiographical element in MacDonald's writing. He himself had come from a distant part of Aberdeenshire to achieve national prominence with his individual interpretation of God's word. We need not put this echoing of himself down to mere self-congratulation: autobiographical elements are common enough in the work of countless novelists, from that day to this. In any case, autobiography alone does not seem sufficient to explain this frequent motif in MacDonald's fiction. What else might be going on here?

It seems possible that, at least in part, MacDonald is making use of one of the perceptions current in his day regarding Scotland, Scottish people, and particularly the special place and style of religion in Scottish life. I suggest that he is taking advantage of a common idea about Scotland, and is building upon an association in the nineteenth-century mind between Scotland and religion. This was not, admittedly, the only Victorian perception of Scotland, or set of associations regarding Scottish people and Scottish life. Indeed, as discussed below, one essay by Margaret Oliphant explores several different 'images' of Scotland and Scottish people current among her contemporaries.[1]

What evidence is there of a widespread vision of Scotland as a country of particular spiritual and moral strength? All that is surely required is a collection of indications – some straws in the wind – of a Victorian perception of Scottish religious piety. It is easy to assume that any special Scottish religious fervour would be regarded as a strength, and viewed with favour and respect, as MacDonald's fiction might seem to imply. However, Scotland's religious intensity was sometimes regarded unfavourably by southern observers. Perhaps MacDonald's implicit claims about the nation's spirituality did not always assume general agreement; at times he may have been depicting Scottish religious instincts in the teeth of more negative perceptions.

Possible sources of evidence regarding attitudes to Scottish religious life include autobiographies – for example, those by Walter Scott, Hugh Miller, Henry Cockburn, Margaret Oliphant, John Ruskin, et al. – books of popular history, such as Robert Chambers' *Traditions of Edinburgh* (1824) or Margaret Oliphant's *Royal Edinburgh* (1890), and classic statements of Victorian ideas such as Arnold's *Culture and Anarchy* (1869). Letters, periodicals and newspapers seem even more useful for an enquiry of this kind. Variety of types of source material is particularly desirable, if it indicates that the association of Scotland with religion and moral fervour was common throughout the conscious outlook of the age. What follows is a diverse collection of scraps of evidence, enough perhaps to allow the claim that MacDonald and his readers did indeed associate and often valued Scotland as a distinctive and influential part of the Victorian religious landscape.

A possible starting-point is found in Wordsworth's 'Resolution and Independence' (1802). In the poem, the traveller describes an old leech-gatherer as speaking with

> [...] a stately speech,
> Such as grave Livers do in Scotland use,
> Religious men, who give to God and man their dues.
> (ll. 96–98)

This seems favourable and appreciative, with Wordsworth associating Scotland with a commendably high religious tone and style. Consequently, it is a little disappointing to discover him commenting more critically in a letter to Henry Crabb Robinson (14 July 1844), though still reflecting his sense of a Scottish tendency towards religious solemnity:

> The Scotch are fond of ceremonials and solemnities and commemorations, partly owing to their nationality, and partly perhaps in opposition to the spirit of the Kirk which is austere and forbidding.[2]

This mixture of responses among English Victorians is to be found elsewhere. When Matthew Arnold, for example, addressed an Edinburgh audience, he was understandably respectful:

> here in the capital of Scotland, of that country which has been such a stronghold of what I call "Hebraism", of deep and ardent occupation with righteousness and religion, you will not complain of my taking for my subject so eminent a doctor in the science of these matters as Butler [...] (*Essays Religious and Mixed*, ed R. H. Super, p. 14)[3]

Elsewhere, however, Arnold was more scathing in his response to an essay by Principal John Tulloch (1823–1886), head of St Mary's College, St Andrews, and a prominent Scottish churchman. This essay had dealt with the latest (and consequently, in Tulloch's view, more sophisticated) tendencies in Scottish religious life. Arnold, however, was not impressed:

> [T]he Puritan Churches have no beauty. This makes the difficulty of maintaining the Established Church of Scotland. Once drop

the false science on which successive generations of Scotchmen have so vainly valued themselves, once convince oneself that the Westminster Confession, whatever Principal Tulloch may think, is a document absolutely antiquated, sterile and worthless, and what remains to the Church of Scotland? Besides the simple elementary truths present in all forms of Christianity, there remains to the Church of Scotland merely that which remains to the Free Church, to the United Presbyterians, to Puritanism in general, – a religious service which is perhaps the most dismal performance ever invented by man. (pp. 342–43)[4]

Nor was Arnold alone: there was criticism of Scottish religious life in plenty emanating from English sources, frequently in the form of a revulsion against the country's Puritan tendencies. Of course, the attitude of MacDonald himself to the austerity of Scottish religious observances was also substantially critical, while at the same time retaining a sense of the spiritual strength which was also part and parcel of Scottish religious life: one thinks particularly of his portrayal of the Missionar Kirk, its people and its services, in *Alec Forbes of Howglen*. Nevertheless, it is not hard to find further comments which reflect an appreciation of the centrality in the national life of a distinctively Scottish brand of religion. Here, for example, is part of a report in *The Times* of a meeting, held in London on the previous day, on the topic of Scottish church extension:

> The Rev. Dr Henderson (of Glasgow) said, he rose for the purpose of laying before the meeting certain statements respecting the spiritual destitution existing in Scotland, more particularly in the large towns and manufacturing districts. To a Scotchman it was a painful and humiliating task to expose the nakedness, in respect of the blessings of religious and moral education, of a land hitherto regarded by its southern neighbours as possessed of them in a high degree [...][5]

This meeting was chaired by Thomas Chalmers (1780–1847), regarded everywhere as the leading Scottish churchman of his day. It was Chalmers who led the Evangelical wing in the Church of Scotland during the great 'Ten Years' Conflict' which eventually resulted in the breakup, or

'Disruption' of the Kirk, and the creation of the Free Church of Scotland, in 1843. By then, however, Chalmers had long been known and respected south of the border for his moral leadership, his preaching, and his innovative social work, as well as for his leadership of the substantial body of Scottish churchgoers vehemently opposed both to patronage in the appointment of ministers and also to the idea that the Church of Scotland was subject in all matters to the civil law of the land. An awareness of Chalmers' gifts, personality, and leadership role in important developments in Scotland's public life must have coloured English perceptions of Scottish religion in the middle decades of the century. It is likely that he reinforced that contradictory division of perception hinted at above, for although he was clearly perceived as a moral and spiritual authority, a figure worthy of immense personal respect, his church was associated with beliefs of backward-facing evangelical fervour and extremism.

An obvious place to search for evidence of English attitudes to Scottish religion is in newspaper accounts of the tumultuous events of May 1843. Attitudes south of the border were predictably contradictory. For example, the new Assembly of the Free Church (which instantly got going in parallel with the Assembly of the now diminished established Church) was addressed, as *The Times* reported, by W. Hamilton of the London Lay Union:

> He said the members of this union, which was yet in its infancy, had all along felt the most intense interest in the contendings of the church of Scotland, and he rejoiced that by the sacrifice they had now made they had been able to rebuke the infidelity of an ungodly age, and bear a noble testimony to the power of religious principle. He complained of the apathy of the public mind in England on this subject, and urged that the Assembly should send a deputation to plead their cause in the metropolis, headed by their rev. Moderator. (Hear, hear.) He also suggested that the assembly should send to London some of their ablest men, to settle there permanently, and enlighten the English mind on this subject.[6]

The meeting was then addressed by others from the south, insisting that this spectacular outbreak of Scottish religious idealism could and should be made a powerful source of regeneration in England:

MR NISBET, bookseller, of Berners-street, London, addressed the house in similar terms, and expressed his desire to aid the cause in which they were engaged. 40 years ago he had passed across the Tweed with his staff in his hand, and now God had blessed his labours. If God should spare his life and prosper his endeavours, it was his intention in the course of five years to give 1,000*l.* to the cause of the protesting church. (Immense cheering.)

DR STEWART, of London [...] next addressed the Assembly, and urged that in their missionary labours they should not forget London.[7]

It was a leading idea amongst these English-based speakers that Scots of the appropriate religious persuasion should be encouraged to travel south and settle, to act as a kind of spiritual leaven in the benighted regions from which their English voices had emerged. It was only two years after this that MacDonald made that very journey, enacting in his own life the pattern eventually to be found in the novels described above.

The issue of *The Times*, however, which reported the supportive and enthusiastic speeches of Messrs Hamilton, Nisbet, and Stewart, spoke in very different terms in its leader article. Apparently, a Mr Dunlop had described to the Free Church Assembly in Edinburgh how there would be major difficulties in establishing and constructing new Free Churches in parishes where landowners were unsympathetic. There would have to be temporary measures in the form of tents, boats, and such, enabling newly 'outed' ministers to address worshippers so that the Free Church message might be preached 'to the people, who might never otherwise hear the message of salvation'. The leader-writer reacted angrily to this last:

> What is the meaning of this? In what land do we live? Is it indeed true, that because one man believes patronage to be a civil right, and presentation by an individual to be preferable to popular election, and another believes the contrary of these propositions to be true, and attests such his belief by relinquishing endowments – is it therefore true that the first of these men (who shall be in all other points every bit as good a Christian as the other, and be acknowledged as his 'brother' up to the moment of separation) – is

> it true that this man can NEVER *by possibility* 'preach the message of "salvation"' while the other shall be indisputably orthodox, so that it is incumbent upon the Non-intrusionist to organise an anti-Christian mission, and to go about the country in boats and with tents, "*converting*" establishment-men to his newly-made creed![8]

That English readers, and leader writers, regularly took an interest in the religious life of Scotland is indicated by evidence from various other sources. For example, in the essay by Principal Tulloch to which Arnold was referring in the earlier quotation, one finds several moments of controversy being handily summarised. Tulloch's essay was entitled 'Progress of Religious Thought in Scotland' and appeared in *The Contemporary Review* in March 1877.[9] His general point was that Scottish religious thought had moved on substantially from the days of the Disruption. He admitted that the leading men of the Disruption (apart from Chalmers himself) had been old-style evangelicals anachronistically embodying the spirit of seventeenth-century Covenanters. After 1843, however, Scottish religious life had increasingly taken its tone from a new generation of establishment churchmen who rejected old evangelical certainties and were open to the influences of such as Coleridge, Maurice, Kingsley, German theology, Carlyle, and Erskine of Linlathen. Tulloch assumed that English readers were likely to be still recollecting the fervour of the Free Church firebrands of the 1840s:

> These were the palmy days of Free Church orthodoxy, when Dr Cunningham was the chief, as he was the ablest, representative of doctrinal opinion in the body; and Dr Candlish adventured as far south as London to deliver the English mind from the snares which Mr Maurice had woven for it in his 'Theological Essays'.[10]

In the place of such bogey-men as Cunningham and Candlish, Tulloch offered Dr Norman Macleod as the best embodiment of the new post-evangelical spirit in the Established Church of Scotland; Macleod, he assured his readers, had been deeply influenced by the advanced thinking of John Macleod Campbell and his writings on the Atonement. Indeed, Tulloch (in 1877) looked back to the period 1863–1865, when Macleod and his periodical *Good Words* had come under heavy evangelical attack in a campaign by a London-based Presbyterian cleric writing in the *Record*. A passage Tulloch quoted from Macleod himself indicated both Macleod's post-evangelical purity, and also just how widespread was the interest throughout Britain in Scottish church matters. Macleod had written:

> The Maledictions of the *Record*, reprinted in the form of a pamphlet, and widely circulated in England and Scotland, were caught up and re-echoed by kindred organs throughout the country, and had the effect of making the editor an object of suspicion to many whose good-will he valued.[11]

Tulloch's attempts to persuade the world that Scotland had moved on in religious terms clearly had an uphill struggle in the face of ingrained English preconceptions, as Arnold's scepticism, quoted above, suggests. Another Victorian literary luminary, George Eliot, had an equally negative perception of Scottish religion, past and present. Her essay 'The Influence of Rationalism' focused on the cruelty which besmirches the history of religion in Scotland:

> Again, the Scotch Puritans, during the comparatively short period of their ascendency, surpassed all Christians before them in the elaborate ingenuity of the tortures they applied for the discovery of witchcraft and sorcery, and did their utmost to prove that if Scotch Calvinism was the true religion, the chief 'note' of the true religion was cruelty. It is hardly an endurable task to read the story of their doings; thoroughly to imagine them as a past reality is already a sort of torture. One detail is enough, and it is a comparatively mild one. It was the regular profession of men called 'prickers' to thrust long pins into the body of a suspected witch in order to detect the insensible spot which was the infallible sign of her guilt. On a superficial view one would be in danger of saying that the main difference between the teachers who sanctioned these things and the much-despised ancestors who offered human victims inside a huge wicker idol, was that they arrived at a more elaborate barbarity by a longer series of dependent propositions. [We] do not share Mr Buckle's opinion that a Scotch minister's groans were a part of his deliberate plan for keeping the people in a state of

terrified subjection; the ministers themselves held the belief they taught, and might well groan over it.[12]

Her view of Scottish religion in her own day could be equally negative, as in her great essay entitled 'Evangelical Teaching: Dr Cumming'. This appeared in the *Westminster Review* in October 1855. It is an astonishing extended attack on both the man and his religious writings, marked as they were by what she saw as his intellectual dishonesty. For forty-seven years, John Cumming was the minister of the National Scottish Church in Covent Garden, and the author of countless books marked by two principal tendencies – unremitting attacks on Roman Catholicism and a belief that Old Testament prophecies actually come true in history, so that he interpreted various historical events and trends as fulfilments of particular prophecies. The atheist George Eliot was far from impressed, either by his arguments themselves or by the Scottish ambience from which they emerged:

> The total absence from Dr Cumming's theological mind of any demarcation between fact and rhetoric is exhibited in another passage, where he adopts the dramatic form:
>
> Ask the peasant on the hills – *and I have asked amid the mountains of Braemar and Dee-side,* – 'How do you know that this book is Divine, and that the religion you profess is true? You never read Paley?' 'No, I never heard of him.' – 'You have never read Butler?' 'No, I have never heard of him.' – 'Nor Chalmers?' 'No, I do not know him.' – 'You have never read any books on evidence?' 'No, I have read no such books.' – 'Then, how do you know this book is true?' 'Know it! Tell me that the Dee, the Clunie, and the Garrawalt, the streams at my feet, do not run; that the winds do not sigh amid the gorges of these blue hills; that the sun does not kindle the peaks of Loch-na-Gar'; tell me my heart does not beat, and I will believe you; but do not tell me the Bible is not Divine. I have found its truth illuminating my footsteps; its consolations sustaining my heart. May my tongue cleave to my mouth's roof, and my right hand forget its cunning, if I ever deny what is my deepest inner experience, that this blessed book is the book of God.' (*Church Before the Flood*, p. 35)

> Dr Cumming is so slippery and lax in his mode of presentation, that we find it impossible to gather whether he means to assert, that this is what a peasant on the mountains of Braemar *did* say, or that it is what such a peasant *would* say: in the one case, the passage may be taken as a measure of his truthfulness; in the other, of his judgement.[13]

It is not difficult, however, to counterpoise one Great Victorian with another. John Ruskin was also far from being a simple Christian believer, yet his attitude to religion, and particularly to Scottish examples of it, was much more tolerant than George Eliot's. His wonderful autobiography *Praeterita*, written in the 1880s, contains several passages voicing his veneration for Scotland and for what he saw as the essential Scottish personality, a personality which he perceives as suffused with a special brand of Scottish piety. Early on, he admits to 'that slight bias against Evangelical religion, which I confess to be sometimes traceable in my later works; but I never can be thankful enough for having seen, in our own "Old Mause", the Scottish Puritan spirit in its perfect faith and force; and been enabled therefore afterwards to trace its agency in the reforming policy of Scotland, with the reverence and honour it deserves.'[14] Elsewhere, he writes about a 'young Macdonald' – not, it should be said, the novelist. This Macdonald

> was a thin, dark Highlander, with some expression of gloom on his features when at rest, but with quite the sweetest smile for his friends that I have ever seen, [...]
>
> He was zealous in the Scottish Evangelical Faith, and wholly true and upright in it, so far as any man can be true in any faith, who is bound by the laws, modes, and landed estates of this civilised world.[15]

Later still in the book, he sounds the same appreciative note again:

> But neither the Puritanism of Belgravia, nor Liberalism of Red Lion Square, interested, or offended, me, otherwise than as the grotesque conditions of variously typhoid or smoke-dried London life. To my old Scotch shepherd Puritanism, and the correspondent

> forms of noble French Protestantism, I never for an instant failed in dutiful affection and honour.[16]

For Ruskin, the Scottish character, clearly associated with his perception of the country's old-style religion, was a source of immense respect. Writing of his friend Dr John Brown, he thinks that Brown's account of his father will seem strange to modern readers, for 'there are few now who can understand a good Scotchman of the old classic breed'. The father had suddenly lost his wife while John Brown and his sister were still very young; Ruskin says about the bereaved man: 'he had a precious sister left to him; but his life, as the noblest Scottish lives are always, was thenceforward generously sad, – and endlessly pitiful'.[17] The nostalgic-cum-lugubrious note is one of which Ruskin seems particularly fond in this part of *Praeterita*: a little further on we find him discussing a clergyman-tutor who had taught the young Thomas Carlyle, as Carlyle himself recorded. But it is Ruskin who refers to the old tutor as 'a Scotch gentleman of old race and feeling, an Andrea Ferrara and some silver-mounted canes hanging in his study, last remnants of the old times'. And on the next page Ruskin continues:

> Assuredly the strength of Scottish character has always been perfected by suffering; and the types of it given by Scott in Flora MacIvor, Edith Bellenden, Mary of Avenel, and Jeanie Deans, – to name only those which the reader will remember without effort, – are chiefly notable in the way they bear sorrow; as the whole tone of Scottish temper, ballad poetry, and music, which no other school has ever been able to imitate, has arisen out of the sad associations which, one by one, have gathered round every loveliest scene in the border land. Nor is there anything among other beautiful nations to approach the dignity of a true Scotswoman's face, in the tried perfectness of her old age.[18]

Ruskin's sense of Scotland is made up partly from his own earliest recollections of the country, partly from the religious temper he believes he encountered there, and partly from his veneration for the writings of Walter Scott. Admittedly, he indicates how in his adult life he has rejected the Puritanism which had formed the ground of his own religious instincts, because that Puritanism seemed to have no place for the aesthetic values now so central to him. Yet a passage like the one just quoted seems to show him associating the stoical sufferings characteristic of Scottish religious tradition with an aesthetic distinctiveness in the 'beautiful nation' of Scotland. Later still in the book, he speaks of a relative of his own, a widow, and her little daughter who was only five when her father died. Brought up in Wigtown, in south-west Scotland, the little girl (he believes) grew in 'daily happiness' due in part to 'the habits of childish play, or education, then common in the rural towns of South Scotland: of which, let me say at once that there was greater refinement in them, and more honourable pride, than probably, at that time, in any other district of Europe; a certain pathetic melody and power of tradition consecrating nearly every scene with some past light, either of heroism or religion'.[19]

Ruskin's veneration for Scotland emerges from a highly personal mix of feelings and associations, but he was certainly not alone in believing that the strengths of the Scottish national character were due in considerable part to the influence of Scotland's religious traditions. Here for example is a Dr Cook, as reported in *The Times*, addressing (much more prosaically than Ruskin) the diminished General Assembly of the Kirk only a few days after Chalmers and his colleagues had marched out so decisively:

> I conceive that it is of great importance to bear in mind that the testimony which so many among ourselves have borne to the value and excellence of the church, is also borne by members who do not even belong to it; and if one thing is more universally received than another, it is this, – that it is through the influence of this church that the character of the people of Scotland has in a great degree been formed, and that high position attained which she happily holds.[20]

But not everyone held Scottish religion and life in such high esteem. George Eliot, in one of the quotations above, refers to 'Mr Buckle'. This, of course, was Henry Thomas Buckle, whose *History of Civilisation in England* (1857–1861) contains *On Scotland and the Scotch Intellect*, a famous attack on the whole history of religion in Scottish life – surely the Victorian age's most substantial and sustained criticism of Scotland's religion. Buckle believed that it was possible to adopt an entirely scientific, rational approach in writing history, so there is an unbending, thesis-driven quality to his whole discussion, resulting in a lacerating picture of Scotland which must have outraged countless numbers of readers. He believed that he had to confront the paradox whereby the enlightened nation which had achieved so much in all the important fields of human endeavour, including a 'bold and inquisitive literature',[21] should also have been utterly priest-ridden (as he saw it). For him, the Scots are 'men who, in the visible and external department of facts and of practical life, display a shrewdness and a boldness rarely equalled, [...] nevertheless, in speculative life, and in matters of theory, tremble like sheep before their pastors, and yield assent to every absurdity they hear, provided their Church has sanctioned it'.[22] This comes from his opening pages, but the entire book is a historical account of Scotland from the Middle Ages onwards, focusing on the malign role (as he sees it) played in the affairs of the nation by Catholic priests and then by post-Reformation clergy. The clerical interest in any period is portrayed as both an intellectual and political power-bloc, always self-seeking and working against the best interests of the time. His chapters get longer as he approaches his own day, with a culminating chapter on the horrors of religious 'superstition' in eighteenth-century Scotland. It is a devastating picture of the religious life of the Scottish people.

The volume on Scotland appeared in 1861, just two years before MacDonald's *David Elginbrod*. Is that first novel of MacDonald's, in part at least, a response to Buckle? Greville MacDonald tells us that David was partly based on MacDonald's father, but the character can also be seen as an idealisation of the whole tradition of Scottish evangelical religion, shorn of its extremes and cruelty but steeped in fervour and spiritual insight. David's religion is as faith-based as that of Dr Cumming's Deeside peasant, and his influence on others for good explicitly transcends the rationalism to which Buckle is so committed. Robert Lee Wolff, in the first 'modern' account of the novel, was amused, baffled, intrigued, and irritated by a work with, as he saw it, so 'many faults. Disjointed, long-winded, didactic, with an elaborate plot whose clumsy mysteries the author himself robs of their effect by flat-footedly explaining them away at once'.[23] And the 'single greatest fault ... is that David himself disappears from the story after the end of this first part'.[24] But while one might agree that the novel is rather hopeless from a conventional point of view, it is nevertheless possible to see it as a bold, radical attempt to articulate in fiction a vision of the spiritual power and mystery of the Scottish religious instinct which David embodies, supremely among all MacDonald's characters, but which Buckle so totally rejects. The fact that David disappears early and dies out of the novel is obviously the whole point, so that MacDonald can enact his continuing importance in the lives he leaves behind, and in the lives of people of whom he never heard: the model is clearly Christ himself. There is a boldness and originality about this which pleases. Indeed, the startling and wilful breach of normal aesthetic expectations (namely, our expectation that the continuity of the role of this obviously important character will take a conventional narrative form) is surely a way of articulating Christianity's vision of the totally abnormal intervention of the divine into the normality of human life during Christ's brief thirty-three years of earthly life. MacDonald's breach of aesthetic norms associates his story with the radical contravention of earthly nature constituted by the divine presence of God's Son in human history. From each brief existence (Christ's on Earth, and David's as a flesh and blood character in the novel) flows all-powerful spiritual aid and healing for humanity as a whole – even for those who had no direct contact with the fountainhead. And with his near-heavy-handed insistence on David's Scottishness (embodied in his language as much as anything else), MacDonald is apparently claiming some link between nationality and spirituality. Even if he is not ultimately implying that Scotland has a monopoly of spiritual effectiveness, he can certainly be interpreted as insisting (at the very least) that, despite Buckle, Scotland's characteristic spiritual world is capable of embodying the saving essence of Christianity.

MacDonald's saviour-figures emerge from a current perception of Scotland, commonly associated with a particular style, and intensity, of religious observance and feeling – and perceived thus, both for good and for ill. Given the national display of stiff-neckedness to which the Scots treated the world in 1843 and in the years leading up to the Disruption, this is scarcely surprising. And the intensity of feeling they displayed on that occasion was echoed in Buckle's portrayal, less than twenty years later, of a peculiarly malign religious element in the national story. Many of the first readers of *David Elginbrod* must have thought of Scotland as a land marked out by the regrettable form of its Christianity. Others again, however, will have regarded Scotland's religious character as an embodiment of true spiritual vitality.

There was about MacDonald, in any case, something of that self-belief which characterised the Scottish Reformers of the sixteenth century, that sense of Scotland's 'own superiority to all other developments of Christianity', that hope that Scotland should be 'a chosen nation like that people, long ago dispersed by a sufficiently miserable catastrophe, to whom was given of old the mission of showing forth the will of God before the world'.[25] The words are those of Margaret Oliphant in her account of John Knox in one of her later books (of so many), *Royal Edinburgh* (1890). That indefatigable woman was a friend of MacDonald, and was influential in persuading a publisher to take on *David Elginbrod* in the first place. She was also outraged by Buckle, and immediately attacked his account, with great energy and confidence, in the essay of hers mentioned above. It is not difficult to believe that for Margaret Oliphant the vision of triumphant Scottish religious feeling in MacDonald's first novel seemed an effective and wholly appropriate counterweight to Buckle's negativity. Nor is it difficult to believe that MacDonald was also fully aware of the kind of disparagement of Scotland's religious essence which writers such as Buckle and George Eliot encouraged, and that a constant impulse behind many of his best novels from *David Elginbrod* onwards was the desire to modify that perception.

Notes

1. Margaret Oliphant, 'Scotland and her Accusers', *Blackwood's Edinburgh Magazine*, July–December 1861, pp. 267–83.
2. *The Letters of William and Dorothy Wordsworth*, ed Alan G. Hill, vol 7 (Oxford: Clarendon Press, 1988), pp. 571–72.
3. Matthew Arnold, 'Bishop Butler and the Zeit-Geist', *Matthew Arnold: Essays Religious and Mixed*, ed R. H. Super (Ann Arbor: University of Michigan Press, 1972), pp. 11–62 (p. 14).
4. Arnold, pp. 342–43.
5. *The Times*, 8 May, 1838.
6. *The Times*, 26 May, 1838.
7. *The Times*, 26 May, 1838.
8. *The Times*, 26 May, 1838.
9. John Tulloch, 'Progress of Religious Thought in Scotland', *The Contemporary Review*, March 1877, pp. 535–51.
10. Tulloch, p. 538.

11. Tulloch, p. 541.
12. George Eliot, 'The Influence of Rationalism', *Fortnightly Review*, 15 May 1865, reprinted in *Essays of George Eliot*, ed Thomas Pinney (London: Routledge & Kegan Paul, 1963), pp. 397–414 (p. 404).
13. George Eliot, 'Evangelical Teaching: Dr Cumming', *Westminster Review*, October 1855, reprinted in Pinney, pp. 158–89 (pp. 172–73).
14. John Ruskin, *Praeterita*, ed A. O. J. Cockshut, Whitehouse Edition of John Ruskin (Keele: Ryburn Publishing, 1994), p. 48.
15. Ruskin, p. 332.
16. Ruskin, p. 387.
17. Ruskin, pp. 161–62.
18. Ruskin, pp. 364–65.
19. Ruskin, p. 426.
20. *The Times*, 27 May, 1843.
21. Henry Thomas Buckle, *On Scotland and the Scotch Intellect*, ed H. J. Hanham (Chicago & London: University of Chicago Press, 1970), p. 26.
22. Buckle, pp. 26–27.
23. Robert Lee Wolff, *The Golden Key: A Study of the Fiction of George MacDonald* (New Haven: Yale University Press, 1961), p. 182.
24. Wolff, p. 195.
25. Margaret Oliphant, *Royal Edinburgh: Her Saints, Kings, Prophets and Poets* (London: Macmillan, 1890), p. 346–47.